Ulysses S. Grant:
A Victor, Not a Butcher

ULYSSES S.
GRANT

A VICTOR, NOT A BUTCHER

EDWARD H. BONEKEMPER III

REGNERY
HISTORY

Regnery® is a registered trademark of Salem Communications Holding Corporation
Regnery History™ is a trademark of Salem Communications Holding Corporation

Cataloging-in-Publication data on file with the Library of Congress

ISBN 0-89526-062-X (hard cover)
ISBN 978-1-59698-641-1 (paperback)
This paperback edition published in 2017, ISBN 978-1-62157-303-6

Published in the United States by
Regnery History
An imprint of Regnery Publishing
A Division of Salem Media Group
300 New Jersey Ave NW
Washington, DC 20001
www.RegneryHistory.com

Manufactured in the United States of America

10 9 8 7 6 5 4 3 2 1

Books are available in quantity for promotional or premium use. For information on discounts and terms, please visit our website: www.Regnery.com.

Distributed to the trade by
Perseus Distribution
www.perseusdistribution.com

Maps by David Deis, Dreamline Cartography. Photos from the Library of Congress and the National Archives.

This book is dedicated to my loving wife,
Susan Weidemoyer Bonekemper;
my ever-supportive parents,
the late Edward H. Bonekemper II and Marie H. Bonekemper;
my inspirational Muhlenberg College history professor,
Dr. Edwin R. Baldrige;
and my departed British/Bermudian Civil War
connoisseur and friend, John W. Faram.

CONTENTS

Maps

INTRODUCTION

Many casual readers of Civil War history come to the conclusion that Robert E. Lee wrought miracles with an outnumbered army and that, by contrast, Ulysses S. Grant was a butcher who slaughtered his own men and won solely by brute force and sheer numbers. Over decades of reading about the Civil War, I have come to contrary conclusions about both men.

Discussions about Robert E. Lee with my late father-in-law, Alfred W. Weidemoyer, led to our concluding that Lee had escaped blame for his many failures during the war and to my writing *How Robert E. Lee Lost the Civil War*. A brilliant and well-read friend's insistence that Grant was a butcher has encouraged me to write this book. As I wrote this book, my continuing research only deepened my conviction that Grant was a great general whose reputation was besmirched by early Civil War historians who had motives of their own and that his generalship has never received the credit it deserves for winning the Civil War.

In these pages, I attempt to summarize Grant's Civil War battles and campaigns with a particular focus on whether his casualties reflected butcher-like conduct. I conclude that he conquered the western third of the Confederacy with a minimum of casualties, drove a stake into the middle of the Confederacy with minimal losses again, and then came east to win the war with tolerable casualties in less than a year. Far from being a butcher, Grant relied on maneuver, speed, imagination, and persistence—in addition to force—to win the Civil War.

In addition to my narrative and arguments, I have included three appendices that support my position. Appendix I contains a summary of historians' treatment of Grant—from the "Lost Cause" historians of the early post-war period to those who have reconsidered and revived his record. Appendix II contains a comprehensive summary of various parties' estimates of the casualties that both sides suffered in the battles and campaigns in which Grant was involved; it provides casualty estimates drawn from a variety of Civil War books, articles, and documents. Finally, Appendix III discusses the surprising closeness of the presidential election of 1864, an election that affected Grant's approach to battle in 1864 and the outcome of which was affected by Grant's aggressive nationwide campaign of that year.

THE GREATEST
CIVIL WAR GENERAL

Why has Grant so often been labeled a butcher and Robert E. Lee a hero? Accusations that Grant was butchering his own soldiers first began during the war—particularly during his aggressive 1864 campaign against Lee to secure final victory for the Union. During that campaign (the Richmond or Overland Campaign), Mary Todd Lincoln said, "[Grant] is a butcher and is not fit to be at the head of an army." On June 4, 1864, Union Secretary of the Navy Gideon Welles wrote in his diary, "Still there is heavy loss, but we are becoming accustomed to the sacrifice. Grant has not great regard for human life." One Southerner said at the time, "We have met a man this time, who either does not know when he is whipped, or who cares not if he loses his *whole* army."[1]

The "butcher" accusations continued in the early post-war period. As early as 1866, a southern writer, Edward Pollard, referred to the "match of brute force" to explain Grant's victory over Lee. Even northern historians criticized Grant. In 1866, *New York Times* war correspondent William Swinton wrote in his *Campaigns of the Army of the Potomac* that Grant relied "exclusively on the application of brute masses, in rapid and remorseless blows." John C. Ropes told the Military Historical Society of Massachusetts that Grant suffered from a "burning, persistent desire to fight, to attack, in season and out of season, against entrenchments, natural obstacles, what not."[2]

Beginning in the 1870s, former Confederate officers played a prominent role in criticizing Grant—especially in comparison to Lee. Lieutenant General Jubal A. Early, in an 1872 speech on Lee's birthday, said, "Shall I compare General Lee to his successful antagonist? As well compare the great pyramid which rears its majestic proportions in the Valley of the Nile, to a pygmy perched on Mount Atlas." In the 1880s, Lieutenant General Evander M. Law wrote, "What a part at least of his own men thought about General Grant's methods was shown by the fact that many of the prisoners taken during the [Overland] campaign complained bitterly of the 'useless butchery' to which they were subjected. . . ."[3]

Likewise, Lee's former adjutant, Walter H. Taylor, elevated Lee at Grant's expense in *General Lee: His Campaigns in Virginia 1861–1865 with Personal Reminiscences*, which was published in 1906. Of the Overland Campaign, Taylor said: "It is well to bear in mind the great inequality between the two contending armies, in order that one may have a proper appreciation of the difficulties which beset General Lee in the task of thwarting the designs of so formidable an adversary, and realize the extent to which his brilliant genius made amends for the paucity of numbers, and proved more than a match for brute force, as illustrated in the hammering policy of General Grant." Taylor also claimed that "[Grant] . . . put a lower estimate upon the value of human life than any of his predecessors. . . ."[4]

Sometimes the accusation has been more subtle, as in Robert D. Meade's 1943 book on Judah Benjamin: "In the spring of 1864 Grant took personal command of the Union Army in Virginia and, with a heavily superior force, began his bludgeoning assaults on Lee's weakened but grimly determined troops." A 1953 dust jacket on a Bruce Catton book said (contrary to Catton's own views): "[The Army of the Potomac's] leader was General Ulysses S. Grant, a seedy little man who instilled no enthusiasm in his followers and little respect in his enemies." In 1965, pro-Lee historian Clifford Dowdey said of Grant: "Absorbing appalling casualties, he threw his men in wastefully as if their weight was certain to overrun any Confederates in their path. In terms of generalship, the new man gave Lee nothing to fear," and described Grant as "an opponent who took no count of his losses." A 1993 article in *Blue & Gray Magazine* referred to the "butcher's bill" of the first two weeks of the Overland Campaign.[5]

Historian Gregory Mertz said it well:

> Grant enjoyed little of the "glory" for his contributions to the [Army of the Potomac's] ultimate success, and was the recipient of much of the blame for the "disasters." Despite moving continually forward from the Wilderness to Petersburg and Richmond, ultimately to Appomattox, and executing the campaign that ended the war in the East, Grant has received little credit, and is most remembered for the heavy losses of Cold Harbor, which tagged him with the reputation of a "butcher."[6]

Even today, examples abound. In 2001, a reporter wrote: "Despite occasional flashes of brilliant strategy and admirable persistence, Grant still comes off looking like a butcher in those final months." Another reporter, writing in 2002 and regarding him as an intellectual lightweight, referred to "last-in-class types, such as Ulysses S. Grant."[7]

The "butcher" label has indeed been tenacious. Civil War historian Don Lowry explained, "Grant has often been depicted as a butcher whose only strategy was to overcome the smaller enemy force by attrition, knowing that he could replace his losses more easily than Lee." As military historian Gordon C. Rhea put it, "The ghost of 'Grant the Butcher' still haunts Civil War lore." An earlier historian, E. B. Long, reluctantly concluded, "Grant the butcher is a hard myth to extinguish." Proving his thesis, an early 2003 Associated Press release stated, "Ask most schoolchildren and they will tell you that Robert E. Lee was a military genius while Ulysses S. Grant was a butcher who simply used the North's advantage in men and material to bludgeon the Confederates into submission."[8]

Grant's armies incurred the bulk of their casualties in the war-ending 1864 Overland Campaign from the Washington area to Richmond/Petersburg against Lee's army. This campaign reflected Grant's war-long philosophy that "The art of war is simple enough. Find out where your enemy is. Get at him as soon as you can. Strike him as hard as you can and as often as you can, and keep moving on."[9] That campaign also represented a deliberate effort by Grant and President Abraham Lincoln to take advantage of the fact that, during the prior two years, Robert E. Lee had chewed up his Army of Northern Virginia and rendered his army, and the Confederacy, vulnerable to a nationwide offensive campaign that would bring the hostilities to a final halt. The Overland Campaign was part of

Grant's national effort to demonstrate Union strength and ensure the reelection of Lincoln. However, it resulted in Grant's being accused of "butchery."

In fact, an average of "only" 15 percent of Grant's Federal troops were killed or wounded in his battles over the course of the war—a total of slightly more than 94,000 men. In contrast, Grant's major Confederate counterpart, Robert E. Lee, who is often treated far more kindly by historians, had greater casualties both in percentages and real numbers: an average of 20 percent of his troops were killed or wounded in his battles—a total of more than 121,000 (far more than any other Civil War general). Lee had 80,000 of his men killed or wounded in his first fourteen months in command (about the same number he started with). All of these casualties have to be considered in the context of America's deadliest war; 620,000 military men died in that war, 214,938 in battle, and the rest from disease and other causes.[10]

Both Grant and Lee were aggressive generals, but only Grant's aggressiveness was consistent with the strategic aims of his government. The Confederacy needed only to avoid conquest, but Lee acted as though the Confederacy had to conquer the North. On the contrary, the Union had the burden of conquering the South, and Grant appropriately went on the offensive throughout the war. He won in the West, won in the Middle, won in the East, and won the war. In summary, Lee needed a tie but went for the win, while Grant needed a win, went for it, and achieved it.

Grant's successes also have been seriously slighted. He accepted the surrender of three entire Confederate armies—at Fort Donelson in 1862, Vicksburg in 1863, and Appomattox Court House in 1865. No other general on either side accepted the surrender of even one army until Sherman, with Grant's blessing, accepted the

North Carolina capitulation of the remnants of the Confederate
Army of Tennessee in mid-April 1865.

Also overlooked by many are the numerous 1862 and 1863 successes of Grant in the West (Kentucky, Tennessee, and Mississippi).
Acting on his own, he occupied Paducah, Kentucky, in early 1862.
He then moved on to quickly capture Forts Henry and Donelson,
gain control of the Tennessee and Cumberland Rivers, and thereby
put a dagger in the left flank of the Confederacy. Shortly thereafter,
he recovered from a surprise Confederate attack, saved his army in
a vicious two-day battle, and thus won a major victory at Shiloh,
Tennessee.

The next year, Grant, again without approval from above,
moved his army from the west bank across the Mississippi River to
get below Vicksburg, took a daring gamble to feed his army off the
countryside, won a series of five battles in eighteen days against
Confederate forces that cumulatively outnumbered his, and
accepted the surrender of Vicksburg and a nearly 30,000-man army
on July 4, 1863. This brilliant campaign resulted in splitting the
Confederacy, opening the Mississippi to Union commerce, and
impeding the flow of supplies and foodstuffs from Mexico and the
Trans-Mississippi to Confederate armies east of that river. Just as
significantly, the capture of Vicksburg and the simultaneous Union
victory at Gettysburg had a combined devastating impact on morale
throughout the South.

In late 1863, Grant moved successfully into the "Middle Theater" of the war (the area from Nashville, Tennessee, to Atlanta,
Georgia). That autumn Lincoln called upon Grant to save a Union
army that was virtually besieged at Chattanooga in southeastern
Tennessee. When Grant arrived there, Union troops and their surviving animals were on the verge of starvation. Under his leader-

ship, the Federal forces quickly opened a new supply line, captured Lookout Mountain, carried Missionary Ridge, and drove the Rebel Army of Tennessee into the hills of northern Georgia. This November 1863 victory at Chattanooga set the stage for Sherman's 1864 campaign toward Atlanta.

Having ended Confederate control in the Mississippi Valley and eastern Tennessee and having won Lincoln's confidence in his willingness to fight and ability to win, Grant was summoned to the East in early 1864 to close out the war. There the Union Army of the Potomac had squandered opportunities to pursue Lee's Army of Northern Virginia after the battles of Antietam (1862) and Gettysburg (1863), and it had recoiled after the first major battle of each offensive campaign against Lee (Seven Days', Fredericksburg, and Chancellorsville). That army had demonstrated that "... superior numbers and equipment alone did not win the war. Success was contingent upon the outcome of battles and campaigns, and the Army of the Potomac only became successful when it found someone who could use its resources to the utmost."[11] Grant was that someone.

Appendix II of this book contains various estimates of the casualties incurred by Grant's armies and their opponents. My best estimate is that Grant's western casualties (1861–1863) were 36,688 while he imposed 84,187 casualties on his opponents; that his eastern casualties (1864–1865) were 116,954 while he imposed 106,573 casualties on Lee's troops; and that Grant's total Civil War casualties were 153,642 while he imposed 190,760 on the enemy. In light of the fact that strategy and tactics compelled him to be on the offensive throughout the war, these totals are convincing evidence of his intelligent execution of his mission.

Far from being the butcher of the battlefield, Grant determined what the North needed to do to win the war and did it. Grant's record of unparalleled success—including Belmont, Forts Henry and Donelson, Shiloh, Iuka, Corinth, Raymond, Jackson, Champion's Hill, Vicksburg, Chattanooga, the Wilderness, Spotsylvania Court House, Petersburg, and Appomattox—establishes him as the greatest general of the Civil War.

One

LIVING A TROUBLED LIFE

Ulysses Grant lives an industrious boyhood, reluctantly attends West Point, fights courageously in the Mexican War, leaves the Army, and struggles in civilian life.

Hiram Ulysses Grant was born in the Ohio River town of Point Pleasant, Ohio, on April 27, 1822. The family of Ulysses' father, Jesse Root Grant, had moved from Connecticut to Pennsylvania and then to Ohio; the family of his mother, Hannah Simpson Grant, made a similar move from Pennsylvania to Ohio. The year after Ulysses' birth, his father established a tannery east of Point Pleasant in Georgetown, Ohio, and the family moved there.[1]

Young "Ulysses," as he was called, loved working with horses but detested the tannery. By the age of nine or ten, he was earning respectable sums of money breaking horses and driving passengers all over Ohio. Beginning in 1827 or 1828, he attended a series of subscription schools and supplemented them with a year of study at the Maysville Seminary in Maysville, Kentucky (1836–1837), and another at the Presbyterian Academy in Ripley, Ohio (1838–1839).[2]

In his memoirs, Grant described his childhood as a pleasant one, saying, "I did not like to work; but I did as much of it, while young, as grown men can be hired to do in these days, and attended school at the same time. I had as many privileges as any boy in the village, and probably more than most of them. I have no recollection of ever having been punished at home, either by scolding or by the rod."[3]

Unbeknownst to Ulysses, his father arranged with an old friend and local congressman, Thomas L. Hamer, for an appointment to the U.S. Military Academy at West Point, New York. Rather than looking forward to this opportunity, Ulysses was apprehensive about the appointment. Although four local appointees had succeeded there, Ulysses had heard the story of a fifth who, after being twice dismissed from the academy, had been forbidden to return home by his father. Hamer succeeded in securing Ulysses an appointment, and submitted Grant's name to the Academy as Ulysses Simpson (his mother's maiden name) Grant. Although Grant signed some Academy documents as "U. H. Grant," he signed his eight-year enlistment oath as "U. S. Grant" and was on his way to being known to history as Ulysses S. (or U. S.) Grant. William Sherman, a cadet three years ahead of Grant at West Point, remembered "U. S. Grant" appearing on a list of new cadets, and several cadets making up names to fit the initials—"United States" and "Uncle Sam"—finally settling on the moniker "Sam," which became Grant's nickname for life.[4]

A few months after arriving at the Academy, Grant wrote that he was adjusting well. "On the whole, I like the place very much. so much that I would not go away on any account. The fact is that if a man graduates here he safe fer life. let him go where he will. There is much to dislike but more to like. I mean to study hard and stay if it be possible. if I cannot—very well—the world is wide [sic]."[5]

At West Point between 1839 and 1843, Grant made many life-long friends, including James Longstreet, who would later command the First Corps in Lee's Army of Northern Virginia, and Rufus Ingalls, who would serve as Quartermaster of the Army of the Potomac. He knew all the cadets in the classes that graduated between 1840 and 1846; those classes included over fifty men who would be generals in the Civil War.[6] Grant's great horse riding, middling grades, and below-average conduct marks resulted in his graduating twenty-first in his 1843 class of thirty-nine.[7] Perhaps the highlight of his West Point years was his graduation ceremony, during which he rode a large, unmanageable horse and jumped a bar higher than a man's head. Grant was the only cadet who could ride that horse well, and the jump astounded the crowd at the ceremony.[8]

Grant took his post-graduation leave of absence in Ohio, where he was twice mocked for his new military uniform. These incidents, in Grant's own words, "gave me a distaste for military uniform that I never recovered from." Thereafter, he never wore a sword unless ordered to do so. During the Civil War, Grant was notorious for his rumpled, informal, and plain uniforms.[9] He generally wore a private's blouse with the indicia of his rank stitched on the shoulder.

As a junior officer, Grant was assigned to Jefferson Barracks outside St. Louis with the Fourth U.S. Infantry. While there, he visited the nearby home of an Academy roommate, Frederick T. Dent. Dent's younger sister, Julia Boggs Dent, quickly caught the eye of the recently graduated Ulysses, and he began courting her. Grant's attentions toward Julia took up much of his time, and sometimes caused him to be late for dinner at the officers' mess. Each time he was late, Robert C. Buchanan, the strict presiding officer of the mess, made Grant pay for a bottle of wine. This dispute started a long feud between the two officers that was only temporarily halted by the Mexican War.[10]

In May 1844, just as the Mexican War was beginning to erupt, Ulysses and Julia became engaged, though her father gave only his conditional approval to the match.[11] After proposing to Julia, Ulysses left almost immediately for Louisiana and four years of separation to assist in the growing dispute and ultimate war with Mexico.[12] Grant was soon awash in the politics that were leading his country down the path to war. Later, he would write in his memoirs that he had no romantic illusions about the nature of his country's conduct that led to the annexation of Texas and war with Mexico:

> For myself, I was bitterly opposed to [the annexation of Texas], and to this day regard the war, which resulted, as one of the most unjust ever waged by a stronger against a weaker nation. . . . Even if the annexation itself could be justified, the manner in which the subsequent war was forced upon Mexico cannot. The fact is, annexationists wanted more territory than they could possibly lay any claim to. . . . The Southern rebellion was largely the outgrowth of the Mexican war. Nations, like individuals, are punished for their transgressions. We got our punishment in the most sanguinary and expensive war of modern times.[13]

During the Mexican War, Grant served under both Winfield Scott and Zachary ("Old Rough-and-Ready") Taylor. He clearly preferred Taylor. Historians McWhiney and Jamieson concluded that Grant and Taylor shared several characteristics: opposition to plundering, willingness to work with available resources, informality of uniform, attention to detail on the battlefield, reticence in conversation, ability to quickly compose clear and concise written orders, and calmness in the face of danger and responsibility.[14] Grant put that feeling in his own words when he retrospectively praised the quality of Taylor's army: "A more efficient army for its number and armament, I do not believe ever fought a battle than the one commanded by General Taylor in his first two engagements on Mexican—or Texan soil."[15]

Perhaps in part because of a famous incident in which Grant rode a wild horse for three hours and thereby tamed it, Taylor selected Grant as the Fourth Infantry Regiment's quartermaster and commissary officer. Grant protested the appointment because he feared it would remove him from combat. However, the military logistics experience he gained as a result of the position proved invaluable. Historian Jean Edward Smith concurred: "During the Civil War Grant's armies might occasionally have straggled, discipline might sometimes have been lax, but food and ammunition trains were always expertly handled. [Grant's victories] depended in no small measure on his skill as a quartermaster."[16]

Serving with Taylor's high-quality army in 1846 gave Grant an opportunity to demonstrate his skills, as in the case of the battles at Palo Alto and Resaca de Palma, and even to act heroically, as when, with his support, the Americans captured the Mexican city of Monterrey. In the battle at Monterrey, Grant volunteered to ride through the city streets, under fire, to carry a vital message requesting a resupply of ammunition.[17] All told, Grant was elated about his successes. It was clear that his time at West Point had prepared him not only for the logistics of waging war, but had instilled in him a capacity for exhilaration as a participant as well. After the first two battles, he wrote to Julia, "There is no great sport in having bullets flying about one in every direction but I find they have less horror when among them than when in anticipation."[18]

In his memoirs, Grant described his admiration for Zachary Taylor in words that may just as well have applied to Grant himself:[19]

> General Taylor was not an officer to trouble the administration much with his demands, but was inclined to do the best he could with the means given him. He felt his responsibility as going no further. If he had thought that he was sent to perform an impossibility with the means given him, he would probably have informed the authorities of his opinion and left them to determine what should be done. If the judgment was against him he would have gone on and done the best he could with the means at hand without parading his grievance before the public. No soldier could face either danger or responsibility more calmly than he. These are qualities more rarely found than genius or physical courage. General Taylor never made any great show or parade, either of uniform or retinue. In dress he was possibly too plain...; but he was known to every soldier in his army, and was respected by all.[20]

General Taylor's no-frills leadership garnered him much respect, and his successes were bringing some at the highest levels of government to worry about this ever-growing public sentiment. For his part, President James K. Polk feared that General Taylor would capitalize on battlefield victories to win the presidency as a Whig candidate in the upcoming 1848 presidential election. For this reason, Polk spread out the laurels by shifting most of Taylor's force, including Grant's regiment, to another Whig general, Major General Winfield Scott.[21]

Early in 1847, therefore, Grant's regiment joined Scott's famous campaign from Vera Cruz, on the coast, to Mexico City. After Vera Cruz surrendered, Grant fought in the major campaign battles of

Cerro Gordo, Churubusco, Molino del Rey, Chapultepec, and Mexico City. Just outside Mexico City, Grant outflanked Mexican artillery with a small detachment, hauled a mountain howitzer to the top of a church belfry, and enfiladed the Mexican position.[22] His heroism, about which he wrote nothing in his correspondence to Julia, earned him two brevet (temporary) promotions. Grant learned several military lessons from his experiences in the Mexican War, a war in which the United States (like the Union in the Civil War) was obliged to go on the offensive, and these lessons would shape his entire philosophy on war strategy.

From both Taylor and Scott, he learned that aggressiveness on the offensive led to victory. According to Jean Edward Smith, Grant "saw how time and again Zachary Taylor and Winfield Scott moved against a numerically superior foe occupying a fortified position, and how important it was to maintain the momentum of the attack."[23] From Taylor in particular, Grant learned that speed and the ability to maneuver were real assets. From both, he learned the value of being cunning and deceptive about planned offensives. From Scott's abandoning his supply line midway through his march on Mexico City, Grant learned that an army could live off the countryside—a lesson that he aptly applied during his 1863 Vicksburg Campaign.[24]

Grant also came to terms with the fact that death was a normal occurrence among soldiers at war; in fact, death was all around him. 13,283 (16.8 percent) of the 78,718 American soldiers engaged in the Mexican War perished—the highest percentage of any war the United States Army has fought (including the Civil War and both World Wars). However, he may have noted that most deaths came from causes other than battle—only 1,721 of the Americans who died in the Mexican War were killed in action. His personal experience

with death was quite real—only four of the twenty-one officers originally assigned to his regiment survived the war.[25]

The Mexican War experience was also teaching Grant how to
manage life without many of the comforts of home. During the war
and his duty in Texas, Grant was compelled to live outdoors for a
couple years, a way of life that he credits with saving his life and
restoring his health.

But Grant never forgot Julia, at home in Missouri. His extensive
correspondence with Julia between 1845 and 1847 is filled with
almost desperate pleas for her father to approve their marriage.
Finally, in the midst of the Mexico City campaign, Grant learned
that Julia's father had at last given his consent. The happiness that
this news must have given Grant on his journey back home was
somewhat tempered by an event that created a black mark on
Grant's military record. During the Fourth Infantry's return to the
United States, someone stole $1,000 in quartermaster's funds from
the trunk of a friend of Grant's. As quartermaster, Grant was held
accountable. Although a board of inquiry convened at his request
cleared Grant, he was still legally required to reimburse the government for the loss—a requirement that would prove difficult to
meet. Grant would spend the next several years trying to get that
debt invalidated.[26]

When the war was at last over, Ulysses Grant married Julia Dent
on August 22, 1848, with James Longstreet as his best man. Soon
after, Grant and his new wife visited his family in Ohio and then
moved on to his stations in Sackets Harbor, New York (on Lake
Ontario), and Detroit, Michigan. It was in these early years of marriage that Grant first realized he had a drinking problem. Stationed
at Sackets Harbor, Grant decided to battle his problem by joining
the Sons of Temperance, which apparently provided him with sup-

port until he was transferred. The drinking problems may have returned after he moved to Detroit. That at least was the impression generated when he fell on an icy sidewalk in January 1851 and sued the merchant who owned the sidewalk. The merchant said of Grant, "If you soldiers would keep sober, perhaps you would not fall on people's pavement and hurt your legs." Grant won the case but came under suspicion in the military community.[27]

The togetherness that Ulysses and Julia shared ended when Grant received orders to go to the Pacific Northwest; Grant decided against taking his pregnant wife and infant son on the dangerous journey to frontier country.[28]

Before sailing west from New York in July 1852, Grant attempted to clear up the quartermaster funds issue. He visited Washington in an unsuccessful effort to resolve the problem; he was stymied by Senator Henry Clay's funeral, which closed the entire city for one of the two days that he was there.[29] Grant would have to deal with the matter later.

Grant scarcely had time to reflect on the issue as his journey to the Pacific got underway with a harrowing crossing of Panama. Grant helped fight a cholera epidemic and was moved by the death of a hundred persons, including his friends and their children.[30] After staying at the Presidio in San Francisco, he traveled north and assumed his duties as commissary officer at Columbia Barracks (renamed Fort Vancouver), where he invested in a store, cattle, hogs, and a farm. These investments, a common practice in those days, brought only losses to Grant. He sold firewood to steamers and rented horses, but the farm was flooded by the Columbia River. Separated from his family, Grant joined many of his fellow officers in heavy drinking. His small size and apparent sensitivity to alcohol made him more prone to intoxication, and his behavior was observed by visiting officers such as the future general George B. McClellan.[31]

His September and October 1853 requests to go to Washington to settle the old $1,000 debt were denied. Instead he received orders to Fort Humboldt in northern California, where he reported on January 5, 1854. As a company commander at Fort Humboldt in 1854, Grant served under Lieutenant Colonel Robert Buchanan, the same officer with whom he had feuded in Missouri. Buchanan made life miserable for Grant. Receiving little mail and anxious to return east, Grant was lonely and depressed, and again he reportedly often drank heavily.[32]

Separated from his wife and family, Grant reflected on his depression in his letters to Julia. On February 2, he wrote to her, "You do not know how forsaken I feel here.... I got one letter from you since I have been here but it was some three months old."[33] Four days later he voiced greater concern and frustration:

> A mail come in this evening but brought me no news from you nor nothing in reply to my application for orders to go home. I cannot conceive what is the cause of the delay. The state of suspense that I am in is scarsely bearable. I think I have been from my family quite long enough and sometimes I feel as though I could almost go home "*nolens volens.*" I presume, under ordinary circumstances, Humboldt would be a good enough place but the suspense I am in would make paradice form a bad picture. [*sic*][34]

In a March 6 letter, he said he was "almost tempted to resign." On March 25, he said that he had received only one letter from Julia at Fort Humboldt (written the prior October) and added, "How very anxious I am to get home once again. I do not feel as if it was possible to endure this separation much longer."[35]

By April 11 Grant had reached his breaking point. Upon receiving notice of his promotion to captain and possibly a threat from Buchanan of a court-martial for being intoxicated while on duty, Grant acknowledged receipt of his new commission, resigned his Army commission (effective July 31, 1854), and requested a leave of absence.[36] He then returned to New York via Nicaragua. Grant's public drinking throughout much of his fifteen-year army career and the circumstances surrounding his resignation had tarred him with a reputation as a heavy drinker.[37] His financial situation deteriorated, as he was unable to collect a $1,750 debt owed to him in San Francisco and $800 owed to him by an Army sutler. He ended up borrowing money from a friend, Captain Simon Bolivar Buckner.[38]

After reentering civilian life, Grant endured the most trying and frustrating years of his life. For several years his primary sources of income were sales of firewood cut on the land that had been given to Julia by her father, Frederick Dent. Grant was an unsuccessful farmer and rent collector. He built a ramshackle house—that he appropriately named Hardscrabble—which Julia despised. He tried to borrow money from his father. A particularly low point occurred in the midst of the 1857 depression when he pawned his gold watch for $22. Throughout this period, Grant was quite dependent upon Julia's father, with whom he had an acrimonious relationship. After giving up farming in 1858, Grant dabbled in real estate until 1860. Finally, he twice applied unsuccessfully for the position of St. Louis County engineer. All in all, these were depressing times.[39] Although it was difficult for him to do, Grant went to his father for help and finally escaped the clutches of Frederick Dent. In May 1860 Ulysses began working under his younger brothers, Simpson and Orvil, in the Grant family's successful leather-goods store in Galena, Illinois. He moved his family into a rented house, led a sober life, and apparently began rebuilding his self-respect.[40] Although he became friends with attorney John A. Rawlins, a Federal elector pledged to the Democrat Stephen A. Douglas, Grant did not meet the Illinois residency requirement for voting in the November 6, 1860, presidential election.

On the eve of the Civil War, Ulysses Grant had a less-than-successful record as a peacetime Army officer, a distant history of Mexican War heroism, and a well-known drinking problem when separated from his wife and children. Although he had proven his dogged determination and persistence, there was not yet any indication of the military greatness he would demonstrate during the nation's most important war.

Two

1861: SEEKING A CHANCE TO FIGHT

As the Civil War breaks out, Grant desperately seeks a meaningful command, settles for a training position, excels at it, obtains a regimental command, and leads his troops into the Battle of Belmont.

braham Lincoln's November 1860 election as the first Republican president of the United States led South Carolina and six other southern states to secede from the Union before he was sworn in as president on March 4, 1861. Grant perceived the Republican Party's opposition to extension of slavery to the territories as the primary cause of secession.[1]

After the Confederates initiated hostilities by firing on Fort Sumter on April 12, 1861, Grant, like many Midwesterners, was anxious to enter the fray in response to Lincoln's call for 75,000 volunteers. Grant attended and was called upon to preside over a public meeting in Galena on April 16 and chaired a recruiting rally two days later. Grant refused to become a mere ordinary captain in the company[2] of volunteers; instead, he drilled them in Galena and at Camp Yates near Springfield. Although he initially declined to seek political intervention in order to obtain a senior military position, he did not refuse an offer of assistance from the powerful local Congressman Elihu B. Washburne, the senior Republican in the House of Representatives. With Washburne's help, Grant became a military aide to Illinois Governor Richard Yates on April 29. That position had high promotion potential. Grant took charge of mustering ten regiments into Illinois service.[3]

When that assignment was completed, Grant still had no military command or position. Grant hoped that his fifteen years of Army service would quickly earn him a position of leadership and responsibility in the United States Army, but those hopes were soon dashed. First, he wrote a letter dated May 24 to the adjutant general in Washington, offering his services for the duration of the war and stating his competence to command a regiment. Next, he personally applied in Cincinnati for a position with Major General George McClellan, who commanded Ohio's militia but may have remembered Grant as a heavy drinker. Hearing nothing from McClellan, Grant next applied to Brigadier General Nathaniel Lyon in St. Louis. Again, he received no reply.[4]

While Grant desperately sought a position, Confederate Brigadier General Richard S. Ewell in Richmond warned a friend, "There is one West Pointer, I think in Missouri, little known, and whom I hope the Northern people will not find out. I mean Sam Grant. I knew him well at the Academy and in Mexico. I should fear him more than any of their officers I have yet heard of. He is not a man of genius, but he is clear-headed, quick and daring."[5]

Grant resigned himself to returning home and somehow creating his own opportunity. However, his work had caught the attention of Congressman Washburne, who would prove to be Grant's dependable sponsor and protector throughout the war. Washburne had seen Grant's performance, realized his military potential, and helped convince Governor Yates to name Grant a colonel and regimental militia commander. Perhaps even more significant was the request to Yates from the officers of the 21st Illinois Volunteers that Grant replace their commander. Their colonel had lost control of the volunteers; the men had become notorious for their drunken rowdiness, petty thefts, and lack of any military discipline. Yates consulted his aides, who had been impressed by Grant's professional direction of that and other regiments, and then offered the command to Grant. After his June 15 appointment, Grant quickly brought discipline to the previously unruly regiment, which was then mustered into national service on June 28. To convince his troops to extend their ninety-day enlistments to three years as a condition of undertaking national service, Grant arranged for speeches by Congressmen (and later generals) John A. McClernand and John A. ("Black Jack") Logan.[6]

Grant immediately recognized that lack of leadership was the fundamental problem in the regiment he was to command. He addressed that issue in his first order of the war: "In accepting this command, your Commander will require the co-operation of all the commissioned and non-commissioned Officers in instructing the command, and in maintaining discipline, and hopes to receive also the hearty support of every enlisted man."[7] Jean Edward Smith perceptively analyzed the significance of this order and what it represented in Grant's approach to commanding units primarily consisting of volunteers:

> The phraseology is vintage Grant. The cooperation of officers and noncommissioned officers was *required*; the support of the enlisted men was something to be *hoped for*. That

distinction became a hallmark of Grant's leadership. No West Point-trained officer understood the nature of the Union's volunteer army better than Grant. Having survived a number of years on the bottom rung in civil life, he had developed an instinctive feel for how civilians behaved. He recognized that volunteer soldiers were not regulars and never tried to impose the spartan discipline of the old army.[8]

Grant used experience and common sense to establish his credibility in numerous ways. When ordered to move his men one hundred sixteen miles to the Mississippi River, Grant declined rail transportation and had his men march the distance. He told Yates, "The men are going to do a lot of marching before the war is over and I prefer to train them in friendly country, not in the enemy's." Based on his Mexican War experience, his supply requisitions were complete and required no changes. When his men were unprepared for an early morning march, he started without many of them and the laggards hurriedly dressed and ran to catch up; the next morning they were ready on schedule.[9]

In early July, Grant's regiment was ordered to Quincy, Illinois, then to Ironton, Missouri, and finally to Florida, Missouri. Grant was to move on the latter two locations to dislodge Confederate forces that were reported to be there. It was during those two movements that Grant first experienced the pre-battle anxiety of a Civil War commander. In his memoirs, he described those emotional experiences:

> My sensations as we approached what I supposed might be "a field of battle" were anything but agreeable. I had been in all the engagements in Mexico that it was possible for one person to be in; but not in command. If some one else had been

colonel and I had been lieutenant-colonel I do not think I would have felt any trepidation. . . . As we approached the brow of the hill from which it was expected we could see Harris' camp, and possibly find his men ready formed to meet us, my heart kept getting higher and higher until it felt to me it was in my throat. [After finding the enemy camp abandoned,] [m]y heart resumed its place. It occurred to me at once that Harris had been as much afraid of me as I had been of him. This was a view of the question I had never taken before; but it was one I never forgot afterwards. From that event to the close of the war, I never experienced trepidation upon confronting an enemy, though I always felt more or less anxiety.[10]

During the summer and early autumn, Grant commanded several regiments in Missouri, was appointed brigadier general of volunteers on August 5 (based on Washburne's recommendation), and named his Galena friend, John Rawlins, his adjutant.[11] While in Missouri, Grant told his headquarters he was, contrary to orders, not building fortifications for his troops. He wrote, "I am not fortifying here at all. . . . Drill and discipline is more necessary for the men than fortifications . . . . I have . . . very little disposition to gain a 'Pillow notoriety' for a branch of service that I have forgotten all about."[12] As Jean Edward Smith noted, "Fortifications reflected a defensive mentality alien to his nature."[13]

Major General John C. Fremont, Union commander in the West, passed over more senior generals and appointed Grant to be the commander of the District of Southeast Missouri. This appointment put Grant in charge of the critical Mississippi River region with Missouri on the west and Kentucky and Illinois on the east. He established his headquarters in Cairo, Illinois, where the Mississippi and Ohio rivers intersect.[14]

Grant immediately faced a crisis and converted it into a strategic success. He learned that Confederate soldiers had breached Kentucky's neutrality and had occupied and were fortifying Columbus, a strong position on the Mississippi a mere twenty miles south of Cairo. More critically, Grant heard from a supposedly reliable spy that Confederates were marching on Paducah, a key Kentucky town at the junction of the Ohio and Tennessee rivers. As soon as he learned of the Confederate occupation of Columbus and the apparent threat to Paducah, Grant wired Fremont of the developments and his intent to move on Paducah unless instructed otherwise.

Within a day, Grant organized an expedition and on September 6, 1861, took possession of Paducah with troops and gunboats. Grant seized Paducah, "a masterful countermeasure to the Confederate occupation of Columbus," in the words of Donald J. Roberts II,[15] without any orders to do so. Grant did not wait for an answer to his wire to Fremont; Fremont's orders to take Paducah were awaiting Grant at Cairo when he returned from Paducah.[16] Although Confederate troops had not actually been marching on Paducah, Grant's initiative in quickly seizing the town reflected its vulnerability, Grant's concern about the damage its loss could impose, and his belief in its utility to the Union.[17]

Fremont transferred Grant and replaced him at Paducah with Brigadier General Charles F. Smith (Grant's commandant at West Point and his early Civil War mentor). Shortly thereafter, Smith's troops occupied Smithland, where the Cumberland meets the Ohio. Thus, the scene was set for Grant's early 1862 thrust into Kentucky and Tennessee via the two riverine highways, the Tennessee and the Cumberland.

For now, however, Fremont was more concerned about, and directed Grant to focus on, the Mississippi River—in particular the

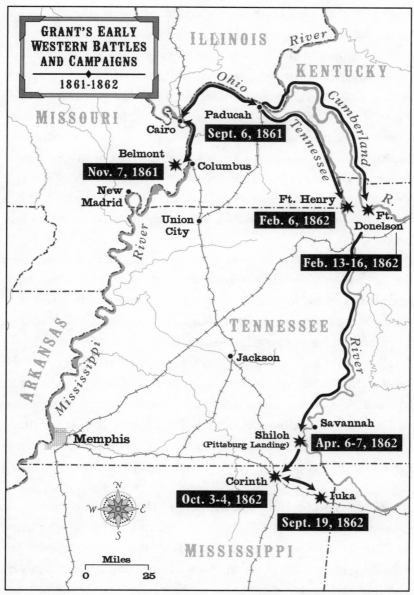

GRANT'S EARLY
WESTERN BATTLES
AND CAMPAIGNS
◆ 1861-1862 ◆

ILLINOIS

River

Ohio

KENTUCKY

Cumberland

MISSOURI

Cairo

Paducah
Sept. 6, 1861

Tennessee

Belmont
Nov. 7, 1861   Columbus

New
Madrid

Ft. Henry
Feb. 6, 1862   Ft.
Donelson   R.

River

Union
City

Feb. 13-16, 1862

TENNESSEE

River

• Jackson

ARKANSAS

Mississippi

Memphis

Shiloh
(Pittsburg Landing)   • Savannah
Apr. 6-7, 1862

Corinth
Oct. 3-4, 1862   ✹ Iuka

Sept. 19, 1862

MISSISSIPPI

N
W · E
S

Miles
0   25

DAVID DEIS, DREAMLINE CARTOGRAPHY

Confederates at Columbus. Beginning on September 8, 1861, Grant used army and naval forces to probe Confederate positions on both banks of the Mississippi. Hoping to take the offensive, Grant sought permission from Fremont to undertake a campaign against Columbus. Fremont, however, had other problems. Reacting to the surrender of 3,500 Union soldiers to a vastly superior Confederate force at Lexington, Missouri, Fremont assembled a 38,000-man Union force, marched into the heart of Missouri, and drove the Confederates into the southwestern part of the state. Fremont, however, had alienated Missouri's Unionists and lost the confidence of President Lincoln, who relieved him of command on November 2.[18]

The day before, Grant finally had received orders to proceed to the vicinity of Columbus. His assignment was to "demonstrate" against the enemy in order to discourage a westward movement of Confederate troops from Columbus into Missouri. Grant's idea of a demonstration was an attack—even though his orders specifically said he was not to do this. Therefore, he planned to assault the Confederate position across the river from Columbus at Belmont, Missouri. His decision to attack in violation of orders was based on two months of intelligence-gathering, his interpretation of enemy intentions, and his increasing willingness to take the initiative, reinforced by his earlier success in seizing Paducah without orders to do so.[19]

Grant would be attacking with only 3,100 troops, whereas the Columbus citadel had 17,000 defenders and 140 artillery pieces. But Grant kept Major General Leonidas ("Bishop") Polk, the Confederate commander, guessing about his intentions. He did this by ordering three columns to move south in Kentucky and two more to do so in Missouri. With his multiple diversionary columns on the move, on November 6, Grant dispatched his 3,100 attackers on steamboats and moved south from Cairo, Illinois. That night he tied up his vessels on the Kentucky (eastern) shore, an action that threatened Columbus. The next morning, however, Grant's men landed at Belmont on the Missouri (western) shore. They came under fire from Columbus artillery and Belmont small arms. Under Grant's personal direction, his men successfully drove the Confederate defenders back to and ultimately through their camp. However, Grant lost control of his neophyte force as they looted the abandoned camp.[20]

Grant's officers and men were restored to order and frightened by Confederate shells that began falling among them. They were cut off from their transports by the Rebels who had fled, moved upstream, and then been reinforced by troops from the Kentucky shore. Suddenly the Union troops realized they had to get back to their transports quickly. Grant reorganized them and they fought through the Confederates again—just in time to get back to their steamboats before being overwhelmed by a superior Confederate force sent across in two more steamers from Columbus.

Grant was the last man aboard the departing Union transports as his horse leaped over the riverbank edge, slid down the bank and trotted aboard the boat on a single gangplank.[21] As Major General Lewis ("Lew") Wallace later wrote, Grant's actions at Belmont were noteworthy, and "the addendum that he had lingered in face of the enemy until he was hauled aboard with the last gang-plank, did him great good."[22]

Grant's foray had created quite a stir among Polk and the Confederates at Columbus. Polk telegraphed President Davis that he had driven away 8,000 attackers and that Grant was reported to have been killed. Three days later, Polk wrote in his official report that "the battle was fought against great odds" and that the Union attackers had lost at least 1,500 men. However, Confederate dead and wounded poured into Memphis, and Grant miraculously reappeared. As soon as it became known that Grant had attacked with only 3,100 troops, an embarrassed Polk ceased claiming victory. He called in his outlying troops and hunkered down in Columbus. The momentum was with Grant—as it would be throughout the war.[23]

Grant's deceptive hit-and-run attack kept Polk from effectively using his superior numbers and amazingly resulted in slightly more casualties for the defenders than the attackers—an unusual occurrence in the Civil War. Of the 3,100 men engaged by Grant, only about 500 were killed, wounded, or missing in the battle. The Confederate force of 7,000, including reinforcements from Columbus, reported about 640 men killed, wounded, or missing.[24]

On the down side, Grant had underestimated the Rebels' ability to counterattack his men; this tendency to overlook the potential for enemy attacks would haunt him again at Fort Donelson and Shiloh. Grant was pleased with the results: his soldiers gained self-confidence, the Rebel forces at Columbus were at least disconcerted, and the Confederates canceled any plans to move troops across the Mississippi to assist their comrades in Missouri. Even more importantly for the North, Belmont brought Ulysses Grant's name to the attention of President Lincoln, who was desperate for any kind of action by a Union general.[25] By the end of 1861, Ulysses Grant had established a good foundation for the great achievements that lay ahead. He had reentered the army, been promoted to brigadier general, and carried out his duties with great initiative and a modicum of casualties. Using tactics that presaged his later Vicksburg Campaign, Grant had used multiple diversions to keep General Polk at Columbus guessing at his intentions while he attacked

Belmont. Most noteworthy during this period was his prompt action, solely on his own initiative, to seize control of the mouths of the Tennessee and Cumberland Rivers—a bloodless movement that laid the groundwork for significant progress in early 1862.

Three

WINTER 1862: CAPTURING FORTS HENRY AND DONELSON

Grant overcomes General Halleck's reluctance, captures Fort Henry, besieges Fort Donelson, counterattacks after a Confederate assault, demands the Fort's unconditional surrender, and wins national fame—all with minimal losses.

From his headquarters at Cairo, Illinois, Grant conceived a brilliant strategy to bypass the Confederate Mississippi stronghold at Columbus, Kentucky, and use more easterly rivers to take the war all the way into Tennessee. His plan was to coordinate waterborne and overland troop movements with naval gunboats to capture Fort Henry on the Tennessee River and Fort Donelson on the Cumberland River. If successful, this campaign would not only force General Polk to abandon Columbus on the Mississippi, but also open the way for Union capture of Nashville, the Tennessee capital, and sever the major east-west railroad from Memphis to Charleston, South Carolina. In addition, a successful move would open western Tennessee to occupation and enable Union gunboats to reach as far south as northern Mississippi and Alabama.[1]

Grant's major problem was the reluctant Major General Henry W. Halleck, the new commander of the Department of the Missouri. After his November 19 appointment, Halleck spent two months probing the enemy and discouraging any offensive action. When Grant went to St. Louis on January 23, 1862, to propose his offensive, Halleck abruptly cut off Grant's discussion of an up-river campaign and told him that such a matter was not Grant's business. After returning to Cairo, Grant persisted and won support from his Navy counterpart, Navy Flag Officer Andrew H. Foote. Therefore, he was prepared to act when a frustrated President Lincoln issued a January 27 order calling for a general advance by all U.S. forces, including "the Army and Flotilla at Cairo."

The next day Grant sent Halleck a telegram—endorsed by Foote—requesting permission to initiate the assault jointly with Foote's riverboat flotilla. The following day Grant sent a follow-up message telling Halleck, "The advantages of this move are as perceptible to the General Commanding the Department as to myself therefore further statements are unnecessary. [sic]"[2] Seeing that he had no other course of action, Halleck sent a January 30 telegram and letter to Grant directing him to "move with the least possible delay" to take and hold Fort Henry. "In three days Grant organized his command for battle, issued rations and ammunition, provided for resupply, procured river transportation, and coordinated the movement of seven Union gunboats. . . ."[3]

Early on the morning of February 3, Grant was already in a position to sail up the Tennessee River from Paducah. Foote's fleet consisted of four ironclad and three timber-clad gunboats, as well as nine transports carrying Grant's 15,000 troops, animals, supplies, and artillery. As the fleet left Paducah, Grant told his aide Rawlins how relieved he was that they were now beyond recall by Halleck.[4]

As General C. F. Smith had advised Grant, Fort Henry was so poorly situated on the Tennessee that much of it was under high water when its defenders learned of the impending attack. Its guns, however, posed a substantial threat and almost killed Grant when he ordered the gunboat *Essex* to move within two miles of the fort to test the range of those guns. Faced with these obstacles, Grant ordered McClernand's troops to disembark three miles north of the fort. McClernand gathered intelligence that the fort had been reinforced with as many as 20,000 troops, but, contrary to this information, there had been no such reinforcements.[5]

Shortly after noon on February 6, Foote's fleet began its bombardment of the fort. His fifty-four guns out-dueled the seventeen heavy guns inside the flooded fort. The bombardment was so horrific that the 3,400-man garrison panicked and fled east toward Fort Donelson, about eleven miles away on the Cumberland River. Within two hours, Brigadier General Lloyd Tilghman hoisted the white flag of surrender. Foote's sailors actually rowed into the fort to accept its surrender. Embarrassed by the flight of his soldiers, Tilghman formally reported that he had transferred them to Fort Donelson the previous day. Not proud of McClernand's mud-marching soldiers' failure to cut off the Rebels' escape, Grant never contested Tilghman's lie, which has become the commonly accepted version of what occurred at Fort Henry.[6]

Grant had to be thrilled at the quickness of the victory but disappointed that his soldiers, who had been disembarked miles downstream and encountered swampy marching conditions, did not intercept the fleeing Confederates. Nevertheless, Grant sent out patrols and then decided on his next step. He called a meeting of his commanders, C. F. Smith, Lew Wallace, and McClernand, who he hoped would quickly agree to a cross-country march on Fort

Donelson. McClernand, who was lobbying Washington for Grant's job, delayed the proceedings by reading a verbose declaration he pulled from his pocket. But Grant had no trouble ignoring him and deciding to move his army on to Fort Donelson.[7]

Although he had no orders from Halleck authorizing his action, Grant quickly ordered his troops to follow the retreating Confederates to Fort Donelson. "In doing so," in Jean Edward Smith's words, "he disregarded explicit instructions to entrench at Fort Henry, ignored Halleck's order to prepare to receive a Confederate attack, and took virtually all of his command with him."[8] Bad roads and heavy rains, however, hindered the movement of Grant's troops to Fort Donelson.

Grant and Foote took advantage of their control of the Tennessee by sending three wooden gunboats twenty-five miles upriver to destroy the Memphis and Ohio Railroad bridge (linking Memphis with Bowling Green, Kentucky) and a total of one hundred and fifty miles south into northern Alabama and Mississippi—all the way to the head of navigation at Muscle Shoals, Alabama. The mini-fleet captured a fast steamboat, destroyed or captured five other vessels, destroyed a wealth of shipbuilding supplies, revived Union sentiment, and spread discontent among Confederate supporters.[9]

Meanwhile Foote's fleet had to steam northward down the Tennessee to the Ohio, eastward up the Ohio to the Cumberland, and southward up the Cumberland to threaten Fort Donelson from the north. On the way, they diverted down the Ohio for repairs at Cairo.[10]

General Albert Sydney Johnston, the Confederate Departmental Commander, played into Grant's hands by neither withdrawing from Fort Donelson to enable his troops to fight another day, nor forcefully reinforcing that position with all his available troops.

Instead, he temporized and sent three brigades to boost the Confederate force there to 17,000. Perhaps shocked by the unexpectedly sudden loss of Fort Henry, Johnston, in Jean Edward Smith's words, had committed "an error of catastrophic proportions."[11]

Grant's troops laid siege to Fort Donelson on February 12. They were reinforced and resupplied by General Sherman from Smithland and from other commands throughout the Midwest. Although as soon as Fort Henry had fallen, Grant had advised Halleck of his intention to take Fort Donelson and Halleck had ordered reinforcements to his command, Halleck sent no communication to Grant either approving or disapproving his plans. Grant was on his own.[12]

February 13 brought fighting on land and water. Despite Grant's orders not to bring on a battle until they had received reinforcements, both Smith and McClernand sent some troops on senseless and unsuccessful assaults of the Confederate line. Meanwhile, Foote initiated an exchange of long-range fire between his ships and the fort's batteries. The unimpressive Union efforts that day were followed that night by the arrival of bitterly cold weather, including snow, sleet, and freezing rain, that brought suffering to the men of both armies.[13]

In recognition of the new situation created by the fall of Fort Henry, on February 14 Grant was appointed Commander of the District of West Tennessee, and his troops became the Army of the Tennessee. Valentine's Day also brought Grant more reinforcements, which he formed into a third division and placed under the command of Lew Wallace between Smith on the left and McClernand on the right. That same busy day, Foote unsuccessfully launched his major gunboat assault on Fort Donelson. He learned to his dismay that, unlike Fort Henry, Donelson, which had been built on high ground, had an artillery advantage over attacking gun-boats. The 32-pounder guns of the fort raked the Union vessels, which had ventured too close. Fifty-four men on the ships were killed. The Confederate defenders were heartened by the sight of Union vessels falling back down the river—badly damaged and clearly out of control.[14]

The next morning Grant was miles downriver from Fort Donelson with the wounded Foote on his flagship planning their next actions when the Confederates successfully attacked from Donelson and pushed back McClernand's troops on Grant's right flank. Wallace eventually sent help from the center of Grant's line, and the Confederate attack was halted by fifty-five rounds of shot and shell from Wallace's guns. The Confederates had an opportunity to flee south toward Nashville away from the Fort Donelson trap, but they failed to do so. Their hesitation provided Grant with the opportunity to regroup, counterattack, and seal off their escape route.[15]

When Grant arrived on the deadlocked scene after a seven-mile ride from Foote's location, he immediately saw that the battle hung in the balance and took the initiative to win it. Initially he was inclined to entrench, but, when informed that the enemy had an open escape route, he ordered the position on the Union right to be retaken.[16] He reassured his subordinates that the enemy would no doubt be equally demoralized and that victory belonged to the aggressor. Grant's own description of the events demonstrates his quick grasp of the situation and his hands-on battlefield tactics:

> I turned to Colonel J[oseph].D. Webster, of my staff, who was with me, and said: "Some of our men are pretty badly demor-alized, but the enemy must be more so, for he has attempted to force his way out, but has fallen back: the one who attacks first now will be victorious and the enemy will have to be in

a hurry if he gets ahead of me.".... I directed Colonel Webster to ride with me and call out to the men as we passed: "Fill your cartridge-boxes, quick, and get into line; the enemy is trying to escape and he must not be permitted to do so." This acted like a charm. The men only wanted some one to give them a command.[17]

Grant reasoned that the Fort Donelson troops had been seeking to break out to the south and probably had left a thin line of defenders on the northern portion of their defensive line. Therefore, he ordered Smith to attack that weakened quarter while Wallace and McClernand recovered the lost ground on the Union right (south). Smith forced his way into the north end of the Confederate lines and bivouacked there in a threatening position that night, while the other two division commanders drove the Rebels back into their entrenchments. The Confederate escape route to Nashville appeared to be blocked.[18]

Late that afternoon Grant demonstrated his sympathy for the wounded of both sides. He discovered an injured Union officer trying to give a drink to a wounded Confederate soldier. Grant dismounted, gave each of them a swig of brandy, ordered corpsmen to remove them on stretchers, and told the reluctant stretcher-bearers to "take the Confederate too. The war is over between them." Continuing his ride among the wounded, Grant told his aide, Colonel Webster, "Let's get away from this dreadful place. I suppose this work is part of the devil that is left in us all." He then quietly recited words of poet Robert Burns: "Man's inhumanity to man/Makes countless thousands mourn."[19]

In the meantime, Confederate Brigadier Generals John B. Floyd, Gideon J. Pillow, and Simon Buckner (Grant's old friend) argued about whether to attempt another breakout, maintain and defend their position, or surrender. Deciding that surrender was probably the wisest course, the incompetent and fearful Floyd (a former disloyal U.S. Secretary of War) and Pillow fled in transports with 1,500 to 3,000 troops and left Buckner to negotiate terms of surrender. Fort Donelson's cavalry commander, Lieutenant Colonel Nathan Bedford Forrest, escaped along the river with 700 to 1,000 Confederate riders.[20]

When, on February 16, Buckner requested negotiation of terms for Fort Donelson, Grant (following Smith's advice) succinctly replied, "No terms except an unconditional and immediate surrender can be accepted. I propose to move immediately upon your works." As a result of this response and the Confederate capitulation on Grant's "ungenerous and unchivalrous terms" (in the words of Buckner in his response to Grant), Grant's West Point-imposed initials suddenly stood for "Unconditional Surrender" Grant.[21]

From Fort Donelson, Grant took away an important lesson. He realized that in every battle there comes a critical time when the issue hangs in the balance, when both sides are exhausted, and that is the time when the outcome is decided. He realized, said T. Harry Williams, that "the general who had the moral courage to continue fighting would win."[22] Historian Benjamin Franklin Cooling concurred with that analysis: "A crisis had been reached in the battle—in Grant's very career, in fact. Calling upon every resource at his command, the general did not waver or vacillate. Here was an opportunity to counter-attack, and Grant seized it."[23]

In the time between the battles of Fort Sumter and Appomattox Court House, three Civil War armies surrendered to their foes. All three were Confederate armies that surrendered to Grant. Buckner's remaining army of 14,000 at Fort Donelson was the first. Those soldiers were soon on their way to Union prison camps in the

North.[24] The news of the fall of Forts Henry and Donelson hit Confederate President Jefferson Davis "like an earthquake," and the impact grew worse as he realized that his armies were thereby being compelled to abandon all of Kentucky and much of Tennessee. The abandonment of Tennessee may have cost the South many additional conscripts.[25]

Grant wired the good news to Halleck's Chief of Staff in St. Louis: "I am pleased to announce to you the unconditional surrender this morning of Fort Donelson, with twelve to fifteen thousand prisoners, at least forty pieces of Artillery and a large amount of stores, horses, mules and other public property."[26] Ominously, Halleck never acknowledged Grant's telegram or congratulated him on his victories. The northern press hailed "Unconditional Surrender" Grant and his twin victories. President Lincoln immediately awarded Grant's success by promoting him to major general of volunteers (a temporary wartime position). In his brilliant, flowing prose, Shelby Foote described how the Northern public, so desperate for victory, ignored all the mistakes Grant had made:

> They saw rather, the sweep and slam-bang power of a leader who marched on Wednesday, skirmished on Thursday, imperturbably watched the fleet's repulse on Friday, fought desperately on Saturday, and received the fort's unconditional surrender on Sunday. Undeterred by wretched weather, the advice of the tactics manuals, or the reported strength of the enemy position, he had inflicted about 2000 casualties and suffered about 3000 himself—which was as it should have been, considering his role as the attacker—and now there were something more than 12,000 rebel soldiers, the cream of Confederate volunteers, on their way to northern prison camps

to await exchange for as many Union boys, who otherwise would have languished in southern prisons under the coming summer sun. People saw Grant as the author of this deliverance, the embodiment of the offensive spirit, the man who would strike and keep on striking until this war was won.[27]

In the Confederate capital, however, the news was a blow. Word of Donelson's fall came at the same time as Jefferson Davis' inauguration, and Confederate War Department clerk J. B. Jones tried to put a brave face on the Confederate calamity: "At last we have the astounding tidings that Donelson has fallen, and Buckner, and 9000 men, arms, stores, everything are in possession of the enemy! Did the President know it yesterday [the inauguration]? Or did the Secretary keep it back until the new government (permanent) was launched into existence? Wherefore? The Southern *people* cannot be daunted by calamity!"[28]

A harbinger of troubles to come between Grant and Halleck was Halleck's wide dispersal of praise for the victories on the rivers— even to generals subordinate to Grant or barely involved in the fighting—coupled with Halleck's simultaneous failure to send Grant a message of congratulations. Even while Grant was campaigning against the twin forts, Halleck had tried to replace Grant with three other generals: Brigadier General William Sherman, who declined; Major General Ethan Allen Hitchcock, an elderly Mexican War veteran who also declined; and Brigadier General Don Carlos Buell, who did not respond to Halleck. After Donelson, Halleck had the gall to wire General-in-Chief McClellan: "Make Buell, Grant, and [John] Pope major generals of volunteers and give me command of the West. I ask this in return for Forts Henry and Donelson." Stanton and Lincoln, aware of who deserved credit, agreed to promote only Grant, who then ranked tenth among Union generals. However,

Halleck had clearly demonstrated that he was jealous and mistrustful of Grant.[29]

Making sure not to rest on his laurels or be dismayed by Halleck's snub, Grant moved his soldiers southward up both rivers until they occupied Clarksville, Tennessee, on February 19 and finally the capital, Nashville, on February 25. Halleck delayed Grant's occupation of Nashville and thereby enabled Forrest to remove commissary and quartermaster stores there.[30] However, Grant's delayed but swift movements angered the slow-footed Buell, whose Army of the Ohio had targeted Nashville as its own goal. On March 1, Halleck belatedly ordered Grant to proceed south on the Tennessee to disrupt Confederate railroads.

Grant's quick thrust against and capture of Forts Henry and Donelson achieved his goals of forcing Polk from Columbus and the Confederates from most of Kentucky, capturing Nashville, seriously disrupting Confederate rail communications, opening western Tennessee to Union occupation, and threatening northern Mississippi and Alabama. He had thrust a dagger into the Confederate left flank.

Civil War historians Herman Hattaway and Archer Jones went so far as to say, "We suggest that Grant's capture of the forts, early in 1862, might justly be regarded as the major turning point [of the war]. . . . "[31] Most impressively, Grant had done all of this while incurring minimal casualties. Of his 27,000 troops, only 2,600 were killed or wounded, while another 224 were missing or captured. In addition, his troops killed or wounded 2,000 Confederates and captured another 14,000.[32] Grant's first major victory was a harbinger of many victories to come—victories that he would achieve with a minimal or reasonable loss of manpower.

Four

Spring 1862: Salvaging
a Victory at Shiloh

Grant pursues the Confederates, is surprised by a massive Confederate attack at Shiloh, saves his army in a day-long battle, and retrieves victory from defeat by launching a successful counterattack that drives the enemy from the field the next day.

rant hoped to capitalize on his successes at Forts Henry and Donelson with an immediate move up the Cumberland to seize the Tennessee capital of Nashville. Instead, Halleck ordered Grant and Foote to remain at Fort Donelson and the neighboring Clarksville and not to move on Nashville. Halleck told them he was awaiting instructions from Washington, but actually Halleck was pressuring General-in-Chief McClellan and Secretary of War Edwin M. Stanton to put him in charge of all the western Union armies. Grant and Foote's forward movement was being held hostage by the ambitions of one man. A frustrated Grant nevertheless resolved the Nashville situation by sending a division of Buell's troops, which had arrived to reinforce him at Fort Donelson, upriver to occupy the city of Nashville, recently abandoned by the Confederates.[1]

Fuming after Washington's brusque rejections of his self-promotion efforts, Halleck took out his frustrations on Grant. As William S. McFeely observed, "Halleck wanted Grant pushed aside; once a victor, Grant became a rival." Halleck was given his opportunity to besmirch Grant's reputation after a Confederate-sympathizing telegraph operator apparently sabotaged Grant's communications to Halleck. On March 3, Halleck wired McClellan that Grant was non-communicative, negligent, and inefficient, and that his army was demoralized. As Grant was moving forces deeper into western Tennessee, Halleck tried to push Grant aside, substituted General Smith as commander of an expedition up the Tennessee, and again accused Grant of failing to report his strength and positions. On March 4, he sent Grant a blunt and accusatory telegram that read: "You will place Major Gen. C.F. Smith in command of expedition [up the Tennessee], & remain yourself at Fort Henry. Why do you not obey my orders to report strength & positions of your command?" For about a week, Grant was onboard a steamer in virtual, but unguarded, arrest.[2]

This was the first indication to Grant that Halleck had not been receiving his reports. Grant stayed at Fort Henry to direct operations while vehemently denying Halleck's charges. In a March 6 telegram, Halleck repeated his allegations and expanded them to include a claim that Grant had exceeded his authority by advancing to Nashville. Not only was the latter claim false, it was a ludicrous complaint given that the occupation of Nashville was both a huge military and political success. Over the next two days Grant sent further denials and requested that he be relieved from serving under Halleck's command.[3]

Meanwhile, "Old Brains" Halleck complained to McClellan that Grant's army lacked discipline and order. Of Grant himself, Halleck wrote, "I never saw a man more deficient in...organization. Brave & able on the field, he has no idea of how to regulate & organize his forces before a battle or to conduct the operation of a campaign." Later Halleck wrote to McClellan of a rumor that Grant "has resumed his former bad habits." McClellan, with Secretary Stanton's approval, authorized Halleck to remove Grant from command. However, in light of Grant's victories and Lincoln's apparent opposition (aided by Congressman Washburne's intervention) to Halleck's anti-Grant actions, Halleck backed down. Halleck explained to Grant that he (Halleck) had been getting pressure from McClellan, who had received reports of Grant's misbehavior and wanted a full investigation. Halleck advised Grant that, instead of conducting an investigation, he was restoring Grant to his command. Only after the war did Grant learn that Halleck himself had initiated the reports to Washington of Grant's alleged misbehavior and had backed down when told to either submit formal charges or reinstate Grant to command.[4]

On March 17, Grant headed south up the Tennessee to Savannah, Tennessee. Before Grant's arrival there, Sherman had traveled thirty miles south on the river in an attempt to destroy the Eastport railroad bridge east of Corinth, Mississippi. His efforts, however, were foiled by high waters. From Savannah, Grant sent reinforcements farther south on the river to Crump's Landing and Pittsburg Landing, where Sherman was organizing them for an offensive against Corinth, a crossroads of north-south and east-west railroads critical to transportation in the southwestern Confederacy. Grant delayed the offensive until he could be joined by Buell's Army of the Ohio, which was advancing from Nashville. Most of Grant's troops camped between Pittsburg Landing and a small church at a place called Shiloh.[5]

Meanwhile, the Confederates were planning an offensive of their own. General Albert Sidney Johnston, a man senior to Robert E. Lee and all other Confederate generals except one, was assembling an impressive force at Corinth. He was gathering troops from across the South, including the Gulf Coast, the southeastern Atlantic Coast (including Beauregard and many troops from Charleston, South Carolina), and the Mississippi Valley (including Polk's forces that had abandoned Columbus, Kentucky). On April 2, Johnston began moving his 44,000 troops the twenty miles toward Pittsburg Landing. In those first few days of April, Johnston's cavalry sporadically encountered Grant's pickets, but this was not enough to lead Grant to expect a Confederate offensive. One day before this surprise attack was to occur, still unaware of Johnston's plan, Grant told a fellow officer, "There will be no fight at Pittsburg Landing; we will have to go to Corinth, where the rebels are fortified." In his memoirs, he later explained: "The fact is, I regarded the campaign we were engaged in as an offensive one and had no idea that the enemy would leave strong entrenchments to take the initiative when he knew he would be attacked where he was if he remained."[6]

The frequency of skirmishes continued to increase, and on April 4 Grant was injured as he rode back to his headquarters in the dark. He had been meeting with officers from the front lines when his horse fell on his leg; he was unable to walk without crutches for two or three days. At that time, Grant was spending his nights downriver from Crump's and Pittsburg Landings at Savannah, where Buell's Army was expected to arrive. On April 5, Brigadier General William ("Bull") Nelson and the lead division of Buell's Army arrived at Savannah. Grant ordered Nelson to proceed down the east bank of the Tennessee so that he could be ferried across to Crump's or Pittsburg Landing.[7]

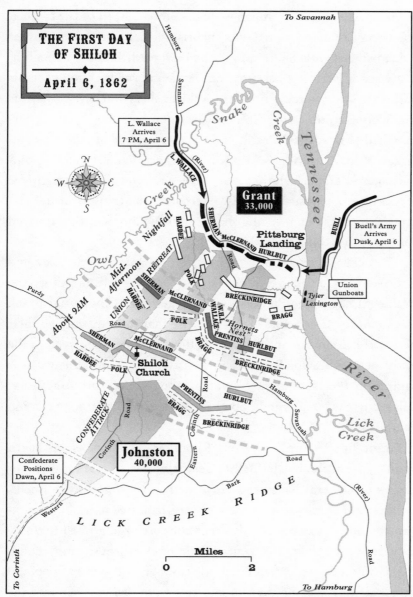

THE FIRST DAY
OF SHILOH

April 6, 1862

To Savannah

Snake Creek

L. Wallace
Arrives
7 PM, April 6

Tennessee

Grant
33,000

Buell's Army
Arrives
Dusk, April 6

Pittsburg
Landing

L. WALLACE

SHERMAN

McCLERNAND

HURLBUT

BUELL

Creek

Nightfall

HARDEE

Owl

Mid-Afternoon

SHERMAN

RETREAT

POLK

Road

McCLERNAND

BRECKINRIDGE

Tyler
Lexington

Union
Gunboats

Purdy

About 9AM

UNION

HARDEE

Road

POLK

McCLERNAND

W.H.L.
WALLACE

"Hornets
Nest"
PRENTISS

BRAGG

HURLBUT

BRAGG

SHERMAN

HARDEE

McCLERNAND

POLK

Shiloh
Church

BRAGG

Hamburg - Savannah

BRECKINRIDGE

River

PRENTISS

HURLBUT

BRAGG

Lick
Creek

Corinth Road

CONFEDERATE ATTACK

BRECKINRIDGE

Corinth

Eastern

Confederate
Positions
Dawn, April 6

Johnston
40,000

Bark

Road

Western

L I C K   C R E E K   R I D G E

To Corinth

(River)

Road

Miles

0   2

To Hamburg

N W E S

MAP BY DAVID DEIS, DREAMLINE CARTOGRAPHY

Grant was still at Savannah early on Sunday, April 6, 1862, when Johnston launched a massive surprise attack on the troops of Brigadier Generals Sherman and Benjamin M. Prentiss at Shiloh, just west of Pittsburg Landing.[8] Sherman and other Union generals had tragically ignored reports from skirmishers and cavalry patrols that Confederates were present in large numbers. On April 5, Sherman had even advised Grant, "I do not apprehend anything like an attack on our position." Grant, for his part, had sent late April 5 messages to Halleck stating that, "The Main force of the enemy is at Corinth. . . ." and "I have scarsely [sic] the faintest idea of an attack, (general one), being made upon us but will be prepared should such a thing take place."[9]

The unsuspecting Union troops were an easy target. They had not even dug defensive trenches, and by the early morning, the onslaught had swept Prentiss's troops backward. The initial attack so caught the Union soldiers by surprise that they abandoned their personal belongings and their campfires, many fleeing even in the midst of cooking breakfast, as an indication of the toll the war was taking on the Confederate soldiers, their follow-up attack was delayed as the hungry and poorly clad soldiers plundered the Union camp.[10]

Grant hurried upriver from Savannah as soon as he heard artillery from the battle. Before departing, he sent another set of orders to General Nelson to move with his division from Buell's Army south along the east bank of the Tennessee to a point opposite Pittsburg Landing. He also sent couriers urging Buell to hurry the rest of his army to the scene. After a brief stop at Crump's Landing, Grant hastened on to Pittsburg Landing and spent a long and desperate day keeping the Union forces from being driven into the Tennessee River.[11]

One problem arose early in the day that could have had disastrous consequences. As soon as Grant arrived at Pittsburg Landing and determined the serious nature of the situation inland there, he sent his quartermaster, Captain Algernon S. Baxter, back to Crump's Landing with an order for General Lew Wallace to march immediately to the battlefield. Wallace's and other troops had previously built an inland bridge on the Shunpike Road across Snake Creek for that very purpose. Wallace, therefore, tried to use that inland road instead of the road along the river.[12]

After hearing nothing from Wallace by midday, Grant sent two more officers, Lieutenant Frank R. Bennett and Captain William R. Rowley, to hasten Wallace's arrival. When Wallace had not arrived by 2:30 p.m., Grant sent Lieutenant Colonel James B. McPherson and Captain Rawlins of his staff to bring Wallace to Pittsburg Landing. At the same time, Captain Rowley reached Wallace at the head of his column miles inland in what had been an unsuccessful attempt by Wallace to enter the fray on the enemy's left (northwest) flank. Even though he was then made aware of the extreme jeopardy Grant's army was in, Wallace proceeded to delay his division's march almost another hour by ordering a countermarch (the head of his misdirected column passing back through the entire column) rather than a simple about-face. During the march, Wallace caused additional delay by ordering his lead soldiers to await slower troops in order to keep the column closed up.

Thus, it wasn't until 7:00 p.m. that Wallace crossed Snake Creek on Grant's right. He eventually arrived after the day's fighting was over, having unintentionally deprived Grant of the use of one of his six divisions at the most critical time and place of what was to become a two-day battle.[13] It appears that Grant erred in relying on oral orders that failed to specify the road Wallace was to take. The use of oral—let alone vague—orders was something Grant tried to avoid for the rest of the war. In an 1885 note written shortly before his death, Grant admitted that he had in fact relied on oral orders to first specify Wallace's route, and that "if the position of our front had not changed, the road which Wallace took would have been somewhat shorter to our right than the River road." As Stacy Allen concluded, "One fact is known: A 6-mile march which might have been made in just over two hours had required seven hours and fifteen miles. This undeniable fact would haunt Lew Wallace for the rest of his life."[14]

With Wallace's division out of the battle for its first day, Grant's 40,000 remaining defenders consisted of five other divisions: Sherman's on the right near Shiloh Church, McClernand's on Sherman's rear and later his left, Prentiss's on Sherman's and then McClernand's left, Brigadier General Stephen A. Hurlbut's in reserve behind Prentiss, and C. F. Smith's (under Brigadier General William H. L. Wallace) in reserve behind all the other divisions. Three of Grant's division commanders were Illinois lawyer-politicians who were new to their commands; Hurlbut had commanded his division for six weeks, Prentiss for eleven days, and William Wallace for all of two days.[15]

Immediately upon arriving at Pittsburg Landing, the injured Grant was assisted onto his horse and rode into the battle with crutches strapped to his saddle. After learning from General William Wallace that his army faced a full-scale attack, Grant quickly sent his appeals for help to Lew Wallace and Bull Nelson and issued an order for ammunition wagons to be moved inland. He then visited his division commanders in the field, told them to hold their ground, and advised them that reinforcements were on the way.[16]

To the west of the attack on Prentiss, several Confederate brigades attacked Sherman's line of green recruits. For hours, Sherman's men inflicted severe casualties on the Rebel attackers. But the defenders finally gave way to the attackers, who swept into Sherman's abandoned camp and then spent valuable time looting it. Requesting reinforcements if available, Sherman had ordered a fighting retreat and told Grant, "We are holding them pretty well just now—but it's hot as hell."[17]

The Union left flank was never turned. Initially, half the Confederate forces attacked that wing in an attempt to get between the Federal soldiers and Pittsburg Landing. One of Sherman's brigades (separated from the rest of Sherman's division), under Colonel David Stuart, held the far left of the Union line along Lick Creek—to the left of Prentiss—until later reinforced.

After the initial shock of, and subsequent retreat from, the surprise attack, Grant's army carried out a desperate, day-long fighting retreat and established a series of defensive positions that were protected on the flanks by Lick Creek and the Tennessee River on its left, and Snake Creek and its Owl Creek tributary on its right. Grant later summarized the strength of his position: "The water in all these streams was very high at the time and contributed to protect our flanks. The enemy was compelled, therefore, to attack directly in our front. This he did with great vigor, inflicting heavy losses on the National side, but suffering much heavier on his own."[18]

A major problem plaguing the Confederates was their disorganization. They had approached the battlefield division by division up the Corinth Road, and each brigade and regiment had been sent to the place of greatest immediate need without regard to any sort of divisional or other organization. By 10:30 that morning, the senior

Confederate generals addressed this problem by informally dividing the battlefield into sectors commanded, from their left to right,
by Generals William J. ("Old Reliable") Hardee, Polk, Braxton
Bragg, and Johnston.[19]

By the same time, two-thirds of the Confederates had drifted to
their left and, with heavy casualties, pushed back Sherman and
McClernand. However, their position and actions were inconsistent
with General Johnston's plan to have the Confederate right flank
turn the Federal left flank, which was putting up fierce resistance.
In fact, throughout the late morning and early afternoon, Johnston
personally directed the efforts on the Confederate right flank to
turn the Union line. He made a fatal mistake by sending his surgeon
away to help wounded troops. Thus, when Johnston was shot in
the leg, no one realized the gravity of his wound. By the time its
seriousness became apparent, it was too late to save Johnston, who
apparently bled to death from a severed artery. Johnston, who was
possibly shot by his own men, may not even have realized that he
had been shot because his leg was numb from an 1837 dueling
wound. An unused field tourniquet was in his coat pocket when he
died. General Beauregard then assumed the Confederate command.[20]

At the other end of the lines, Sherman and McClernand, having
received fresh ammunition and reinforcements, successfully counterattacked, inflicting many casualties on the Confederates to their
front as they drove them back. While the Confederates were themselves regrouping and getting ammunition, Sherman and McClernand, realizing that they were over-extended, drew back to strong
defensive positions they would hold the rest of the day.[21]

The major fighting, however, would occur in an area that started
as the center of the Union line and became the left of that line as the

battle progressed. Prentiss, who commanded the Army of the Tennessee's Sixth Division in that sector, would play a key role in the battle. Although he had initially rebuked a subordinate for apparently bringing on the attack by sending out an unauthorized patrol, he quickly focused on feeding units into defensive positions to stem the Confederate tide. As the Confederates overran Sherman's and then McClernand's camps, they stopped to loot and eat. This delay was crucial in giving Prentiss and other Union leaders valuable time to organize a defense. While his troops were being flanked or overpowered, Prentiss reorganized them, obtained reinforcements from other divisions, and finally put together an extremely effective defensive position, which achieved lasting fame as "the Hornets' Nest."[22]

In that location, the divisions of Hurlbut, William Wallace, and Prentiss formed a semi-circle facing south and west in ravines behind an old wagon-road on the southern (left) end of Grant's line. In their center were what was left of the Fifth Ohio and the First Minnesota Light Artillery regiments. These 5,500 infantrymen and twenty-seven guns formed the anchor of Grant's critical mid-day defense against the Confederate attackers.[23]

The first Confederates to feel the sting of the Hornets' Nest were Tennessee and Kentucky troops of Colonel William Stephens' brigade of Major General Benjamin F. Cheatham's division. Around 11:00 a.m. they moved through thick underbrush toward the Union position, but they were devastated by camouflaged Union firepower at eighty paces. Sixth Tennessee Private R. W. Hurdle described the effects of the vicious firestorm:

> Then came an incessant hail of lead and iron until our line
> was strewn with the dying and the wounded. The remainder

had to lie down for protection. In a few minutes a Mississippi
Regiment dashed up and they passed over our line, and called
out: "get out of the way, Tennessee, and let Mississippi in!"
They passed on a short distance and returned on the double
quick, and as they passed a Tennessee fellow said, "get out of
the way, Tennessee, and let Mississippi out!"[24]

Shortly thereafter, Grant arrived to check out the Hornets' Nest.
After observing that the position was a strong one and that Prentiss had deployed the troops effectively, Grant told Prentiss to
"maintain that position at all hazards." For the next several hours,
that is exactly what the men in the Hornets' Nest did.[25]

Between 11:30 a.m. and noon, Prentiss's troops repelled a 3,600-
man, four-brigade attack led by Brigadier General Alexander P.
Stewart. The attackers were stopped by blistering fire after advancing only 100 yards.[26] Next, General Bragg ordered a series of suicidal charges by Colonel Randall Lee Gibson's Louisiana and
Arkansas Brigade; those four charges came no closer than sixty
yards to the inaccessible position of the Blue troops, and the attackers fell like leaves. Although Confederate bullets took their toll on
Iowa infantry defending the Union guns, two more Confederate
brigades made mid-afternoon assaults and were bloodily repulsed.
Grant recalled being with Prentiss late that afternoon, and described
him "as cool as if expecting victory."[27]

When it became clear that the Confederates were not about to
go through the Hornets' Nest with infantry, they changed their tactics. Brigadier General Daniel Ruggles assembled fifty-two pieces of
artillery that bombarded the Yankee stronghold, destroyed or drove
off many Federal batteries, and convinced many infantrymen to flee
to the rear. Simultaneously, Confederate infantry flanked the left
end of the Union line and caused Hurlbut's Division to retreat

toward Pittsburg Landing. The final Confederate assault on the Hornets' Nest involved parts of fourteen of the sixteen Rebel brigades on the field.[28] Military historian Herman Hattaway calculated that the final assault on the Hornets' Nest involved 10,000 Confederate troops, who incurred about 2,400 casualties.[29]

Finally, Grant's line north of the Hornets' Nest (McClernand's Division) gave way, causing Wallace's Division to retreat and permitting Confederates to outflank Prentiss's right as well as his left. Soon the Hornets' Nest was surrounded. Some of the Union troops fought their way out of the trap, but finally Prentiss and 2,200 troops surrendered at about 5:30 p.m. As the Confederates cheered the mass surrender, a proud Benjamin Prentiss exclaimed to his captors, "Yell, boys, you have a right to shout for you have this day captured the bravest brigade in the United States Army." The men under his command had done their job and held that position "at all hazards" for six hours—and stymied the Confederate attack for a total of twelve hours since the 5:00 a.m. initiation of hostilities.[30]

Having finally bypassed the Hornets' Nest, the Confederates made a final attempt to break Grant's left wing and capture Pittsburg Landing. But Grant himself had long before prepared a warm reception for them. At 2:30 that afternoon, he had directed his chief of staff, Colonel Webster, to create a line of defense for the Landing. For the next three hours, Webster assembled artillery pieces along Dill Branch of Lick Creek near Pittsburg Landing in a successful attempt to stem the Confederate tide. Using every gun in the reserve artillery and in the retreating units that approached the Landing, Webster assembled a seventy-gun line that included five 24-pounder siege guns that had been hauled up from the Landing.[31]

By 5:30 p.m., 20,000 Union troops had joined those guns in "Grant's Last Line." The assembled defenders repelled a six-gun

Alabama battery and a final assault by 4,000 of the 8,000 Confeder-ates poised to capture the Landing. As a result, Grant's Army held the Landing, maintained a strong and compact defensive position as night fell, and had begun receiving "Bull" Nelson's reinforcements at the Landing from Buell across the Tennessee.[32] Grant had continually moved about the battlefield and visited each of his division com-manders several times during the day.[33] He creatively used all of his forces, his cavalry, his artillery, and his infantry—and even two naval gunboats. During the battle, Grant found a crucial use for his cavalry. He stationed them behind his infantry to discourage straggling and desertion by troops fleeing the heat of battle. He later wrote:

> The nature of this battle was such that cavalry could not be used in front; I therefore formed ours into line, in rear, to stop stragglers—of whom there were many. When there would be enough of them to make a show, and after they had recov-ered from their fright, they would be sent to reinforce some part of the line which needed support, without regard to their companies, regiments or brigades.[34]

Beauregard believed, as turned out to be the case, that Grant's use of massed artillery at the close of the day was a significant factor in the Rebels' failure to force a surrender of Grant's army. Those artillery pieces were assisted by the firing of 32-pounder cannonballs and eight-inch shells from the two Union gunboats, *Tyler* and *Lex-ington*, at the mouth of Dill Branch. Those same vessels provided moderately effective support earlier in the day and intermittent shelling during the night after the first day of battle, but they were constantly hindered by an inability to determine the Confederates' position because of the nature of the terrain (including woods, hills, and high riverbanks).[35] Grant's infantry had provided the bulk of the resistance to the Confederate onslaught. Again and again during the long day, determined collections of Union infantrymen halted the Confederate advance until they either ran out of ammunition or were surrounded by the enemy. Most of them retreated from one defensive position to another and were able to impose severe casualties on the attacking Confederates. The Confederates suffered between 8,000 and 8,500 casualties in the day's fighting.[36]

The battle had taken its toll on the Union forces as well. Prentiss's Division was gone—mostly surrendered along with the Division Commander. General William Wallace had been mortally wounded, and his division was scattered among the others. Union forces had suffered a remarkably similar 8,500 casualties. The three "intact" divisions in the Union line at dusk were those of Hurlbut on the left, McClernand in the center, and Sherman on the right. However, as Grant stated in his memoirs, "All three divisions were, as a matter of course, more or less shattered and depleted in numbers from the terrible battle of the day." He also described the relative losses of the two sides:

> The reports of the enemy show that their condition at the end of the first day was deplorable; their losses in killed and wounded had been very heavy, and their stragglers had been quite as numerous as on the National side, with the difference that those of the enemy left the field entirely and were not brought back to their respective commands for many days. On the Union side but few of the stragglers fell back further than the landing on the river, and many of these were in line for duty on the second day.[37]

By nightfall, Grant's army had been driven at least a mile closer to the Tennessee than it had been at dawn. But it had survived a ferocious and unexpected attack; there were even reasons to be optimistic. By dusk, Buell's first 5,000 troops (specifically, Nelson's Division) had begun arriving, and Grant hurried them toward the front. On the right, Lew Wallace at long last arrived with his own 5,000 unscarred troops. By the next morning, Alexander M. McCook's and Thomas L. Crittenden's divisions of Buell's Army had come upriver from Savannah and joined Grant's troops.[38]

During the evening following that first day at Shiloh, Grant had an experience that brought home to him the events of the day, which involved the only truly significant number of casualties that his troops would suffer in any of his western campaigns in the first three years of the Civil War:

> During the night rain fell in torrents and our troops were exposed to the storm without shelter. I made my headquarters under a tree a few hundred yards back from the river bank. My ankle was so much swollen from the fall of my horse the Friday night preceding, and the bruise was so painful that I could get no rest.... Some time after midnight, growing restive under the storm and the continuous pain, I moved back to the loghouse under the bank. This had been taken as a hospital, and all night wounded men were being brought in, their wounds dressed, a leg or an arm amputated as the case might require, and everything being done to save life or alleviate suffering. The sight was more unendurable than encountering the enemy's fire, and I returned to my tree in the rain.[39]

That same night Beauregard wired Richmond the news of what he perceived to be his glorious victory:

We this morning attacked the enemy in strong position in front of Pittsburg, and after a severe battle of ten hours, thanks be to the Almighty, gained a complete victory, driving the enemy from every position. Loss on both sides heavy, including our commander-in-chief, General A.S. Johnston, who fell gallantly leading his troops into the thickest of the fight.

But the reality was that the Confederates had suffered debilitating casualties and were, as Bragg wrote to his wife two days later, "disorganized, demoralized, and exhausted." Assured by an incorrect dispatch that Buell was not coming to join Grant, the Confederate commanders were satisfied to let their exhausted troops get some sleep and to reorganize in the morning. On the other side of the lines, Grant was heard to mutter, "Not beaten by a damn sight."[40]

Instead of being shocked into inaction by the massive attack that he had failed to anticipate and his army had barely survived, Grant resolved to go on the offensive the next morning. In his own words:

So confident was I before firing had ceased on the 6th that the next day would bring victory to our arms if we could only take the initiative, that I visited each division commander in person before any reinforcements had reached the field. I directed them to throw out heavy lines of skirmishers in the morning as soon as they could see, and push them forward until they found the enemy, following with their entire divisions in supporting distance, and to engage the enemy as soon as found.[41]

When asked by Lieutenant Colonel McPherson whether the army should retreat across the Tennessee, Grant responded, "Retreat?

No, I propose to attack at daylight and whip them." A little later Sherman approached Grant and said, "Well, Grant, we've had the devil's own day, haven't we?" and Grant replied, "Yes. Yes. Lick 'em tomorrow though."[42] In the words of Jean Edward Smith, "If anyone other than Grant had been in command Sunday night [between the two days at Shiloh], the Union army certainly would have retreated."[43]

Soldiers of both armies spent a restless night as the Union gunboats fired shells inland, the rain fell, and the cries of the wounded came from the battlefield and the makeshift hospitals. But Grant had been reinforced by Wallace's 5,000 troops and another 13,000 from Buell's three divisions. Confederate Cavalry Colonel Nathan Bedford Forrest observed thousands of reinforcements arriving by ferry across the river and from downstream, but his warnings to General Hardee were ignored.[44]

Ignoring the possibility of reinforcements from Buell and expecting to conduct mopping-up operations in the morning, Beauregard and his fellow Confederate generals were shocked when Grant's artillery opened the Union counterattack before six o'clock the next morning. The Union goal was to drive the enemy from the ground they had fought so hard to gain the prior day. Casualties and desertions had already reduced the Rebel force to 28,000, and it wasn't until 10 a.m. that the disorganized and scattered Confederate units formed a respectable defensive line. While John C. Breckinridge commanded all units of his corps, Hardee, Bragg, and Polk commanded mixed-bag contingents that contained virtually no one from their own corps.[45]

Before the unexpected and overwhelming onslaught by four of Grant's divisions and three of Buell's, the disorganized Confederates conducted a fighting retreat that was much more chaotic than the one their Union counterparts had just conducted the previous day. The Confederates kept moving back all day (except for periodic costly counterattacks), fell back on the Corinth Road, and halted for the night on that road, five miles from Pittsburg Landing. While overseeing the progress of the battle, Grant came under fire and had a bullet hit and break the scabbard of his sword.[46]

The next day Grant conducted a reconnaissance-in-force down the Corinth Road. Although some critics have contended that he should have aggressively pursued and destroyed Beauregard's Army, that was not a realistic possibility. Grant was under prior orders from Halleck to stay on the defensive, there were good defensive positions along the Corinth Road, Grant lacked sufficient cavalry and horses for rapid pursuit, and Grant's troops were totally exhausted. Thus, Beauregard and his survivors retreated all the way to Corinth. But Grant's "stubborn pugnacity," in the words of military historian Russell F. Weigley, had turned defeat into victory.[47] As the result of two days of ferocious fighting, the two armies suffered a total of 19,900 killed and wounded. Grant described the battle's ferocity:

> Shiloh was the severest battle fought at the West during the war, and but few in the East equaled it for hard, determined fighting. I saw an open field, in our possession on the second day, over which the Confederates had made repeated charges the day before, so covered with dead that it would have been possible to walk across the clearing, in any direction, stepping on dead bodies, without a foot touching the ground.[48]

Grant, fighting on the defensive the first day and on the counteroffensive the second, incurred about 1,750 casualties and another 8,400 wounded (15–16 percent) among his 63,000–65,000 troops.

At the same time, his troops killed 1,730 and wounded 8,000 (22–24 percent) of the 40,000–45,000 Rebels. Three months later, Grant's casualties were nearly doubled by Robert E. Lee, who incurred 19,700 killed and injured (21 percent) during the Seven Days' Campaign—while killing and wounding "only" 9,800 (11 percent) of his enemy.[49]

Grant had not brought on the Battle of Shiloh. Rather, he had survived it and done so in a way that caused his enemy to suffer casualties at a rate almost 50 percent in excess of his own. Because the Confederate armies had only half the manpower of Union armies, the Confederates could not afford to take such high casualties—especially at a one-to-one ratio with their counterparts. Historians Smith and Stacy Allen summarized the impact of Shiloh's casualties: "The difference was the Union could replenish its men and equipment, the Confederacy could not,"[50] and "Therefore, the Confederacy suffered a substantial, even decisive defeat in the war of attrition."[51]

After Shiloh, the northern press was filled with venomous, inflated, and inaccurate criticisms of Grant—including claims that he was drunk when Johnston launched his surprise attack. Many newspapers called for his resignation or dismissal. Perhaps realizing the value of Grant but more likely saving his own hide, Halleck falsely claimed that Grant had not been surprised and thus helped shut down the calls for his removal. Grant's critics were reacting to the unprecedented number of casualties at Shiloh (more than any four other Civil War battles fought thus far and more than in all of the nation's preceding wars combined). They also were responding to false reports from ill-informed reporters and vicious rumors spread by officers jealous of Grant's ascension and success. Lincoln, however, stood behind Grant and said, "I can't spare this man; he fights."[52] Few other senior Union commanders met that basic standard.

Five

1862–1863:
SURVIVING FRUSTRATION
UPON FRUSTRATION

Grant is demoted by Halleck, regains major command, wins victories at Iuka and Corinth, and encounters numerous setbacks and frustrations as he attempts to capture Vicksburg, Mississippi.

What was to be a year of frustrations for Grant began on April 11, 1862, when Halleck arrived at Pittsburg Landing and took command of Grant's and Buell's armies. Denounced by the press for Shiloh and mourning the recent death of his friend and mentor, General Charles Smith, Grant was disconsolate. Halleck added to Grant's woes with an April 14 letter to him stating that his "army is not now in condition to resist an attack" and directing him to achieve that condition,[1] as well as a petty directive that same day saying, "The Major General Commanding desires that, you will again call the attention of your officers to the necessity of forwarding official communications through the proper military channel, to receive the remarks of intermediate commanders. Letters should relate to one matter only, and be properly folded and indorsed." Looking back on those mid-April days, Grant recalled,

"Although next to [Halleck] in rank, and nominally in command of my old district and army, I was ignored as much as if I had been at the most distant point of territory within my jurisdiction...."[2]

Grant's morale would soon hit a new wartime low when, on April 30, Halleck relieved Grant of his command, named him his (Halleck's) deputy, and replaced him with newly promoted Major General George H. Thomas as commander of the Army of the Tennessee. In Russell Weigley's words, "Halleck appears to have been jealous of [Grant] for his early successes..., and he did all that he could to deny Grant full credit for his achievements at Henry, Donelson, and Shiloh and kept him under a shadow as second in command in the West, practically a supernumerary, through the Corinth campaign."[3]

Having thrived as a commander of troops, Grant was extremely frustrated by what he regarded as a demotion to a meaningless and powerless position under Halleck. His frustration was aggravated by Halleck's overly cautious, excruciatingly slow "march" on Corinth, Mississippi, the place to which Beauregard's Confederates had retreated after Shiloh. Corinth, where the east/west Memphis & Charleston Railroad intersected with the north/south Mobile & Ohio Railroad, was so critical that it had been called "The Crossroads of the Western Confederacy."[4]

Beginning on April 30, it took four weeks for the 120,000 Union troops to advance twenty-two miles to Corinth, as they entrenched daily and none of the three constituent armies (those of the Tennessee, the Ohio, and the Mississippi) was permitted to edge ahead of the others. On May 11, Grant wrote to Halleck requesting either a field command or relief from duty. Halleck denied the request. Grant told a fellow officer from Galena that he felt like "a fifth wheel to a coach."[5]

During May, the Federal armies, with deliberate and frustrating slowness, arrived near Corinth, partially invested the town, cut off the railroads north and east of town, and engaged in some minor fighting with Beauregard's troops. Meanwhile, Beauregard faced greater challenges: bad water, typhoid fever, dysentery, and desertions. Army of Tennessee Private Sam R. Watkins reported, "We became starved skeletons; naked and ragged rebels. The chronic diarrhoea [*sic*] became the scourge of the army. Corinth became one vast hospital. Almost the whole army attended the sick call every morning. All the water courses went dry, and we used water out of filthy pools." Apparently still in shock from the events at bloody Shiloh, neither Halleck nor Beauregard seemed anxious to engage in combat. Finally, Beauregard ended the standoff with a cleverly executed retreat from Corinth.[6]

The strategic ineffectiveness of Halleck's slow-motion movement against, and partial encirclement of, Corinth became obvious when the 50,000 Confederates escaped by abandoning the city on May 29 and 30. In executing their retreat, the Confederates made Halleck appear even more ridiculous by running their evacuation in a manner that caused Halleck to fear they were reinforcing, not evacuating, Corinth. This was done by cheering the arrival of empty evacuation trains as though they were bringing reinforcements. In fact, on the morning of May 30, Halleck had his entire army prepared for defensive battle and issued orders indicating that the Union left was likely to be attacked.

The Confederates' movement south to Tupelo, Mississippi, left Corinth in Union hands and forced the Confederate military abandonment of the subsequently unprotected city of Memphis. But their retreat also allowed Beauregard's soldiers to fight future battles. Despite having a war-high total of 137,000 troops in Corinth,

Halleck failed to pursue the 50,000 Confederates to Tupelo or to move on significant locations such as Vicksburg, Chattanooga, or Atlanta. Instead, he stayed at Corinth and ordered his troops to dig even more extensive fortifications than the Rebels had abandoned.[7]

Grant was frustrated and disgusted by Halleck's month-long "movement" to cover a distance that he believed should have taken two days. These feelings were reinforced by the Rebels' successful evacuation from Corinth of all their healthy troops, their wounded, and their supplies—with only a few log "Quaker guns" left behind for Halleck's army. As a *Chicago Tribune* correspondent commented, "General Halleck has thus far achieved one of the most barren triumphs of the war. In fact, it was tantamount to a defeat." During the cautious siege, Halleck had sent orders directly to Grant's wing of the army without going through Grant. He had also abruptly rejected a suggestion from Grant about how to attack the enemy.[8] Believing that he was nothing more than an observer, and embarrassed by his position, Grant made several applications to be relieved.

But Grant's concerns went deeper than his own welfare. He feared that the Army of the Tennessee felt the capture of Corinth was hollow: "They could not see how the mere occupation of places was to close the war while large and effective rebel armies existed. They believed that a well-directed attack would at least have partially destroyed the army defending Corinth." As he wrote in his memoirs, Grant was also disappointed in Halleck's tepid pursuit of the enemy after Corinth and his failure to pursue other opportunities with his large army:

> After the capture of Corinth a movable force of 80,000 men,
> besides enough to hold all the territory acquired, could have
> been set in motion for the accomplishment of any great cam-

paign for the suppression of the rebellion. . . . If [Buell] had been sent directly to Chattanooga as rapidly as he could march . . . he could have arrived with but little fighting, and would have saved much of the loss of life which was afterwards incurred in gaining Chattanooga. Bragg would then not have had time to raise an army to contest the possession of middle and east Tennessee and Kentucky; the battles of Stones River and Chickamauga would not necessarily have been fought; Burnside would not have been besieged in Knoxville without the power of helping himself or escaping; the battle of Chattanooga would not have been fought. These are the negative advantages, if the term negative is applicable, which would probably have resulted from prompt movements after Corinth fell into the possession of the National forces. The positive results might have been: a bloodless advance to Atlanta, to Vicksburg, or to any other desired point south of Corinth in the interior of Mississippi.[9]

A dismayed Grant took leave to visit his family and perhaps to seek transfer to another theater. His friend Sherman told him to be patient and to hope for reinstatement. That is exactly what happened when on June 10 Halleck restored him to command of the Army of the Tennessee. However, Halleck's intervention after Shiloh stopped the momentum of Grant's offensive into the Confederacy and threat to the Mississippi. After Shiloh, Weigley said, "Halleck dispersed the western armies on garrison and railroad-building work. . . . it was Halleck who sneered at Lincoln for wanting to violate the principle of concentration by maintaining pressure against the Confederacy everywhere."[10]

On June 21, Halleck granted Grant's long-standing request to move his headquarters away from Halleck—to Memphis, and on

June 23 Grant established his headquarters there. It was there that his growing impatience with guerilla activities against his troops incited him to issue an order stating that Confederate guerillas captured out of uniform would not be treated as prisoners of war, and that Confederate sympathizers would have their property seized.

Meanwhile, good fortune smiled on Grant. On June 10, Congress relieved him of the liability for the missing Mexican War monies. Even more significantly, Halleck headed for Washington and left the western theater for good after being appointed General-in-Chief on July 11. Before departing for Washington, Halleck summoned Grant to Corinth to establish his headquarters there. Grant now commanded the District of West Tennessee (Tennessee and Kentucky between the Cumberland and Mississippi rivers), but had no department commander and thus reported directly to Halleck.[11] Historian T. Harry Williams commented on Halleck's legacy to the western theater:

> Before he left he split the Western Department into two commands under Buell and Grant. Characteristically, he assigned to Buell, who had done practically no fighting, a fighting mission—the seizure of well-guarded Chattanooga. To Grant, who had done much hard and victorious fighting, he gave the relatively inactive mission of protecting communications along the Mississippi River.[12]

Grant arrived in Corinth on July 17. At that time, he commanded about 64,000 scattered troops of the Armies of the Tennessee (commanded by Grant) and the Mississippi (commanded by Major General William S. ["Old Rosy"] Rosecrans). They were tasked with defending a 115-mile front and over 360 miles of railroad track.[13] Then Grant's scattered force was weakened by the transfer of troops to another theater.

Not only had Halleck stopped Grant's momentum, but his wait-and-see approach left the North vulnerable to Confederate offensives. In the fall of 1862, Confederates took advantage of this weakness and went on the offensive. While Lee moved into Maryland on his Antietam Campaign, Bragg and [Edmund] Kirby Smith moved northward into central Tennessee and eastern Kentucky. As Buell moved north to intercept Bragg and Smith in Kentucky, Grant was directed to send three of Rosecrans's divisions as reinforcements to Buell. This left Grant to face the challenge of defending his assigned territory with reduced forces.[14] The Confederates were east and south of Grant, who was headquartered at Corinth. Thus, Confederate Major Generals Sterling "Old Pap" Price (Army of the West) and Earl Van Dorn (Army of Mississippi) together posed a possible threat to Grant's remaining and scattered 50,000 troops.

Price had conflicting orders from Bragg, who wanted him to threaten Nashville and thus protect Bragg's invasion flank, and from Van Dorn, who wanted Price to come join him in a western Tennessee offensive. On September 14, the hesitant Price and his 12,000 to 14,000 Confederate troops occupied the town of Iuka, about twenty miles east of Corinth on the Memphis & Charleston Railroad. Grant characteristically saw the situation as an opportunity and went on the offensive.[15]

Halleck ordered Grant to keep Price from crossing the Tennessee River to join with Bragg's forces in Tennessee. Grant's plan was to trap Price in Iuka before Van Dorn could come to his aid from the south. From Corinth, Grant accompanied Major General Ord with 8,000 men down the Memphis & Charleston Railroad to attack from the northwest and directed William Rosecrans with 9,000 troops to attack from the southwest and southeast. To prevent a surprise attack by Van Dorn on the critical rail hub of Corinth, Grant kept some troops in locations where they could detect such a movement by Price. He also kept locomotives and railcars ready to move Ord back to Corinth if necessary.[16]

Ord arrived first and demanded Price's surrender. Price refused, only to realize that he faced not only Ord to the northwest but also Rosecrans, who would be arriving soon from the south. Rosecrans, who had been slow in reaching Iuka, was under orders to block the southern roads out of Iuka. Ord was under orders to engage the enemy the moment he heard guns from Rosecrans's direction. Rosecrans moved on the Confederate pickets southwest of Iuka starting at about 2:00 p.m. on September 19. Despite initial success, Price's troops were able to rally with a counterattack that drove the Federals back. A fierce battle raged for several hours, both sides incurring hundreds of casualties.[17] Ord, however, did not simultaneously attack from the northwest because he never actually heard the sounds of fighting between Price and Rosecrans. The wind and weather conditions had created an "acoustic shadow" that prevented both Ord and Grant from hearing the sounds of battle.[18]

Price intended to resume his attack the next morning. However, the death of his best division commander and the advice of his other generals about the threat from Ord caused him to reconsider. Instead he decided to retreat and join up with Van Dorn. Fortunately for Price, Rosecrans had left open the road to the southeast— thereby allowing Price to escape Grant's planned pincers attack. Grant came up after the battle and had to direct Rosecrans to pursue the retreating enemy.[19]

Unlike Halleck, when Grant saw an opportunity to attack he did so—and did so promptly. Grant aggressively sought a fight at Iuka, and the battle was a strategic and tactical victory. Although Rose-crans's dilatory nature coupled with the acoustic shadow had squandered an opportunity to inflict even more damage on Price's force, Rosecrans's men suffered only 800 casualties while imposing about 1,600 on the enemy. Grant also had succeeded in defending his territory without any need to recall the three divisions that had been sent to Buell in Kentucky.[20]

After Iuka, Grant moved his headquarters to Jackson, Tennessee. Meanwhile, Van Dorn compelled a reluctant Price to join him in an attack on Rosecrans at Corinth. Under the command of Van Dorn, 22,000 Confederates with sixty-four guns moved fourteen miles northwest of Corinth and then turned to march east and south on the key rail hub. Realizing the threat this posed, Grant ordered reinforcements to Corinth from Jackson and Bolivar. The 23,000 Union defenders also would be aided by an effective series of fortifications—batteries and redoubts—that Rosecrans had recommended and Grant had approved. Those facilities constituted a final defensive line, the College Hill Line, which was inside the middle "Halleck Line" from earlier days and the outer line of fortifications constructed by the Confederates when they had been defending Corinth against Halleck after Shiloh.[21]

On October 3, Van Dorn pressed a three-division attack against Corinth. Amidst ferocious fighting that lasted all day, the Confederates drove Rosecrans's defenders back almost two miles. That advance proved to be problematic, however, as it enabled Rosecrans to effectively deploy his four divisions in shortened and extremely strong defensive positions for the next day's battle. Having endured terrible loss of life, Van Dorn's divisions attacked again the next day, overran Union batteries (even, for a time, the staunchly defended Battery Robinett), entered the town itself, but were driven out by a fierce Union counterattack. As Van Dorn withdrew his troops from the town, Price wept on seeing the scant remnants of his troops retreat. At Corinth he had lost 2,500 of 3,900 men in one of his divisions, and he lost another 600 who deserted during the retreat. In the end, the bloody, vicious Battle of Corinth was a decisive Union victory.[22]

Grant tried to follow up that victory by trapping and destroying Van Dorn's retreating army. He sent Major General Hurlbut with 8,000 men from Bolivar to the Davis Bridge on the Hatchie River to block the retreat. Grant, careful to ensure the safety of Hurlbut's forces, also hastily dispatched Rosecrans to pursue Van Dorn. But, instead of following these orders post-haste and pursuing the fleeing enemy, Rosecrans delayed pursuit and rode along his lines to assure his men that the report of his death was wrong. Even the arrival of McPherson and his five regiments of reinforcements, sent by Grant from Jackson, could not convince Rosecrans to initiate the chase until the next morning. Having meticulously planned specific actions for a Rebel retreat and a subsequent Union chase, Grant was understandably frustrated by Rosecrans's lack of effort.[23] As Grant later recalled:

> General Rosecrans, however, failed to follow up the victory, although I had given specific orders in advance of the battle for him to pursue the moment the enemy was repelled. He did not do so, and I repeated the order after the battle. In the first order he was notified that the force of 4,000 men which was going to his assistance would be in great peril if the enemy was not pursued.[24]

General Ord arrived to take command of Hurlbut's force and was able to keep Van Dorn's troops from retreating across the

Hatchie River at the bloody Battle of Davis' Bridge.[25] It was at this point that the repercussions of Rosecrans's lack of haste became clear, as the Confederates, who might have been trapped in the Mississippi swamps if Rosecrans had followed his orders, broke free from General Ord's grip. Rosecrans, who had delayed pursuit until the next day and who even took the wrong road, gave Van Dorn the opportunity to cross the Hatchie and to retreat to Holly Springs, Mississippi, thus escaping Grant's carefully planned trap. In the river-crossing battles that ensued, Ord's men were forced to attack a strong Rebel position, incurring about five hundred casualties.[26] In light of this unnecessarily difficult chase, brought about by Rosecrans's failure to capitalize on Union strengths after the Battle of Corinth, a permanent coolness developed between Grant and Rosecrans.[27]

Ironically, after having just thwarted Grant's orders to aggressively pursue, Rosecrans decided that he wanted to do just that, and ignored Grant's new orders to halt the pursuit. Grant raised the issue to Halleck, who allowed Grant to decide. Grant, again ordering Rosecrans back, reasoned that "had he gone much farther he would have met a greater force than Van Dorn had at Corinth and behind intrenchments [*sic*] or on chosen ground, and the probabilities are he would have lost his army." It appears that there were serious miscommunications between Grant and Rosecrans, and that Grant may have erred in not allowing Rosecrans to continue after Van Dorn—an atypical lack of aggressiveness on Grant's part. But, by this time, Grant apparently had lost all confidence in Rosecrans and doubted that he could effectively pursue and engage Van Dorn.[28]

At Corinth, Grant (as Rosecrans's commander) once again had achieved a significant victory while incurring few casualties. His troops had suffered 355 killed, 1,841 wounded, and 324 missing, and the Confederates had 505 killed, 2,150 wounded, and 2,183 missing or captured.[29] The defeat cost Van Dorn his command, and he was replaced by Lieutenant General John C. Pemberton as Commander of the Department of Mississippi and East Louisiana.

Disappointed with Rosecrans's failure at Iuka and his off-and-on pursuit at odds with Grant's orders after Corinth, Grant was ready to remove him from command when, on October 23, Rosecrans was transferred eastward to relieve Buell as commander of the Army of the Ohio, which then became the Army of the Cumberland. Shortly thereafter, on October 25, Grant was given command of the newly formed Department of Tennessee (Tennessee and Kentucky west of the Tennessee River and northern Mississippi) with headquarters at Jackson, Tennessee.[30]

Grant's numerous victories and the September 22, 1862, announcement of President Lincoln's Emancipation Proclamation inspired many African-American slaves to flee and seek refuge behind Union lines. In December 1862, Grant reported that 20,000 Black refugees were being housed, fed, and protected in his Department. Men among the former slaves, joined by free Blacks, began to play significant support, and then active military, roles in Grant's Department.[31]

First Attempts to Capture Vicksburg

That November, bolstered by reinforcements, Grant began an undertaking that would both consume him and require his dominating trait—perseverance—more than ever before. He set his sights on the capture of Vicksburg, and began organizing his first attempt to capture the citadel city that, along with Port Hudson to its south, blocked Union control of the Mississippi River. Vicksburg occupied the first high ground adjacent to the river south of Memphis and was home to a railroad junction that, crucially, enabled food and other imports to move from Mexico and the Trans-Mississippi to the eastern portions of the Confederacy.[32] For that reason, Grant's next six months would be filled with frustration upon frustration as he struggled to find a way to seize Vicksburg.

Historian Russell Weigley put Grant's long-term focus on Vicksburg and the Mississippi in perspective:

> [Grant's] Vicksburg campaign, which extended from the autumn of 1862 into the summer of 1863, was a model of persistent long-range planning. He did not draw inflexible plans, because war is too unpredictable for that, and his progress toward Vicksburg did suffer many reverses. But while always retaining a variety of options in preparation for the unexpected, nevertheless Grant kept pursuing consistently a well-defined strategic goal, the opening of the Mississippi; and viewing battles as means rather than as ends, he refused to be diverted from his goal by the temporary fortunes of any given battle.[33]

Grant's first thrust toward Vicksburg was a two-pronged assault from the north. His plan was to lead troops overland along the Mississippi Central Railroad from Grand Junction, Tennessee, while Sherman took others down the Mississippi for an amphibious attack. Wasting no time after assuming his departmental command, Grant began the Vicksburg campaign on November 2, 1862, when he wired Halleck from Jackson, Tennessee, "I have commenced a movement on Grand Junction with three 3 [*sic*] divisions from Corinth and two from Bolivar. Will leave here tomorrow evening and take command in person. If found practicable I will go on to Holly Springs and may be [*sic*] Grenada completing Railroad & Telegraph as I go."[34]

Grant had three major generals as his wing commanders: James McPherson commanding his left wing, Charles S. Hamilton the center, and Sherman on his right at Memphis on the Mississippi. By November 8, Grant's force had occupied Grand Junction and LaGrange (just north of the Mississippi border), as well as eight miles of the Mississippi Central Railroad south of LaGrange.

Back in Washington, meanwhile, Illinois politician and Major General John McClernand was lobbying Lincoln and Stanton for an independent command on the Mississippi that would overlap with Grant's area of responsibility. Grant learned of McClernand's efforts through newspaper stories and dreaded the chaotic effects such an arrangement would create. Therefore Grant was relieved to receive, on November 12, a dispatch from Halleck giving him command over all troops in his department and the freedom to dispatch them where he chose. Little did he know that a few weeks earlier, on October 21, Stanton had given McClernand a confidential and potentially conflicting order authorizing him to raise troops in the Midwest for a campaign that he would command against Vicksburg. Only later did McClernand realize, to his chagrin, that the fine print in that order made his actions subject to approval by both Grant and General-in-Chief Halleck.[35]

The next day Grant's cavalry occupied Holly Springs, Mississippi, farther south on the Mississippi Central. Grant chose that location for a supply depot, and from there he planned to move across the Tallahatchie River toward Vicksburg. To do so, Grant ordered Sherman to bring most of his troops southeast from Memphis so that he would have a sufficient force to challenge Pemberton, who was fortified on the south side of the Tallahatchie. Grant's cavalry crossed upstream to the east of Pemberton, who in turn retreated south beyond Oxford. Delaying at Oxford to repair the railroad, Grant learned that Halleck had approved a simultaneous water-borne movement from Memphis to Vicksburg.[36]

Intent on ensuring that this expedition was not led by the conniving McClernand, and having been authorized by Halleck to go himself or send Sherman, Grant chose to give the command to Sherman. Sherman would proceed south on the Mississippi while Grant continued his inland trek in the same direction—separated from Sherman by massive bayous. Thus, on December 8, from Oxford, Mississippi, Grant issued orders to his right-wing commander that simply and lucidly stated:

> You will proceed with as little delay as practicable to Memphis, Ten. taking with you one Division of your present command. On your arrival at Memphis you will assume command of all the troops there, and that portion of [Major] Gen. [Samuel R.] Curtis' forces at present East of the Mississippi river and organize them into Brigades & Divisions in your own way. As soon as possible move with them down the river to the vicinity of Vicksburg and with the cooperation of the Gunboat fleet under command of Flag Officer [David Dixon] Porter proceed to the reduction of that place in such manner as sircumstances [*sic*] and your own judgement may dictate.
>
> The amount of rations, forage, land transportation &c. necessary to take will be left entirely to yourself.
>
> The Quartermaster in St. Louis will be instructed to send you transportation for 30.000 [*sic*] men. Should you still find yourself deficient your Quartermaster will be authorized to make up the deficiency from such transports as may come into the port of Memphis.

On arriving in Memphis put yourself in communication
with Admiral Porter and arrange with him for his cooperation. Inform me at the earlyest [*sic*] practicable day of the
time when you will embark and such plans as may then be
matured.

I will hold the forces here in readines[s] to cooperate with
you in such manner as the movements of the enemy may
make necessary.

Leave the District of Memphis in the command of an efficient officer and with a garrison of four regiments of Infantry,
the siege guns and whatever Cavalry force may be there.[37]

Grant's plan was to maintain contact with Pemberton's main
body of troops—either by keeping them away from Vicksburg or
following them to Vicksburg if they retreated to that city. In his
memoirs, Grant reflected on that time:

It was my intention, and so understood by Sherman and his
command, that if the enemy should fall back I would follow
him even to the gates of Vicksburg. I intended in such an
event to hold the [rail]road to Grenada on the Yallabusha
[River] and cut loose from there, expecting to establish a new
base of supplies on the Yazoo, or at Vicksburg itself, with
Grenada to fall back upon in case of failure. It should be
remembered that at the time I speak of it had not been
demonstrated that an army could operate in an enemy's territory depending upon the country for supplies.[38]

On the 18th of December, Grant received orders to divide his
command into four corps and assign one of them to McClernand
as part of the Mississippi River assault force. Grant obeyed those
orders and sent dispatches to McClernand, who was back in

Springfield, Illinois. No doubt anxious to move out for Vicksburg before the arrival of McClernand, who was senior to him, Sherman left Memphis on December 19 with 20,000 men, picking up 12,000 more reinforcements when he reached Helena, Arkansas.[39]

Disaster struck, however, the day after Sherman left Memphis, when Van Dorn's Confederates destroyed Grant's supply depot back at Holly Springs. The 1,500-man garrison there had been forewarned, but fought incompetently and surrendered. The Rebel cavalry destroyed massive supplies of munitions, food, and forage. Grant was further isolated by a simultaneous cavalry raid to the north, led by Forrest, on Grant's rail connection between Columbus, Kentucky and Jackson, Tennessee. As a result, Grant had to retrace his steps northward along the railroad and was unable to contact Sherman about the collapse of the eastern prong of the campaign.[40] Grant found a silver lining in this cloud of disaster. Along the march from Oxford back to Grand Junction, Grant had his troops bring in supplies of food and forage for fifteen miles on each side of the railroad and was surprised at the successful results:

> I was amazed at the quantity of supplies the country afforded. It showed that we could have subsisted off the country for two months instead of two weeks without going beyond the limits designated. This taught me a lesson which was taken advantage of later in the campaign when our army lived twenty days with the issue of only five days' rations by the commissary. Our loss of supplies was great at Holly Springs, but it was more than compensated for by those taken from the country and by the lesson taught.[41]

However, the disruption of Grant's supply line and his retreat north left Pemberton free to return to Vicksburg. And so it was that

Sherman found Pemberton waiting for him when he arrived at Vicksburg. During the last week of the year, Sherman carried out an assault on Confederate forces between the Yazoo River and Vicksburg. The Confederates held the high ground on bluffs, and high water flooded the bottom lands and forced the attackers into narrow corridors that were well-defended. Perhaps hoping that Grant would soon come to his aid, Sherman continued attacking until his heavy casualties revealed the hopelessness of the situation. In this Battle of Chickasaw Bluffs, Sherman incurred 1,780 casualties while the well-entrenched Confederates lost a mere 190. He then retreated back up the Mississippi. Grant's first grasp at Vicksburg had failed ignominiously.[42]

Grant returned to Holly Springs by December 23, and, after railroad repairs had been made, moved his command to Memphis on January 10. From then on, he would stay on or near the Mississippi until he succeeded in capturing Vicksburg. Meanwhile McClernand had gone downriver, assumed command of Sherman's and his own troops, and led a successful expedition up the Arkansas River to capture Fort Hindman at Arkansas Post, along with about 5,000 prisoners. When Grant complained to Halleck that McClernand was on "a wild goose chase," Halleck authorized Grant to remove McClernand from command; Grant wrote an order doing so but inexplicably did not send it. McClernand would remain a thorn in his side for several more months.[43]

After McClernand returned to the mouth of the Arkansas River, both Sherman and Admiral Porter sent messages to Grant urging him to join them and take personal command. They doubted McClernand's competence to do it himself. On January 17, Grant journeyed downriver, met with McClernand and others, and realized he would have to assume personal command. Grant could not put Sherman in command of the expedition because he was junior to McClernand, and Grant chose not to exercise the authority recently given to him by Halleck to relieve McClernand. Even when McClernand responded disrespectfully upon Grant's assuming personal command on January 29 at Young's Point near Vicksburg, Grant chose not to relieve him because of his political value as a strong, pro-Union Democrat from President Lincoln's home state.[44]

Although the safe thing to do would have been to return to Memphis and Holly Springs and launch another overland campaign against Vicksburg, Grant was concerned that this would be demoralizing for the North:

> It was my judgment at the time that to make a backward movement as long as that from Vicksburg to Memphis, would be interpreted, by many of those yet full of hope for the preservation of the Union, as a defeat, and that the draft would be resisted, desertions ensue and the power to capture and punish deserters lost. There was nothing left to be done but to *go forward to a decisive victory*. This was in my mind from the moment I took command in person at Young's Point.[45]

Rather than be seen as retreating northward, Grant initiated a series of experiments intended to secure a base on the east bank of the Mississippi for an attack on Vicksburg. This time, it was geography that made the chore difficult. The city was protected on the north by the Yazoo River and associated swamps, as well as by heavily fortified Haines' Bluff. Its western edge consisted of high bluffs overlooking the Mississippi. Grant orchestrated the experiments to divert the attention of his troops, the enemy, and the public; he had doubts about their success but was prepared to take advantage if any succeeded.[46]

The first of these experiments was the digging of a canal to divert the river in a straight north-south path across a peninsula and away from the bend at the base of Vicksburg. Four thousand soldiers struggled to dig this canal between late January and March 8, when the river broke through a dam that had been built on the north end of the canal to protect the excavation. Even had the canal been completed, its effectiveness would have been reduced by the fact that it was within range of Confederate guns about a mile away.[47]

Slightly farther to the west, Grant ordered General McPherson and his troops to flood Lake Providence and to attempt to clear a waterway through Bayous Baxter and Macon and the Tensas, Washita, and Red Rivers in order to reach the other remaining Confederate military position on the river. This project, which began on January 30, was no sooner started than it was seen as unrealistic by Grant on February 4 and discontinued at the same time as the failed canal project.[48]

These two projects west of the Mississippi were matched in futility by two others on the east side of the river. In the first of these, Grant sought back-door access to the Yazoo River by destroying a levee across from Helena, Arkansas, far north of Vicksburg. The plan was to restore a previously navigable waterway through Moon Lake, Yazoo Pass, and the Coldwater, Tallahatchie, and Yallabusha Rivers about 250 miles to the Yazoo River. A Union expedition of 4,500 troops on transports made it all the way to Confederate Fort Pemberton at the juncture where the Tallahatchie and Yallabusha join to form the Yazoo. They, however, were repelled by Confederate fire from the fort. After destroying another levee on the Mississippi in an unsuccessful effort to flood Fort Pemberton, the Union fleet retreated.[49]

Grant's second effort on the east side of the Mississippi consisted of an Admiral Porter-led fleet of five gunboats, four mortar-boats, and troop-carrying river steamers trying to wend its way through Steel Bayou, Black Bayou, Deer Creek, Rolling Fork, and the Big Sunflower River to the Yazoo River about ten miles above Haines' Bluff. Grant himself accompanied the fleet at the start of the mission but went back to hurry up reinforcements under Sherman. The smaller gunboats got too far ahead of the steamers, which were impeded by the heavy, overhanging swamp trees and the sharp turns in the bayous. Just as the lead vessels were about to break into open water, they ran into more obstructions and a 4,000-man contingent of Confederates. The gunboats were no match for the Rebel sharpshooters, so Sherman's infantry left their delayed steamers and marched along the riverbanks to rescue the gunboats and their crews. The Union vessels were lucky to be able to back out of the hazardous waterways, and as Edwin Bearss concluded, "thus ended in failure the fourth attempt to get in rear of Vicksburg."[50]

In fact, Grant made one final effort—back on the west bank—to use waterways to bypass Vicksburg. He had his men dredging and widening natural bayou channels from Milliken's Bend, northwest of Vicksburg, through Richmond, Louisiana, and back to the Mississippi at Carthage, twenty-five or more miles above Grand Gulf, Mississippi, and a few miles below Vicksburg. He halted the work when it became clear that a useable channel could not be developed. Deteriorating levees and abnormally high water in the river created an excess of water everywhere and made dry land a rarity. As a result, Union soldiers were afflicted with malaria in addition to the usual measles and chicken pox.[51]

Reports of these conditions—and the several failed projects—caused grumbling back home and new calls for Grant's replacement. Many northern newspapers called for Grant's removal and suggested that he be replaced with McClernand, John C. Fremont, Brigadier General David Hunter, or George McClellan. The *New York Times* reported on March 12, "There is no symptom of any plan of attack on Vicksburgh [*sic*]." Later that month the paper reported that "Nothing visible...has been done lately toward the reduction of Vicksburgh [*sic*]."[52]

On March 15, McClernand launched a personal campaign against Grant by writing to Lincoln. McClernand told the president that Grant had been "gloriously drunk" on March 13 and sick in bed all the next day. If the president had decided to remove Grant, McClernand, the next senior officer, would have succeeded him.[53] Lincoln had other ideas.

McClernand wasn't the only one critical of Grant. Congressman Washburne's brother, Cadwallader C. Washburn,[54] a brigadier general in McPherson's corps, wrote that "All Grant's schemes [against Vicksburg] have failed. He is frittering away time and strength to no purpose. The truth must be told even if it hurts. You cannot make a silk purse out of a sow's ear." A Cincinnati newspaper editor wrote to Secretary of the Treasury Salmon P. Chase that Grant was "a jackass in the original package. He is a poor drunken imbecile. He is a poor stick sober, and he is most of the time more than half drunk, and much of the time idiotically drunk." But Lincoln had the final word: "What I want, and what the people want, is generals who will fight battles and win victories. Grant has done this and I propose to stand by him."[55]

Regardless of what his critics had to say, Grant had a definite purpose in occupying his men with these operations—in addition to the possibility they just might succeed. As British Major-General and historian J. F. C. Fuller explained, "All were extremely difficult, entailed immense labor on the part of the army and the fleet; and though all failed in their object, they undoubtedly formed admirable training for Grant's army, hardening and disciplining the men, in fact turning them into salted soldiers."[56]

A year of frustration had begun with Halleck's assumption of command and demonstration of what not to do with a 120,000-man army. It had taken him three weeks to move from Shiloh and another four to "advance" twenty miles to Corinth, where he allowed the outnumbered enemy to escape unscathed. Halleck's breakup of the huge Union force preceded his promotion to Washington and left Grant with decreasing numbers of troops to hold the gains he had previously made.

At the Battle of Iuka, Grant had seen his best-laid plans go awry in the hands of an incompetent subordinate. The great success at Corinth had been a disappointment because of Rosecrans's failure to promptly pursue. Then Grant launched his first campaign against Vicksburg—only to be thwarted by aggressive Confederate cavalry and a pusillanimous Union commander at Holly Springs. That episode led to Sherman unsuccessfully attacking near Vicksburg without the expected support from Grant's stymied overland march. Grant had endured a series of frustratingly unsuccessful efforts to get at the Confederates in Vicksburg.

Grant kept his troops active, kept pressure on his adversaries, and did so with minimal casualties as he preserved his resources for opportunities for significant victory. With each disheartening experience, however, Grant demonstrated his characteristic tenacity and even seemed to draw lessons from each setback. His persistence and experience would soon reap huge dividends.

Six

May–July 1863:
Vanquishing Vicksburg

***

Grant conducts his brilliant Vicksburg Campaign by launching a series of diversionary actions, moving troop transport vessels past Vicksburg's guns, undertaking a daring amphibious movement, living off the countryside, driving between two Rebel armies, winning five battles in eighteen days, besieging Vicksburg, and accepting the surrender of that city and a 29,500-man army—all with minimal casualties to his own army.

During the spring and early summer of 1863, Grant carried out the finest campaign of the Civil War and one of the greatest campaigns in military history. Two of the Civil War's preeminent historians shared that view. James M. McPherson called the Vicksburg Campaign "the most brilliant and innovative campaign of the Civil War," and T. Harry Williams called it "one of the classic campaigns of the Civil War and, indeed, of military history." In fact, the *U.S. Army Field Manual 100-5* (May 1986) described it as "the most brilliant campaign ever fought on American soil" and said, "It exemplifies the qualities of a well-conceived, violently executed offensive plan."[1]

Vicksburg, the Gibraltar of the West, was the key to Union control of the Mississippi. Along with Port Hudson to the south, Vicksburg constituted the only remaining Confederate stronghold on the river. Early in the war, Lincoln himself had pinpointed Vicksburg's importance when he pointed to a national map and said, "See what a lot of land these fellows hold, of which Vicksburg is the key. The war can never be brought to a close until that key is in our pocket."[2]

Having been stymied in his earlier efforts to reach and capture Vicksburg, Grant made sure every detail of the campaign was extremely well thought out. His first course of action was to march his army southward down the west bank of the Mississippi to get well below Vicksburg. He planned to load his men on transports—after having floated them past the guns of Vicksburg—and then move this army to the east bank of the Mississippi shore south of Vicksburg. From there he would strike inland against any Confederate forces brought to bear and eventually attack and capture Vicksburg. He had spent months poring over maps and charts single-handedly to devise this approach. Grant believed that by carrying out this campaign plan he would accomplish phenomenal achievements with a surprisingly small loss of Union personnel. This plan, both daring and extremely risky, was opposed by Grant's subordinate commanders, including Sherman, McPherson, and Logan—a respectable group of fairly experienced generals.[3]

They all understood that Vicksburg was a bastion of fortification. Surrounded by numerous defenses (including nine major forts or citadels), the city had 172 guns that commanded all approaches by water and land and was protected by a 30,000-troop garrison. Grant had three options for attacking it: (1) return to Memphis for an overland approach from the north and east, (2) cross the river and directly assault the city, or (3) march his troops down the west bank of the Mississippi, cross the Mississippi, and approach the city from the south and east. Grant rejected the first option because going back would be morale-deflating (Grant hated to retrace his steps) and the second because it involved, Grant said, "immense sacrifice of life, if not defeat." Grant was left with only one option. Historian Edwin C. Bearss writes, "The third alternative was full of dangers and risks. Failure in this venture would entail little less than total destruction. If it succeeded, however, the gains would be complete and decisive."[4]

Early April brought receding waters and with that, the emergence of roads from Milliken's Bend northwest of Vicksburg to other west bank points on the Mississippi downriver from that city. Grant planned to march his troops over those roads to a location where he could ferry them to the east bank of the river. To do that, he had to enlist the support of Admiral Porter to engage the Navy in getting steamships and transport vessels from north of Vicksburg past that city to the location where Grant's troops would be awaiting ferry transportation.[5]

He had reason to trust this important mission to Porter, who had demonstrated his creativity in an earlier episode. In February, Confederate engineers at Vicksburg were attempting to raise and repair a Union gunboat that had been sunk along the Mississippi shore. On February 25, Porter sent a barge disguised as a gunboat downriver past Vicksburg to frighten the engineers into thinking they were being attacked. The ruse succeeded, and the Rebels burned the ship.

The cooperative Porter agreed to Grant's plan and eagerly set about organizing the vessels for a much larger maritime parade past Vicksburg. He warned Grant that the ironclad vessels did not have sufficient power to return upstream past Vicksburg's guns—that this transit would be the point of no return. In preparation for the transit, Porter directed that the boilers on the steamships be hidden and protected by barriers of cotton and hay bales, as well as bags of grain. The hay and cotton would also be useful later. Beginning at 10:00 p.m. on April 16, Porter led the fleet of seven ironclad gunboats, four steamers, and an assortment of towed coal barges downstream. Coal barges and excess vessels were lashed to the sides of critical vessels to provide additional protection.[6]

Confederate bonfires illuminated the Union vessels that were under fire for two hours as they ran the gauntlet past the Vicksburg guns. Those guns fired 525 rounds and scored 68 hits. Miraculously, only one vessel was lost, and no one on the vessels was killed. The Vicksburg guns had been surprisingly ineffective considering that Pemberton had been selected for the command because of his "supposed experience using artillery against ships."[7] Grant now had his marine transportation in place. Passage of the vessels south of Vicksburg caused the withdrawal to the east bank of Confederates who had been opposing McClernand's progress southward along the west bank.[8]

Fortunately for Grant, Pemberton did not connect the passage of Porter's vessels with the possibility of a Union march down the west bank and an amphibious crossing. Back in Richmond, Robert E. Lee told President Davis that Grant "can derive no material benefit" from Porter's movement and predicted that the addition of more artillery at Vicksburg would prevent Porter from repeating his performance. It was a nineteen-year-old Vicksburg gunner who perceptively wrote in his diary, "Their object, I think, in going below is to cross troops and try and get in the rear of Vicksburg."[9]

Beginning on March 31, Grant had started McClernand's four-division corps on the land route from Milliken's Bend via Richmond, Louisiana, to New Carthage below Vicksburg. Despite muddy roads and broken levees, one of McClernand's divisions reached New Carthage by April 6. From there, his men continued

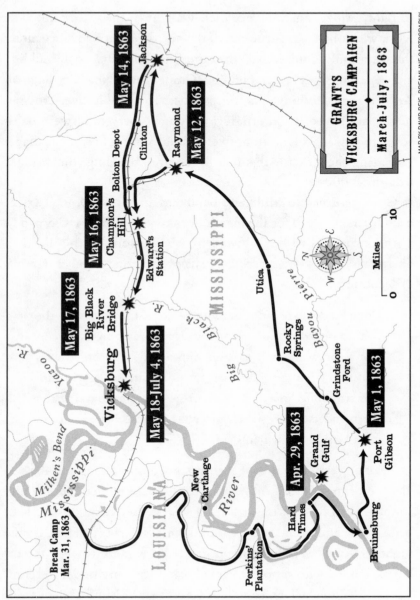

to fight, bridge, and advance their way down the west bank. The work was tough. Construction of the narrow line of advance along the west bank required backbreaking canal digging, road building and repairing, and bridge building. Grant visited New Carthage on April 17, and, to move his troops closer to a viable river-crossing point, approved an alternate but longer forty-mile west bank route to Perkins' Plantation, twelve miles south of New Carthage. Preparing the way for this march required building four bridges totaling 2,000 feet across bayous.[10]

Grant returned to Milliken's Bend and, on April 20, issued Special Orders No. 110 for the march by his entire army. McClernand's 13th Corps was to be followed by McPherson's 17th, and then Sherman's 15th.[11] On the critical issue of gathering supplies, Grant's order stated:

> Commanders are authorized and enjoined to collect all the beef cattle, corn and other necessary supplies on the line of march; but wanton destruction of property, taking of articles useless for military purposes, insulting citizens, going into and searching houses without proper orders from division commanders, are positively prohibited. All such irregularities must be summarily punished.

Realizing that the area of their intended operations and the single line of march that they had created were inadequate to fully supply his troops, Grant ordered a second collection of vessels to bring some additional supplies south past Vicksburg. Thus, on the night of April 22, six more protected steamers towing twelve barges loaded with rations steamed past Vicksburg under the command of Colonel Clark Lagow of Grant's staff. Most of the vessels were commanded and manned by army volunteers from "Black

Jack" Logan's division because the civilian vessel crews did not want to run the now-notorious Vicksburg gauntlet.[12] Despite General Lee's prediction, five of the steamers and half of the barges made it through the gauntlet of artillery batteries, which fired 391 rounds.

Grant now had his transportation (seven transports and fifteen or sixteen barges), a modicum of supplies, and a gathering invasion force. However, Sherman and Porter had serious doubts about the viability of eventually supplying Grant's army via a poor, swampy road on the west bank of the Mississippi River and then across the river and into Mississippi. Nevertheless, Grant pressed forward with his plan and started McPherson's Corps south from New Carthage on April 25.[13]

GRANT'S DIVERSIONS

Meanwhile, Grant had created several diversions to the north and east of Vicksburg to deflect Confederate attention from his campaign plans. First, he had sent Major General Frederick Steele's troops in transports one hundred miles northward up the Mississippi River toward Greenville, Mississippi. This movement led General Pemberton in Vicksburg to conclude that Grant was retreating (to reinforce Rosecrans in eastern Tennessee) and to allow about 8,000 Rebel troops to be transferred from Mississippi back to Bragg in Tennessee.[14]

Second, Grant had initiated a cavalry raid from Tennessee to Louisiana through the length of central and eastern Mississippi. Incurring only a handful of casualties, Colonel Benjamin H. Grierson, a fellow Illinoisan, conducted the most successful Union cavalry raid of the entire war. Grant had devised this diversionary mission back on February 13, when he sent the following simple, flexible, and brilliant suggestion in a dispatch to General Hurlbut in Tennessee:

> It seems to me that Grierson with about 500 picked men might succeed in making his way South and cut the railroad East of Jackson Miss. The undertaking would be a hazardous [sic] one but it would pay well if carried out. I do not direct that this shall be done but leave it for a volunteer enterprise.

On April 17, Grierson rode out of LaGrange, Tennessee, in command of 1,700 cavalrymen (the Sixth and Seventh Illinois and the Second Iowa cavalries) and a six-gun battery (Battery K of the First Illinois Artillery).[15]

In the early days of the raid, Grierson deftly split off part of his force, primarily to confuse the Confederates as to his location and intentions. First, on April 20, he sent 175 men determined to be incapable of completing the mission (deemed the "Quinine Brigade") and a gun back to LaGrange with prisoners and captured property. Then the next day he sent the Iowa regiment and another gun east to break up the north/south Mobile & Ohio Railroad, creating even more confusion. Before sending them east, Grierson had that third of his contingent ride along with his two-thirds and then reverse their path, obliterating Grierson's trail to a point at which Grierson left the road to ride cross-country for some time. The diversion worked so well in drawing off trailing Confederate cavalry from Grierson that the Iowa regiment was followed and had to fight its way clear to return north. To ensure that significant enemy forces were not present in towns that he raided, Grierson assembled a group of nine hand-picked men, the "Butternut Guerillas," who scouted ahead dressed in Confederate uniforms and clothes.[16]

Grierson also was aided by a Union scout (spy) named Charles S. Bell. To establish Bell's "Confederate" credentials, Union General Hurlbut, in January 1863, had arrested Bell in Jackson, Tennessee, and then allowed him to escape. Relying upon his then-established relationship with Confederate Brigadier General James R. Chalmers, Bell worked with Hurlbut on a feint within a feint to divert Chalmers' attention from Grierson's raid. While Hurlbut sent 1,500 troops toward Chalmers' position in northwestern Mississippi, Bell went directly to Chalmers to "warn" him of their approach. Chalmers went for the bait and kept his cavalry focused on this minor distraction while Grierson moved freely to the east on his major diversionary mission.[17]

With still another thirty-five-man detached force drawing substantial Confederate infantry and cavalry away from his main force, Grierson continued to Newton on the east/west Southern Railroad (the eastern extension of the Vicksburg and Jackson Railroad) in the heart of Mississippi. There, on April 24, he destroyed two trains (both filled with ammunition and commissary stores). He also destroyed the railroad and tore down the telegraph line—both linking Meridian to the east with Jackson and Vicksburg to the west. With the disruption of the key railroad to Vicksburg and the destruction of millions of dollars worth of Confederate assets (including thirty-eight railcars), Grierson's mission was complete— except for his final escape.[18]

Pemberton, who had sent troops to head off Grierson before he reached the railroad, now sent additional soldiers to try to cut off the escape of the raiders. Grierson moved southwest to the north/south New Orleans & Jackson Railroad, along which he created such destruction that it went unused for the balance of the war.[19] The raid's effect on Pemberton is reflected in the fact that on

April 27 he sent seventeen messages to Mississippi commands about Grierson's raiders and not a single one about Grant's build-up on the west bank of the Mississippi River. By the 29th, Pemberton had further played into Grant's hands by sending all his cavalry in pursuit of Grierson; he advised his superiors:

> The telegraph wires are down. The enemy has, therefore, either landed on this side of the Mississippi River, or they have been cut by Grierson's cavalry, which had reached Union Church, on road from Hazelhurst to Natchez. All the cavalry I can raise is close on their rear. Skirmishing with them yesterday.[20]

Sixteen days and six hundred miles after starting their dangerous venture, Grierson's men reached the Union lines at Baton Rouge, Louisiana, on May 2—two days after Grant's amphibious landing at Bruinsburg on the Mississippi. They had survived several close calls, created havoc in their wake, and performed their primary mission of diverting attention from Grant's movements west and south of Vicksburg. They had also inflicted one hundred casualties and captured over five hundred prisoners. Miraculously, all this had been accomplished with only three killed, seven wounded, and between five and fourteen missing, captured, or sick and left behind. There was good reason for Sherman to call it the "most brilliant expedition of the Civil War."[21]

Grant's third diversion involved another cavalry foray. At the same time as Grierson was traveling the length of Mississippi, other Union forces went on the offensive far to the east. Colonel Abel D. Streight led a "poorly mounted horse and mule brigade" from Middle Tennessee into Alabama and drew the ever-dangerous cavalry of Nathan Bedford Forrest away from Grierson and his various detachments.[22]

To completely confuse Pemberton, Grant used a fourth diversion. While he was moving south with McClernand and McPherson on the west bank (Louisiana shore), Grant had Sherman's 15th Corps threaten Vicksburg from the north. On April 27, Grant ordered Sherman to proceed up the Yazoo River and threaten Snyder's Bluff northeast of Vicksburg. On the 29th, Sherman did so; he dispatched ten regiments of troops and appeared to be preparing an assault while eight naval gunboats bombarded the Confederate forts at nearby Haines' Bluff. Having suffered no casualties, Sherman withdrew on May 1 to hastily follow McPherson down the west bank of the Mississippi. His troops were ferried across the river on May 6 and 7.[23]

AMPHIBIOUS ASSAULT

Grant, meanwhile, had joined McClernand at New Carthage on the west bank on April 23. When Colonel James H. Wilson of Grant's staff and Admiral Porter determined that there were no suitable landing areas east of Perkins' Plantation, Grant on April 24 ordered the troops to proceed south another twenty-two miles to Hard Times, a west bank area sixty-three miles south of Milliken's Bend and directly across the river from Grand Gulf, Mississippi. According to Stanton's special observer and former *New York Tribune* reporter and editor, Charles A. Dana, McClernand moved his troops slowly and disobeyed Grant's orders to preserve ammunition and to leave all impediments behind, but the facts don't bear this out. McClernand had guns fired in salute at a review and tried to bring his wife and servants along. Ten thousand soldiers were moved farther south by vessel, and the rest of the men bridged three bayous and completed their trek to Hard Times by April 27.

On April 28, Confederate Brigadier General John S. Bowen at Grand Gulf spotted the Union armada gathering across the river and urgently requested reinforcements from Pemberton in Vicksburg. But Pemberton was focused on Grierson and Sherman and refused to send reinforcements south toward Grand Gulf. He at last gave in and sent the troops on April 29, but they were already too late to halt the Union amphibious crossing.[24]

Two days later, with 10,000 of McClernand's troops embarked on vessels for a possible east bank landing, Porter's eight gunboats attacked the Confederate batteries on the high bluffs at Grand Gulf. The Union vessels fired for five and a half hours and suffered the loss of eighteen killed and about fifty-seven wounded. The Union fleet managed to eliminate the guns of Fort Wade but not those of Fort Coburn, which stood forty feet above the river and had a forty-foot-thick parapet. A disappointed Grant watched from a small tugboat, and Porter eventually halted the attack.[25]

The persistent Grant, however, did not give up; he simply moved south. That night, the 10,000 troops left the vessels and marched across a peninsula while Porter slipped all his vessels past the Confederate guns. Grant was planning to load his troops again and land them at Rodney, about nine miles south of Grand Gulf. Instead, he changed his mind when he sent a landing party to the Mississippi shore and thereby learned from a local Negro that Bruinsburg, a few miles closer, offered a good landing site and a good road inland to Port Gibson. Convinced of what he was going to do the next day, Grant sent orders that night to Sherman to immediately head south with two of his three corps. On the morning of April 30, Grant moved across and down the Mississippi with McClernand's Corps and one of McPherson's divisions from Disharoon's Plantation (near Hard Times), Louisiana, took them six miles south to Bruinsburg,

Mississippi, and landed them without opposition.[26] In his memoirs, Grant explained the great relief he felt after the successful landing:

> When this was effected I felt a degree of relief scarcely ever equaled since. Vicksburg was not yet taken it is true, nor were its defenders demoralized by any of our previous moves. I was now in the enemy's country, with a vast river and the stronghold of Vicksburg between me and my base of supplies. But I was on dry ground on the same side of the river with the enemy. All the campaigns, labors, hardships and exposures from the month of December previous to this time that had been made and endured, were for the accomplishment of this one object.[27]

Using the cover of several diversions, Grant had daringly marched his army through Louisiana bayous down the west bank of the Mississippi and launched one of the largest amphibious operations (involving 24,000 troops) ever conducted prior to D-Day on June 6, 1944. Historian Terrence J. Winschel concluded:

> The movement from Milliken's Bend to Hard Times was boldly conceived and executed by a daring commander willing to take risks. The sheer audacity of the movement demonstrated Grant's firmness of purpose and revealed his many strengths as a commander. The bold and decisive manner in which he directed the movement set the tone for the campaign and inspired confidence in the army's ranks.[28]

Moving Inland: Port Gibson and Raymond

The first day ashore, Grant pushed McClernand two miles inland to high, dry ground and then onward toward the town of Port

Gibson, which had a bridge across Big Bayou Pierre that led to Grand Gulf (which Grant coveted as a supply base on the Mississippi). Meanwhile, Grant oversaw the continuous transport of more of his troops across the Mississippi well into the night. Aided by the light of huge bonfires, McPherson's soldiers were transported until 3:00 a.m., when a collision between two transports stopped the operation until daylight.[29]

Back upriver Sherman was beginning to move south but remained skeptical of the feasibility of the long, vulnerable supply-line. There was reason to be skeptical. As historian James R. Arnold observed, "Grant was at the end of an exceedingly precarious supply-line, isolated in hostile territory, positioned between Port Hudson and Vicksburg—two well-fortified, enemy-held citadels—outnumbered by his enemy, and with an unfordable river to his rear. Few generals would have considered this anything but a trap. Grant judged it an opportunity."[30]

The next day, May 1, brought conflict and the first of Grant's five victories in battles leading to the siege of Vicksburg: the Battle of Port Gibson.[31] Two Confederate brigades, which had belatedly marched as many as forty-four miles from near Vicksburg, and the garrison from Grand Gulf had crossed the bridge over the North Fork of Bayou Pierre at Port Gibson. They confronted McClernand's troops about three miles west of Port Gibson. McClernand split his forces along two parallel roads leading toward town and ran into strong opposition. General Bowen arrived from Grand Gulf to command the defenders.

The Confederate left fell back under intense attack from three of McClernand's divisions as Union sharpshooters picked off the brave and effective Rebel gunners manning the defenders' artillery. Following the initial Rebel retreat, McClernand and visiting Illinois

Governor Yates delivered victory remarks and did some politicking with the troops. Grant put an end to those proceedings and ordered the advance to resume. Meanwhile, Grant had reinforced McClernand's left wing with two of McPherson's brigades, and that wing similarly drove the Confederates back toward Port Gibson in the face of persistent Confederate artillery. Victory was confirmed the next morning (May 2), when Grant's soldiers found Port Gibson abandoned by the Confederates, who had crossed and burned the bridges across Big Bayou Pierre (to Grand Gulf) and Little Bayou Pierre.[32]

Although Grant's troops were on the offensive all day at Port Gibson, the two sides' casualties were surprisingly comparable. Grant had lost 131 killed, 719 wounded, and 25 missing—a total of 875. Based on incomplete reports, the Confederate defenders had at least 68 killed, 380 wounded, and 384 missing—a total of at least 832.[33]

Despite narrow roads, hilly terrain, and dense vegetation that aided the defenders, Grant's superior force had gained the inland foothold it needed and access to the interior. The battle set the tone for those that followed in the campaign and affected the morale of both the winners and the losers. Grant would consistently bring superior forces to each battlefield although his troops were outnumbered by the Confederates scattered around western Mississippi. From Vicksburg, Pemberton accurately and somewhat desperately telegraphed Richmond: "A furious battle has been going on since daylight just below Port Gibson. . . . Enemy's movement threatens Jackson, and, if successful, cuts off Vicksburg and Port Hudson from the east. . . ." With minimal losses, Grant was moving inland. Meanwhile, a rattled Pemberton sent an urgent message to his field commanders directing them to proceed at once— but neglecting to say to where.[34]

In addition to his mid-battle political speech, McClernand demonstrated other problems of competence and attitude. His men went ashore with no rations instead of the standard three days of rations. He rejected a recommendation from one of his brigadiers that he attack the enemy flank and instead ordered a frontal assault. When Grant ordered McClernand's artillery to conserve ammunition, an angry McClernand countermanded the order.[35] Having just crossed the Mississippi to initiate a challenging campaign of unknown duration, a subordinate military commander would be expected to honor the commanding general's concern about conserving ammunition for future contingencies. McClernand was setting himself up for a big fall. In fact, Stanton, aware of the previous problems with McClernand, had sent Charles Dana a May 6 telegram authorizing Grant "to remove any person who by ignorance in action or any cause interferes with or delays his operations."[36]

After his troops had quickly built a bridge across Little Bayou Pierre, Grant accompanied McPherson northeast to Grindstone Ford, the site of the next bridge across Big Bayou Pierre. Fortunately, they found the bridge still burning and only partially destroyed. They made rapid repairs and crossed Big Bayou Pierre. Because Grant was now in a position to cut off Grand Gulf, the Confederates abandoned that port town and retreated north toward Vicksburg. At Hankinson's Ferry, north of Grand Gulf, the Confederates retreated across a raft bridge over the Big Black River, the only remaining geographical barrier between Grant and Vicksburg.[37]

On May 3, Grant rode into the abandoned and ruined town of Grand Gulf, boarded the *Louisville*, took his first bath in a week, caught up on his correspondence, and rethought his mission. He had learned of the successful completion of Grierson's diversionary mission[38] and also of the time-consuming campaign of General Nathaniel P. Banks up the Red River. He decided to deviate radically from his orders from General Halleck, which called for him to send McPherson's corps south to Port Hudson to await the return of Banks and cooperate with Banks in the capture of Port Hudson—all of this before a decisive move on Vicksburg. Grant realized that, in waiting to cooperate with Banks in taking Port Hudson, he would lose about a month and would gain only about 12,000 troops from Banks. He understood also that in the intervening time he would give the Confederates, under Department Commander Joseph E. Johnston, the opportunity to gather reinforcements from all over the South to save Vicksburg. Instead, Grant decided to move inland with McPherson's and McClernand's corps, and he ordered Sherman to continue moving south to join him with two of his three divisions.[39]

Therefore, before leaving Grand Gulf at midnight on May 3, Grant wrote to Halleck:

> The country will supply all the forage required for anything like an active campaign and the necessary fresh beef. Other supplies will have to be drawn from Millikin's [sic] Bend. This is a long and precarious route but I have every confidance [sic] in succeeding in doing it.
>
> I shall not bring my troops into this place but immediately follow the enemy, and if all promises as favorably hereafter as it does now, not stop until Vicksburg is in our possession.[40]

Grant was going for Vicksburg—now! Until Sherman's troops arrived, Grant had only 25,000 troops across the river to face 50,000 Confederates in Mississippi with as many as another 20,000 on the way.[41]

When he moved inland to Hankinson's Ferry at daybreak on May 4, Grant learned that McPherson's men had captured intact the bridge across the Big Black River and established a bridgehead on the opposite shore. While awaiting the arrival of Sherman's corps, Grant ordered McPherson and McClernand to probe the countryside. McClernand's patrols soon discovered that the Confederates were fortifying a defensive line south of Vicksburg. Their patrols also were designed to create the impression that Grant would directly attack Vicksburg from the south. With the arrival of Sherman and the bulk of his corps on May 6 and 7 (via the 63-mile march from Milliken's Bend to Hard Times and ferrying across to Grand Gulf), Grant was ready to move in force.[42]

Realizing that Vicksburg by now was well defended to the south and that its defenders could flee to the northeast if he attacked from the south, Grant decided on a more promising, but riskier, course of action. In the words of T. Harry Williams, "Then the general called dull and unimaginative and a mere hammerer executed one of the fastest and boldest moves in the records of war."[43] He cut loose from his base at Grand Gulf, withdrew McPherson from north of the Big Black River, and ordered all three of his army's corps to head northeast between the Big Black on the left and Big Bayou Pierre on the right. His goal was to follow the Big Black, cut the east/west Southern Railroad (also known as the Vicksburg and Jackson Railroad in this stretch) between Vicksburg and Jackson, and then move west along the railroad to Vicksburg. In what historian Thomas Buell called "the most brilliant decision of his career," Grant "would attack first Johnston and then Pemberton before they could unite and thereby outnumber him, the classic example of defeating an enemy army in detail."[44]

Given the poor condition of the dirt roads, the tenuous supply situation, and the threat of Confederate interference from many directions, according to Ed Bearss, Grant's "decision to move northeast along the Big Black-Big Bayou Pierre watershed was boldness personified, and Napoleonic in its concept."[45] William B. Feis concluded: "From the outset, Grant designed his movements to sow uncertainty in Pemberton's mind as to the true Federal objective. The key to success, especially deep in Confederate territory, was to maintain the initiative and make the enemy guess at his objectives."[46] Noteworthy is Grant's determination not only to occupy Vicksburg, but to trap Pemberton's army and keep its soldiers from escaping to fight again. As he would do later in Virginia, Grant stayed focused on defeating, capturing, or destroying the opposing army—not simply occupying geographic positions. This approach was critical to ultimate Union victory in the war.

General Fuller pointed out that Grant's plan was not only daring and contrary to his instructions from Halleck, but, just as importantly, it required immediate execution. Grant insisted that his commanders move with haste to execute it, and his orders to them in those early days of May were filled with words urging them to implement his orders expeditiously. He made it clear that he wanted to move quickly inland to negate any forces other than Pemberton's, destroy Vicksburg's supply-line, and then quickly turn on Vicksburg with his own rear protected.[47]

As Grant moved inland, he planned to live off the previously untouched countryside. His troops slaughtered livestock and harvested crops and gardens to obtain food and fodder. They also gathered an eclectic collection of buggies and carriages to assemble a crude and heavily guarded wagon train that would carry salt, sugar, hard bread, ammunition, and other crucial supplies from Grand

Gulf to Grant's army. Grant would depend on those intermittent and vulnerable wagon trains to meet some of his needs for two weeks until a supply-line was opened on the Yazoo River north of Vicksburg on May 21.[48]

From May 8 to 12, Grant's army moved out of its Grand Gulf beachhead and up this corridor with McClernand hugging the Big Black on the left and guarding all the ferries, Sherman in the center, and McPherson on the right. They gradually swung in a more northerly direction (pivoting on the Big Black) and moved within a few miles of the critical railroad without serious opposition. Then, on May 12, McPherson ran into stiff opposition south of the town of Raymond.[49] Aggressive assaults ordered by Confederate Brigadier General John Gregg, who believed he was facing a single brigade, threw McPherson's soldiers into disarray. Strong counterattacks led by Major General "Black Jack" Logan drove the outnumbered Confederates back into and through Raymond. Gregg's aggressiveness cost him one hundred dead, three hundred five wounded, and four hundred fifteen missing for a total of eight hundred twenty casualties. McPherson reported his casualties as sixty-six killed, three hundred thirty-nine wounded, and thirty-seven missing for a total of four hundred forty-two. Grant's campaign of maneuver and his concentration of force were resulting in progress at the cost of moderate casualties.[50]

Even more significantly, Grant's daring crossing of the Mississippi and inland thrust were wreaking havoc at the highest levels of the Confederacy. Pemberton, in command at Vicksburg, was caught between conflicting orders from President Jefferson Davis and his Department Commander, General Joseph Johnston. Davis told Pemberton that holding Vicksburg and Port Hudson was critical to connecting the eastern Confederacy to the Trans-Mississippi. The northern-born Pemberton, who had been eased out of his Charleston, South Carolina command for suggesting evacuation of that city, decided to obey the president and defend Vicksburg at all costs. He did this despite May 1 and 2 orders from Johnston that, if Grant crossed the Mississippi, Pemberton should unite all his troops to defeat him. Grant was the unintended beneficiary of Pemberton's decision because Pemberton kept his fifteen brigades in scattered defensive positions behind the Big Black River while Grant moved away from them toward Jackson. Meanwhile, Johnston sat in Tullahoma, Tennessee, with little to do and only moved to oppose Grant when belatedly ordered to do so by Davis and Secretary of War James A. Seddon on May 9—and did so with only 3,000 troops at first.[51]

CAPTURING JACKSON, THE STATE CAPITAL

The battle at Raymond caused Grant to realize the seriousness of the Confederate threat to his right flank, and then to his rear, if he simply continued north to the railroad and then turned west toward Vicksburg. He had received reports (including one from scout Charles Bell) that General Johnston had arrived in Jackson, and reinforcements from the east and south were headed for that town. Jackson, was the obvious rail junction for any additional Confederate troops and supplies headed for Vicksburg. Thus, Grant decided to attack Jackson and eliminate it and the troops there as a threat to his Vicksburg campaign. On the evening of May 12, therefore, he issued orders for McPherson to move on Clinton (on the railroad ten miles west of Jackson) and then on to Jackson, and for Sherman to move on Jackson from the southwest through Raymond. They carried out their orders on the 13th and threatened Jackson by nightfall.[52]

That very evening Johnston arrived at Jackson in accordance with orders from Confederate Secretary of War James A. Seddon, despite Johnston's initial protestations of illness. Advised by Gregg that Union troops were astride the railroad to Vicksburg, that only 6,000 Confederate troops were in the Jackson vicinity, and that Confederate reinforcements were on the way (which he already knew), Johnston hoped to assemble 12,000 troops at Jackson within a day and trap Grant between Pemberton's force and his. To accomplish this, he sent three couriers with messages directing Pemberton to organize a converging attack and, if practicable, to attack the Federal troops at Clinton. He stressed that "time is all important." Johnston concluded in a concurrent telegram to Seddon, "I am too late."

In light of Grant's initiative and Pemberton's hesitance to carry out Johnston's order or abandon Vicksburg, Johnston was indeed too late.[53] Partly because Grant's spy network had advised him of Johnston's arrival and plans for reinforcement, Grant did not hesitate to continue his expedited offensive.[54]

Because of Grant's concentration of force at Jackson, and despite torrential downpours, his troops were able to drive the Confederates from Jackson in a May 14 battle that lasted less than a day.[55] McPherson fought his way in from the west and Sherman from the southwest; they occupied the city by mid-afternoon. Jackson cost the Union 42 killed, 251 wounded, and 7 missing (a total of 300) while the Confederates suffered an estimated 500 casualties and the loss of 17 cannons. Confederate industrial losses in Jackson were significant. Johnston himself burned all the city's cotton and five million dollars in railroad rolling stock, and Sherman followed that up by burning an arsenal, foundries, machine shops, and cotton factories and warehouses. During the assault, Grant had used McCler-

nand to protect his western exposure against an attack by Pember-
ton that never came. Pemberton spent the day probing southeast of
Vicksburg for Grant's non-existent line of communication with
Grand Gulf, and Johnston retreated from Jackson to the north
away from Pemberton's movement. Even worse for the Rebels,
Johnston turned back reinforcements that were moving toward
Jackson by rail.[56]

Grant then learned from McPherson that one of Johnston's three
couriers carrying his May 12 "attack" message to Pemberton was
a Union spy—almost certainly the same Charles Bell who a few
months earlier had been ceremoniously ejected from Memphis for
supposed Confederate sympathies. Thus, Grant learned of Johnston's order and immediately turned his army westward to deal
with Pemberton. He ordered McClernand to Bolton Station, about
twenty miles west of Jackson and the nearest point to Jackson on
the railroad where Johnston might merge his and Pemberton's
forces. He also ordered McPherson to swiftly move west along the
railroad and Sherman to destroy the railroads[57] and enemy property
in and around Jackson. These actions were all accomplished without delay on May 15, and Grant at last was prepared to march
directly toward Vicksburg.[58]

CHAMPION'S HILL AND THE BIG BLACK RIVER

At five o'clock in the morning on the 16th, Grant learned from two
railroad workers that Pemberton was supposedly moving toward
him with about 25,000 troops; he actually had 23,000. Grant
immediately sent Sherman orders to cease his destructive work at
Jackson and move hastily west to join him, McClernand, and
McPherson. Meanwhile, Pemberton, having wasted his time on the

southward movement to cut off Grant's non-existent base, had finally decided to obey his orders from Johnston and move east toward Jackson to confront Grant. Pemberton occupied a strong defensive position at Champion's Hill, astride the Vicksburg and Jackson Railroad, the main road between the two towns, and two parallel roads. Pemberton's men were exhausted from their confused handling on the 15th while Grant's troops were efficiently moved into a threatening position.[59]

At the May 16 Battle of Champion's Hill, Grant's 32,000 troops, contained in McPherson and McClernand's corps, moved against 23,000 Confederate defenders. McClernand pushed his 13th Corps ahead on the Raymond Road and the Middle Road, a parallel road to the north. They encountered Confederate troops who were linked by a connecting road. An aura of uncertainty hung over the Confederate troops as word spread of General Pemberton's belated decision, made that morning, to attempt to disengage from the enemy and move northeast to join Johnston. His decision (his third different strategic decision in three days as he tried to figure out what Grant was doing) came too late, and the armies were soon locked in battle.[60]

After the initial blocking action on the Raymond and Middle roads, Pemberton gave orders for some infantry to follow his wagon train back toward Vicksburg, away from the conflict, and eventually to turn northeast and link up with Johnston. Quickly thereafter, however, he discovered a new Federal threat that caused him to cancel that order. Coming in from the east toward Champion's Hill, farther north on the Jackson Road and angling toward a crucial intersection with the Middle Road, was McPherson's 17th Corps. Pemberton had no choice but to attempt to block their march as well as McClernand's.[61]

Under Grant's oversight and McPherson's control, Union soldiers launched a late morning assault on the north side of the battlefield. By early afternoon, they not only had carried Champion's Hill, but they also had gained control of Jackson Road west of the crossroads, thereby cutting off one of Pemberton's only two escape routes back toward Vicksburg. In the process, they had shattered one Confederate division and captured sixteen precious guns.[62]

Seeing the north end of his line collapsing, Pemberton ordered reinforcements from his right. Despite reluctance and delay on the part of Generals Bowen and William Wing ("Old Blizzards") Loring, who were facing McClernand on the south end of the lines, they at last ordered two of their brigades to march north toward the Jackson Road/Middle Road crossroads. At 2:30 that afternoon, those veteran Arkansas and Missouri brigades launched a furious assault on the Union soldiers who only recently had taken control at the crossroads. The two Rebel brigades drove the Yankees not only out of the crossroads, but all the way back beyond the crest of Champion's Hill.[63]

Grant and McPherson organized yet another attack to regain the lost ground. As at Belmont, Donelson, and Shiloh, Grant took charge at a critical moment to turn adversity into victory. He said, "[Brigadier General Alvin P.] Hovey's division and [Colonel George] Boomer's brigade are good troops. If the enemy has driven them he is not in good plight himself. If we can go in here and make a little showing, I think he will give way." Led by a newly arrived division of McPherson's Corps, the Federals made that "little showing" and drove the stubborn Rebels off Champion's Hill and out of the crossroads. To ensure the success of this counter-attack, Grant even recalled the advance troops that blocked the Jackson Road toward Vicksburg. The success of the Union counterattack was aided by

Loring's additional delay in reinforcing Pemberton with troops from the right wing—apparently due to an ongoing dispute between Pemberton and Loring.[64]

With Union forces pressing them all along the front and only one retreat route open (the Raymond Road that McClernand still had not blocked), Bowen's and Major General Carter L. Stevenson's divisions fled southwest to the Raymond Road and then westward to and across the Big Black River. Loring's division, covering the retreat, was cut off by an Indiana battery (part of McClernand's corps) that had pursued fleeing Rebels west on the Jackson Road and then had cut south across the countryside to get to the Raymond Road. As a result, Loring took his 7,000-man division farther south, was unsuccessful in crossing Bakers Creek to get back to Pemberton, abandoned his twelve guns (which Union soldiers retrieved the next day), and headed toward Jackson. By the time he joined Johnston at Jackson, Loring's force had melted away to 4,000.[65]

The Battle of Champion's Hill involved about three hours of skirmishing and four hours of fierce fighting on Grant's center and right. Aggressive assaults by McPherson's corps had compelled a Confederate retreat. However, McClernand's failure to aggressively advance on the left first allowed Confederate reinforcements to be sent against McPherson, and later permitted many of the hard-pressed Rebels to flee back to the Big Black River. Instead of aggressively pushing forward on his front, McClernand sought reinforcements from the already engaged center and right of the battlefield—an effort Grant vetoed. Although Grant was on the offensive throughout the battle and attained his goal of pushing back the enemy toward Vicksburg, the numbers of his dead and wounded were remarkably similar to his enemy's: both sides had about 400 killed and 1,800 wounded, but Grant's 200 missing paled alongside the Confederates' 1,700 missing. In addition, Grant captured 30 pieces of artillery and cut Loring's 7,000-man division off from the rest of Pemberton's army.[66]

This battle closed the door on possible escape by Pemberton's army and cleared the way for the siege of Vicksburg. It has been described by James R. Arnold as "arguably the decisive encounter of the war." While Pemberton kept 40 percent of his troops behind the Big Black River, Grant had pressed forward with all available troops and thereby gained a crucial and decisive 3 to 2 manpower advantage. Grant later described the military significance of the victory: "We were now assured of our position between Johnston and Pemberton, without a possibility of a junction of their forces."[67]

With the demoralized Confederates having moved back to the Big Black River, Grant sent word to the trailing Sherman to head northwest to cross that river at Bridgeport with his 15th Corps and thereby flank Pemberton's troops. Before Sherman arrived on their flank, the Confederates had been beaten again. At the Big Black River in front of Grant, the Confederates again had a respectable defensive position from which to confront Grant's assault. Inexplicably, however, they built a parapet of cotton bales and dirt on the east side of the river instead of on the higher ground west of the river. Thus they failed to fully utilize the river's defensive potential during the brief battle that ensued. Pemberton kept his men east of the river in hopes that Loring would show up and need protection crossing the river. Pemberton's over-commitment to the east bank was offset by his withdrawal of all the artillery horses to the west bank, making withdrawal of those guns east of the river difficult or impossible.[68]

On the morning of May 17, Grant's troops arrived near the river and came under fire as the Battle of the Big Black River began.[69] A brigade of Iowa and Wisconsin troops scurried under fire to an old river meander scar near the center of the battlefield. From there they launched a dramatic three-minute charge through a swamp and abatis (an obstacle of cut trees with sharp points aimed at attackers) and entered the Confederate lines to the shock of everyone on the field. They captured many startled defenders while the rest of the Rebels east of the deep river started a major "skedaddle." A few of them tried to swim across the river while most scrambled back across two "bridges" (one being a converted steamboat), which the Confederates then burned behind them as they fled to Vicksburg.

Although the bridge-burning prevented Grant's immediate pursuit across the high river, fast-moving Union troops and the river trapped at least a thousand Confederates on the east side of the river. Thus, Grant captured those soldiers, 18 guns, and the last obstacle between his army and Vicksburg at the relatively small cost of 39 killed, 237 wounded, and 3 missing.[70]

As the Battle of the Big Black River was about to begin, an officer from General Banks's staff had arrived with a May 11 letter to Grant from General-in-Chief Halleck ordering Grant to return to Grand Gulf and cooperate with General Banks in capturing Port Hudson. Grant told the startled officer he was too late and that Halleck would not have given the order if he had known of Grant's position. The next day, May 18, Grant crossed the Big Black and met Sherman, who had crossed miles above as planned. They rode together hastily toward their long-sought position on the Yazoo River northeast of Vicksburg, where they could establish a base for supplies moved in from the Mississippi.[71] In his memoirs, Grant remembered the moment of elation he shared with Sherman:

In a few minutes Sherman had the pleasure of looking down from the spot coveted so much by him the December before on the ground where his command had lain so helpless for offensive action. He turned to me, saying that up to this minute he had felt no positive assurance of success. This, however, he said was the end of one of the greatest campaigns in history and I ought to make a report of it at once. Vicksburg was not yet captured, and there was no telling what might happen before it was taken; but whether captured or not, this was a complete and successful campaign.[72]

As Grant approached Vicksburg, he could look back on the past eighteen successful days with satisfaction. He had entered enemy territory against a superior force and with no secure supply-line, fought and won five battles, severely damaged the Mississippi capital, driven away Johnston's relief force, driven Pemberton's Army back into Vicksburg, inflicted over 7,000 losses (killed, wounded, and missing) on the enemy, separated Loring's 7,000 troops from the main enemy army, and thus reduced Pemberton's Army by 14,000 troops. Grant's own casualties were between 3,500 and 4,500. Historian Ed Bearss succinctly summarized the greatness of Grant's campaign to that point:

> During these 17 days, Grant's army had maneuvered and fought while dependent upon a dangerously exposed and tenuous supply line, and the men lived in part off the country. Union losses during this period had been about 3,500 officers and men. Students of history up to that time had to go back to the campaigns of Napoleon to find equally brilliant results accomplished in the same space of time *with such corresponding small losses.*[73]

ASSAULTING AND BESIEGING VICKSBURG

Wasting no time, Grant immediately moved on Vicksburg with all three of his corps and ordered the first assault at 2:00 p.m. on the 19th. Riding the momentum of his string of successes, Grant wanted to catch the defenders before they had an opportunity to fully organize. Although that assault tightened the noose around the town and resulted in Grant's troops achieving covered and advanced positions, it also demonstrated that capture of the town by assault would be difficult. It cost Grant 900 casualties to the Rebels' 200.

Nevertheless, Grant decided on a second assault because of the threat presented by Johnston's army in his rear, his desire to avoid having to bring in reinforcements from elsewhere, and his knowledge that his soldiers believed they could carry the town's fortifications and needed an opportunity to try doing so. Therefore, on May 22, all three corps launched simultaneous attacks, bravely approached the enemy fortifications, and were repulsed. In response to dubious claims of success by McClernand, Grant sent him reinforcements and continued attacks elsewhere, thus causing additional casualties. Grant had 3,200 casualties, while the defenders incurred about 500. With that final assault having failed, Grant settled in for a siege.[74]

In his memoirs, Grant expressed regret for the May 22 assault, but explained his reasons for doing it:

> We were in a Southern climate, at the beginning of the hot season. The Army of the Tennessee had won five successive victories over the garrison of Vicksburg in the three preceding weeks.... The Army of the Tennessee had come to believe that they could beat their antagonist under any circumstances. There was no telling how long a regular siege might

last. As I have stated, it was the beginning of the hot season in a Southern climate. There was no telling what the casualties might be among Northern troops working and living in trenches, drinking surface water filtered through rich vegetation, under a tropical sun. If Vicksburg would have been carried in May, it would not only have saved the army the risk it ran of a greater danger than from the bullets of the enemy, but it would have given us a splendid army, well equipped and officered, to operate elsewhere with.[75]

General Fuller pointed out that Grant had seven reasons to attack rather than simply besiege Vicksburg: (1) Johnston was gathering an army in his rear; (2) a quick victory would allow Grant to attack Johnston; (3) Union reinforcements would be required to perfect the siege; (4) the troops were impatient to take Vicksburg; (5) the weather was getting hotter; (6) water was scarce; and (7) the men were not anxious to dig entrenchments. Although he has been criticized in hindsight for initiating the May 22 assault, Grant had sufficient reasons to justify his attempt to take the town by assault. Even though his casualties that day were 500 killed and 2,550 wounded, Grant's casualties in the three prior weeks of fighting had been a mere 700 killed and 3,400 wounded. Cumulatively, these casualties were a fair price to pay for having struck at the heart of the western Confederacy and trapping a 30,000-man army in the citadel on the Mississippi, the capture of which would culminate in an extraordinarily significant Union victory.[76]

From afar, Robert E. Lee gave President Davis some belated advice on the Vicksburg situation and paid a tribute to Grant's speedy execution of his campaign. On May 28, Lee wrote, "I am glad to hear that the accounts from Vicksburg continue encouraging—I pray & trust that Genl Johnston may be able to destroy

Grant's army—I fear if he cannot attack soon, he will become too strong in his position—No time should ever be given them to fortify. *They work so fast.*"[77]

About this time, separated from Julia since April, Grant may have resumed his drinking. On May 12, 1863, *Chicago Times* reporter Sylvanus Cadwallader allegedly observed Grant drinking three cups of whiskey from a barrel maintained for him by his chief of artillery, Colonel William L. Duff. And in early June, during the siege of Vicksburg, Cadwallader allegedly saw Grant go on a two-day "bender" on board the steamboat *Diligence* while Grant was on an inspection tour on the Yazoo River. Cadwallader claimed that he had tried unsuccessfully to keep Grant from drinking during the trip, but Grant sobered up when he returned to his headquarters. Cadwallader's account was far from contemporaneous, and he is not regarded as a reliable witness. However, there is evidence that Grant did do some drinking during the uneventful portions of the Vicksburg siege.[78]

There are many reports of Lincoln humorously rebuffing complaints about Grant's alleged drinking problem. In the midst of the Vicksburg campaign, Colonel T. Lyle Dickey of Grant's cavalry was sent to Washington with dispatches for the president and secretary of war. When meeting with the president, Colonel Dickey assured the president that rumors about Grant's drinking were false. The president allegedly responded, "[I]f those accusing General Grant of getting drunk will tell me where he gets his whiskey, I will get a lot of it and send it around to some of the other generals."[79]

Grant's drinking episodes did not interfere with the business at hand—bringing about the surrender of Pemberton's army and Vicksburg itself. Grant, after the May 22 attack on Vicksburg, ordered his troops to dig in for a sustained siege. They dug trenches and protected them with sandbags and logs while Union sharp-shooters kept the besieged defenders from interfering with the construction. With only four engineering officers in his army, Grant directed every West Point graduate to actively supervise the siege line construction. With Johnston assembling an "Army of Relief" consisting of 31,000 troops from all over the South to trap him, Grant received reinforcements of his own from Missouri, Tennessee, and Kentucky. His army grew from 51,000 to 77,000. As reinforcements arrived, Grant used them to cut off all communication out of Vicksburg south along the Mississippi, secure the country-side back to the Big Black River, destroy bridges across that river, and thus protect his army from being attacked by Johnston's force from the east.[80]

Grant's gambling campaign left him somewhat vulnerable to a Confederate counter-attack between May 22 and June 8, when the first division of Union reinforcements arrived. During that time, Grant had about 51,000 troops between Pemberton, with 30,000 men, and Johnston, with 22,000 that increased to 30,000 by June 3. But Johnston's temerity and the lack of Confederate coordination kept Grant from being attacked. In Virginia, Lee learned that Grant had reached the Yazoo and optimistically speculated, "The enemy may be drawing to the Yazoo for the purpose of reaching their transports and retiring from the contest, which I hope is the case." As Kenneth P. Williams concluded, "Grant's persistence during the winter and his brilliant campaign behind Vicksburg had taught Lee nothing about the character of the soldier he would a year later have to face."[81]

As Grant's troops advanced their lines, particularly on the eight roads into Vicksburg, he at last found a means of ridding himself of the conniving McClernand. McClernand had issued a congratulatory order to his troops that effectively disparaged the troops of McPherson and Sherman. The latter two generals complained to Grant when their men read the order in northern newspapers. Grant asked McClernand for a copy of the order and on June 18 relieved him of command for violating prohibitions on publishing unapproved orders. When McClernand received the relief order, he exclaimed "Well, sir, I am relieved," and then, noting a hint of satisfaction on the delivering officer's face, added, "By God, sir, we are both relieved!" Major General Ord replaced McClernand as corps commander.[82]

On June 22, Grant learned that some of Johnston's cavalry had crossed the Big Black River to threaten his rear. Immediately Grant put Sherman in charge of the half of his army protecting against such an attack and readied other forces to reinforce Sherman if needed. With 30,000 men and 72 guns, Sherman's "Army of Observation" guarded all of the Big Black River crossings. Johnston backed off. Johnston may have been reluctant to attack Grant because Union scout and double-agent Charles Bell had personally told Johnston that Grant had 85,000 troops (an exaggeration of over 20,000 at the time). Bell also had reported more accurately to Grant on Johnston's own strength and disposition.[83]

On June 25 and July 1, Union troops exploded mines in tunnels they had dug under the Confederate lines. Although these explosions did not afford the besiegers an opportunity to enter the city, they did force the defenders to further constrict their lines. For forty-seven days, the Confederate forces and Vicksburg residents were subjected to continuous Union fire from ships and shore that may have totaled 88,000 shells and killed perhaps twenty civilians. With deserters reporting that morale and food supplies were running low in Vicksburg, and with his trenches having been advanced as far as possible, Grant planned an all-out assault for July 6. Coincidentally, Johnston had chosen that same date for his own long-delayed assault on Grant.[84]

For six weeks, Grant's soldiers dug day and night in order to advance their lines, set off explosions beneath the Rebel defenses, and improve their prospects for a final assault. Grant rejected some officers' views that another assault should have been launched before the one planned for July 6. After May 22, the siege of Vicksburg was a relatively bloodless one for Grant's army, despite the fact that a siege is usually costlier for the besiegers than the defenders. Between May 23 and July 3, Grant's forces had 104 killed, 419 wounded, and 7 missing, while they killed more than 805 and wounded more than 1,938 of the enemy, which also had at least 129 missing.[85]

CONFEDERATE SURRENDER

With the noose tightening and food running low, Pemberton finally gave up. On the morning of July 3, he raised white flags and sent out a pair of officers to arrange an armistice during which capitulation terms could be negotiated. "Unconditional Surrender" Grant rejected that proposal and wrote Pemberton: "The useless effusion of blood you propose stopping by this course can be ended at any time you may choose, by the unconditional surrender of the city and garrison."[86]

That afternoon Grant and Pemberton met to discuss the possibility of the latter's surrender. Although they could not agree on terms, Grant promised to send a letter that night giving final terms. In that letter he proposed paroling, instead of imprisoning, Pemberton's soldiers. Grant apparently made that concession, which Pemberton had requested, to save Union transportation resources and to encourage desertions by the freed and demoralized Rebel troops. In fact, Pemberton's signalmen had decoded Porter's signals to Grant that he lacked adequate vessels to transport almost 30,000 prisoners to the North, and thus Pemberton held out for parole rather than imprisonment. Pemberton accepted Grant's offer of parole, and Pemberton's July 4 surrender of his 29,500-man army (along with 172 guns and 60,000 rifles)[87] made the national holiday a memorable one for the North—especially in conjunction with Lee's July 1–3 defeat at Gettysburg. As a result of Vicksburg's fall, the Confederate commander at Port Hudson surrendered to Banks his 6,000 soldiers on July 9, thereby relinquishing the last Confederate position on the Mississippi.[88]

Grant's decision to parole Pemberton's demoralized men placed a burden on the South to support them—even though hundreds of Confederates declined to be paroled and elected Union prison camp rather than face the possibility of fighting again. Thousands were ill and hardly able to move. Thousands of others spoke with their feet and headed home never to fight again. Faced with a disaster and having no weapons to enforce his orders, Pemberton gave his entire army a thirty-day furlough, which President Davis countermanded. Pemberton switched to staggered furloughs—after which most of his soldiers did not reappear to be "swapped" for Union prisoners captured elsewhere. The deserting troops became a public safety hazard throughout Mississippi, and Pemberton ordered railroad depot guards to shoot them if they did not leave the trains on which they had swarmed to return home.[89]

After the fall of Vicksburg, Grant sent Sherman back to Jackson in order to drive out Johnston and his troops and complete the city's destruction. As early as July 3, Grant had wired Sherman of the anticipated surrender and told him to "make your calculations to attack Johnston; destroy the railroad north of Jackson." Sherman was aided by specific and accurate information on Johnston's forces provided by scout Charles Bell. The first of Sherman's 50,000-man force left their lines east of Vicksburg on July 5. The three-pronged army approached Jackson by July 9 and then besieged and bombarded the town. They forced Johnston to evacuate Jackson on July 16 and retreat to middle Alabama; by July 19 they had advanced twelve miles east of Jackson to Brandon. Sherman's first successful independent command completed its mission by destroying all railroads within fifty miles of Jackson as well as what little of value remained in that unfortunate town.[90]

In the time between May 1 at Port Gibson and the mid-July return to Jackson, the Union offensive of Grant and Banks resulted in the fall of Vicksburg, Port Hudson, and Jackson, as well as the capture of 241 guns in Grant's campaign and another 51 at Port Hudson—all at a cost of one-third of the losses suffered by the Confederates. Grant's and Banks's battlefield casualties (killed, wounded, missing, or captured) totaled 14,846 while the Confederate casualties were 47,625. Of the 2,153 captured Confederate officers, 15 were generals.[91]

Grant's isolated Vicksburg Campaign ratio is even more impressive. His troops suffered about 9,400 casualties while inflicting about 38,500 on the enemy.[92] Considering that Grant was on the offensive, that he achieved his strategic goals, and that the defenders should have had a tactical advantage, his 1:4 casualty ratio is an amazing tribute to his great generalship.

LEGACY OF THE VICKSBURG CAMPAIGN

Thus ended the greatest campaign of the war. As Hattaway and Jones stated, "Grant succeeded because his superb campaign had embodied all of the elements that had made for Napoleon's victories—

distraction, a penetration to threaten communications and turn the enemy, and the use of interior lines."[93] One third of the Confederacy had been severed; horses and food from Texas, Mexico, and elsewhere beyond the river were denied to the Confederacy's main armies and population centers, and the river could resume its role as a highway for transporting Union produce of the Midwest. Not only did the Union control the Mississippi Valley, but the states of Mississippi and Alabama were no longer major arenas in the war.[94]

To carry out his plan, Grant had had to proceed rapidly, avoid being crushed between two Confederate forces, effectively abandon his supply-line, and live off the land until he had obtained a secure position on the Mississippi in the Vicksburg area. With Grant's direct involvement in all stages, his army crossed the river, fought and won five battles in eighteen days, twice drove the Rebels from the Mississippi capital of Jackson, trapped a 30,000-man army in Vicksburg, besieged that city, and accepted the surrender of both the city and the army on July 4, 1863. That same evening Robert E. Lee's army began its retreat from the Gettysburg battlefield in Pennsylvania.

Historian Alan Nevins observed, "The country had at last the military hero for which it had longed, and Grant's name was on every lip."[95] He was promoted to major general in the regular army, the nation's highest military rank at that time.[96] (Previously he had been a major general of volunteers, a wartime-only position.) Grant also received a letter of thanks and apology from the president, who obviously had been following his activities closely:

> My Dear General:
>
> I do not remember that you and I ever met personally. I write this now as a grateful acknowledgment for the almost ines-

timable service you have done the country. I wish to say a word further. When you first reached the vicinity of Vicksburg, I thought you should do, what you finally did—march the troops across the neck, run the batteries with the transports, and thus go below; and I never had any faith, except in a general hope that you knew better than I, that the Yazoo Pass expedition, and the like, could succeed. When you got below and took Port Gibson, Grand Gulf and vicinity, I thought you should go down the river and join Ge. Banks; and when you turned Northward East of the Big Black, I feared it was a mistake. I now wish to make the personal acknowledgment that you were right, and I was wrong.

Yours very truly

A. Lincoln[97]

While Lee's army of 75,000 was suffering 23,000 killed and wounded (30 percent casualties) in his simultaneous but disastrous Gettysburg Campaign, Grant carried out his brilliant Vicksburg Campaign with the loss of a mere 2,254 of his 29,373 troops (8 percent casualties) killed or wounded at Champion's Hill and 3,052 of his 45,556 troops (7 percent casualties) killed or wounded at Vicksburg itself.[98] For the entire campaign, Grant lost a total of only 9,362 (1,514 killed, 7,395 wounded, and 453 missing or captured). The Confederates opposing Grant lost almost 41,000 men (2,000 killed, 5,000 wounded, and 33,718 captured.)[99]

The impact of the two campaigns on Confederate morale was crushing. In Richmond, War Department Clerk Jones wrote on July 8, "But, alas! we have sad tidings from the West. Gen. Johnston telegraphs from Jackson, Miss., that Vicksburg capitulated on the 4th inst. This is a terrible blow, and has produced much despondency." On July 28, the Confederate Chief of Ordnance, Josiah Gorgas, absorbed the blows of Vicksburg, Port Hudson, and Gettysburg and wrote in his diary, "Yesterday we rode on the pinnacle of success—today absolute ruin seems to be our portion. The Confederacy totters to its destruction."[100]

Although Brigadier General Grenville M. Dodge had obtained intelligence for Grant on the pre-campaign situation in Vicksburg itself and on the mid-campaign position and strength of Johnston,[101] Grant often moved without the full intelligence he might have desired. Feis concluded, "During the campaign, Grant showed that success was possible even without adequate intelligence as long as a commander maintained the offensive and refused to let inevitable uncertainty lead to paralysis. But he also demonstrated at times that there was no substitute for competent collection and use of information."[102]

Perhaps the keys to the campaign's success, in Noah Andre Trudeau's words, were Grant's "bold leadership and shrewd risk-taking," and the facts that he "knew his objective and never lost sight of it."[103] Grant's campaign was noteworthy for its focus, deception, celerity, flexibility, maneuver, and cunning.[104] As Edward C. Bearss, the master historian of Vicksburg, concluded, "The oft told story that Grant was a heedless, conscienceless butcherer, devoid of the skills associated with history's great captains is shown by the Vicksburg Campaign to be a shallow canard."[105] It was Grant, not Lee, who was campaigning—and winning—in a non-butcher-like manner.

Seven

AUTUMN 1863:
SAVING CHATTANOOGA

After a disastrous defeat at Chickamauga and a retreat into
Chattanooga, nearly starving Union troops are revived by the
arrival and operations of Grant, who organizes and oversees
their Missionary Ridge breakout and compels the Rebels to
retreat back into Georgia.

ollowing his Vicksburg victory, Grant proposed that his
army attack Mobile, Alabama, the last open Confederate
port on the Gulf of Mexico. The unimaginative General–in–Chief
Halleck rejected Grant's proposal. The president himself explained
to Grant that he agreed with the concept but that the recent French
establishment of an emperor in Mexico made a Texas movement
more urgent. Grant's reputation was growing in Washington. Lincoln and the newly promoted Assistant Secretary of War Charles
Dana even discussed the possibility of bringing Grant east to command the Army of the Potomac. Grant demurred on the grounds
that he knew the players and terrain in the West and that such an
appointment would upset the eastern generals.[1]

From July to September, Grant was in New Orleans conferring
with General Nathaniel Banks. Banks had given Grant a spirited

horse as a gift, and Grant was seriously injured in early September when the horse, spooked by a locomotive, fell on him while he and Banks were returning to the city after a review of troops. Despite rumors that Grant had been drinking at the time, there is no evidence to support that conclusion. Following the accident, Grant was bedridden in New Orleans and then Vicksburg for several weeks.[2]

His recovery, however, was rudely interrupted by a crisis in Tennessee. All the previous events—Belmont, Donelson, Shiloh, and Vicksburg—had prepared him well for this crisis. Bruce Catton put it well, "Grant was ready, at last. The time of testing was over, and he had reached his full stature. He had developed—through mistakes, through trial and error, through steady endurance, through difficult lessons painfully learned, and through the unbroken development of his own capacities—into the man who could finally lead the way through that open door [to victory]."[3]

On September 19 and 20, Major General Rosecrans's Army of the Cumberland incurred substantial losses at the Battle of Chickamauga, Georgia. Confederate Army of Tennessee Commander Braxton Bragg was belatedly reinforced by General James Longstreet (Grant's best man) with troops from Virginia and attacked the startled Rosecrans. While George ("the Rock of Chickamauga") Thomas prevented the loss of the army by a heroic holding action, Rosecrans led the hasty retreat of his army to Chattanooga, Tennessee. That critical railroad and river crossroads town was a key transportation hub between the Deep South and Virginia, between the Mississippi River and the Carolinas, and between Nashville and the critical industrial city of Atlanta. However, Chattanooga soon became a trap for the Union forces there, as Bragg's army took over the high ground east and southwest of the town.

The Rebels limited the Union forces to a single, mountainous, and inadequate supply-line over a sixty-mile wagon-road from the Union railhead at Bridgeport, Alabama. Rations were cut, animals were dying, and starvation threatened the troops.[4]

Realizing the critical nature of the situation, Lincoln, Stanton, and Halleck looked to Grant to resolve the crisis. In an October 3 dispatch, Halleck told Grant, "It is the wish of the Secretary of War that as soon as General Grant is able he will come to Cairo and report by telegraph." Grant arrived at Cairo on October 16, immediately telegraphed Halleck, and was advised the next day to proceed to the Galt House in Louisville to meet "an officer of the War Department." On his way to Louisville, Grant was met in Indianapolis by none other than Secretary of War Stanton, who had Grant's train flagged down so that he could join him. Stanton accompanied Grant the rest of the way to Louisville and explained the desperate situation in Chattanooga. The secretary then gave Grant the choice of two orders—both naming him commander of a new Military Division of the Mississippi—which included the Departments (Armies) of the Ohio (Major General Ambrose E. Burnside), the Cumberland (Rosecrans), and the Tennessee (Grant), as well as all territory between the Mississippi and the Alleghenies north of Banks in Louisiana.[5]

Following this October 16 appointment, Grant's top priority became saving Chattanooga. His first action was to replace Rosecrans as commander of the Army of the Cumberland with Major General George Thomas, who had saved Rosecrans's army from destruction as it retreated from Chickamauga to Chattanooga. He did this by accepting one of the alternate orders offered to him by Stanton—the one that relieved Rosecrans of command; the other order would have left Rosecrans in command. Grant wired

Thomas, "I will be there as soon as possible. Please inform me how long your present supplies will last, and the prospect for keeping them up." Thomas replied that he and his troops would hold "until we starve."[6]

Meanwhile, on September 24, Secretary of War Stanton had ordered the 11th and 12th corps of the Army of the Potomac, under Major General Joseph ("Fighting Joe") Hooker, to proceed by rail from Virginia to the Chattanooga area. The next day those troops began boarding trains for the 1,200-mile journey over seven railroads through Maryland, West Virginia, Ohio, Indiana, Kentucky, and Tennessee all the way to Bridgeport, Alabama. The movement of 20,000 troops, their baggage, and ten artillery batteries was completed in fifteen days, and their 3,000 horses and transport vehicles followed within about a week. This, the most efficient long-distance movement of troops in the Civil War, resulted in Grant receiving the fully equipped soldiers of Major General Oliver O. Howard's 11th Corps and Major General Henry W. Slocum's 12th Corps, under the command of Hooker, for his Chattanooga operations.[7]

Despite his injuries, Grant, in the company of Sherman, began the painful and arduous sixty-mile trek by horse over the mountains to Chattanooga as soon as he arrived by train at Bridgeport. He had to be carried part of the way because sections of the road were unfit for riding horses. Along the way, the animal-loving Grant must have been dismayed by the sight of thousands of horse and mule carcasses and the wreckage of numerous wagons—all evidence of the need to open a better supply route into Chattanooga. Upon his October 23 arrival in Chattanooga, Grant asked Halleck to promote Sherman to command the Army of the Tennessee in place of Grant; Halleck did so.[8]

GRANT OPENS THE CRACKER LINE

Grant immediately conferred with Sherman, Thomas, and Thomas's staff, including Brigadier General William F. "Baldy" Smith, Chief Engineer of the Army of the Cumberland. After scouting the area with Thomas and Smith the next day, Grant approved Smith's creative plan to open an adequate supply-line to the town. Three nights later that plan was executed. Under the cover of darkness and fog between three and five o'clock on the morning of the 27th, 1,800 Union troops in 60 pontoon boats floated downriver from Chattanooga around Moccasin Bend to Brown's Ferry. There they quickly overcame the surprised Confederate guards, ferried across another brigade of awaiting troops, and coordinated with the first of Hooker's 11th and 12th Corps soldiers coming up Lookout Valley.

They repelled a Rebel counterattack and had a bridge built across the river by 4:30 that afternoon. This virtually bloodless operation (with a mere twenty-one casualties) resulted in Grant's forces taking control of the Lookout Valley and the Tennessee River below Chattanooga, thus opening the "Cracker Line" by which massive rations and supplies could be brought directly and efficiently from Bridgeport to Chattanooga. Grant's troops in Chattanooga celebrated the opening of the Cracker Line as the first barges carrying 400,000 rations and 39,000 pounds of forage arrived behind the steamer *Chattanooga*.[9]

Riding the crest of his Vicksburg fame, Grant received the troops' praise for their sudden change of fortune. He gave the credit for the breakthrough, however, to Thomas and Smith in his dispatches to Washington. But Grant did both deserve and receive credit for the new direction that he brought to the Union troops at Chattanooga.

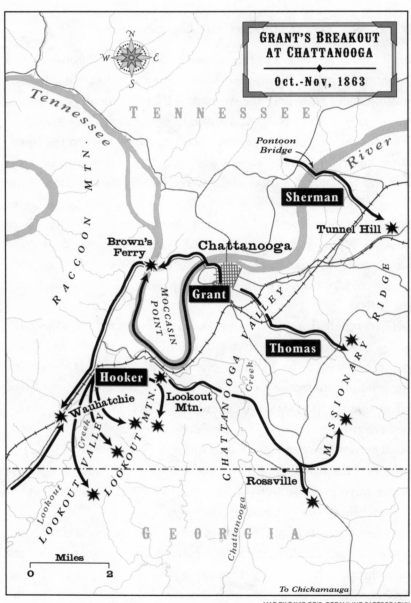

GRANT'S BREAKOUT AT CHATTANOOGA

Oct.-Nov, 1863

MAP BY DAVID DEIS, DREAMLINE CARTOGRAPHY

The just-arrived General Howard wrote later that fall, "This department was completely 'out of joint' when we first arrived.... I cannot be too thankful for the policy that placed these three Depts. under Grant." Years later a veteran said, "You have no conception of the change in the army when Grant came. He opened up the cracker line and got a steamer through. We began to see things move. We felt that everything came from a plan. He came into the army quietly, no splendor, no airs, no staff. He used to go about alone. He began the campaign the moment he reached the field."[10]

Bragg's Confederates must have been shocked by the suddenness and ease with which Grant had altered the Chattanooga situation. Instead of being bottled up in a valley and subsisting on short rations, the Union forces had a wide open supply-line that promised food, rations, forage, clothing, and other provisions—as well as a route for reinforcements from both the East and West. Grant himself later summarized the about–face that had occurred:

> In five days from my arrival in Chattanooga the way was open to Bridgeport and, with the aid of steamers and Hooker's teams, in a week the troops were receiving full rations. It is hard for any one not an eyewitness to realize the relief this brought. The men were soon clothed and also well fed; an abundance of ammunition was brought up, and a cheerfulness prevailed not before enjoyed in many weeks.... I do not know what the effect was on the other side, but assume it must have been correspondingly depressing. [Jefferson] Davis had visited Bragg but a short time before, and must have perceived our condition to be about as Bragg described it in his subsequent report. "These dispositions," he said "faithfully sustained, insured the enemy's speedy evacuation of Chattanooga for want of food and forage. Possessed

of the shortest route to his depot, and the one by which reinforcements must reach him, we held him at our mercy, and
his destruction was only a question of time."[11]

In desperation, the shocked Confederates counterattacked the
second night following the surprise Union assault. Longstreet's men
came down from Lookout Mountain to attack Hooker's troops in
Lookout Valley. Union Brigadier General John W. Geary at the Battle of Wauhatchie was badly outnumbered, but held his position.
Howard moved to the rescue from Brown's Ferry, engaged Confederates attacking from a foothill of Lookout Mountain on his left,
drove them back, and captured the hill. The attack on Geary, meanwhile, was broken up by a stampede of his horses and mules toward
the attackers, who mistook the stampede for a cavalry charge on
the pitch-black night. The Union victory at Wauhatchie kept Lookout Valley open, guaranteed the security of the Cracker Line, and
came at a minimal cost (216 casualties to the Rebels' 355).[12]

There were no further Confederate attempts to impede the supply and reinforcement route Grant had so easily opened—a mas-
terstroke achieved at minimal cost. The initial surprise assault had
cost three Union soldiers killed and eighteen wounded. The later
defense of Lookout Valley cost the Confederates 50 percent more
casualties than Hooker's troops. At a minuscule cost, therefore,
Grant had saved a trapped army, opened and defended a practical
supply and reinforcement route to Chattanooga, and in a short time
posed a serious threat to Bragg's encircling army.[13]

Grant was having such a good time that he made a one-man
reconnaissance of the situation along the Chattanooga Creek west
of Chattanooga and near the base of Lookout Mountain. Union
and Confederate pickets had placed watches on their respective
sides of the creek. When Grant approached the Union pickets, one

recognized him and called out, "Turn out the guard for the commanding general." Grant dismissed the Union pickets who turned out—but not in time to keep the Confederates across the creek from learning what was happening. Thus, a Confederate picket called out, "Turn out the guard for the commanding general, General Grant." The resulting line of Confederate pickets saluted Grant, and he returned their salute.[14]

GRANT ORGANIZES A BREAKOUT

Having solved the supply problem, Grant spent the next month gathering his reinforcements, assembling an army of 80,000, and planning an assault on the six-mile Confederate line semi-encircling Chattanooga. The presence of Hooker's 20,000 troops (the 11th and 12th Corps) and Sherman's two corps from Mississippi swelled Grant's army and demonstrated Grant's grasp of both the national situation and the critical importance of Chattanooga. On the other hand, Robert E. Lee had stymied a Confederate plan to reinforce Chattanooga with 25,000 troops from Lee in Virginia and 10,000 from Johnston in Mississippi. President Davis rejected the plan at an October 11 council of war because Lee refused to provide more troops.[15]

Lee and Davis not only prevented an increase in Bragg's force; they actually reduced it. Anxious to get back the bulk of Longstreet's corps, which Davis had belatedly pried loose from Lee and sent to Chickamauga, Lee had written to Davis on September 23 and 25 suggesting that Longstreet and his two divisions move away from Chattanooga, drive Burnside out of Knoxville (which he had occupied in early September), and then return to Lee. On October 29, Davis passed Lee's suggestion to Bragg, whose command Davis had just saved despite requests from Longstreet and virtually all of Bragg's generals that he be removed. Bragg knew that Longstreet had aggravated the discontent among Bragg's generals and suspected—correctly—that Longstreet wanted his command. On November 3, Bragg discussed and agreed on the Knoxville diversion with Longstreet; two days later Longstreet took 15,000 troops away to the northeast. This gambit reduced Bragg's strength to 36,000 against Grant's ultimate 80,000 and deprived Bragg of a reserve in the event of a Union breakthrough. Lee, Davis, and Bragg seemed determined to make Grant's breakout feasible.[16]

Pressured by Washington to relieve Burnside in Knoxville, Grant devised a plan to drive Bragg away from Chattanooga and put pressure on Longstreet to return to Chattanooga (and away from Knoxville). Therefore, Grant's battle plan involved sending Sherman against the Confederate right (north) wing all the way to the railroad in Bragg's rear (the pathway to Knoxville), sending Hooker against the Confederate left at Lookout Mountain, and having Thomas pressure the Confederate center to keep reinforcements from going to either flank. Unlike McClellan, Grant did not believe in keeping any portion of his available troops idle. Ironically, the arrival of Sherman's troops caused Bragg to think they were headed toward Knoxville and to order 11,000 more of his troops to head there. They were in the process of doing so and were recalled when Grant attacked at Chattanooga.[17]

The first Union step was a November 23 one-mile forward movement by Thomas's troops against the center of the Confederate line when he turned what looked like a drill into a takeover of the advance Confederate lines and a prominent hill called Orchard Knob. That night, to the north, thousands of Sherman's men crossed the river in pontoon boats, established a beachhead, and then built a pontoon bridge for the men behind them. The next day Grant ordered Hooker to take Lookout Mountain, the 1,200-foot-high dominant landmark in the area that towered over the Tennessee River southwest of Chattanooga. His three divisions crossed Lookout Creek and proceeded to take control of the weakly manned mountain in a daylong "Battle Above the Clouds." The fighting on the upper half of the mountain was visible to cheering Union troops in the Tennessee River valley and to Grant and other generals on Orchard Knob in the center of the Union lines. Bragg ordered the mountain abandoned that night and thus ended the Confederates' 63-day occupation of that dominant position. The Rebels suffered 1,251 casualties in its defense. Hooker's success cleared the way for his troops to advance through Chattanooga Valley on the Rebel left flank as part of an all-out assault on the remaining Confederates threatening Chattanooga.[18]

Grant ordered Sherman and his troops, who had marched over 600 miles from Vicksburg and then crossed the Tennessee north of town, to attack Tunnel Mountain on the north end of Missionary Ridge, the dominant Confederate heights overlooking Chattanooga from the east.[19] Grant simultaneously ordered Hooker to drive from Lookout Mountain through Chattanooga Valley to threaten the south end of Missionary Ridge. Meanwhile, Grant held George Thomas's troops in reserve between Sherman and Hooker, prepared to reinforce any breakthrough made by either of them. Sherman's planned offensive made little progress on November 24, but a full eclipse of the moon that evening seemed to auger significant developments the next day.

On November 25, however, Sherman continued to encounter serious problems because Tunnel Hill turned out to be a couple of ridges beyond its expected location—and behind a ravine. A frustrated

Sherman sent small portions of his troops into deadly frontal assaults on well-planned defensive positions conceived by Confederate Major General Patrick R. Cleburne. Sherman's lack of progress was matched on the other end of the line by Hooker, who was having difficulty crossing the now bridgeless Chattanooga Creek in Chattanooga Valley. From his outpost on Orchard Knob between Chattanooga and Missionary Ridge, Grant observed Confederate reinforcements being shifted to deal with Sherman's attack on the north and became concerned about Sherman's welfare.[20]

The Commanding General approached his old Academy roommate, Brigadier General Thomas J. Wood, and said, "General Sherman seems to be having a hard time." To which Wood responded, "Yes, General, he does seem to be in a warm place." Sensing that neither of his primary options was working, the hands-on Grant then ordered Wood and Major General Philip H. Sheridan, under Thomas's command, to "advance your divisions to the foot of the ridge and there halt . . . it will menace Bragg's forces so as to relieve Sherman." Preparing to do so, Wood said, "I think we can carry the entrenchments at the base of the ridge."[21]

Thomas assembled 23,000 infantrymen for an assault on the rifle pits at the base of Missionary Ridge. To Confederates in the pits, in positions halfway up the ridge and atop the ridge, there appeared to be 50,000 troops. The attackers moved out in good order and, despite some defensive fire, quickly made their way to the base of Missionary Ridge, where the defending Rebels fled uphill. Thomas's men, however, soon realized they were in a no man's land where they were under fire from numerous Confederate riflemen and some artillery on the side and top of the ridge. A Union infantryman, Fred Knefler of the 79th Indiana, described the situation: "Nothing could live in or about the captured line of field works; a few minutes of such terrific, telling fire would quickly convert them into untenable hideous slaughter pens. There was no time or opportunity for deliberations. Something must be done and it must be done quickly." Given the option of retreating, dying, or continuing the assault, they scrambled up the ridge to attack the source of the killing rifle fire.[22]

In addition, many officers at the base of the hill thought they had orders to continue the assault. Wood's division quickly began climbing the ridge, and Sheridan's division immediately followed after Sheridan reputedly yelled, "As soon as you get your wind, men, we will go straight to the top of that hill." Other reports are that Sheridan's men (and others) went up the ridge without orders and that Sheridan himself went with them before he could receive an answer to his inquiry about whether to stop at the rifle pits. When the diminutive Sheridan raised a silver whiskey flask in salute to the Rebel gunners, he was just missed by an artillery shell and then retorted, "That's damn ungenerous! I shall take those guns for that!"[23]

Back at Orchard Knob, Grant and numerous generals watched in astonishment as Thomas's men scrambled up the ridge. Grant accusingly asked Thomas, "Who ordered those men up the ridge?" After Thomas denied knowledge, Grant turned to Thomas's deputy, Major General Gordon Granger, and asked, "Did you order them up, Granger?" Granger said he had not and explained, "When those fellows get started, all hell can't stop them." Grant mumbled that someone would "catch it" if the attack failed.[24]

Because of Confederate incompetence, Thomas's men had three things going for them. With Longstreet's 15,000 men having been sent away, and with most Confederates defending their flanks, Bragg did not have the numbers to withstand such a massive assault at the center of his line. The Confederates had also placed their artillery at the geologic, instead of the military, crest of the ridge, thereby causing most of their guns to be too far back from the slope to be lowered and fired at the thousands of men desperately heading their way. Finally, these blunders had been compounded by the wasteful and foolish Confederate placement of a significant number of their troops in indefensible positions at the base of the ridge from which those that survived the initial assault were compelled to retreat.[25]

Virtually as one, hundreds and then thousands of Thomas's troops reached the summit and began wreaking havoc among the fleeing Confederates. They shouted "Chickamauga! Chickamauga!" as they avenged that embarrassing September defeat and retreat. General Wood, General Granger, or both humorously addressed the Union troops: "Soldiers, you ought to be court-martialed, every man of you. I ordered you to take the rifle pits and you scaled the mountain."[26]

As the center of the Confederate line collapsed, troops from all sectors of that line abandoned their positions and fled toward Georgia. Their unpopular commander, Braxton Bragg, rode among his troops in a vain attempt to stop the retreating flood. To his cries of "Here is your commander!" they responded, "Here's your mule." Bragg had completely lost control over his army, many of his soldiers were captured, and thousands threw away their weapons. In total, they abandoned 41 guns (one-third of their Army's total) and 7,000 firearms. By 7:00 p.m. Bragg had reached Chickamauga Station and telegraphed news of the debacle to Richmond. Despite determined pursuit by Phil Sheridan, Cleburne saved the army with an effective rear-guard defense at a strong defensive position. Sheridan's aggressive pursuit nevertheless caught Grant's eye and played a role in a major promotion for him the following year.[27]

The Battle of Chattanooga certainly was not fought and won as Grant had planned. An excellent summary of the planning and execution was provided by "Baldy" Smith, Chief Engineer of Thomas's Army of the Cumberland: "The original plan contemplated the turning of Bragg's right flank, which *was not done*. The secondary plan of Thomas looked toward following up the success of Hooker at Lookout Mountain by turning the left flank of Bragg [through Rossville Gap], and then an attack by Thomas along his entire front. The Rossville Gap was not carried in time to be of more than secondary importance in the battle. The assault on the center before either flank was turned was never seriously contemplated, and was made without plan, without orders...."[28] The bottom line is that the victory did not occur where and how Grant planned, but instead was the result of his aggressive use of all his forces to keep the pressure on the enemy at all points.

One Confederate soldier, captured and taken to the rear, described Grant's compassion for the defeated and demoralized enemy prisoners. After telling how all the other Union officers rode by without paying the prisoners any attention, the soldier wrote, "When General Grant reached the line of ragged, filthy, bloody, starveling, despairing prisoners strung out on each side of the bridge, he lifted his hat and held it over his head until he passed the last man of that living funeral cortege. He was the only officer in that whole train who recognized us as being on the face of the earth."[29]

Consistent with Lincoln's direction to "Remember Burnside," Grant immediately sent a relief expedition and supplies toward Knoxville. Before that expedition, 6,000 of Burnside's troops had avoided being trapped, beaten Longstreet's 12,000 troops to Campbell's Station on the road to Knoxville, held them back in a daylong battle there on November 16, and retreated to Knoxville.[30] Later Burnside had thwarted Longstreet's assault on Knoxville, and the threat of the relief column drove Longstreet into the Tennessee mountains twenty miles east of Knoxville, where his troops spent a hard winter. Eastern Tennessee was now in Union hands.[31] With both Chattanooga and Knoxville secure, Lincoln finally tendered Grant, "and all under your command, my more than thanks—my profoundest gratitude—for the skill, courage, and perseverance with which you and they, over so great difficulties, have effected that important object."[32]

THE LEGACY OF CHATTANOOGA AND GRANT'S WESTERN EXPERIENCES

Having achieved his objectives in eastern Tennessee, Grant issued a December 10 congratulatory order to his troops:

> In a short time, you have recovered from the enemy the control of the Tennessee River from Bridgeport to Knoxville. You dislodged him from Chattanooga Valley, wrested from his determined grasp the possession of Mission[ary] Ridge, repelled with heavy loss to him his repeated assaults upon Knoxville, forcing him to raise the siege there, driving him at all points, utterly routed and discomfited, beyond the limits of the state. By your noble heroism and determined courage, you have most effectually defeated the plans of the enemy for regaining possession of the states of Kentucky and Tennessee. You have secured positions from which no rebellious power can drive or dislodge you.[33]

In Georgia, a retreating Rebel officer observed, "Captain, this is the death knell of the Confederacy. If we cannot cope with those fellows with the advantages we had on this line, there is not a line between here and the Atlantic Ocean where we can stop them."

His captain responded, "Hush, Lieutenant. That is treason you are talking."[34]

More evidence of the despondency Grant's successes at Chattanooga had imposed on Confederate troops is reflected in this December 26, 1863, letter written from winter quarters at Dalton, Georgia, by Dr. John T. Farris, a surgeon in the Army of Tennessee:

> ... Our cause is lost, certain, and I would just now say that I do not know but it will be as well. I am of the opinion that, should we gain independence, that we would have a totering [*sic*] of aristocrat government, and many are of this opinion. From what I can learn, this whole army was yesterday and night before last in the same condition as our Brigade. All drunk, and shame forever. I also understand that one Major and four privates were killed dead by accident shots of drunken rowdys. God knows, you can have no idea of what took place yesterday last night and the night before. . . . I am troubled at the way everyting [*sic*] is going. If I had known at the beginning of the war what I now know, I today would have been in Canida [*sic*] making an honest living. God knows I wish I was there now.[35]

That Confederate despair reached all the way to Richmond, where President Davis reluctantly accepted the resignation of his friend Bragg as Commander of the Army of Tennessee and most grudgingly replaced him with their mutual enemy, Joseph Johnston.[36]

In the amazingly short period of time of about five weeks, Grant had converted a potential Union disaster at Chattanooga into a smashing success by assembling a potent force and keeping incessant pressure on the enemy. Feis concluded that "Grant's conduct of the Chattanooga campaign revealed just how sweet the fruits of intelligence and luck could be if one was unafraid of taking risks."[37]

As he had done in his earlier western campaigns, Grant accomplished his success at Chattanooga with minimal casualties. Of his 56,400 troops engaged between November 23 and 25, Grant had 752 killed, 4,713 wounded, and 349 missing—a total of 5,814 (10.3 percent). On the other side, Bragg's 46,165 troops had 361 killed, 2,160 wounded, and 4,146 missing (most captured)—a total of 6,667 (14.4 percent).[38] Considering that Grant's troops were attacking an enemy entrenched on high ground above them, these statistics are an amazing tribute to Grant's intelligent but persistent pursuit of the enemy.

As 1863 was drawing to a close, Grant could look back at an unbroken series of successes, including Forts Henry and Donelson, Shiloh, Iuka, Corinth, Vicksburg, and Chattanooga. He had lopped off a third of the Confederacy and put Union armies in a position to split the remaining two thirds in half. At Vicksburg alone he had captured almost 30,000 of the enemy. According to McWhiney and Jamieson, Grant had done all this fighting over a two-year period of time at a minimal cost of 23,500 killed and wounded (15 percent of the total 221,000 men who fought under his command in those battles and campaigns). A battle-by-battle breakdown of total Union and Confederate casualties (killed, wounded, and captured/missing) reveals that Grant imposed 84,187 casualties on the western Confederates while his armies suffered 36,688 casualties—a positive difference of 47,499. Far from being a butcher, Grant had demonstrated that a Union general could aggressively maneuver and attack with great success at a relatively minimal cost.[39]

Eight

EARLY 1864: PLANNING A NATIONAL CAMPAIGN

Promoted to lieutenant general and general-in-chief, Grant goes east to meet Lincoln, retrain the Army of the Potomac, and plan a comprehensive national campaign against all Confederate forces.

Immediately after his Chattanooga victory, Grant yet again proposed a winter offensive against Mobile, Alabama, which still remained as the last Confederate port in the Gulf of Mexico. He had proposed a similar effort after capturing Vicksburg. Grant was not satisfied to sit idly by while more Confederate targets beckoned. Thus, on November 29 he proposed the Mobile campaign to Charles Dana, and he repeated the proposal in a December 7 letter to Halleck. In the words of Bruce Catton, "[Grant] had at last reached the point where he could see that final triumph for the Union depended on crowding a beaten foe without respite, permitting no breathing spell in which the weaker antagonist could regain his balance and repair damages—using the superior power of the North, in short, to apply unrelenting pressure of a sort the

Confederacy had not the resources to resist."[1] He soon would have an opportunity to implement his national strategy.

Four Union generals emerged as leaders from the Chattanooga crisis and victory: Grant, Sherman, Thomas, and Sheridan. Their leadership would bring victories to the Union cause all over the nation in 1864 and 1865. But among this illustrious group, there emerged a clear leader of leaders: Grant.

Saving the army trapped in Chattanooga, breaking out of the Confederate trap, and driving Bragg's army back into Georgia guaranteed Grant greater fame and an historic promotion. From Palo Alto in Mexico through Missionary Ridge, he had fought twenty-seven battles without defeat. He had captured two Confederate armies and soundly defeated a third.[2] On December 17, Congress recognized his amazing accomplishments by passing a joint resolution thanking him, his officers, and his soldiers and directing that a gold medal be struck and presented to him.

More significantly, Grant's aggressively achieved successes virtually compelled Congress and President Lincoln to offer him a promotion to lieutenant general—the first three-star American general since George Washington—and General-in-Chief of the Union Armies. The bill reviving that rank was introduced by Washburne in the House of Representatives and James Doolittle of Wisconsin in the Senate. The senator calculated that Grant had won seventeen Civil War battles, captured 100,000 prisoners, and seized 500 artillery pieces.[3]

Promotion, however, did not come immediately, and it was not the only thing on Grant's mind. In the months following Chattanooga, Grant moved his headquarters to Nashville, visited Knoxville, and began planning a movement deeper into Georgia.[4]

Grant and Sherman did not remain inactive. Beginning on February 3, 1864, Sherman and 23,500 soldiers left Vicksburg and penetrated deeply into Mississippi east of Jackson. He followed the Southern Railroad of Mississippi all the way east to its junction with the Mobile and Ohio Railroad at Meridian, Mississippi. In this Meridian Campaign, a prelude to Sherman's more famous later marches, Sherman's troops traveled light and basically lived off the countryside in the fertile, previously untouched "bread-basket" area of northern Mississippi. Casualties to Sherman's men were minimal. Despite the failure of Brigadier General William Sooy Smith to join them with his cavalry, Sherman's men entered Meridian on February 14.

In that vicinity, over a five-day period, Sherman's men destroyed 61 bridges, 20 locomotives, and 115 miles of railroad track. He reported that "Meridian, with its depots, store-houses, arsenals, hospitals, offices, hotels, and cantonments no longer exists." Sherman then withdrew back to Vicksburg with the knowledge that an army could live off the countryside while destroying its resources—a lesson he would apply later in Georgia and the Carolinas. The damage to the Meridian area railroads was so extensive that it cost John Bell Hood's late 1864 campaign into Tennessee a month's delay and contributed to his defeats at Franklin and Nashville.[5]

Meanwhile, leaders of both national political parties expressed an interest in Grant's becoming president. A concerned Lincoln put out feelers on Grant's intentions and was relieved to see a letter Grant had written to an old Galena friend. In that letter, Grant had said, "I already have a pretty big job on my hands, and...nothing could induce me to think of being a presidential candidate, particularly so long as there is a possibility of having Mr. Lincoln re-elected." Lincoln was in fact so relieved that he immediately endorsed the bill creating the position of Lieutenant General of the Army. After congressional passage, the president signed the bill into law on February 26. Lincoln nominated Grant for the position on March 1, and the Senate confirmed him the next day. On March 3, Grant was ordered to Washington.[6]

GRANT TAKES CHARGE

Grant had commanded one army at Vicksburg and three armies at Chattanooga. Now he would command all the armies of the United States. He was in charge of nineteen departments and seventeen commanders.[7] His chief job became coordinating their actions so that they were synchronized and mutually supportive.

Grant and his eldest son, Fred, arrived in Washington unheralded. They went to the Willard Hotel, where the desk clerk reluctantly offered them an inconvenient and ordinary room on the top floor. After Grant signed the register, the clerk quickly changed his tune, offering Grant the best room in the house. Later Grant and his son became the center of attention in the hotel dining room as one enthusiastic patron stood on his chair and led the gawking crowd in three cheers for the general.[8]

That night Grant went to the White House to meet President Lincoln for the first time. The crowd parted for Grant to meet the president, who shook his hand, smiled, and said, "Why, here is General Grant! Well, this is a great pleasure, I assure you." Secretary of State William H. Seward introduced Grant to Mary Todd Lincoln and, when the crowd started chanting for Grant, had the short general stand on a couch to be seen by all. The pandemonium only increased.

The next day, March 9, Grant returned to the White House to receive his commission from the president. In the presence of his Cabinet, Lincoln presented the commission and said:

General Grant, the nation's appreciation of what you have done, and its reliance upon you for what remains to be done in the existing great struggle, are now presented, with this commission constituting you lieutenant-general in the Army of the United States. With this high honor, devolves upon you, also, a corresponding responsibility. As the country herein trusts you, so, under God, it will sustain you. I scarcely need to add that, with what I here speak for the nation, goes my own hearty personal concurrence.[9]

Grant, having seen the president's remarks the prior evening, briefly responded to them:

Mr. President, I accept the commission, with gratitude for the high honor conferred. With the aid of the noble armies that have fought in so many fields for our common country, it will be my earnest endeavor not to disappoint your expectations. I feel the full weight of the responsibilities now devolving on me; and I know that if they are met, it will be due to those armies, and above all, to the favor of that providence which leads both nations and men.[10]

"The turning point of the entire Civil War would be when Grant took command. He had a completely different way of doing things," according to historian Gordon Rhea.[11] The Union now had a general who had a broad national view of the war (something the Confederacy lacked), coordinated the activities of all theaters, and realized that destruction of Lee's army was the primary mission in the Virginia theater. Although Grant kept George Meade as commander of the Army of the Potomac, he usually was its de facto commander. Never again would that army's soldiers be the victims of the incompetence or timidity so often demonstrated by its earlier commanders, Irvin McDowell, George McClellan (twice), Ambrose Burnside, and Joseph Hooker, who had suffered numerous casualties (144,000 including Meade's) without moving the war to conclusion. They would be part of a coordinated nationwide assault on Confederate armies, rather than on mere places. As Rhea said, "Their objective under Grant was the destruction of Confederate armies, and the days of short battles followed by months of inactivity were over. Henceforth, Union armies were to engage the armed forces of the rebellion and batter them into submission, giving no respite."[12]

On the Confederate side, Grant's old friend Longstreet had a similar view. As renowned historian Bruce Catton told it:

> Over in the Army of Northern Virginia, James Longstreet was quietly warning people not to underestimate this new Yankee commander: "That man will fight us every day and every hour till the end of the war." Nobody in the North heard the remark, but the quality which had called it forth had not gone unnoticed. Here was the man who looked as if he would ram his way through a brick wall, and since other tactics had not worked perhaps that was the thing to try. At Fort Donelson and at Vicksburg he had swallowed two Confederate armies whole, and at Chattanooga he had driven a third army in head-long retreat from what had been thought to be an impregnable stronghold, and all anyone could think of was the hard blow that ended matters. Men seemed ready to call Grant the hammerer before he even began to hammer.[13]

Lincoln wanted an aggressive, proven winner to challenge and defeat Robert E. Lee. Grant was his man, and the troops in the

Army of the Potomac agreed. Among them was soldier-artist Charles Ellington Reed, who welcomed Grant's appointment even though he foresaw tough fighting ahead: "Placeing [*sic*] Grant in command is the grandest coup yet. It has inspired all with that confidence that insures success I have not the slightest doubt but that we shall be gloriously successful this comeing [*sic*] campaign. There will be hard fighting without doubt. Many assert that our next battle will eclipse all others in magnitude and slaughter, but that remains to be seen."[14] Dependent on Grant to make substantial progress to ensure his own reelection, Lincoln demonstrated his complete confidence in the general by telling Secretary of War Stanton to "leave him alone to do as he pleases."[15]

On March 10, the day after receiving his three-star commission, Grant visited Meade at the Army of the Potomac's Brandy Station, Virginia headquarters. Meade graciously offered to step aside as army commander so that Grant could name someone of his own choosing. If Grant had any plans of making such a change, Meade's gesture ended them. Grant assured him that he would retain the command. Although Grant avoided the politics of Washington by keeping his command in the field with Meade's army, Grant generally issued orders to the Army of the Potomac through Meade.[16]

Having decided to retain Meade in place and to accompany him in the field, Grant quickly made other important decisions. Sherman would command the three-army march on Atlanta, McPherson would replace him as commander of the Army of the Tennessee, and "Black Jack" Logan would replace McPherson.[17] In an early interview with Lincoln, Grant expressed his dissatisfaction with the eastern Union cavalry and secured the president's consent to bring Phil Sheridan east to command the Army of the Potomac's cavalry corps.[18] Grant's senior team was in place.

By April 6, Grant also had assembled an experienced and professional personal staff consisting of Brigadier General John A. Rawlins, chief of staff; Lieutenant Colonel Theodore S. Bowers, assistant adjutant general; Lieutenant Colonel Cyrus B. Comstock, senior aide-de-camp; Lieutenant Colonels Orville E. Babcock, Horace Porter, and Frederick T. Dent, aides-de-camp; Lieutenant Colonels William Rowley and Adam Badeau, military secretaries; Captains Ely S. Parker and George K. Leet, assistant adjutants general; Lieutenant Colonel William Duff, inspector general; and Captain Peter T. Hudson and First Lieutenant William McKee Dunn, Jr., aides-de-camp. Unlike Lee, Grant had a large, competent staff and used it.[19]

Grant also took care of another important piece of business in Washington. His former superior (and, unknown to Grant until after the war, his opponent in the West), Henry Halleck, requested to be relieved as general-in-chief in light of Grant's promotion. Grant cleverly arranged for Halleck to be chief of staff. Through this deft separation of administration from strategic command, "a crucial innovation in modern warfare," Grant had Halleck handle the political and handholding chores in Washington while Grant was free to command in the field.[20]

Although Meade was left in command of the Army of the Potomac, it quickly became known as "Grant's army." One reason for that may be that changes immediately began to take place. Inspectors general suddenly took an interest in what units were and were not doing; unit commanders had to reduce the discrepancy between "numbers present for duty" and "numbers present for duty, equipped"; discipline became tighter; infantrymen were drilled on how to fire a rifle since so many abandoned weapons on battlefields had contained multiple minie balls indicating they had never been fired; artillerymen were drilled on assembling and disassembling their guns; cavalrymen received new Spencer seven-shot repeater rifles; and the entire army benefited from trainloads of supplies and equipment that arrived at Brandy Station.[21]

In March and April 1864, Grant devised a grand strategy that would put all Union troops on the offensive against their Confederate counterparts, and thereby keep the latter from using their interior lines to transfer troops among theaters. This plan envisioned Sherman's three armies (the Cumberland, the Tennessee, and the Ohio) pushing Joseph Johnston's Army of Tennessee southeastward back toward Atlanta; Nathaniel Banks joining Sherman after capturing Mobile; General Franz Sigel clearing Confederates out of the Shenandoah Valley; Major General Benjamin F. Butler directly attacking Petersburg-Richmond via the James River; and the Army of the Potomac going after Lee's Army of Northern Virginia until it was defeated or destroyed.[22] Every Union soldier and army had a role. As Lincoln told Grant and Grant told Sherman (without attribution), "Those not skinning can hold a leg."[23] Grant told Meade: "Lee's army will be your objective point. Wherever Lee's army goes, you will go also."[24]

This strategy would not only advance the offensive goals of the Union, but it also would preclude the Confederates from having the flexibility to converge their forces in a meaningful counterattack. Remembering earlier Confederate convergences at Shiloh and Chickamauga, Grant and Sherman were determined to prevent a repetition of them.[25]

Grant declined a White House banquet in his honor so that he instead could quickly head west to meet with Sherman.[26] Coordination with Sherman was so important to Grant that he spent March 11 to 23 on a trip to visit him in Nashville, including extended consultations on Grant's return train ride from Nashville to Cincinnati. Grant made it clear that Sherman's primary objective was Johnston's Army of Tennessee, and his secondary objective was Atlanta. Grant's hope was that a successful campaign there would divide the remaining Confederacy in half.[27]

On his return trip, Grant was accompanied to Cincinnati by his friends and confidants, Sherman and Grenville Dodge. There they laid out maps and planned their end-the-war campaigns. Sherman later said that Grant's plan was simple: Grant would go for Lee, and Sherman would go for Joe Johnston.[28] Grant's primary concern then and later was to ensure that Sherman's thrust in Georgia and Meade's in Virginia would keep the Confederates so occupied that they could not reinforce each other. To protect against the possibility of Confederate inter-theater transfers, he wrote to Sherman:

> What I now want more particularly to say is, that if the two main attacks, yours and the one from here, should promise great success, the enemy may, in a fit of desperation, abandon one part of their line of defense, and throw their whole strength upon the other, believing a single defeat without any victory to sustain them better than a defeat all along their line, and hoping too, at the same time, that the army meeting with no resistance, will rest perfectly satisfied with their laurels, having penetrated to a given point south, thereby enabling them to throw their force first upon one and then on the other.
>
> With the majority of military commanders they might do this. But you have had too much experience in traveling light, and subsisting upon the country, to be caught by any such ruse. I hope my experience has not been thrown away. My directions, then, would be, if the enemy in your front shows signs of joining Lee, follow him up to the full extent of your

ability. I will prevent the concentration of Lee upon your front, if it is in the power of this army to do it.[29]

Sherman promised Grant that he would "ever bear in mind that Johnston is at all times to be kept so busy that he cannot, in any event, send no [*sic*] part of his command against you or Banks."[30]

As Grant planned his campaign against Lee, he was relieved to be free from presidential interference. In Grant's first interview with Lincoln, the president told him he was not a military man and would not interfere, but that he was opposed to procrastination.[31] That was a problem he would not have with Grant. Lincoln wrote him, "The particulars of your plans I neither know, or seek to know. You are vigilant and self-reliant; and, pleased with this, I wish not to obtrude any constraints or restraints upon you."[32] Lincoln was confident that he finally had a forceful and effective general in the East, where Union commanders had seen their soldiers suffer 144,000 casualties and had nothing to show for it.[33]

Grant relied upon excellent intelligence developed by the Bureau of Military Information (BMI), originally established by General Hooker in 1863. Under the direction of Colonel George H. Sharpe and his primary subordinate, civilian John C. Babcock, the BMI (or secret service) proved invaluable to Grant.[34] The BMI gathered intelligence from spies, scouts, deserters, prisoners, "cavalry reconnaissances, visual observations, signal intercepts, and captured correspondence."[35]

During the more than eleven months it took Grant to vanquish Lee, he made increasing use of the BMI's excellent intelligence services:

> As a result of the BMI's all-source capability, constant search for corroboration, and intensive source assessment, Meade and

Grant received not an assemblage of undigested bits of news of seemingly equal weight but true intelligence, the finished product of systematic information analysis. Though the BMI would become more sophisticated and efficient than [Grenville] Dodge's network [used by Grant in the western theater], Grant would not fully utilize its services during the campaign from the Rapidan to Petersburg. By midsummer, however, as the war in Virginia lapsed into a protracted siege, Sharpe and his men would play a key role in Grant's eventual success.[36]

BMI intelligence confirmed the arrival of Longstreet's First Corps back in the main Virginia theater and pinpointed its location at Gordonsville, about a day's march from Lee's other two corps near the Rapidan River.[37] As late as March 25, Lee remained doubtful that Grant, the westerner, would direct the primary Union assault against his army in Virginia rather than against Johnston's army in Georgia. Lee reminded Davis of the ruses Grant had used at Vicksburg, told him he doubted the first Union effort would be against Richmond, and concluded that Grant's first efforts would be against Johnston in Georgia or Longstreet in Tennessee. Lee seems not to have contemplated Grant directing the simultaneous assaults by two Union armies of 100,000 apiece.[38]

Grant's primary decision concerning his advance in Virginia was whether to move to the east or west of Lee. An advance to the west was more likely to force Lee to fight in the open, thereby enhancing the value of Grant's supremacy in overall numbers and especially in artillery. That course of action, however, would compel Grant to rely on tenuous overland lines of supply via questionable roads and a single rail line. Grant instead decided to move east of Lee so that he could utilize Union waterborne transportation to supply his troops via all the rivers and streams that fed into the

Potomac River and Chesapeake Bay. That route also would facilitate coordination with the movements on the James River of General Benjamin Butler, in whom Grant had little or no confidence. In
addition, the fords across the Rapidan were more accessible by the
eastern route, Longstreet's corps was farther away, and the previous November Lee had taken thirty hours to defend his right flank
in the same area.[39]

Historian James Epperson pointed to five factors that limited
Grant's flexibility and virtually compelled him not to attempt a
western approach to Lee:

~ Political pressure to protect Washington
~ Need for logistical preparations for an extended stay in the
    field
~ Need to avoid protecting a lengthy supply line
~ Need to keep Lee from staying behind his Mine Run works
~ Need to keep attacking Lee to prevent him from seizing the
    initiative[40]

William Feis captured the gist of Grant's strategy as he began the
Overland Campaign:

> In any event, the endgame for Grant was not the capture of
> strategic points but the destruction of Lee's army, and he
> could achieve this in one of two ways. He could fight him on
> open ground or in the Wilderness, or perhaps force him to
> retreat. Even if Lee withdrew, Grant understood that it would
> only delay the inevitable. To prevail in this war, the military
> might of the Confederacy had to be destroyed. At some point,
> therefore, Grant would have to stand toe to toe with Lee and
> beat him, regardless of the circumstances. Nothing short of
> this would guarantee the death of the rebellion.[41]

As indicated above, on April 9 Grant made clear to Meade his primary objective in the Virginia theater: "Lee's army will be your objective point. Wherever Lee goes there you will go also."[42] In that same letter, Grant advised Meade that Burnside's independent Ninth Corps would be brought east to add another 25,000 men to the Union forces in Virginia.[43] Although Grant would move toward Richmond, he would do so because Lee had to defend the Confederate capital and major rail hub and manufacturing center. "Richmond was to be attacked because it was defended by Lee, not Lee because he defended Richmond."[44] Grant also realized that an army's communications and supply were vital to its survival, and in following this strategy, went after Lee's communications and supply routes whenever possible.[45]

Taking the initiative and clinging to Lee's army, however, would prove costly. In Gordon Rhea's words, "The very nature of Grant's assignment guaranteed hard fighting and severe casualties. Mistakes there were. The facts, however, do not support the caricature of Grant as a general who eschewed maneuver in favor of headlong assaults and needlessly sacrificed his men. Quite the opposite is true."[46] Grant was prepared to pay the price to end the war and get Lincoln reelected. This time, unlike earlier eastern efforts, the price would buy results.

In just two months, Grant took control of all Union armies and worked out his strategy to end the war. Union armies would continuously pressure the Confederates everywhere and continue to do so until the war was won. Grant's strategy became a reality in less than a year.

Nine

SUMMER 1864:
ATTACKING LEE'S ARMY

Grant moves the Army of the Potomac against Lee's Army of Northern Virginia at the Wilderness, Spotsylvania Court House, North Anna River, and Cold Harbor before crossing the James River and threatening Petersburg.

*G*rant's forty-six-day Overland Campaign at long last put him head-to-head against the famous Robert E. Lee, whose army Grant was determined to defeat, if not destroy. It took Grant less than two months to get his army to the Richmond-Petersburg area and less than a year to defeat Lee and end the Civil War. More than twenty years later, Grant looked back at the start of that campaign:

> Soon after midnight, May 3rd–4th, the Army of the Potomac moved out...to start upon that memorable campaign, destined to result in the capture of the Confederate capital and the army defending it. This was not to be accomplished, however, without as desperate fighting as the world has ever witnessed; not to be consummated in a day, a week, a month, or a single season. The losses inflicted, and endured, were destined to be

severe; but the armies now confronting each other had already been in conflict for a period of three years, with immense losses in killed, by death from sickness, captured and wounded; and neither had made any real progress toward accomplishing the final end. . . . So here was a stand-off. The campaign now begun was destined to result in heavier losses, to both armies, in a given time, than any previously suffered; but the carnage was to be limited to a single year, and to accomplish all that had been anticipated or desired at the beginning of that time. We had to have hard fighting to achieve this.[1]

On April 18, Grant reviewed the Sixth Corps and received a mixed review from an observer, Elisha Hunt Rhodes, a Rhode Islander who rose from private to lieutenant colonel during the war: "General Grant is a short thick set man and rode his horse like a bag of meal. I was a little disappointed in the appearance, but I like the look of his eye."[2]

Grant's plans for several simultaneous assaults were undermined by three incompetent political generals who, because Lincoln needed their election-year support, still commanded Union troops. First, Massachusetts Democrat Benjamin "Beast" Butler failed in the direct assault on the Richmond-Petersburg area. After landing his 40,000-man Army of the James at Bermuda Hundred, a peninsula between the Appomattox and James Rivers, Butler foolishly spent a week building fortifications instead of immediately attacking. This delay enabled Beauregard to gather reinforcements from North Carolina, march north from Petersburg, and engage Butler at Drewry's Bluff, about six miles south of Richmond. Beauregard's surprise attack drove Butler away from the Richmond-Petersburg railroad and back into Bermuda Hundred. Butler had failed to occupy the Confederate works at Drewry's Bluff or to take any other action to permanently cut the supply-line from Petersburg to Richmond. As a result of his reticence and incompetence, Butler remained so bottled up in Bermuda Hundred that Grant thereafter withdrew his troops for use under more productive generals elsewhere.[3]

Failure also marked the Shenandoah Valley campaign of the German-American Major General Franz Sigel. He had attracted many German-Americans into joining the Union army; they proudly proclaimed, "I fights mit Sigel."[4] His May 1864 campaign, however, was a disaster. With 9,000 troops, he had headed south up the Shenandoah but was routed by Major General John C. Breckinridge's 5,300 troops (including 247 Virginia Military Institute cadets) at the Battle of New Market on May 15. Grant replaced Sigel with Major General David Hunter on May 26.[5]

Far to the southwest, on the Red River, another Massachusetts Democratic general, Nathaniel Banks, was matching the ineptitude of Butler and Sigel. His second campaign up the Red River in Louisiana was stopped cold by a crushing defeat at Sabine Crossroads (or Mansfield) that was followed by a downriver retreat in which Banks nearly lost his army. Banks's demoralized forces were unable to carry out Grant's plans for an assault on the port city of Mobile, Alabama.[6]

Fortunately for Grant, the other major Union campaign of that spring and summer was in the capable hands of Grant's good friend Sherman. He commanded the armies of the Cumberland, the Tennessee, and the Ohio. During the month of May, Sherman made steady progress, moving from the Tennessee border toward Atlanta in northwestern Georgia. He engaged in fights at Dalton, Resaca, and Dallas, but focused primarily on getting around the flanks of

Johnston's Army of Tennessee and moving closer to Atlanta. Through June and into early July, Sherman avoided frontal assaults (except his costly effort at Kennesaw Mountain) and continued to move around Johnston's flanks. Sherman's maneuvers enabled him to avoid fighting Johnston at rivers or at strong defensive fortifications prepared by Johnston. The decisive moment came on July 8, when Sherman's left flank crossed the Chattahoochee and threatened Atlanta.[7]

THE WILDERNESS: DAY ONE

Back at Culpeper, Virginia, Grant planned and then initiated his campaign against Lee. On the night of May 3, he met with his personal staff and discussed the coming campaign. He wanted to destroy or seriously damage the Army of Northern Virginia before it reached the existing fortifications at Richmond. Grant explained that he wanted all his commanders to focus on enemy *armies* rather than enemy *cities*.[8] Finally, he previewed and invited full staff participation:

> I want you to discuss with me freely from time to time the details of the orders given for the conduct of a battle, and learn my views as fully as possible as to what course should be pursued in all the contingencies which may arise. I expect to send you to the critical points of the lines to keep me promptly advised of what is taking place, and in cases of great emergency, when new dispositions have to be made on the instant, or it becomes suddenly necessary to reinforce one command by sending to its aid troops from another, and there is not time to communicate with headquarters, I want you to explain my views to commanders, and urge immediate

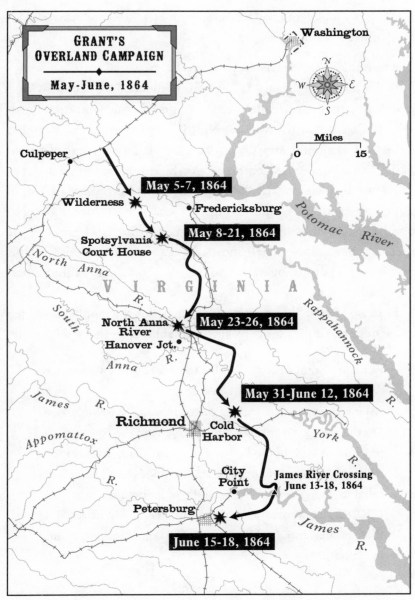

GRANT'S OVERLAND CAMPAIGN
◆
May-June, 1864

Washington

Miles
0   15

Culpeper

May 5-7, 1864

Wilderness   • Fredericksburg

Potomac River

May 8-21, 1864

Spotsylvania
Court House

North Anna

V I R G I N I A

Rappahannock

North Anna
River   May 23-26, 1864
Hanover Jct.

Anna R.

James R.

May 31-June 12, 1864

Richmond   Cold
Harbor   York R.

Appomattox

City
Point   James River Crossing
June 13-18, 1864

Petersburg

June 15-18, 1864   James R.

MAP BY DAVID DEIS, DREAMLINE CARTOGRAPHY

action, looking to cooperation, without waiting for specific orders from me.[9]

Grant, unlike Lee, clearly empowered his personal staff.

Just after midnight on May 4, Grant launched his famous Overland Campaign[10] as Meade's Army of the Potomac and then Burnside's independent (of Meade) Ninth Corps crossed the Rapidan River at Germanna and Ely's fords. Grant had a total of about 120,000 men under his command. As the Union troops crossed the fords and headed toward the Wilderness, Grant received a Union signal-corps intercept indicating that Lee was rushing troops to oppose the advance. A satisfied Grant commented, "That gives me the information I wanted. It shows that Lee is drawing out from his position and is pushing across to meet us."[11] Grant wanted a battle, and Lee obliged.

Epperson provided an insightful analysis of the manner in which the armies of Grant and Lee came into contact in the Wilderness:

> Actually, Grant's plan called for the Army of the Potomac to wheel southwest toward Lee's army, and Grant was quite willing to engage Lee within the confines of the Wilderness. Lee did not figure out Grant's plan. Quite to the contrary, Lee precipitated the battle by essentially ordering his advanced infantry corps to find out Grant's intentions. And there is no reliable evidence from the period to support the notion that Lee actually wanted a battle within the Wilderness, while there is substantial evidence that Lee wanted to fight behind the entrenchments at Mine Run.[12]

Grant was aware that Longstreet's First Corps was some distance beyond the Second and Third corps of Richard Ewell and Ambrose

P. Hill, and he hoped to bring on a battle before Longstreet arrived. Although Lee had a total of 66,000 troops at his disposal,[13] he had put himself at a distinct disadvantage because of Longstreet's location back at Orange Court House. Because of the pre-positioning of Longstreet, Lee only had two-thirds of his troops for the Wilderness conflict on May 5, and Longstreet did not arrive on the battlefield until mid-morning on May 6. Longstreet's men did not start marching toward the Wilderness until 11:00 a.m. on May 4, many hours after many of Grant's troops were south of the Rapidan River. Lee sent his other two corps on a reconnaissance-in-force eastward on the parallel Orange Turnpike and Orange Plank Road.[14] Epperson commented that "[a]pparently, Lee did not think Grant was turning toward him, for he sent two thirds of his army forward on separated roads with no good line of communication between them and with the remaining one-third of his army a full day's march to the rear."[15]

After the entire Union army crossed the Rapidan without interference, fierce fighting erupted in the Wilderness on May 5, and the vicious Battle of the Wilderness continued for two whole days.[16] Grant's operations in that battle were adversely affected by the failure of the Federal cavalry, under the ineffective command of Brigadier General James H. Wilson (Grant's former aide), to provide adequate and accurate information on the approaching Confederates. Despite having orders to send out reconnaissance patrols on each of the major roads in the area, Wilson failed to maintain adequate pickets at key locations and to detect the close proximity of Confederate troops on the evening of May 4 and the morning of May 5. Nevertheless, Grant was determined to attack Lee as soon as the enemy was located and, because of Lee's poor positioning of Longstreet, he wanted to do so before Longstreet's First Corps arrived. Close to 8:30 that morning, Grant urged Meade to attack:

"If any opportunity presents [it]self for pitching into a part of Lee's Army do so without giving time for [di]sposition."[17] Against their wishes, the strung-out, front-line Union troops therefore were ordered to attack and succeeded in engaging the Confederates before Lee was at full strength.[18]

Early on the afternoon of May 5, accordingly, Major General Gouverneur K.Warren's Union Fifth Corps attacked Lieutenant General Richard Ewell's Second Corps at Saunders' Field on the Orange Turnpike, the northern east/west approach to Fredericksburg. Ewell's men held their ground and counterattacked. That fighting spread south to Higgerson's Field and north along Culpeper Mine Road, continued all afternoon and evening, and resulted in tremendous casualties to both sides.[19]

To the south, Major General Winfield Scott Hancock and his Union Second Corps had proceeded south on the Brock Road with plans to turn west toward Lee on a road south of the Orange Plank Road (which nearly paralleled the Orange Turnpike to its north). His plans were disrupted by the fighting well to his rear and the threat posed by General A. P. Hill's Third Corps, which was marching east on the Orange Plank Road. Hill was headed for the intersection of the Plank Road and Brock Road, where he would be able to split the Union forces. While a division from Major General John Sedgwick's Sixth Corps initially delayed Hill's approach, Hancock hastened to carry out orders from Grant and Meade to reverse his course on the Brock Road and get back to the Plank Road to stop Hill.[20]

Of course, Grant did not just want Hill stopped; he wanted an attack on Hill. Hancock's Corps began arriving at the crucial intersection at 3:00 p.m., and his troops launched their major assault down the Orange Plank Road around 4:30. Bloody fighting continued that afternoon and into the darkness. Hill had been firmly stopped and potential disaster averted.[21]

As to the first day's fighting at the Wilderness, Overland Campaign historian Gordon Rhea concluded that Grant had been impatient and his coordination sloppy. However, he said, "there was still something about the quiet man's style that promised a new era of warfare in Virginia.... Grant would keep trying until he got it right."[22] More positively, historian Don Lowry explained how Grant took the initiative: "It was Grant, matching tactics to strategy, who ordered an attack on Lee as soon as his forces were encountered, in order to put him on the defensive and keep him too busy to launch one of his famous flank attacks."[23]

That evening Grant chatted with Henry Wing, a young reporter who was returning to Washington to file his story. Grant gave him a verbal message to deliver to President Lincoln. At two o'clock in the morning of May 7, Wing saw Lincoln and delivered the message: "[Grant] told me I was to tell you, Mr. President, that there would be no turning back." Lincoln happily embraced the reporter.

THE WILDERNESS: DAY TWO

Hill's bruised, exhausted, and disorganized troops had gaps in their line and both flanks exposed as they settled in for the night after the first day's fighting. According to one Confederate sharpshooter, they "lay in the shape of a semi-circle, exhausted and bleeding, with but little order or distinctive organization." Lee declined Hill's request to withdraw and left these troops exposed to attack. That is exactly what Grant planned to do as he ordered Burnside's Ninth Corps to exploit the gap between Ewell and Hill and then roll up Hill's flank with an attack at 5:00 a.m. on May 6. Burnside's attack was to be coordinated with an assault down the Plank Road by Hancock's augmented Second Corps.[24]

Hancock attacked as planned, but Burnside was a "no-show." As Hancock was successfully proceeding with his attack and routing Hill's troops, however, Longstreet arrived to save Lee's army from disaster. Hill's retreating forces were reinforced by Longstreet, who stabilized the Confederate line and then counterattacked. When Confederate artillery shells began landing near Grant's headquarters, an officer there suggested to Grant that the headquarters be moved. Grant responded, "It strikes me it would be better to order up some artillery and defend the present position." Lee later authorized Longstreet to counterattack around the exposed southern (left) flank of the Union forces via an abandoned railroad bed. Longstreet initially surprised the Union defenders and, in Hancock's post-war words, "rolled me [Hancock] up like a wet blanket." Longstreet was driving back the Second Corps troops when he was hit by friendly fire from Confederates on the Plank Road as he dangerously swept across their front. His serious throat and shoulder wounds brought the assault to an immediate halt.[25]

That afternoon, however, Lee once again played into Grant's hands. The Union line at the Brock Road/Plank Road intersection was not as vulnerable as it may have appeared in the initial moments of Longstreet's surprise flank assault. Just after 4:00 p.m., Lee personally launched a thirteen-brigade frontal assault against Union fortifications along Brock Road that were perpendicular to the Orange Plank Road. "At nearly every point of attack, Lee's troops were stopped by a deadly curtain of musketry and cannon fire."[26] The Rebels were repulsed with heavy losses.[27]

That same morning and afternoon, inconclusive fighting continued to the north on and near the Orange Turnpike. The increasingly incompetent Ewell, relying on the unreliable Major General Jubal A. Early, ignored Brigadier General John B. Gordon's accurate, eye-witness information that the Union right flank was open to attack. When Lee finally learned about Gordon's observations and advice, he ordered a late-afternoon attack around the Union right flank. Although the attack was initially successful, all of Gordon's troops eventually were either swallowed up or repulsed by the Union troops and the darkness.[28]

After two days of vicious, confused, and bloody fighting in the wilderness, both armies were further shocked as wounded soldiers were burned alive in the fires spreading through the woods between the lines. Grant's forces had taken almost 18,000 casualties in two days, while Lee had lost about 11,000 troops. Grant, however, had achieved his strategic goal of attaching himself to Lee's army—within forty-eight hours of starting his campaign. Furthermore, Lee lost 20 percent of his men, while Grant was losing 15 percent. The war of adhesion and attrition was under way as Lee's aggression played into Grant's hands, and Lee was compelled to remain on the defensive (with perhaps two exceptions) for the rest of the war.[29]

Lee's losses at the Wilderness were so significant that he had destroyed any reserve he might have hoped to assemble and was forced to go on the tactical defensive for the rest of the Overland Campaign. McWhiney and Jamieson reasoned that "[h]ad [Lee] refrained from attacking Grant on May 5, which was an act of doubtful wisdom, he would have reached Richmond with his army almost intact."[30]

The Wilderness was a learning experience for Grant. There he had sat, smoked, and whittled while allowing Meade to direct the operations of his army. Because Grant was not impressed with

Meade's performance under fire, Grant decided that for the rest of the campaign he would take more direct control of the battles. Meade, to his chagrin, became Grant's de facto executive officer.[31]

GRANT MOVES FORWARD

Unlike his eastern predecessors after Seven Days', Fredericksburg, and Chancellorsville in 1862 and 1863, Grant was not persuaded to retreat or remain stationary as a result of the bloody fighting and great loss of life at the Wilderness. He was determined to carry on— even if some of his officers needed some bucking up. Shortly after Gordon's attack late on the second day of battle, one of Grant's generals told him that a crisis existed, and that Lee would throw his whole army on the Union rear and cut off its communications. Grant sent a message to the entire Army of the Potomac when he responded: "Oh, I am heartily tired of hearing about what Lee is going to do. Some of you always seem to think he is suddenly going to turn a double-somersault and land in our rear and on both of our flanks at the same time. Go back to your command, and try to think what we are going to do ourselves instead of what Lee is going to do."[32]

On May 7, the day after the Battle of the Wilderness, Elisha Hunt Rhodes no longer had any qualms about Grant: "If we were under any other General except Grant I should expect a retreat, but Grant is not that kind of a soldier, and we feel that we can trust him."[33] Another more skeptical soldier said that Grant "has come up from the Western army, where they have been fighting skirmish-lines, and has found that we have lines of battle to fight here, and he is now studying how to get back across the Rapidan."[34] In fact, that very morning Grant had issued orders to Meade to spend the day preparing for a flank movement southeast toward Spotsylvania Court House.[35]

The defining moment of the Overland Campaign was Grant's decision, after engaging in the fierce fight in the Wilderness, to stay his ground and not retreat across the Rappahannock as his eastern predecessors would have done, and instead to move southeast and on toward Richmond.[36] Jean Edward Smith called it "the final turning point of the war."[37] Gordon Rhea explained the impact of Grant's determination and forward movement after the Wilderness:

> Hooker had treated his loss in the Wilderness as a defeat. Grant lost more troops in the Wilderness, but rather than retreat he pushed on. Defensively minded commanders such as McClellan, Burnside, Hooker, and Meade considered as defeats setbacks that Grant shrugged off as mere tactical reverses. It was this new way of thinking that got the Army of the Potomac through stalemates at the Wilderness, Spotsylvania, North Anna, and Cold Harbor, and on to victory.[38]

And Sherman put it in the context of the men Grant had lost and would lose: "Undismayed, with a full comprehension of the importance of the work in which he was engaged, feeling as keen a sympathy for his dead and wounded as anyone, and without stopping to count his numbers, he gave his orders calmly, specifically, and absolutely—'Forward to Spotsylvania.'"[39]

When his troops realized that Grant was ordering an advance, they went wild with enthusiasm. Grant had to order them not to cheer for fear of revealing their movement. As he often did, historian Shelby Foote caught the spirit of that moment:

> But now a murmur, swelling rapidly to a chatter, began to move back down the column from its head, and presently each man could see for himself that the turn, beyond the ruins of the Chancellor mansion, had been to the right. They were headed south, not north; they were advancing, not

retreating; Grant was giving them another go at Lee.... There
were cheers and even a few tossed caps, and long afterwards
men were to say that, for them, this had been the high point
of the war.[40]

Thus, on the night of May 7–8, the Army of the Potomac
marched off to try to outflank the Army of Northern Virginia. Lee
himself expected a retreat and advised Confederate Secretary of
War Seddon that the "enemy had abandoned his position and is
moving toward Fredericksburg."[41]

While riding toward Spotsylvania Court House along the Brock
Road, Grant, Meade, and members of their staffs accidentally left
the main road and drifted toward the Confederate lines. So determined was Grant not to turn back that he at first objected to doing
so. Colonel Horace Porter described the incident: "General Grant
at first demurred when it was proposed to turn back, and urged
the guide to try and find some cross-road leading to the Brock
Road, to avoid retracing our steps. This was an instance of his
marked aversion to turning back, which amounted almost to a
superstition."[42]

Spotsylvania Court House

Unfortunately for Grant and the Army of the Potomac, confusion
reigned on the southeasterly march toward Spotsylvania Court
House.[43] Sheridan's cavalry and Gouverneur Warren's infantry got
in each other's way, Confederate cavalry delayed the Union movement, Meade reversed a Sheridan order that would have blocked a
Confederate advance, and the Confederate First Corps under Major
General Richard H. ("Fighting Dick") Anderson (who had replaced
the wounded Longstreet) started early and kept going toward Spot-

sylvania because fires at the Wilderness prevented them from bivouacking there for the night. As a result of all these factors, Anderson's Confederate force arrived minutes ahead of Warren's Union infantry at Spotsylvania. As Union reinforcements arrived, so did additional blocking Confederates.[44]

One ramification of the confused Union movement toward Spotsylvania Court House was a finger-pointing confrontation between Meade and Sheridan. They each blamed the other for the fiasco. Sheridan, frustrated by Meade's desire to keep the cavalry close to his infantry, told Meade that he could defeat Confederate Cavalry commander and Major General James Ewell Brown ("Jeb") Stuart if given the chance. When Meade repeated what he thought was a ridiculous boast to Grant, the Commanding General shocked Meade by ordering him to take Sheridan up on his offer. As a result, Sheridan was sent off on a mission that resulted in Stuart's death at Yellow Tavern, but left Grant without the eyes of his cavalry during the ensuing days at Spotsylvania.[45]

At Spotsylvania, Grant lost one of his corps commanders in a famous incident. On May 9, General John Sedgwick, while adjusting the alignment of his Sixth Corps troops, observed his men ducking enemy fire coming from a thousand yards away. Jesting with them about their actions, he twice said, "They couldn't hit an elephant at this distance." A few seconds later, a sharpshooter's bullet hit him in the head and killed him instantly. He was the most senior Union officer killed in the war. Brigadier General Horatio G. Wright replaced him as Sixth Corps Commander and was promoted to major general three days later.[46]

In the West, Grant had relied upon great generals as his subordinates: Sherman, Thomas, and McPherson. His eastern corps commanders were not their equal. Wright was untested, Hancock continued to suffer from his Gettysburg wound, and Burnside and Warren both had "the slows," as Lincoln had described one of McClellan's noteworthy traits.[47]

Lee had left his army vulnerable to attack by keeping a significant number of his troops aligned in a major half-mile-by-one-mile salient (a forward projection of the Rebel line), dubbed the "Mule Shoe" because of its shape, which could be attacked on three sides. After unsuccessful attacks on Lee's flanks on May 9 and 10, Union planners decided to attack the Mule Shoe's western flank at a mini-salient (Doles' Salient) in a column formation that would quickly overrun the Confederate front line. Twelve hand-picked regiments were selected for the assault, four of them from the Sixth Corps that had succeeded in similar assaults at Second Fredericksburg in May 1863 (part of the Battle of Chancellorsville) and Rappahannock Station in November 1863.[48]

Colonel Emory Upton led the well-conceived attack late in the afternoon of May 10. His concealed men had to cross a short open field to the Confederate lines, were not within clear artillery field of vision, and were initially free of enfilading fire because they were attacking a salient. With all these advantages, Upton's 5,000 attackers charged without firing until they reached the enemy and then tore through the Confederate front line. Because they were not joined in their attack by more than one other Union regiment, they soon were counterattacked and had to retreat to their original position. During the ninety-minute battle, Upton's thirteen regiments had taken on more than six Confederate brigades, threatened the entire Mule Shoe, taken a thousand prisoners, and killed and wounded many of the enemy. Even more importantly, Upton had planted in Grant's mind the idea for a similar but grander attack on the apex of the Mule Shoe.[49]

On May 11, as he planned for an all-out assault on the Mule Shoe the next morning, Grant apprised Halleck of the situation and expressed his determination to keep fighting. That letter began with this famous paragraph:

> We have now ended the sixth day of very heavy fighting. The result to this time is much in our favor. But our losses have been heavy as well as those of the enemy. We have lost to this time eleven General officers killed, wounded or missing, and probably twenty thousand men. I think the loss of the enemy must be greater we having taken over four thousand prisoners, in battle, whilst he has taken from us but few except stragglers. I am now sending back to Belle Plaines [*sic*] all my wagons for a fresh supply of provisions, and Ammunition, and propose to fight it out on this line if it takes all summer.[50]

Grant set 4:00 a.m. on May 12 as the time for a massive assault on the northern edge of the Mule Shoe to be led by Hancock's Second Corps. He also ordered Burnside and his Ninth Corps to launch an adjoining attack at the same time.[51] Lee had made the Mule Shoe more vulnerable by ordering all its artillery withdrawn the prior evening. There are a variety of explanations for Lee's mistake. He may have mistaken the noise of Grant's preparation for an assault as a retreat toward Fredericksburg—again! He may have interpreted Rebel scouts' reports of a massive movement of Union wagons toward Fredericksburg as separate evidence of a retreat by Grant—although the wagons were going back for rations and ammunition. Or Lee may have intended to launch an attack elsewhere or to guard his flanks against Grant. At the time, Lee told Brigadier General Henry Heth, "My opinion is the enemy are preparing to retreat tonight to Fredericksburg. . . . We must attack those people if they retreat." Thus, it appears that Lee believed Grant was retreating. If so, he had not studied Grant's western campaigns; the word "retreat" was not in Grant's vocabulary.[52]

Well before dawn on May 12, 20,000 Union troops under Hancock's command made their way through the foggy woods and up a slope toward the Confederate fortifications. With a loud cheer, they made the final rush and cleared the Rebel fortifications. They engaged in furious hand-to-hand combat; captured 4,000 prisoners (including two generals), twenty guns (which Lee had returned just in time to be captured and used against his own men), and thirty Rebel colors; and drove the defenders out of the salient.[53]

Burnside's Corps kept pressure on the Rebel right, and Wright's Sixth Corps promptly responded to orders to support Hancock; however, Warren's Fifth Corps apparently was slow to do so.[54] Lee ordered a furious counterattack to retake the captured territory, but five assaults on Hancock failed. The most vicious and deadly fighting occurred at the "Bloody Angle," where hand-to-hand combat resulted in piles of dead and wounded soldiers. Bruce Catton captured the viciousness of the fighting:

> Men fired at one another through chinks in the logs, or stabbed through the chinks with their bayonets, or reached over the top to swing clubbed muskets. Where the Vermont Brigade was fighting, men were seen to spring on top of the logs and fire down on their enemies as fast as their comrades could pass loaded muskets up to them. Each man would get off a few rounds before he was shot, and usually when one of these men fell someone else would clamber up to take his place. Dead men fell on top of wounded men, and unhurt men coming up to fight would step on the hideous writhing pile-up. . . .

.... This was the Bloody Angle, the place where a trench made a little bend, and where the two armies might have clasped hands as they fought; and it was precisely here that the war came down to its darkest cockpit. It could never be any worse than this because men could not possibly imagine or do anything worse. This fighting was not planned or ordered or directed. It was formless, monstrous, something no general could will. It grew out of what these men were and what the war had taught them—cruel knowledge of killing, wild brief contempt for death, furious unspeakable ferocity that could transcend every limitation of whipped nerves and beaten flesh.[55]

The rifle and musket fire of the battle was so fierce that one eighteen-inch-diameter oak tree was cut down by minie balls. The close-in fighting continued until three o'clock the next morning, when Lee withdrew to a new and safer line. While Grant did not lose a single company at the "Mule Shoe," Lee lost a division (and its commander), a brigade, and a regiment.[56]

After Lee's withdrawal, Grant's forces had suffered 32,000 casualties (killed, wounded, and missing) since crossing the Rapidan. However, Grant had imposed similarly proportional casualties on Lee's army, which had lost 18,000 of its 60,000 troops.[57]

Off and on through May 18, Grant ordered continued assaults on sectors of Lee's Spotsylvania line that Grant believed had been weakened by troop movements. None of them proved successful. Grant's infectious aggression and determination, however, kept Union spirits up. For example, on May 17, Elisha Hunt Rhodes reported the loss of half his division but wrote, "I am well and happy and feel that at last the Army of the Potomac is doing good work. Grant is a fighter and bound to win."[58]

On May 18, Grant learned of the Union disasters at Bermuda Hundred and in the Shenandoah Valley that would enable Lee to be reinforced. On that day, Grant ordered the final assault at Spotsylvania Court House. About 12,000 troops attacked over the ground where the Mule Shoe had been, but they were repelled firmly by small-arms and artillery fire. Their casualties were over 1,500, while the Confederate defenders' casualties were negligible. Seeing nothing to be gained by more assaults at Spotsylvania after almost twelve days of them, Grant decided to move southeast once again.[59]

The final battle at Spotsylvania was the Battle of Harris Farm on May 19.[60] Fortunately for Grant, Lee had decided to send Ewell's Second Corps (minus most of its artillery) against and around the supposedly weakened Union right in what was intended as a reconnaissance-in-force, or a disruptive raid. For once, Union soldiers (after recovering from being caught in a scattered and vulnerable condition) could fire on exposed attackers. Newly arrived and inexperienced New York, Massachusetts, and Maine heavy artillery regiments (now fighting as infantrymen), which Grant had received from the defenses of Washington, acquitted themselves well, stopped the progress of Ewell's attack, and imposed heavy casualties on the Second Corps. When Ewell realized that he had overreached, was two miles from the rest of Lee's army, and was in danger of losing his isolated corps, he settled into defensive positions. His corps fought off Union attackers, was perhaps saved by darkness, finally broke off contact, and retreated during the night. Ewell lost at least 900 men, while the "green" Union heavy artillery units suffered about 1,500 casualties and earned the respect of the Army's veterans. Before the end of May, Lee relieved Ewell of command. On the Union side, Grant noted that Warren again was slow and had missed an opportunity to cut off the isolated Second Corps.[61]

As Spotsylvania drew to a close, it was clear that this campaign was going to be costly to both sides. Grant and Lee suffered casualties at Spotsylvania amazingly similar to those they had incurred at the Wilderness—just over a much longer period of time. Grant had lost a militarily tolerable 18,000 men (killed, wounded, missing/captured), while Lee had incurred 12,000 such casualties. Because Grant outnumbered Lee by 2:1 and had more reinforcements available, he could tolerate that 3:2 ratio of casualties as he moved toward his goal of defeating or destroying Lee's army. Lee, on the other hand, was seeing his Army disappear through casualties that he could not tolerate, and the South had begun to use up its last reinforcements. Virtually all Confederate soldiers in South Carolina, coastal Georgia, and eastern Florida were ordered to Virginia, and Lee also received reinforcements from the Shenandoah Valley. Lee's army was back up to numbers between 50,000 and 55,000, but that number would decline for the rest of the war because the supply of reinforcements had virtually been exhausted. Lee's heavy losses impaired his ability to reinforce Johnston against Sherman—and, in fact, were draining troops from the region Johnston was defending.[62]

Grant's persistence in pursuing his campaign came as a surprise to many Confederates. Evander M. Law, one of Lee's generals, later said that he knew that Grant had been aggressive in the West, "but we were not prepared for the unparalleled stubbornness and tenacity with which he persisted in his attacks under the fearful losses which his army sustained at the Wilderness and at Spotsylvania."[63]

Grant's attacks had just about wrecked Ewell's Second Corps. Ewell had started the campaign with 17,000 troops and had only 6,000 left after the first two battles. Lee's corps commanders also were in bad shape. Longstreet was wounded and out of action for many months, Ewell had become increasingly erratic and undependable before he was replaced, and Hill was sick during Spotsylvania and not in command until May 21. In fact, after these first two battles of the campaign, Lee had lost twenty of his fifty-seven corps, division, and brigade commanders, while Grant had lost only ten of sixty-nine.[64]

A Union officer's letter from Spotsylvania described the Confederate defenses that the Union forces faced: "It is a rule that, when the rebels halt, the first day gives them a good rifle-pit; the second, a regular infantry parapet with artillery in position; and the third a parapet with an abattis in front and entrenched batteries behind. Sometimes they put this three days' work into the first twenty-four hours."[65] He explained, "Our men can, and do, do the same," but he cautioned, "but remember, our object is offense—to advance."[66] Grant's critics sometimes forget that.

THE NORTH ANNA RIVER

On May 20, Grant sent Hancock's Corps ahead alone in hopes of drawing Lee out in an attack on an isolated corps. Grant sent Warren's Corps after Hancock's and invited Lee to attack someone somewhere. When the invitation was not accepted, Burnside and Wright's corps followed the other two. The movement of all Grant's corps compelled Lee to respond in order to protect Richmond.[67] The Union forces came upon Lee at the North Anna River. On May 23, Hancock successfully attacked Lee's rear-guard posted north of the river at the Chesterfield Bridge on Telegraph Road, drove them into and across the river, and captured hundreds of prisoners.[68]

Upstream from the bridge, near Jericho Mill, other Union troops crossed the river and repulsed an attack by A. P. Hill's corps. The next day, an ill Lee rebuked Hill with the stinging words: "Why did you let these people cross the river? Why did you not drive them back as General [Thomas J. ("Stonewall")] Jackson would have done?"[69]

After Grant's flanks crossed the river, he realized that he faced a difficult position: "Lee now had his entire army south of the North Anna. Our lines covered his front, with the six miles separating the two wings guarded by but a single division. To get from one wing to the other the river would have to be crossed twice. Lee could reinforce any part of his line from all points of it in a very short march; or could concentrate the whole of it wherever he might choose to assault. We were, for the time, practically two armies besieging."[70]

Some of Burnside's troops (under drunken Brigade Commander James H. Ledlie) recklessly attacked the point of this inverted "V" on May 24 and lost heavily for their efforts. The next day Lee could have attacked the spread-out and divided Union troops, but his ill and bedridden condition, combined with his failure to delegate, prevented him from overseeing or initiating such an attack. No attack, therefore, was made, and a disappointed Lee kept muttering, "We must strike them a blow. We must not let them pass us again. We must strike them a blow."[71]

By May 26, Grant had the divided wings of his army protected with newly dug earthworks and better connected by a series of pontoon bridges. Hancock's Corps had been the most vulnerable to a Rebel attack, but its troops' entrenching ended any vulnerability. In addition, Grant's flanks were patrolled by Sheridan's cavalry, which had returned to him on May 24. Thus, Grant and Lee were stalemated. Neither could easily attack the other without heavy losses.[72]

Meanwhile, an encouraging event for the Union had occurred on May 24. On that day, 1,100 men of Brigadier General Edward A.

Wild's all-Black "African Brigade" of Butler's Army of the James repulsed an attack on Fort Pocahontas at Wilson's Wharf, twenty miles downriver from Bermuda Hundred on the north side of the James River. Confederate Major General Fitzhugh Lee, Robert E. Lee's nephew, attacked them with 3,000 cavalry and was particularly anxious to overwhelm the Union position when he learned that the defenders were an all-Black unit. The Rebels launched three separate attacks on the fort between noon and 6:00 p.m., but were repelled by heavy fire from the defenders. After the first attack, Lee sent a message to Wild demanding surrender, stating that the Black soldiers would be treated as prisoners of war in that event, and warning that otherwise Lee "would not be answerable for the consequences." After his three failed assaults, Lee ordered a retreat. Lee's division lost twenty killed, perhaps two hundred wounded, and nineteen captured. The Federal defenders lost two killed, nineteen wounded, and one missing. Butler's line of communication to Fort Monroe was preserved, and the fighting ability of Black soldiers was confirmed.[73]

Given his inability to effectively attack Lee's inverted "V" at the North Anna River, and the fact that Lee had been reinforced, Grant decided it was once again time to move on. He did so on May 27. His optimism was reflected in a dispatch he sent the prior day: "Lee's army is really whipped.... Our men feel that they have gained morale over the enemy and attack with confidence. I may be mistaken but I feel that our success over Lees [sic] army is already insured."[74] Grant's hopes were premature.

Under cover of darkness on the night of May 26–27, Grant had Meade delicately withdraw his troops from their positions opposite Lee's Army and move again toward the southeast. After considering the possibility of moving around Lee's left flank and crossing several small rivers, Grant decided in favor of crossing a single river, the Pamunkey, which had the additional advantage of providing

White House Landing as a base of supply off the Chesapeake Bay.[75] According to Rhea, "Grant's virtually bloodless withdrawal from the North Anna and his shift to Hanovertown ranks among the war's most successful maneuvers."[76]

Most of the Union troops crossed the Pamunkey River at Hanovertown and Nelson's Crossing just above the Totopotomoy Creek on May 28. Southwest of the crossing, screening Union cavalry, commanded by Brigadier General David M. Gregg, engaged in a fierce battle at Haw's Shop. They fought Wade Hampton's cavalry, which Lee had moved to block Grant from coming west to attack the Virginia Central Railroad. Hampton's cavalry slowed the Union march for five hours and confirmed for Lee that Grant was across the Pamunkey. Hampton and Sheridan both missed opportunities to seriously damage their opponents, the result was a draw, and each side suffered several hundred casualties.[77]

On May 29, the still-ailing Lee replaced the ill and ineffective Ewell with Jubal Early as commander of his Second Corps. When Warren's Corps crossed the Totopotomoy that same day, Lee saw an opportunity to counterattack that isolated corps. He ordered Early to do so and told Early, "We must destroy this Army of Grant's before he gets to [the] James River. If he gets there it will become a siege, and then it will be a mere question of time."[78]

On May 30, therefore, Early pushed his Corps forward into a collision with the Union Fifth Corps. However, after driving back some Pennsylvania Reserves near Bethesda Church, the brigade of Colonel Edward Willis charged up the Walnut Grove Road into a deadly Union trap. They were hit by rifle and artillery fire from ahead and both flanks. Colonel Willis (who had been approved for promotion to brigadier) was killed, and his brigade, "perhaps the cream of the Confederate [Second] Corps," according to Gordon Rhea, was decimated. Union casualties were about 420 and

Confederate about 450. This Union victory at Bethesda Church may have encouraged Grant to think that Lee's army was demoralized and ready to be broken.[79]

Meanwhile, Grant had ordered General "Baldy" Smith's 18th Corps to sail from Bermuda Hundred to Grant's new supply base at White House Landing on the Pamunkey River and then to join Grant and Meade. With 10,000 troops, Smith arrived at White House Landing on May 30. Looking ahead, Grant on that same day requested Halleck to send all the pontoons in Washington to City Point near Bermuda Hundred on the James River. For his part, Lee told President Davis he needed reinforcements to prevent "disaster" and was successful in getting Major General Robert F. Hoke's 7,000-man division sent to him from Beauregard in Richmond/Petersburg.[80]

By the end of May, Grant's casualties were pouring back into Washington by the boatload. The wounded filled twenty-one Washington area hospitals. There was "dark talk that Grant, although dogged, was also a butcher who harbored too little regard for human life."[81] The northern press was calling Grant a "butcher."[82] The fighting and bloodshed did not cease. In the running battles and skirmishes from the North Anna to the Totopotomoy and then Cold Harbor between May 26 and June 2, Grant and Lee each took about 5,000 casualties.[83]

COLD HARBOR

That "dark talk" certainly increased after the next development: Cold Harbor. Sheridan's cavalrymen arrived at the Cold Harbor crossroad on May 31, forcefully repelled the advance of a Confederate brigade on the morning of June 1, and were then relieved by Wright's Sixth Corps, which had orders from Grant to attack immediately. Wright's corps began arriving at 10:00 a.m. that morning. Believing his men to be too tired and deciding to wait for Baldy Smith's reinforcements from Bermuda Hundred, Wright did not attack until later.[84]

Belatedly reinforced by Smith (who had marched on the wrong road from White House Landing under outdated or erroneous orders), Wright finally attacked the partially organized Confederate Cold Harbor line at 5:00 p.m. on June 1. The 30,000 troops of Wright and Smith's corps were repelled in most places, broke through a gap in the Rebel lines, captured hundreds of prisoners, and were finally sealed off by a counterattack. The Union attackers' casualties may have been in the thousands, while the Rebel defenders lost between five and six hundred.[85]

Despite Grant's desire to attack again quickly as both armies converged on Cold Harbor, the Confederates ended up with a day and a half to construct seven miles of fortifications as protection against the expected Union attack. Grant's plans to attack at 5:00 a.m. on June 2 were delayed by the 6:30 a.m. arrival of Hancock's Corps, and his plans to attack at 5:00 p.m. that day were delayed until 4:30 the following morning by the exhausted condition of Hancock's men. Therefore, the Confederates were well-prepared for the expected attack. Fearing the worst, many Union troops wrote farewell letters to their loved ones and pinned their names on their uniforms to ensure that their bodies were well-marked for identification in the event they did not survive the attack.[86]

Grant was seven miles from Richmond, had just been reinforced, and believed he had no choice but to attempt to break Lee's army and perhaps win the war. He gave Meade another chance to demonstrate his command skills by placing him in operational charge for the day; Meade failed to reconnoiter, coordinate, or command. Some of the Union forces launched a frontal assault on the southern end of Lee's line at 4:30 a.m. on June 3. The well-entrenched defenders shot down any exposed Union soldier. Large numbers died in a short period, and the attack lasted no more than an hour. Hours later, Burnside attacked on the north end of the line. Grant lost about 3,500 to 4,000 men in the early morning assault and about another 2,500 during the rest of the day.[87] After several hours of waffling by Meade about whether to call off the assaults, Grant interviewed the corps commanders and then ordered an end to the attacks. Rhea observed, "Far from behaving like an uncaring 'butcher,' Grant intervened to save lives when Meade, seemingly paralyzed by indecision, appeared incapable of acting."[88]

In his immediate June 3 post-action report to the War Department, Grant stated, "Our loss was not severe nor do I suppose the Enemy to have lost heavily."[89] It is likely that he was trying some routine damage control in light of northern press criticism of his casualties.[90] Grant's more honest, later brief summary of the attack was: "The assault cost us heavily and probably without benefit to compensate; but the enemy was not cheered by the occurrence sufficiently to induce him to take the offensive."[91]

Cold Harbor has been the major black mark on Grant's record.[92] As Harold Simpson wrote, "In a little over *eight minutes*, Grant lost almost 7,000 men and earned for himself the sobriquet, 'The Butcher.'"[93] Grant himself later said in his memoirs:

> I have always regretted that the last assault at Cold Harbor was ever made.... At Cold Harbor no advantage whatever was gained to compensate for the heavy loss we sustained. Indeed, the advantages other than those of relative losses, were on the Confederate side. Before that, the Army of Northern Virginia seemed to have acquired a wholesome regard for the courage, endurance, and soldierly qualities generally of the Army of the Potomac... This charge seemed to

revive their hopes temporarily; but it was of short duration. The effect upon the Army of the Potomac was the reverse. When we reached the James River, however, all effects of the battle of Cold Harbor seemed to have disappeared.[94]

His Army's disappointing performance at Petersburg two weeks later, however, casts some doubt on Grant's last statement.

Gordon Rhea, who has exhaustively studied the Overland Campaign, explained that Grant was only seven miles from Richmond, Lee's weakened army had a river at its back, and Bethesda Church and the June 1 breakthrough seemed to indicate Lee's army was on the verge of collapse. Meade ineffectively oversaw the uncoordinated attack by only half the Union troops against unexplored Confederate lines. Rather than the 7,000 to 15,000 men Grant is alleged to have lost in that early morning assault,[95] Rhea stated that battlefield records show that Grant lost no more than 3,500 to 4,000 troops—many less than Lee in similar assaults at Gettysburg and Chancellorsville.[96] "The traditional figure of 7,000 Union casualties in the first thirty minutes certainly is too high. While Grant's army definitely absorbed tremendous casualties in that time, the grand total probably fell several thousand short of 7,000."[97]

In his writings on Cold Harbor, Rhea explored the Union casualty record in detail and concluded that the early morning assault on June 3 cost Grant approximately 3,500 to 4,000 killed, wounded, and missing. For the entire day, Rhea calculated that Grant suffered slightly more than 6,000 casualties, while Lee took about 1,000 to 1,500.[98] Rhea went on to put Cold Harbor in perspective:

Severe as Grant's losses were on June 3, the two years preceding Cold Harbor had seen a host of days in which Union and Confederate armies each sustained far more casualties in a single day. Lee's subtractions in three days fighting at Gettysburg, for example, exceeded 22,000, with Confederate losses on the last day of the battle topping 8,000. Pickett's famous charge at Gettysburg—a frontal attack that lasted about as long as Grant's main morning attack at Cold Harbor—cost the Confederates between 5,300 and 5,700 men, a number well in excess of Grant's casualties during his June 3 attack. And while cumulative casualties in Grant's successive battles against Lee were high, no single day of Grant's pounding saw the magnitude of Union casualties that McClellan incurred in one day at Antietam, and no three consecutive days of Grant's warring proved as costly in lives to the Union as Meade's three days at Gettysburg.

Assistant Secretary of War Charles Dana, who was with Grant at Cold Harbor, later analyzed that battle:

> This was the battle of Cold Harbor, which has been exaggerated into one of the bloodiest disasters of history, a reckless, useless waste of human life. It was nothing of the kind. The outlook warranted the effort. The breaking of Lee's lines meant his destruction and the collapse of the rebellion. Sheridan took the same chances at Five Forks ten months later, and won; so did Wright, Humphreys, Gibbon, and others at Petersburg [on April 2, 1865].[99]

Even after Cold Harbor, morale remained high among many officers and soldiers in Grant's force. On June 3 Elisha Hunt Rhodes wrote: "Nothing seems to have been gained by the attack today, except that it may be that it settles the question of whether the enemy's line can be carried by direct assault or not. At any rate General Grant means to hold on, and I know that he will win in the end."[100] Captain Charles Francis Adams, Jr. wrote that "so far Grant has out-generalled Lee and he has, in spite of his inability to start Lee one inch out of his fortifications, maneuvered himself close to the gates of Richmond." Even a soldier in one of the decimated corps wrote, "We have the gray backs in a pretty close corner at present and intend to keep them so. There is no fall back in Grant."[101] He certainly had that right.

Union Major General Jacob D. Cox noted that, "Grant was slower than Sherman in learning the unprofitableness of attacking field-works, and his campaign was by far the most costly one.... There were special reasons which led Grant to adhere so long to the more aggressive tactics, which need to be weighed in any full treatment of the subject...."[102] On May 22, Sherman explained, "Grant's battles in Virginia are fearful but necessary. Immense slaughter is necessary to prove that our Northern armies can and will fight."[103]

Others, however, were unhappy with Grant's generals. Cavalry Brigadier James Wilson told Grant that his army could be greatly improved by having Colonel Ely Parker, a full-blooded Indian on Grant's staff, scalp the first six major generals he encountered.[104]

After the abortive attack of June 3, and following an unseemly dispute between Grant and Lee about conditions for retrieving wounded from between the lines, the troops on both sides settled into a deadly standoff in which sharpshooters picked off anything that moved in the enemy lines. The broiling sun, the danger of being shot, and the smells of the battlefield made the conditions unbearable. Within ten days Grant would move on once again.[105]

As the confrontation at Cold Harbor came to a close, both sides could look back at almost six weeks of virtually incessant fighting. During the final two weeks, along the Totopotomoy and at Cold

Harbor, Lee at long last achieved something close to the 3:1 casualty ratio he needed for victory. During that time, Grant's forces had suffered almost 16,000 casualties to Lee's more than 7,000. However, those results were too little and too late to affect the ultimate outcome of the war. Between the Wilderness and Cold Harbor, Grant had lost 50,000 of his 122,000 troops to death or wounds, while Lee's 70,000 troops (including reinforcements) had incurred 32,000 such casualties. Thus, Lee had lost an irreplaceable 46 percent while Grant had lost a replaceable and militarily tolerable 41 percent. In addition, the Army of Northern Virginia had lost twenty-two of its fifty-eight generals (eight killed, twelve wounded, and two captured).[106]

CROSSING THE JAMES RIVER

Grant quickly determined to restore the morale of his soldiers and to threaten Richmond by making a surprise crossing of the James River. "For Grant, Cold Harbor had been a setback, not a defeat."[107] On June 5, Grant revealed his movement plans to Halleck and said, "My idea from the start has been to beat Lee's Army, if possible, north of Richmond, then after destroying his lines of communication North of the James river to transfer the Army to the South side and besiege Lee in Richmond, or follow him South if he should retreat."[108] Given the Rebels' continuous use of defensive fortifications since their abortive attacks at the Wilderness, Grant stated that such a movement was necessary in order to avoid "a greater sacrifice of human life" than he was willing to make.[109]

As a prelude to his secret move, Grant on June 6 sent Sheridan on his "Second Raid" to destroy much of the Virginia Central Railroad, a key supply connection between Richmond and the Shenandoah Valley, and to connect with General Hunter, whose troops were to destroy the James River Canal at Lynchburg. Both Sheridan and Hunter failed. Confederate cavalry commanded by Wade Hampton kept Sheridan from reaching his critical goal of Gordonsville and drove him into retreat at the Battle of Trevilian's Station on June 11 and 12. Jubal Early and the Second Corps arrived from Richmond in time to save Lynchburg from the dawdling Hunter and to drive him back into West Virginia. The one positive result for Grant of Sheridan's expedition was that Hampton's response deprived Lee of the eyes of his own cavalry for a critical period when Grant moved his army again.[110]

Back at Cold Harbor, Grant planned for and then began his secret back-door assault on Petersburg via a crossing of the James River. On June 5, he requested more vessels from Washington and ordered Horace Porter and Cyrus Comstock of his staff to locate a suitable crossing of the James River. They reported their findings to Grant on June 12. Behind a massive screen of cavalry and one corps (Warren's Fifth), Grant evacuated his line one corps at a time. First, W. F. Smith's 18th Corps marched east back to White House Landing and traveled by vessel via the Pamunkey and York rivers, Chesapeake Bay, Hampton Roads, and the James River to Bermuda Hundred, where they arrived on June 14.[111]

Meanwhile, all the other corps moved out from Cold Harbor without being discovered and, behind a screen established at Malvern Hill by Warren's corps, crossed the Chickahominy River via three separate crossings—two fixed bridges and a pontoon bridge. Confederate Brigadier General [Edward] Porter Alexander described how the Rebels could have pounced on and crushed the isolated Fifth Corps on the afternoon of June 13—but for one problem: "The only trouble about that was that we were entirely ignorant of the fact that it was isolated. On the contrary. . . . War-ren's corps had taken up its line so near to Riddell's Shop as to give us the idea that it was the advance corps of Grant's whole army pushing toward Richmond on the road from Long Bridge."[112] As Jean Edward Smith observed, "The Army of the Potomac—115,000 men—had marched away so quietly that Confederate pick-ets had not observed its departure."[113]

On June 14, Hancock's corps crossed the James by boat from Wilcox's Landing and established a bridgehead around Windmill Point on the south shore. Those actions cleared the way for con-struction of—at that time—the world's longest pontoon bridge, over which the rest of Grant's army crossed on the 15th and 16th. Grant took a tremendous gamble that he would be able to detach his large army from Lee's, construct and use a 2,100-foot bridge across a river with a four-foot tidal range, and cross that river without being attacked with his army split on two sides of the river. As the cross-ing succeeded, Dana wired Stanton, "All goes on like a miracle."

As early as 7:00 p.m. on June 15, Grant's advance troops were attacking Petersburg, with Lee twenty-five miles away. Only incompetence on the part of Grant's corps commanders prevented the seizure of that key railroad junction so critical to Richmond's survival.[114]

How badly had Grant fooled Lee with his unprecedented mas-sive crossing of the mile-wide James? Beauregard at Petersburg had predicted Grant's movement in June 7 and 9 dispatches, sent tele-graphic warnings and a personal emissary to Lee on the 14th, and continued to send dire reports and reinforcement requests on the 15th and 16th. Confederate General Porter Alexander later con-cluded that Grant's initial attack at Petersburg late on the 15th could have been another Cold Harbor, but "General Lee did not have a soldier there to meet him! Grant had gotten way from US [*sic*] completely & was fighting *Beauregard*. The Army of Northern Virginia had lost him, & was sucking its thumbs by the roadside 25 miles away, & wondering where he could be!"[115] In General Fuller's words, "*Lee* had been completely out-generalled."[116]

Even after the assaults on Petersburg began, Lee continued to doubt Beauregard's claims. He sent the following telegrams to Beauregard in the days *after* Grant's troops began attacking Petersburg:

> *June 16 at 10:30 a.m.:* "I do not know the position of Grant's army and cannot strip north bank of James River. Have you not force sufficient?"[117]
>
> *June 16 at 4:00 p.m.:* "The transports you mention have probably returned Butler's troops. Has Grant been seen crossing James River?"[118]
>
> *June 16–17 at midnight.:* "Until I can get more definite information of Grant's movements, I do not think it prudent to draw more troops to this [south] side of the river."[119]
>
> *June 17 at 6:00 a.m.:* "Can you ascertain anything of Grant's movements?"[120]
>
> *June 17 at 4:30 p.m.:* "Have no information of Grant's crossing James River, but upon your report have ordered troops up to Chaffin's Bluff [still north of the James]."[121]

At 6:40 that evening, more than two days after Grant's first attack on Petersburg, Beauregard sent an attention-grabbing dispatch to Lee indicating that he would attempt that night to fall back from outer to inner lines and might have to abandon the city. That night, while he indeed was falling back, Beauregard sent, one after the other, two colonels and a major as personal emissaries to convince Lee that the situation was desperate. The last effort succeeded at 3:00 a.m. on the 18th, and Lee then started arranging rail transportation for reinforcements to Petersburg.[122]

Meanwhile, a number of Grant's corps commanders displayed incredible incompetence and timidity that cost them the opportunity to capture a severely undermanned Petersburg. The first attack, on the 15th, was made by W. F. Smith's Corps with Hancock's Corps in support. After Smith wasted most of the day, he finally attacked with 16,000 troops against a mere 2,200 defenders. His overwhelming superiority forced Beauregard to fall back to new positions, but Smith failed to take the entire garrison, allowed his "weary" men to be replaced by Hancock's soldiers, and rested them before their goal had been achieved. Hancock's arrival to support Smith apparently had been delayed by a missing order and delayed rations. The next day saw half-hearted attacks by the Second, 18th and newly arrived Ninth Corps. Even the arrival of the Fifth Corps on the 17th was followed by uncoordinated and unsuccessful attacks. Union troops and commanders may have been suffering from "Cold Harbor fever."[123]

On the 18th at dawn, with the newly arrived Sixth Corps further bolstering their strength, the Federals launched a 70,000-man, five-corps assault on Petersburg. They overran the recently abandoned Confederate outer lines and seriously threatened to at last take the town. As at Spotsylvania, Lee's troops appeared on scene just in time to stop a Federal advance and save the day. Four hours after Lee began arranging for their transportation from north of Richmond, Confederates began pouring into their comrades' defensive lines at 7:30 that morning. They continued to do so until 11:00 a.m. About an hour later, the attackers tried again. After another unsuccessful assault at 4:00 p.m., a frustrated and perhaps angry Grant called off the attacks.[124] Not until April 2 of the next year would

Grant order another frontal assault; in fact, he expressly prohibited such assaults.[125] Siege warfare would commence.

One of those gravely wounded in the Petersburg assaults was Colonel Joshua L. Chamberlain, who had been one of the heroes at Gettysburg. Upon hearing of Chamberlain's apparently fatal wounding, Grant issued him a battlefield promotion to brigadier general.

Some analysts have dramatically—and somewhat inaccurately—criticized Grant's Overland Campaign: "Grant had covered some sixty miles and lost nearly 60,000 men—a thousand per mile, 2,000 a day, three [actually two] for every one of Lee's men—a number equal in size to the entire Confederate army he faced. Now, after all of that, the war in the South had come down to a siege."[126] Although Grant's forces had lost between 60,000 and 65,000 killed and wounded between May 5 and June 18, Lee's Army had suffered between 33,000 and 37,000 casualties during the same period.[127] While both armies lost about half their troops during that time, Grant could count on more reinforcements. Lee's army, however, had begun a downward spiral in strength that would continue till the war's end. The war had evolved to a condition that Lee had wanted to avoid.

Lee's casualties were so significant that units from elsewhere totaling 24,495 men had come to reinforce him.[128] These reinforcements to Lee weakened critical areas to which Sherman would be heading, and the South was now essentially out of reinforcements. Besides his hard-to-replace manpower losses, Lee had another serious problem. In May 1864, eight of his generals were killed—three at the Wilderness, two at Spotsylvania, two at Yellow Tavern, and one at Bethesda Church. Leadership in his army had become a serious problem.[129]

The authoritative Gordon Rhea analyzed Grant's losses in the campaign:

> Did Grant pay too great a human cost in waging his Overland Campaign? Critics emphasized that he lost approximately 55,000 soldiers in forty days, nearly as many men as Lee had in his army at the beginning of the campaign. Lee, however, lost about 33,000 troops in that same period. While Grant's subtractions were numerically greater than Lee's, his percentage of loss was smaller. Grant's losses amounted to about 45 percent of the force he took across the Rapidan; Lee's reached slightly over 50 percent. And while Grant could draw upon a deep manpower pool for reinforcements, Lee's potential was limited. In the game of numbers, Grant was coming out ahead. He was losing soldiers at a lower percentage than was his adversary, and he possessed greater capacity to replace his losses.[130]

Although the Overland Campaign had not yet resulted in the surrender of Richmond or Lee's army, Grant had succeeded in bottling up the bulk of Lee's troops in Richmond and Petersburg—a situation that Lee himself had said would be fatal[131]—and in seriously damaging Lee's army. James M. McPherson provided a perceptive analysis of that campaign:

> Grant did not admit culpability for the heavy Union casualties in the whole campaign of May and June 1864. Nor should he have done so, despite the label of "butcher" and the later analyses of his "campaign of attrition." It did turn out to be a campaign of attrition, but that was more by Lee's choice than by Grant's. The Union commander's purpose was to maneuver Lee into a position for open-field combat; Lee's

purpose was to prevent this by entrenching an impenetrable line to protect Richmond and his communications. Lee was hoping to hold out long enough and inflict sufficient casualties on Union forces to discourage the people of the North and prevent Lincoln's reelection. Lee's strategy of attrition almost worked. That it failed in the end was owing mainly to Grant, who stayed the course and turned the attrition factor in his favor. Although the Confederates had the advantage of fighting on the defensive most of the time, Grant inflicted almost as high a percentage of casualties on Lee's army as vice versa.[132]

Gordon Rhea concluded: "Contrary to the image urged by Grant's detractors, the general's campaign against Lee reveals a warrior every bit as talented as his famous Confederate counterpart. Grant understood the importance of seizing the initiative and holding tight to his offensive edge to keep Lee off balance and prevent him from going on the offensive."[133]

In summary, Grant had taken high, but militarily acceptable, casualties as the price of seriously weakening Lee's army, compelling Lee to retreat to a siege situation at Richmond and Petersburg, and keeping Lee from reinforcing the Confederates facing Sherman in Georgia. His game plan for Lee's defeat and Lincoln's reelection was working.

Ten

1864–1865:
TIGHTENING THE NOOSE

While Grant pins Lee down in Petersburg and Richmond, Union forces capture Atlanta, the Shenandoah Valley, and Mobile Harbor; Lincoln wins reelection; Sherman marches through Georgia, and George Thomas virtually destroys John Bell Hood's Army of Tennessee.

During the second half of 1864, Grant kept Lee pinned down in Petersburg and Richmond, encouraged Sherman's success in Georgia, and finally drove the Confederates out of the Shenandoah Valley. Incurring minimal casualties, Grant tightened the noose around Lee's Army and readied the way for victory in 1865. Grant never let up the pressure on Lee's supply-lines, continuing to threaten them by extending his own left flank and making cavalry raids beyond the lines.[1]

After the siege began, the first problem that Grant faced was that Early and his Second Corps were on the loose—without Grant's knowledge. His intelligence system had broken down, and Grant was not made aware of his position until Early neared Frederick, Maryland, on an ill-conceived approach to Washington. At the same time that Grant was moving his army to and across the James

River, Lee had sent Early's corps west to defend Lynchburg against David Hunter's attack out of the Shenandoah Valley. Outnumbering Hunter 14,000 to 11,000, Early drove Hunter away from Lynchburg and back into the Kanawha Valley of West Virginia.[2]

At that point, Lee could have ordered Early to return to Richmond, to reinforce Johnston at Atlanta, or to do something else. The best strategic move would have been to reinforce Johnston who, overwhelmed by Sherman's numerical superiority, needed to hold Atlanta if Lincoln was to be defeated in the November presidential election. That was, consequently, the move most feared by Grant and Sherman. Instead, on June 27, Lee authorized Early to proceed north through the Shenandoah Valley to threaten Washington. Early's orders even contained a ludicrous authorization for him to go around Washington and free Confederate prisoners at the isolated Point Lookout prison camp far southeast of Washington.[3]

Although the fortifications surrounding Washington made it unlikely that Early would accomplish much, he did create quite a stir. As directed, his 18,000 troops made their way north through the Shenandoah and entered Maryland. Once there, Early demanded and received ransoms of $20,000, $1,500, and $200,000, respectively, from the citizens of Hagerstown, tiny Middletown, and Frederick.

At first Grant refused to believe reports that Early was in Maryland. He briefly reported on July 3 that "Early's corps is now here." Two days later, Grant, apparently concerned about continuing reports of Early's possible movement, told Stanton and Halleck that he would send a full corps to Washington if the city was threatened; they, however, declined the assistance. Nevertheless, after Meade reported to Grant that deserters claimed Early was heading for Maryland and Washington, Grant sent Brigadier General James B.

Ricketts' Third Division of the Sixth Corps north by vessel to Baltimore as an insurance policy.[4]

Having at last discerned where Early was positioned, Grant ordered the rest of the Sixth and all of the Nineteenth Corps to head north to defend Washington. Ricketts' 5,000-man division greatly strengthened the force that General Lew Wallace had scraped together at Monocacy Creek, south of Frederick, to oppose Early's advance. These men supplemented the 2,800 untested soldiers Wallace had under his own command. With a force now more prepared to fight, Wallace carefully picked the battlefield site, where the Baltimore & Ohio Railroad, the Georgetown Pike to Washington, and the Baltimore Pike (National Road) all crossed the river.[5]

As the July 9 Battle of Monocacy began,[6] Wallace's makeshift force fiercely held all three bridges at those crossings. After hours of fighting at the bridges, Early decided to have his cavalry cross the river at a ford a mile downstream from the fighting and then attack the Union left flank. After the cavalry were driven back, Confederate Major General John Gordon's division attacked that same flank with several charges by his three brigades of infantry. Their overwhelming numbers finally drove Wallace's men back toward Baltimore after seven hours of fighting.[7]

The Battle of Monocacy cost Early a day, and in the meantime two divisions of seasoned Sixth Corps troops from Grant had arrived to defend Washington and were waiting for him there by the time he arrived at midday on July 11. Early then undertook a long retreat—plus a detour to burn Chambersburg, Pennsylvania, on July 30 when the residents were unable to raise sufficient tribute money.[8] The net result of Early's raid was that Lee had used one of his three corps to cause Grant to send two of his seven corps away from Richmond.

For his part, Grant was relieved that Early was wasting time burning Chambersburg instead of reinforcing Johnston at Atlanta. In early July, Grant had written Sherman about his concern that Early's Corps would be sent to Atlanta, and on July 15 Grant also wrote Halleck, reiterating that his greatest fear was such a movement.[9] Fortunately for Grant and Sherman, Lee kept Early's 14,000 to 18,000 troops in his own theater. Confederate General Porter Alexander later criticized Lee for his use of Early to try to bluff Grant, whom he said could not be bluffed, and for not sending Early's Corps to Georgia, "the very strongest play on the military board. Then every man sent might have counted for his full weight in a decisive struggle with Sherman &, if it proved successful, then Early might return bringing a large part of Johnston's army with him to reinforce Lee."[10]

Grant's friend Sherman also was being helped by Confederate President Jefferson Davis. On July 17, with Lee's agreement, Davis replaced Joseph Johnston with Lieutenant General John Bell Hood. Davis was dissatisfied with what he perceived to be Johnston's lack of aggressiveness. Hood, who had lost the use of an arm at Gettysburg and a leg at Chickamauga, was notorious for his aggressiveness (some said recklessness) on the battlefield. That aggressiveness explains why his appointment was unwelcome in the Confederate Army of Tennessee but greeted with cheers among the Union officers who knew him.[11] Their hopes were rewarded as Hood, who was immediately promoted to full general, went on the offensive three times in his first twelve days of command. Although his strategic mission was defensive and his soldiers were not expendable, Hood attacked—as he usually did. Those three attacks (Peach Tree Creek on July 20, Decatur on July 22, and Ezra Church on July 28) cost Hood 14,000 casualties to Sherman's 4,000, earned him an ironic rebuke from Davis for attacking the enemy in entrenchments, and made his army likely to lose Atlanta.[12]

At Peach Tree Creek, Hood attempted to catch the Federals as they crossed the creek, but his attack was delayed by repositioning of his troops. The massive two-corps attack first hit the New Jersey 33rd Regiment, the most forward Union unit. The overwhelming force of the attackers drove the New Jersey troops back into the main Union line, which turned back Hood's attack and inflicted severe casualties on the Rebel attackers.[13] At Decatur (also known as Bald Hill or Atlanta), Hood directed a major attack on what he thought would be the Union flank or rear but turned out to be entrenchments; he suffered 5,000 casualties. Finally, at Ezra Church, Hood's plan to once again attack the Union flank resulted instead in six separate Confederate assaults on strong Union lines and the decimation of Lieutenant General Stephen D. Lee's corps. As Sherman expected, Hood had immediately gone on the offensive, and, as Sherman hoped, Hood had so weakened his army that Atlanta was vulnerable.

Toward the end of June, meanwhile, Grant authorized Pennsylvania Volunteer miners under Burnside's command to dig a 500-foot tunnel under the Confederate fortifications at Petersburg. By July 23, they had finished their digging and were ready to detonate eight tons of explosives directly under the Confederate lines. In the latter days of July, Grant transferred troops north toward Richmond. By doing so, he duped Lee into moving four of seven infantry divisions from Petersburg to Richmond and thereby weakened that sector of Lee's line. Then, on the night of July 29–30, Grant surreptitiously brought most of his troops back to the Petersburg front in an effort to exploit the expected breakthrough from the planned explosion. Early on the morning of July 30, Union troops set off a massive explosion under the Confederate lines, thereby creating a huge opening and an opportunity for a break-through.[14]

However, Meade had ordered a last-minute replacement for the African-American troops who had been trained to lead the assault. General James Ledlie, the division commander of the replacement troops, cowered in a bunker behind the lines—drunk again (as he had been at the North Anna River). Therefore, contrary to Grant's orders stressing "the absolute necessity of pushing entirely beyond the enemy's present line," after Ledlie's men entered "The Crater" they hesitated to move farther. The belated and ineffective Union advance provided the initially shocked Confederates with time to reorganize and counterattack. The Rebel response resulted in a slaughter of Union troops in the Crater. What Grant later called "this stupendous failure" resulted in 4,000 Union casualties while the Confederates suffered only 1,500. Ledlie at last was removed from command.[15]

Grant was more successful in establishing and maintaining con-trol of the James River north of his City Point base at the inter-section of the James and Appomattox Rivers. From June 20 onward, his forces held a fortified bridgehead on the northwest bank of the James at the narrow horseshoe curve called Deep Bot-tom (because the James River was very deep at that point). For the next two months, they cleared Confederate mines from the river and blocked the creeks flowing into it. Lee declined Early's request for artillery and infantry that were necessary to dislodge Grant's forces, and the Union troops thus prevented a Rebel blockade of the river, safeguarded their City Point base of opera-tions, and kept viable their ability to transfer troops between the Petersburg and Richmond fronts.[16]

In late July, Grant sent Hancock and Sheridan on a mission to challenge the northern end of Lee's lines, divert Lee's attention from the planned mine explosion in Petersburg, widen the Union bridgehead on the north side of the James River, and thus more effectively threaten Lee's Richmond lines. At what became known as the First Battle of Deep Bottom, aggressive Rebel defenders caused Hancock to hesitate and to refrain from using his overwhelming numerical advantage. Although Hancock failed to achieve his mission (except to divert Lee's attention), he did impose more casualties than he incurred. He lost 62 killed, 340 wounded, and 86 missing, while the Confederates lost 471 killed or wounded and 208 captured.[17]

During August, Grant began to fully comprehend the sorry state of the enemy forces, especially in terms of manpower. In mid-August, he wrote to his friend and political advocate, Congressman Elihu Washburne:

> The rebels have now in their ranks their last man. The little boys and old men are guarding prisoners, guarding rail-road bridges and forming a good part of their garrisons for intrenched [sic] positions. A man lost by them can not be replaced. They have robbed the cradle and the grave equally to get their present force. Besides what they lose in frequent skirmishes and battles they are now loosing [sic] from desertions and other causes at least one regiment per day.[18]

Grant recognized that prisoner exchanges benefited the Confederates, who had limited manpower. On August 18, he wrote, "If we commence a system of exchanges which liberates all prisoners taken we will have to fight on until the whole South is exterminated. If we hold those caught they amount to no more than dead men. At this particular time to release all rebel prisoners [in the] North would insure Sherman's defeat and would compromise our safety here."[19] The next day he wrote, "We ought not to make a single exchange nor release a prisoner on any pretext whatever until the war closes. We have got to fight until the military power of the South is exhausted and if we release or exchange prisoners captured it simply becomes a War of extermination."[20]

By mid-August, Grant was aware from the Bureau of Military Intelligence (BMI) that Lee had sent reinforcements to the Shenandoah and believed he could take advantage of their absence. By threatening Richmond on the north end of the battle-lines, Grant thought Lee would have to so weaken Petersburg in response that Petersburg could be taken. Thus he directed Hancock, with 29,000 troops, to move on Richmond, which was defended by a well-entrenched force of 7,700. Due to serious bungling and lack of coordination, this Second Battle of Deep Bottom, from August 14 to 20, resulted in little progress (other than overrunning and capturing eight large guns that threatened Union control of the James) being made by the Union forces, which incurred 2,900 casualties while imposing about 1,500 on the defenders.[21] But Grant was keeping the pressure on Lee.

That approach was consistent with a Grant–Lincoln exchange of views that occurred that same month. Halleck initiated the communications by writing that possible northern draft riots would necessitate the withdrawal of troops from the Army of the Potomac to deal with the insurrections. Grant strongly disagreed, contended that state militias would have to deal with any riots, and said, "If we are to draw troops from the field to keep the loyal states in the harness it will prove difficult to suppress the rebellion in the disloyal states. My withdrawel [sic] now from the James River would insure the defeat of Sherman." Lincoln then chimed in and wired Grant, "I have seen your despatch expressing your unwillingness to break your hold where you are. Neither am I willing. Hold on with a bull-dog gripe [*sic*], and chew & choke, as much as possible.[22]

The end of August brought favorable developments near Atlanta. On August 31 at Jonesboro, south of Atlanta, Hood lost 4,000 more troops unsuccessfully trying to drive Union troops away from the last open railroad serving Atlanta. True to his character, Hood afterward criticized his subordinate Hardee's assault as feeble because of the low percentage of casualties (15 percent). Because Sherman's armies now controlled all railroads into and out of Atlanta, Hood was compelled to abandon the city on September 1. Sherman occupied it the next day, the North went wild in celebration, and Lincoln's reelection was virtually assured.[23] Ironically, the Democrats had nominated George McClellan as his opponent only the day before at their Chicago convention.

As in Virginia, the Atlanta Campaign had not been a bloodless one for either side. Sherman incurred casualties of 31,687, while his Confederate opponents lost 34,979—almost 20,000 of those after Hood replaced Johnston.[24] On September 12, Grant sent a personal letter to Sherman that was delivered by Colonel McPherson of Grant's staff. He closed by congratulating Sherman on his Atlanta campaign: "In conclusion [*sic*] it is hardly necessary for me to say that I feel you have accomplished the most gigantic undertak[ing] given to any General in this War and with a skill and ability that will be acknowledged in history as unsurpassed if not unequalled." Grant told Sherman that he was sending McPherson to get Sherman's views on future actions, but Grant did suggest the possibility of moves on Mobile and Savannah.[25] Grant was thinking ahead on a national scale.

After Early's July 30 burning of Chambersburg, Pennsylvania, Grant took action to end the Confederate use of the Shenandoah Valley as an avenue for raiding the North and as a means of supplying Lee. Secretary of War Stanton had previously rejected Phil Sheridan as commander of all the forces there because of Sheridan's young age. Grant, nevertheless, was determined to get his aggressive cavalryman directly involved. Thus, he sent Sheridan and another division of cavalry to the Shenandoah and wired Halleck, "Unless Gen. Hunter is in the field in person I want Sheridan put in command of all the troops in the field with instructions to put himself south of the enemy and follow him to the death. Wherever the enemy goes let our troops go also."[26]

After reading this dispatch, Lincoln sent Grant an August 3 wire quoting the above words and then prodding Grant to do more:

> This, I think, is exactly right, as to how our forces should move. But please look over the despatches [sic] you may have receved [sic] from here, even since you made that order, and discover, if you can, that there is any idea in the head of any one here, of "putting our army *South* of the enemy" or of ["]following him to the *death*" in any direction. I repeat to you it will neither be done nor attempted unless you watch it every day, and hour, and force it.[27]

Taking the president's not-so-subtle hint, Grant immediately left his City Point headquarters and headed north to resolve this situation. He went directly to Monocacy, Maryland, where he met General Hunter. Since Hunter was unable to tell Grant where the enemy was, Grant decided to smoke out the enemy troops by sending a trainload of soldiers four miles west of Harper's Ferry to draw them out. After Grant also ordered Hunter's cavalry and wagons to move west in search of Confederates and explained that Sheridan would command in the field, Hunter requested that he be relieved of command. Grant gladly complied and thus had Sheridan where he wanted him—in charge of 30,000 troops charged with clearing the Valley of Confederates. Grant would not be disappointed.[28] Between August 13 and 20, Grant moved troops north of the James to keep Lee from reinforcing the Shenandoah.[29]

From June 22 to August 21, Grant intermittently focused on extending his south-of-Petersburg lines westward to block the north/south Weldon Railroad, over which Lee's Army was receiving many of its supplies from Weldon, North Carolina. After unsuccessfully moving on that railroad in late June with a loss of 3,000 troops, Grant's forces tried again in August. Warren's Fifth Corps extended its line three miles to the west, took and fortified a position on the railroad, and then held on against a Confederate counterattack at the Battle of Globe Tavern (or Weldon Railroad) on August 18 to 21. Thereafter the Confederates had to bypass the section of that railroad held by Grant's troops via a thirty-mile detour by wagon, making Richmond/Petersburg more difficult to supply. The battle had cost Lee 1,200 killed or wounded out of his almost 15,000 soldiers involved, while Grant had used over 20,000 troops and had 1,303 killed or wounded. Also, Grant's missing and captured exceeded Lee's 400 by about 2,600.[30]

On September 15, Grant left City Point for another visit with Sheridan. In his memoirs, Grant said he went to Harper's Ferry to discuss an offensive greater than anything Stanton or Halleck would have authorized if he had tried to communicate by telegraph. Grant brought a campaign plan with him, but kept it in his pocket when Sheridan produced a plan of his own—another indicator of Grant's willingness to delegate authority. Grant wanted an end to years of pussyfooting by Union generals in the Valley, and he was now certain that Sheridan was the man to do it. Thus began Sheridan's successful 1864 Shenandoah Valley campaign.[31]

On September 19, at Opequon Creek (Third Winchester), Sheridan took 5,000 casualties to impose 4,000 casualties on Early and drive him south. Three days later, at Fisher's Hill, Sheridan repeated his assault and, at a cost of only 500 casualties, imposed 1,200 casualties on Early and drove him farther south.[32]

Sheridan chased Early so far up the Valley that Sheridan lost contact with Washington. To allay Lincoln's fears that Lee would successfully reinforce Early against Sheridan, Grant told him he would prevent this by attacking Lee. To do that, Grant issued September 28 orders to Ord's 18th and Major General David B. Birney's Tenth corps and Brigadier General August V. Kautz's cavalry to threaten the Richmond end of Lee's lines.[33]

Between September 29 and October 2, Grant launched simultaneous offensives on both ends of the Petersburg/Richmond siege lines, captured important Fort Harrison outside Richmond, induced Lee to launch a costly and unsuccessful counterattack against that fort, and compelled Lee to extend his lines three miles farther west of Petersburg, thereby thinning and weakening Lee's defensive perimeter. Utilizing excellent BMI intelligence, Grant and Sheridan caught Major General Joseph B. Kershaw's Division in transition between Richmond and the Shenandoah Valley while Grant was conducting his successful dual assaults against Lee's weakened army. A few days later, Grant's troops used Spencer repeating rifles to repulse a Lee-directed assault along Darbytown Road.[34]

A month later, on October 19, Early surprised Sheridan's troops at Cedar Creek in the Shenandoah and drove them in retreat toward Winchester. The absent Sheridan arrived just in time to stop the panicked retreat, organize a counterattack, and rout and drive Early's soldiers from the Lower Valley for the final time. Both sides withdrew most of their remaining troops to the Richmond/Petersburg front, and significant fighting in the Shenandoah was over. Although Sheridan had suffered 5,900 casualties to Early's 2,900, his third and final major victory in the Valley in about thirty-five days provided more grist for the Lincoln reelection mill.[35]

After all the September fighting, Lee the next month again proposed to Grant that prisoner exchanges be resumed. Grant responded that exchanges could be resumed if Lee agreed that African-American prisoners would be exchanged "the same as white soldiers." Lee, in turn, replied that ". . . negroes belonging to our citizens are not considered subjects of exchange and were not included in my proposition." Grant, therefore, declined resumption of exchanges, in accordance with Lincoln's policy on the matter—a policy that cost Lincoln votes in the November election.[36]

In the Deep South, meanwhile, Admiral David Glasgow Farragut had taken major actions against Mobile, Alabama, a key port and rail center that had long been on Grant's list of primary targets. Not only was it the last major open port on the Gulf, but Mobile was the only extant rail connection point between the remaining eastern and western segments of the Confederacy. Lincoln's reelection prospects were enhanced by Farragut's "Damn the torpedoes—Full speed ahead" charge into Mobile Bay on August 5 and the August 23 capture of Fort Morgan, which controlled that bay. Although the city itself was not occupied until April 1865, it was useless as a Confederate port after Farragut's assault.[37] The morale-boosting impact of the Mobile Bay victory was captured by Secretary of State William H. Seward, who said, "Sherman and Farragut have knocked the bottom out of the [Democrats'] Chicago platform."[38]

In late October, Grant made his final pre-winter effort to cut Lee's supply-lines. On the 24th, he ordered Meade on an October 27 movement west from the Weldon Railroad toward the South Side Railroad. Meade incurred over 1,700 casualties compared to the enemy's fewer than 1,000.[39] Grant protected Meade's movement with a simultaneous effort by Butler on the far north end of the lines. Butler made some progress but was similarly rebuffed when he tried to drive headlong down the Darbytown Road instead of first turning the Confederate flank.[40]

Riding the wave of Atlanta, Mobile Bay, and Shenandoah military victories, Lincoln respectably won reelection with 2,200,000 votes (55 percent) to McClellan's 1,800,000 (45 percent). More decisive results came from the electoral college, where Lincoln's advantage was 212 to 21. On top of that, the 78 percent of the military vote received by Lincoln apparently reflected the soldiers' satisfaction with how the war was going. Although these statistics seem to reflect a landslide, the election was much closer than it appeared. The switch of less than 1 percent of the votes (29,935 out of 4,031,195) in Connecticut, Illinois, Indiana, New York, Oregon, and Pennsylvania would have given McClellan the 97 additional electoral votes he needed to barely win with 118 electoral votes.[41]

After occupying Atlanta, Sherman deliberated over what to do next. As early as September 10, Grant talked about sending Union troops to Savannah. Sherman's response mentioned several possible Georgia targets and the possibility that he could "sweep the whole State of Georgia." On September 12, Grant sent Lieutenant Colonel Porter to visit Sherman and get his views on future operations.[42]

Sherman watched and then followed as Hood moved north and then west to Alabama. Initially Hood went after Sherman's supply-line, the Western and Atlantic Railroad, from Chattanooga to Atlanta. Finally, Sherman decided that pursuing Hood

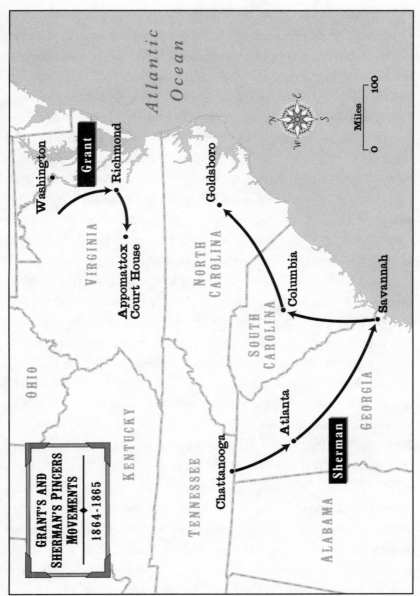

GRANT'S AND
SHERMAN'S PINCERS
MOVEMENTS
♦
1864-1865

Atlantic Ocean

Washington
Grant
Richmond
VIRGINIA
Appomattox
Court House
NORTH
CAROLINA
Goldsboro
Columbia
SOUTH
CAROLINA
Savannah
OHIO
Atlanta
GEORGIA
Sherman
Chattanooga
KENTUCKY
TENNESSEE
ALABAMA

Miles
0   100

MAP BY DAVID DEIS, DREAMLINE CARTOGRAPHY

and protecting his own extended supply-line was getting him nowhere. Instead, on October 9, Sherman made a radical proposal to Grant: Sherman should break loose from his supply-line, destroy the railroad between Chattanooga and Atlanta (his supposed life-line), and "move through Georgia smashing things to the sea." Sherman told Grant, "I can make Savannah, Charleston or the mouth of the Chattahoochee" and asked for quick approval.[43] That same evening, Grant succinctly gave his conditional approval: "Your dispatch of to-day received. If you are satisfied the trip to the sea coast can be made holding the line of the Tennessee River firmly you may make it destroying all the rail-road South of Dalton or Chattanooga, as you think best."[44] Perhaps reluctant at first, Grant gave final approval to Sherman's proposal after Sherman sent George Thomas and John Schofield (with the 12,000-man Army of the Ohio) to defend Tennessee against a likely incursion by Hood.[45]

It was on November 2 that Grant unconditionally approved Sherman's proposed campaign through Georgia. Only two weeks later, on November 16, Sherman left Atlanta with about 60,000 troops, deftly feinted moves toward different destinations, and wreaked a path of destruction sixty miles wide from Atlanta to Savannah. General Slocum commanded the two-corps (14th and 20th) Left Wing, General Howard commanded the two-corps (15th and 17th) Right Wing, and Brigadier General Hugh Judson ("Kill Cavalry") Kilpatrick commanded the cavalry. They destroyed railroads, factories, and Confederate arsenals and seized anything that could be eaten by men, horses, or mules. Despite orders to the contrary, they burned and pillaged at will. When Lincoln grew concerned about Southern press reports that Sherman's men were demoralized and starving, Grant told Lincoln not to worry.[46]

Confederate General Hardee, a Georgia native, came back to his home state, raised some troops, and harassed Sherman's unstoppable force as it continued toward Savannah. Sherman arrived at Savannah's outskirts and began his siege of that city on December 10. In order to establish contact with the Federal fleet that had arrived off Savannah, Union Brigadier General William B. Hazen's Division had to assault and capture Fort McAllister—Sherman's first hard fighting since Atlanta. Once he had access to the shipboard mail, Sherman was able to read a December 3 letter from Grant. In that letter, Grant expressed his confidence in Sherman and his awareness of the relationship of their mutual activities:

> Not liking to rejoice before the victory is assured I abstain from congratulating you and those under your command until bottom has been struck. I have never had a fear however for the result.
>
> Since you left Atlanta no very great progress has been made here. The enemy has been closely watched though and prevented from detaching against you.[47]

Although Hardee's 10,000 defenders inexplicably and inexcusably were allowed to escape the city into South Carolina, Sherman occupied Savannah in time to make it a Christmas present to the president. He wired the president: "I beg to present to you as a Christmas-gift the city of Savannah, with one-hundred and fifty heavy guns and plenty of ammunition, also about twenty-five thousand bales of cotton." The greatest significance of the capture of Savannah was that it gave Sherman an ocean base for supplies. For the balance of the war, his army could be supplied with ammunition and other essentials by sea and rail through Atlantic Ocean ports.[48]

Sherman's march from Atlanta to Savannah had a devastating effect on the Georgia countryside and towns and demoralized the inhabitants, their soldier relatives, and the entire South. In his memoirs, Grant gave full credit to Sherman for the conception and execution of this critical march: "[T]he question of who devised the plan of march from Atlanta to Savannah is easily answered: it was clearly Sherman, and to him also belongs the credit of its brilliant execution. It was hardly possible that any one else than those on the spot could have devised a new plan of campaign to supersede one that did not promise success."[49]

Meanwhile, in Tennessee, Grant's national campaign achieved yet more success. George Thomas had the good fortune to be facing a veritable madman in John Bell Hood. After Major General John M. Schofield's two Union corps escaped a trap set by Hood's army of 23,000 at Spring Hill, Tennessee, on November 29, a furious Hood ordered a suicidal assault the next day at Franklin, Tennessee. The results were devastating; the Confederates lost twelve generals (including six killed), 1,750 Confederate soldiers were killed, another 5,500 were wounded or captured, and more than 60 of their 100 regimental commanders were killed or wounded. Hood's 32 percent casualty rate at Franklin made this perhaps the dumbest attack of the war and certainly exceeded Cold Harbor and Pickett's Charge at Gettysburg in its self-inflicted damage.[50]

Still not satisfied, Hood ordered his battered army to proceed toward Nashville. With his inadequate force, Hood fortified in front of Nashville while Thomas consolidated and received reinforcements. For the next two weeks, Grant urged Thomas to attack; his attempted micro-management of Thomas demonstrates that Grant had less confidence in Thomas than he did in Sherman.[51] On December 15 and 16, Thomas launched a massive assault on

Hood's forces and inflicted another 6,600 casualties (including captured soldiers)—26 percent of the remaining Army of Tennessee. The broken remnants of Hood's army headed back to Alabama in frigid winter conditions. Aided by two rivers and the horrid weather, Hood escaped—much to Grant's chagrin. In five months, however, Hood had reduced the Army of Tennessee from 50,000 to 18,000.[52]

During the second half of 1864, therefore, Grant tightened the noose around Richmond and Petersburg and oversaw successful operations in other theaters. Nowhere did Union forces suffer significant casualties compared with those they imposed on the enemy—especially when considered in light of their offensive missions and significant accomplishments. By the end of 1864, Grant's nationwide campaign had succeeded in capturing Atlanta, Savannah, Mobile, and the Shenandoah Valley; reelecting President Lincoln; virtually destroying the Army of Tennessee; and laying the groundwork for the final defeat of Lee and the Confederacy.

Eleven

EARLY 1865:
WINNING THE WAR

Sherman marches through the Carolinas, Wilmington falls, Grant's troops extend the Confederates and break through at Petersburg, Confederates abandon Richmond, and Lee surrenders at Appomattox Court House.

In the first months of 1865, Grant concentrated virtually all his forces in the Carolina/Virginia theater with the single goal of bringing the war to a decisive end. As the year began, Grant had Lee pinned down in Richmond and Petersburg, Sherman was poised to march through the Carolinas from Savannah, and George Thomas was prepared to send tens of thousands of troops eastward after his rout of Hood at Franklin and Nashville.

Ignoring the wishes of President Davis, the Confederate Congress passed a January 19 law effectively making Lee the Confederate Commander-in-Chief. He, however, had dwindling forces to command, since 40 percent of Confederates east of the Mississippi had deserted during the fall and early winter. On New Year's Eve, less than half of the Confederacy's soldiers were present for duty with their units. Lee himself requested that Lieutenant General E. Kirby Smith's Trans-Mississippi Army be transferred to Virginia.[1]

As the Confederacy's condition deteriorated in early 1865, a half-hearted effort to fashion a peace agreement brought about a February 3 conference on board the *River Queen* steamer in Hampton Roads, Virginia. Before leaving for those talks, Lincoln had wired Grant, "Let nothing which is transpiring change, hinder, or delay your Military movements or plans." Grant responded that he would keep his soldiers "in readiness to move at the shortest notice if occasion should justify it."[2] Lincoln brought the same resolve to the meeting, and made it clear to the Confederate representatives that the southern states were required both to return to the Union and to put an end to slavery. The talks went nowhere.

Grant's Army and the threat it posed to Richmond seemed to be the sole concern of Lee and the paralyzed Confederate Government. They were slow to respond to the danger represented by Sherman and his resupplied 60,000-man army. Optimistically, Lee had sent one dispatch in which he spoke of achieving two incompatible goals: stopping Sherman and holding Charleston.[3] Achieving both was unrealistic with the few Confederate troops available in the Carolinas. Besides Hardee's small force that had escaped Savannah, there were only local militia and the reassembled remnants of the Army of Tennessee, which had come northeast from Alabama to oppose Sherman.

Initially Grant had intended to move Sherman's troops by vessel from Savannah to either Richmond or North Carolina. When Sherman realized how long it would take to gather the necessary transports, however, he instead proposed a march through the Carolinas. Grant promptly approved. As early as January 21, Grant was making arrangements for up to 30,000 western troops to be brought east to the ports of Wilmington and New Bern, North Carolina, from which they could move inland to reinforce Sherman.[4]

Sherman later explained the importance of his intended march through the Carolinas: "Were I to express my measure of the relative importance of the march to the sea and of that from Savannah northward, I would place the former at one, and the latter at ten, or the maximum."[5] The plan was brilliant; it allowed Sherman to destroy the railroads supplying Lee from the Carolinas as he moved to close Lee's back door.[6]

Late in December, with Sherman outside Savannah, Grant had analyzed Lee's vulnerability to Sherman's actions. On December 18, Grant wrote to Sherman about Lee's focus on Richmond: "If you capture the garrison of Savannah it certainly will compel Lee to detach from Richmond or give us nearly the whole South. My own opinion is that Lee is averse to going out of Virginia, and if the cause of the South is lost he wants Richmond to be the last place surrendered. If he has such views it may be well to indulge him until everything else is in our hands."[7]

Lee meanwhile was seeing his army melt away. On February 25, he wrote, "Hundreds of men are deserting nightly...."[8] Union Colonel Elisha Hunt Rhodes provided confirmation of that; he reported continuing Confederate desertions, including the arrival of ten deserters on February 21 and 160 of them on February 25.[9] Between February 15 and March 18, there were 3,000 deserters from Lee's army, a loss of 8 percent.[10] The situation became so bad that in March Lee reported 1,094 desertions in a 10-day period, and one entire division left en masse.[11] During March, numerous regimental and brigade commanders requested the Confederate Adjutant's Office in Richmond to drop from the rolls captains and lieutenants who had deserted.[12] Appomattox Campaign historian

William Marvel calculated that, between March 10 and April 9, from 14,400 to 20,400 of Lee's soldiers deserted.[13]

These desertions did not simply result from the strains of trench warfare and military life. A major factor was the impact of Sherman's campaign: it caused a reduction of food and supplies coming to Lee's Army, and, as Bevin Alexander observed, it resulted in "letters from home, which reflected the despair and helplessness of families and friends who had watched Sherman's unchecked progress and witnessed the destruction of their property."[14] Lee's manpower situation became so desperate that in January he and Davis agreed to exchange their African-American prisoners, and in March the Confederate Congress belatedly passed a bill to recruit African-American soldiers.[15]

Because of the continued incompetence of General Benjamin Butler, Wilmington, North Carolina, remained open to blockade-runners as 1865 began. After Sherman captured Atlanta and Mobile was blocked, Grant had given his approval for troops to be used in an amphibious assault designed to close Wilmington. Similarly, Lee had sent a division of troops to defend the city; President Davis overruled Lee's choice of a commander and put his friend, Braxton Bragg, in command there instead of his enemy, P. G. T. Beauregard.

On Christmas Eve, Butler exploded a naval vessel near Fort Fisher, guarding the approach to Wilmington, in an effort to destroy that fort. As early as December 3, Grant had expressed his skepticism about the exploding-ship tactic: "Owing to some preparations Admiral Porter and Gen. Butler are making to blow up Fort Fisher, and which, whilst I hope for the best, do not believe a particle in.... "[16]

The ship explosion was a fiasco—as was Butler's Christmas Day amphibious assault on Fort Fisher. Infuriated that Butler had ignored his orders to at least besiege the fort, Grant urged Lincoln to relieve Butler of his command. On January 4, 1865, Lincoln at long last removed the political general, who had, in the words of Chris Fonvielle, a "singular blend of arrogance and military ineptitude." Having approved Sherman's plans for a march up through the Carolinas, Grant was determined not only to close Wilmington to Confederate commerce, but to capture and open it as a means of resupplying Sherman via the Cape Fear River and Wilmington's three railroads. Grant then designated Brigadier (Brevet Major) General Alfred H. Terry as Butler's replacement to cooperate with Admiral Porter in taking Fort Fisher and Wilmington.[17]

On January 13, Terry landed his 9,000 troops four miles north of the fort. The next day, Porter softened the Confederate land defenses by shelling the fort's guns protecting that side. On January 15, Terry and Porter continued their coordination and successfully stormed the weakened fort with a combined force of soldiers, sailors, and marines. Bragg, who had ignored numerous pleas from Fort Fisher for reinforcements, simply returned to Richmond.[18]

In order to get the additional manpower needed to complete the capture of Wilmington, Grant assigned General Schofield and his 23rd Corps, which only recently had come east from Tennessee after helping to repel Hood. Schofield, who superseded Terry as the Union commander by virtue of his seniority, arrived with one division on February 7 and began his advance on February 11. A combined naval and ground assault resulted in the February 19 capture of Fort Anderson, close to the city. The Union forces continued their assaults as they approached the city. As the Federals drew closer, Bragg returned from Richmond just in time to evacuate Wilmington, the Confederacy's last port city, on the night of February 21–22.

The fall of Wilmington opened three rail routes for possible resupply of Sherman's ongoing advance into the Carolinas. Grant seized upon this new opportunity, and sent railroad rolling stock by water from Virginia to reinforce and supply Sherman. The city's fall also opened the Cape Fear River, which also immediately was used to supply Sherman at Fayetteville. Conversely, no more foreign supplies would come to Lee or Johnston through the Union blockade.[19] Grant's investment of troops in the Wilmington campaign, therefore, paid real dividends. As Fionvielle concluded, "The fall of Wilmington did not end the Confederacy, but it hastened its downfall by guaranteeing the success of Sherman's Carolinas Campaign."[20]

SHERMAN MARCHES THROUGH THE CAROLINAS

On February 1, Sherman left Savannah for the major offensive thrust of 1865. His men were eager to wreak havoc in South Carolina. One Union soldier exclaimed, "Here is where treason began, and by God, here is where it will end!"[21] Sherman wrote to Halleck that he almost trembled at the fate of South Carolina.[22] With that fervor, Sherman's soldiers advanced through the wintry swamps of southern South Carolina at a pace that amazed their opponents. In a manner similar to the March to the Sea, Slocum's Army of Georgia made up the left wing of the advance, Howard's Army of the Tennessee was the right wing, and Brevet Major General Kilpatrick led the Third Cavalry Division. They headed for the South Carolina capital of Columbia while cavalry bluffed movements toward Augusta, Georgia, on the left and Charleston, South Carolina, on the right.[23]

As in 1864, Sherman still had concerns about the possibility of Lee shifting troops to oppose his advance:

.... [T]he only serious question that occurred to me was, would General Lee sit down in Richmond (besieged by General Grant), and permit us, almost unopposed, to pass through the States of South and North Carolina, cutting off and consuming the very supplies on which he depended to feed his army in Virginia, or would he make an effort to escape from General Grant, and endeavor to catch us inland somewhere between Columbia and Raleigh?[24]

The answer was the same as in 1864: Lee would not move any troops from his beloved Virginia to oppose Sherman. He did, however, allow the 14,000 troops who had been defending Fort Fisher, Wilmington, and its environs to remain in North Carolina.[25]

Virtually unopposed, therefore, Sherman raced over the rivers and through the swamps of South Carolina to the capital at Columbia. The only delays were to rebuild burned bridges, corduroy roads, and fend off cavalry skirmishers. Columbia was burned on February 17; controversy still exists as to whether the wind-driven fire's primary cause was Confederates' torching of their cotton stockpiles or arson by drunken Union soldiers and other looters. Sherman's juggernaut moved on.[26]

Sherman's march on Columbia cut many of the railroad connections to Charleston and compelled the military evacuation of that "Cradle of the Confederacy" on February 15. Beauregard positioned his forces forty-five miles north of Columbia to protect Charlotte, North Carolina. Sherman, however, moved northeast toward Goldsboro and unification with Schofield and at least 21,000 soldiers who previously had entered North Carolina to capture Wilmington and were now moving inland.[27]

As Sherman approached and then moved into North Carolina, Jefferson Davis belatedly and reluctantly allowed Lee to reinstate Davis's old enemy, Joseph Johnston, as commander of the remnants of the Army of Tennessee, Hardee's corps, Hampton's cavalry, and ultimately Bragg's Department of North Carolina. Thus, it was not until February 22 that Lee recalled Joseph Johnston to once again serve as commander of the Army of Tennessee. Lee optimistically ordered him to "concentrate all available forces and drive back Sherman."[28]

Johnston proposed that Lee bring a large number of his troops to North Carolina to join him in his mission to defeat Sherman. This was exactly the merger that Grant and Sherman had been so concerned about since the beginning of their simultaneous campaigns in May 1864. Sherman said, "If Lee is a soldier of genius, he will seek to transfer his army from Richmond to Raleigh or Columbia; if he is a man simply of detail, he will remain where he is, and his speedy defeat is sure."

Hence on March 1, 1865, Johnston posed this critical question to Lee, who declined the prospect and chose instead to wait to turn on Sherman until the Federals had crossed the Roanoke River, a mere fifty-five miles south of Petersburg. At the time of Lee's decision, Johnston had about 21,000 troops to take on Sherman's forces: 60,000 soldiers of his own and perhaps another 30,000 with Schofield coming inland from the North Carolina coast. As it turned out, each Confederate army would lose separately.[29]

From March 8 to 10, Bragg's 8,500 troops halted Schofield's westward movement at Kinston, North Carolina. The delay was temporary only because Sherman's overwhelming force was moving farther northeast with little hindrance. He took Fayetteville on March 11, crossed the Cape Fear and Black rivers, and continued northeast toward a rendezvous with Schofield at Goldsboro. Grant earlier had selected Goldsboro as Sherman's goal because it was the junction of two railroads, the Wilmington & Weldon and the Atlantic and North Carolina, that would facilitate troop and supply movements from Wilmington, New Bern, and Morehead City on the coast.[30]

Slocum's left wing of Sherman's army was delayed by Hardee's troops at Averasboro between the Black and Cape Fear rivers on March 15 and 16.[31] Then from March 19 to 21, two isolated divisions of that wing were attacked by Johnston's combined forces at Bentonville. Sherman's forces incurred 1,500 casualties while inflicting 2,600 on the Confederates. Seeking to avoid a costly end-of-the-war frontal assault on Johnston's lines, Sherman passed up an opportunity to reinforce a breakthrough by one of his divisions.[32]

To avoid the merging Federal forces, Johnston retreated north to Smithfield. As a result, on March 23, Sherman and Schofield merged their forces at Goldsboro into a 90,000-man threat to Johnston's less than 20,000 troops. Sherman's army thus completed its 425-mile march, which historian Bevin Alexander described as "the greatest march in history through enemy territory."[33]

UNION PROGRESS IN VIRGINIA

Things were going no better for the Confederates in the Shenandoah. The forces of both Early and Sheridan had been reduced by wintertime transfers to the Richmond area. At this point, Sheridan decided to end Confederate occupation of any part of the Shenandoah Valley and promptly did so. He moved south on February 25 and pushed aside Early's cavalry at Mount Crawford on March 2. The next day, Sheridan decimated Early's infantry at Waynesboro. Early retreated through the Blue Ridge Mountains toward

Charlottesville, thereby ending any Confederate army presence in the valley that had once been its primary breadbasket in the East.

On the Petersburg front, meanwhile, Grant was making survival more difficult for the Army of Northern Virginia. His Army of 118,000 faced Lee's army of 68,000 (56,000 fit for fighting) along more than a 30-mile front.[34] On February 5 to 7, Grant pushed back the Confederates at Hatcher's Run on the far western end of the lines below and west of Petersburg and then extended his (and, in response, the Confederate) lines an additional two miles. Grant's army was inching closer to the South Side Railroad and the Boydton Plank Road, key supply routes for Lee's army.[35]

In addition, Grant's continual extension of his line was weakening Lee's defensive strength by stretching out his defenders. In August 1864, Lee had about 65,000 soldiers defending a 27-mile front—2,500 men per mile. By March 1865, however, Lee was defending a 35-mile front with 53,000 troops—a greatly reduced 1,500 men per mile.[36]

Not only was Grant stretching and weakening Lee's line, he also was fortifying his own so efficiently that he freed up men to launch the final campaign of the war. David W. Lowe explained this development:

> In the war's last months, Federal engineers strengthened every fort on the Petersburg front into a self-sufficient fortress capable of meeting an assault from any direction. Artillery fields of fire were carefully refined, using diverse facings and restricting embrasures to generate the maximum degree of mutual support among the forts. The engineers proposed to denude the connecting parapets of troops and place the brunt of defense on the artillery and garrisons of 150-300 men— about 900 men per mile of front—certainly the most efficient use of entrenchments of the war.[37]

In a desperate attempt to force Grant to shorten his lines and perhaps aid an escape of Lee's army to North Carolina, Lee launched a March 25 pre-dawn assault from his Petersburg lines on Fort Stedman. Although initially successful in capturing that fort (perhaps because the defenders thought the attackers were deserters coming over to their lines), the Confederate attackers were driven back or surrounded by an immediate counterattack and deadly crossfire from every direction—particularly from the well-positioned nearby forts. The survivors who were not trapped retreated without the 4,000 of their comrades who were killed, wounded, or captured. Grant's army had lost a few more than a thousand men. That was to be Lee's last offensive.[38]

On March 26, Lieutenant Colonel Elisha Hunt Rhodes reported on the previous day's happenings:

> We had a very exciting day yesterday. At daylight the Rebels charged upon Fort Stedman on the 9th Corps front and got possession. Our division was ordered to march to the relief of the 9th Corps. The distance was about five miles, and we made it at a double quick most of the time and arrived in season to see a Division commanded by [Brigadier] Gen. John [F.] Hartranft of Penn. recapture the fort with many prisoners. We got a good shelling as we passed the Rebel forts and lost two horses from our division.[39]

The failure of this desperate Confederate assault on Fort Stedman affected both Lee and Grant. Lee finally argued to Davis that his army should attempt to join with Johnston to defeat Sherman and then turn on Grant. On the other side of the lines, Grant sensed an enhanced opportunity to end the stalemate. On March 24, he had issued orders to Meade for a movement by Ord and Sheridan that was to begin on the 29th, with Ord bringing three divisions from the far right to the far left of Grant's lines. Grant said that the movement was "for the double purpose of turning the enemy out of his present position around Petersburg, and to insure the success of the Cavalry under general Sheridan . . . in its efforts to reach and destroy the South Side and Danville rail-road[s]."[40] Lee's losses at Fort Stedman improved the prospects for success on the far left.[41]

Using Ord's men to fill the lines vacated by the Second Corps, Grant completed the shift of manpower to create a mobile force of Major General Andrew A. Humphreys' Second and Warren's Fifth infantry corps, plus Sheridan's 9,000-man cavalry corps. With that force, Grant intended to finally get around the Confederate right flank and cut off the Southside and Danville railroads, the last ones supplying, respectively, Petersburg and Richmond. The Union troops started moving west on the 27th, and Lee sent Fitzhugh Lee's cavalry and Major General George E. Pickett with five brigades of infantry to oppose them. By moving at least 5,500 cavalry and 5,000 infantry southwest out of the Petersburg fortifications, Lee was fulfilling one of Grant's goals: drawing the Confederates into a fight with few, if any, fortifications.[42]

On March 29, Elisha Hunt Rhodes expressed anticipation of a movement and confidence in his commanders: "Still on picket and very quiet, although every man is on the alert. Something is about to happen. We are all ready to move, and if I did not know our leaders I should feel that we were in trouble and about to retreat. But I feel sure that the enemy are [sic] about to leave Petersburg, and we are held in readiness to pursue them."[43]

March 29 saw a successful advance by two of Warren's Fifth Corps divisions onto the key Boydton Plank Road as a result of their success at the Battle of Lewis' Farm. Encouraged by this development, Grant told Sheridan to forget a railroad raid and instead work with the Fifth Corps to turn the Confederate flank. When

Sheridan asked instead for the Sixth Corps, with which he had worked in the Shenandoah Valley, Grant pointed out the Fifth Corps' position closer to Sheridan and declined his request.[44]

The Fifth Corps stayed in place on March 30 because of heavy rain, the issuance of three days' rations, and confusion about their orders. On the 31st, however, at White Oak Road (Gravelly Run or Hatcher's Run), Warren allowed two of his four divisions to be separately attacked and routed before he finally drove back Confederate Major General Bushrod R. Johnson's infantry division across White Oak Road. Union casualties totaled almost 1,900, while Johnson reported that he lost 800. The action, however, did prevent Johnson from reinforcing Pickett, who faced Sheridan farther west. Grant and Meade took critical note of Warren's performance and wondered why he had allowed the enemy troops to entrench after their retreat.[45]

DINWIDDIE COURT HOUSE AND FIVE FORKS

To the west of the Fifth Corps on that same day, Pickett and Fitzhugh Lee hit Sheridan's strung-out 9,500 troopers hard in the Battle of Dinwiddie Court House[46] and forced them back until Sheridan actively oversaw a last-ditch stand to avoid collapse. With the Confederates on the offensive throughout that day, Sheridan imposed 750 to 1,000 casualties on them while suffering only 360 to 400 himself. Although he had been stymied by Pickett from reaching Five Forks, Sheridan saw an opportunity. That evening he told one of Grant's aides, "[Pickett's] force is in more danger than I am in—if I am cut off from the Army of the Potomac, it is cut off from Lee's army, and not a man in it should ever be allowed to get back to Lee."[47]

Nearby, Colonel Elisha Hunt Rhodes heard the fighting and wrote, "The fight has raged all day on the 2nd Corps front to our left, and we have been under arms waiting for something to turn up. It means fight within a few hours, and may God give us a victory. Grant knows what he is doing and I am willing to trust him to manage Army affairs."[48] Colonel Rhodes would not be disappointed.

On the evening of March 31, Grant agreed with Sheridan's assessment of Pickett's isolation and vulnerability. Therefore, Grant ordered Warren, through Meade, to withdraw a division and send it to reinforce Sheridan. Meade at first sent only a brigade, but within hours Grant accepted a Meade recommendation and ordered Warren to move his entire corps west to strike Pickett. Due to delayed and confused orders and the prior destruction of a key bridge, Warren's corps arrived on the morning of April 1—well after Sheridan expected them. As soon as he was ordered to reinforce Sheridan, Warren had told Meade that he would have to build a replacement bridge over the swollen Gravelly Run; that forty-foot bridge was completed at 2:00 a.m. Sheridan, unaware of Warren's difficulties, wanted to attack immediately but had to delay until the arrival of all Warren's troops. Warren inexplicably and foolishly waited three hours before personally reporting to Sheridan at 11:00 a.m., and Sheridan's anger at Warren increased as the day progressed.[49]

During the night, Pickett had learned of the approach of Warren's infantry, which threatened to isolate him, and withdrew from Dinwiddie Court House back to a more secure line at Five Forks. During that movement, Pickett received a forceful and unfriendly message from Robert E. Lee: "Hold Five Forks at all hazards. Protect road to Ford's Depot and prevent Union forces from striking the Southside Railroad. Regret exceedingly your forced withdrawal, and your inability to hold the advantage you gained."[50]

Lee correctly appreciated the value of Five Forks in protecting the South Side Railroad, but he probably failed to appreciate the difficult situation faced by Pickett with only about 10,000 soldiers defending a mile and three-quarter line and opposed by an increasingly superior adversary. Pickett advised Lee of his situation and requested a diversionary action. Inexplicably, he and his cavalry commander, Fitzhugh Lee, negligently left the front lines and joined Major General Thomas L. Rosser at his shad bake behind Hatcher's Run, perhaps a mile from the front. Fitzhugh Lee went even after being advised that Union cavalry had driven away the Confederate cavalry between the Confederates at Five Forks and the rest of the Army of Northern Virginia. It was to be a costly fish fry.[51]

At 4:00 p.m., the Battle of Five Forks finally got under way. Sheridan's 10,000 cavalry generally dismounted, manned the bulk of the attacking Union line, and took the brunt of the Rebel defenders' fire. To Sheridan's right, Warren's 12,000 troops were to come in on the left flank of Pickett's infantry. Because of an erroneous map and faulty reconnaissance, Warren's troops were misaligned and got into the fight only after changing the direction of their march. Warren desperately directed his divisions toward the fighting and even chased down one that had marched well past the battle. Brigadier General Joshua Chamberlain worked with Sheridan on the front lines to throw all available troops into the struggle as Pickett's leaderless troops bravely held on but finally broke and ran. One reason they broke is that the bulk of Warren's troops finally appeared on their flank and rear. Back at the shad bake, Pickett and Fitzhugh Lee learned of the battle from couriers. Pickett got through to Five Forks to participate in the rout while Lee was trapped behind Hatcher's Run with Rosser's cavalry.[52]

After the prior night's delayed march by Warren's Fifth Corps, although primarily the fault of Meade and a missing bridge, Grant had authorized Sheridan to relieve Warren of command. Sheridan had no qualms about using that authority after Warren's "tardy" arrival, his misdirected attack, and his absence from the front lines while he retrieved his errant divisions. When Warren's chief of staff reported to Sheridan late in the battle, Sheridan told him, "By God, sir, tell General Warren he wasn't in the fight." When a subordinate suggested that he rethink his decision, Sheridan roared, "Reconsider, hell! I don't reconsider my decisions. Obey the order!" At 7:00 p.m. a messenger brought Warren written orders replacing him as corps commander with Brigadier General Charles Griffin, who was promptly promoted to major general.[53]

With the sacking of Warren behind him, Grant had completed a clean sweep of all his senior commanders except Meade as he entered the final phase of the war. A. A. Humphreys had succeeded the ailing Hancock as Second Corps commander; Wright had replaced the dead Sedgwick at the Sixth Corps; John G. Parke had replaced Burnside, who had long commanded the Ninth Corps; John Gibbon had replaced Baldy Smith at the 24th Corps; and Ord had replaced the incompetent Butler as Commander of the Army of the James.[54] All involved were major generals. The new leadership guaranteed there would be no hesitation in the war's last days.

Sheridan's cavalry and Warren's infantry had achieved a great victory at Five Forks, devastated Pickett's command, killed or wounded more than 500, taken between 2,000 and 2,500 prisoners, turned Lee's right flank, and opened the way to the South Side Railroad. Remnants of Pickett's five brigades were in full retreat, and Grant ordered artillery fire all along the line in anticipation of a full-scale attack the next day. After receiving news of the Sheridan/Warren victory from Colonel Porter, Grant quietly retired to his tent, drafted orders, and then announced to the celebrating officers, "I have ordered a general assault along the lines."[55]

BREAKTHROUGH AT PETERSBURG

April 2 was a critical day in the history and ultimate demise of the Army of Northern Virginia. Following up on the victory at Five Forks the preceding day, Union troops captured Sutherland Station on the South Side Railroad, four miles east of Five Forks, and thereby severed Lee's last lifeline to Petersburg. More significantly, Union forces executed Grant's order for an all-out assault on the Confederate lines at Petersburg, which he assumed would be weakened by Lee's manpower shifts to the west. Grant also attacked to preclude any possible counterattack on Five Forks by the ever-aggressive Lee.[56]

Wright's Sixth Corps exploited a weakness where a creek breached the Confederate line, used a 14,000-man wedge to attack at first light (about 4:40 a.m.) along a one-mile front, and by 5:15 a.m. had achieved a complete breakthrough. Alongside Wright, Ord and Humphreys's corps were likewise successful in overrunning the Confederate lines in their fronts. At midday, Grant's forces assaulted two Confederate forts at Petersburg; they captured one, and the defenders of the other then fled. Lee sent President Davis a message, saying, "I think it is absolutely necessary that we should abandon our position to-night...." It was delivered to Davis as he attended Sunday church services in Richmond. Davis immediately began preparations for the Confederate Government and treasury to leave Richmond by rail.[57]

Grant's well-conceived assault broke Lee's line, killed Lieutenant General A. P. Hill, compelled the evacuation of Petersburg and

Richmond, and sent Lee's army in a westward retreat. He accomplished these tasks with fewer casualties than he imposed on the Rebels. While Grant may have suffered casualties of about 4,000, Lee's army lost between 5,000 and 5,500—about 10 percent of Lee's remaining force. As A. Wilson Greene concluded, "The engagements of April 2 doomed the Confederate war effort in Virginia."[58]

THE CHASE TO APPOMATTOX

Before abandoning Richmond, Lee ordered the burning of large quantities of Confederate supplies in the city. The resulting fires burned much of Richmond. As Grant's troops occupied the city on April 3, Lee's army fled westward. The Appomattox Campaign had begun.[59] The Rebel troops generally followed the Appomattox River on their 90-mile retreat, but were slowed by having to cross and re-cross the river and its tributary creeks. Their flight was accompanied by Union cavalry and infantry moving on their left flank in order to keep them from moving toward North Carolina and Johnston—as well as by Union forces following directly behind them.

Lee's plan was to have his forces head for Amelia Court House on the Richmond and Danville (R&D) Railroad, where Lee later claimed rations and supplies were supposed to be waiting. None were there, however, when the Confederates arrived on April 5. It is quite possible that Lee's staff, specifically Colonel Walter Taylor, failed to issue an order for those materials in the haste of evacuating Richmond (and Taylor's haste to get to his evening wedding on April 2). More significantly, Lee had to wait an extra day at Amelia Court House for Ewell's column, which was delayed in crossing the Appomattox River by a missing pontoon bridge.[60] Lee's predicament was worsened by the fact that some of Grant's cavalry had

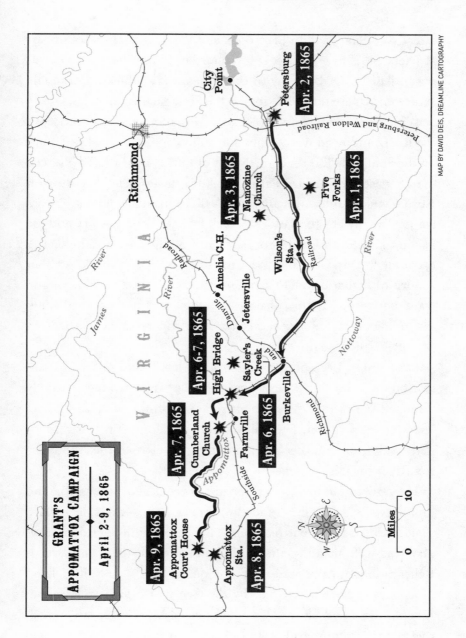

GRANT'S
APPOMATTOX CAMPAIGN
————◆————
April 2-9, 1865

Apr. 9, 1865
Appomattox
Court House

Apr. 8, 1865
Appomattox
Sta.

Apr. 7, 1865
Cumberland
Church

Apr. 6-7, 1865
High Bridge

Apr. 6, 1865
Burkeville

Sayler's
Creek

Farmville

Jetersville

Amelia C.H.

Apr. 3, 1865
Namozine
Church

Wilson's
Sta.

Richmond

City
Point

Petersburg
Apr. 2, 1865

Five
Forks
Apr. 1, 1865

VIRGINIA

James River

Appomattox

Nottoway River

Danville Railroad

Southside Railroad

Richmond and Danville Railroad

Petersburg and Weldon Railroad

Miles
0   10

MAP BY DAVID DEIS, DREAMLINE CARTOGRAPHY

already gotten ahead of his troops and were eight miles southwest at Jetersville astride the R&D. Even farther southwest, by the morning of April 6 Ord's Army of the James was at Burke (Burkeville Junction), where the R&D joined the Southside Railroad.[61]

With the R&D forcefully blocked, Lee had no choice but to leave the R&D and head west. Hoping to find supplies from Lynchburg on the Southside Railroad northwest of Burke, Lee ordered a forced march westward toward Farmville. But disaster befell his army on April 6 when Anderson's and Early's divisions fell behind and were trapped at Sayler's (or Sailor's) Creek by Sheridan's cavalry and the Second and Sixth Union corps. Overlooking the battlefield, Lee exclaimed, "My God, has the army dissolved?" He did lose about a third of it that day. The Confederates lost most of their wagon train, had about 2,000 killed or wounded, and had another 7,000 (including at least nine generals) taken prisoner—at a cost to Grant of only 1,200 casualties.[62]

On April 6, Lee's hungry survivors at last found rations in railcars on the Southside Railroad at Farmville. They had only partially removed the rations when the arrival of trailing Federal soldiers ended that operation. The railcars were moved west toward Appomattox Station, and Lee's remaining forces crossed the Appomattox River for the last time.[63]

Lee now found his army trapped between the Appomattox and James rivers. His soldiers headed west once again—this time toward a place called Appomattox Court House. But Phil Sheridan's cavalry was well ahead of them. He had captured the trainloads of Rebel rations at Appomattox Station on the Southside Railroad and blocked any farther advance by the Army of Northern Virginia. Lincoln, who had been at City Point since March 24, saw a positive report from Sheridan and on the morning of April 7 wired

Grant, "Gen. Sheridan says 'If the thing is pressed I think that Lee will surrender.' Let the *thing* be pressed."[64] That apparently was Lincoln's last written communication to Grant, who did indeed press the thing.

Grant recognized that the human chess match was nearly over, and on the afternoon of April 7 made his first overture to Lee:

> General, The result of the last week must convince you of the hopelessness of further resistance on the part of the Army of Northern Va. in this struggle. I feel that it is so and regard it as my duty to shift from myself, the responsibility of any further effusion of blood by asking of you the surrender of that portion of the C. S. Army known as the Army of Northern Va.[65]

That night, his Army's third consecutive night of marching, Lee responded with an inquiry about the terms Grant would allow:

> General, I have recd your note of this date. Though not entertaining the opinion you express of the hopelessness of further resistance on the part of the Army of N. Va. I reciprocate your desire to avoid useless effusion of blood & therefore before Considering your proposition ask the terms you will offer on condition of its surrender.[66]

Lee's response was delayed by delivery difficulties and did not arrive until the morning of April 8. Grant promptly responded with a minimal requirement:

> Your note of last evening, in reply to mine of same date, asking the conditions on which I will accept the surrender of the Army of N. Va. is just received. In reply I would say that *peace* being my great desire there is but one condition I insist

upon, namely: that the men and officers surrendered shall be disqualified for taking up arms again, against the Government of the United States, until properly exchanged.

I will meet you or will designate Officers to meet any officers you may name for the same purpose, at any point agreeable to you, for the purpose of arranging definitely the terms upon which the surrender of the Army of N. Va. will be received.[67]

In a response to Grant that night, Lee expressed an unrealistic view that the end was not necessarily imminent but then reluctantly agreed to a meeting with Grant:

General, I recd at a late hour your note of today—In mine of yesterday I did not intend to propose the Surrender of the Army of N. Va—but to ask the terms of your proposition. To be frank, I do not think the emergency has arisen to call for the Surrender of this Army; but as the restoration of peace should be the Sole object of all, I desired to know whether your proposals would lead to that end. I cannot therefore meet you with a view to Surrender the Army of N– Va—but as far as your proposal may affect the C. S. forces under my Command & tend to the restoration of peace, I should be pleased to meet you at 10 A m tomorrow on the old stage road to Richmond between the picket lines of the two armies—[68]

Although Lee may not yet have been willing to accept the inevitable, several of his officers were. They held an informal council, and one of them, Brigadier General William Nelson Pendleton, approached Longstreet about advising Lee to surrender. Refusing to do so, Longstreet responded, "If General Lee doesn't know when to surrender until I tell him, he will never know."[69]

The next morning everyone knew that the time for surrender had arrived. As Confederates attempted a massive breakout under orders from Lee and challenged Sheridan's cavalry, they clearly observed six infantry brigades of Ord's Army of the James behind the cavalry, poised to attack. The Second, Fifth, and Sixth corps all were circling Lee's beleaguered army. Escape was not possible. Grant had Lee's army bottled up.[70]

Earlier that same morning, before the final military confrontation, Grant had declined to meet Lee on Lee's terms. Instead, based on his instructions from Lincoln, Grant rejected Lee's peace discussion overture in a note he sent to Lee:

> Your note of yesterday is received. As I have no authority to treat on the subject of peace the meeting proposed for 10 a.m. to-day could lead to no good. I will state however General that I am equally anxious for peace with yourself and the whole North entertains the same feeling. The terms upon which peace can be had are well understood. By the South laying down their Arms they will hasten that most desirable event, save thousands of human lives and hundreds of Millions of property not yet destroyed.
>
> Sincerely hoping that all our difficulties may be settled without the loss of another live [*sic*] I subscribe myself . . .[71]

After receiving Grant's response and receiving the reports of his surrounded Army's hopeless condition, Lee finally decided to surrender and went into the Union lines looking for Grant. As Lee went through the Union lines under a flag of truce, he belatedly remembered that the outgunned Confederates facing Ord and others ought to send out a flag of truce of their own. As Lee directed, Longstreet sent an officer with the white flag just as a Federal offensive was about to start. That officer was accompanied back to the Rebel lines by a brash Union cavalry commander, Major General George A. Custer, who made a pompous demand for the Confederate army's unconditional surrender. When Custer repeated his demand to Longstreet, the First Corps commander dressed down Custer and told him he could either wait for Lee or attack. A humbled Custer returned to his lines, and all awaited developments at the highest level.[72]

When he was unable to find Grant, Lee wrote to him: "General: I received your note of this morning on the picket line, whither I had come to meet you and ascertain definitely what terms were embraced in your proposal of yesterday with reference to the surrender of this army. I now request an interview in accordance with the offer contained in your letter of yesterday, for that pu[r]pose."[73]

Their subordinate officers quickly arranged for the historic meeting of Grant and Lee in Appomattox Court House at the home of Wilmer McLean. (The unfortunate Mr. McLean had moved to that peaceful town after his home had been hit by artillery during the First Battle of Bull Run [Manassas] in 1861.) During the rather awkward meeting, Grant extended generous terms to Lee. He paroled Lee's 28,000 remaining men and allowed his officers to keep their horses. The only condition was that the Confederates not again take up arms against the United States. After confirming Lee's acceptance of his terms, Grant asked for writing materials and reduced the terms to writing on the spot. He agreed to Lee's additional request that any artilleryman or cavalryman who had brought his own horse to war could take one horse back home; Grant said that would help in the planting of crops. At Lee's request, Grant ordered Sheridan to provide rations for Lee's men. They then signed the surrender agreement, and Lee departed.[74]

Although there were about one hundred minor engagements elsewhere before all fighting ceased, Lee's surrender to Grant on April 9, 1865, effectively ended the Civil War. Once again Grant had achieved his goal with a reasonable loss of men. During the entire expanded Appomattox Campaign (including Five Forks), about 9,000 of Grant's 113,000 soldiers (8 percent) were killed or wounded as they broke through the Petersburg lines and pursued Lee to Appomattox. They killed or wounded almost 7,000 of Lee's almost 50,000 troops (13.5 percent) and took thousands of prisoners along the way.[75]

In the chase from Petersburg to Appomattox Courthouse, Grant used about 80,000 troops to pursue more than 50,000 Confederates. Appomattox Campaign historian William Marvel described how, on April 9, Confederate General Gordon claimed in an address to his troops that Lee surrendered only 8,000 troops to Grant's 60,000 and thus started the myth of Appomattox Campaign numbers relied upon by defenders of The Lost Cause. Rejecting claims by Lee's adjutant, Colonel Walter Taylor, that Lee faced 6:1 odds and had only 25,000 troops as the Appomattox pursuit began, Marvel carefully reviewed the official records and other sources and concluded that Lee started the chase with between 51,000 and 57,000 men. Marvel pointed out that the numbers of Gordon and Taylor are difficult to reconcile with the published list of 28,231 Confederates who surrendered and were paroled at Appomattox. Similarly, Marvel demolished Taylor's claim that Grant had 162,000 troops and instead concluded that Grant started the chase with about 80,000 men—less than a two-to-one edge.[76] Thus, Lee still had a huge force at his disposal as he abandoned Petersburg and Richmond, but Grant's aggressive pursuit with a somewhat larger force quickly brought Lee's army to bay.

As Assistant Secretary of War Charles A. Dana concluded, "Grant in eleven months secured the prize with less loss than his predecessors suffered in failing to win it during a struggle of three years."[77] To the end, therefore, Grant had not been a butcher. He was persistent, aggressive, dogged, and determined, but he rarely incurred unnecessary casualties. During the Appomattox Campaign, as was his usual practice, he maneuvered his army and avoided frontal assaults as best he could and attacked when he believed he had to. With Lee's surrender, Grant had demonstrated that he knew what had to be done to achieve victory, and he had done it.

Twelve

GRANT'S WINNING
CHARACTERISTICS

Ulysses Grant acquired the unfortunate and unfair label of "butcher" because of the 1864 campaign of adhesion he conducted against Robert E. Lee to secure final victory for the Union. It was toward the end of that campaign that some began using the word "butcher" or "murderer" to describe him.[1] However, as Russell F. Weigley concluded, "There is no good reason to believe that the Army of Northern Virginia could have been destroyed within an acceptable time by any other means than the hammer blows of Grant's army."[2] Such an aggressive campaign inevitably would result in heavy Union losses, and, again in Weigley's words, "[i]t was the grim campaign to destroy the Confederacy by destroying Lee's army that was to give Grant his reputation as a butcher."[3]

Writing in 1898, Charles Dana, assistant secretary of war during the Civil War, examined the specific casualties suffered by Union troops in the East under Grant's predecessors and then under Grant. Under Generals McDowell, McClellan, Pope, Burnside, Hooker, and Meade, the Union's eastern armies, according to Dana's table of statistics, had 15,745 killed, 76,079 wounded, and 52,101 missing or captured for a total of 143,925 casualties between May 24, 1861, and May 4, 1864. Dana then calculated Grant's losses between May 5, 1864, and April 9, 1865, as 15,139 killed, 77,748 wounded, and 31,503 missing or captured for a total of 124,390. Dana concluded that these numbers show that "Grant in eleven months secured the prize with less loss than his predecessors suffered in failing to win it during a struggle of three years."[4]

Grant's direct, aggressive approach to war was reflected in his statement, "The art of war is simple enough. Find out where your enemy is. Get at him as soon as you can. Strike at him as hard as you can and as often as you can, and keep moving on." As renowned Civil War scholar T. Harry Williams concluded, Grant, however, was an enigma to many: "He hated war, and yet found his place there above all his fellows. No wonder he is difficult to understand, and no wonder he has not been more fully appreciated." While the strategy fascinated him, he loathed the actual slaughter.[5]

GRANT VERSUS LEE

Both Grant and Lee were proactive, aggressive generals,[6] but it was only Grant whose aggressiveness was consistent with the strategic aims of his government. The Confederacy only needed to keep from being conquered;[7] Lee acted as though the Confederacy had to conquer the North. On the contrary, the Union had the burden of conquering the South, and Grant appropriately went on the offensive throughout the war. Lee needed a tie but went for the win, while Grant needed a win, went for it, and achieved it.

Not only did Grant recognize the need for the Union armies to be on the offensive, but he also was cognizant of the need for them to damage, destroy, or capture Confederate armies—instead of merely gaining control of geographical positions. He had, in Jean Edward Smith's words, an "instinctive recognition that victory lay in relentlessly hounding a defeated army into surrender."[8] Only three armies surrendered while the Civil War raged: Buckner's at Fort Donelson, Pemberton's at Vicksburg, and Lee's at Appomattox. They all surrendered to Ulysses S. Grant.

According to T. Harry Williams, Lee, unlike Grant, had little interest in a global strategy for winning the war, and

> what few suggestions [Lee] did make to his government about operations in other theaters than his own indicate that he had little aptitude for grand planning. . . . Fundamentally Grant was superior to Lee because, placed in the situation of a modern total war, he had a modern mind, and Lee did not. . . . The modernity of Grant's mind was most apparent in his grasp of the concept that war was becoming total and that the destruction of the enemy's economic resources was as effective and legitimate a form of warfare as the destruction of his armies.[9]

The other sharp contrast between Grant and Lee was in the use of their manpower resources. Although the Confederacy was outnumbered 4:1 in white men of fighting age, Lee decimated his army in a continuous series of offensives, lost 80,000 wounded and killed in his first fourteen months in command, and lost a total of 121,000 wounded and killed during the war—far higher than any other Civil War general.[10] "Lee lost more troops than any other general in the war and 'if a general could be called a butcher, Lee is probably more of a butcher than Grant,' said [historian Gordon] Rhea."[11] Geoffrey Perret commented on this paradox: "After Cold Harbor, [Grant] was an easy target for those who called him 'Butcher Grant.' Lee was more reckless with men's lives, yet got away with it. The list of costly, doomed frontal assaults in Lee's career is remarkably long, but he was not known as 'Butcher Lee.'"[12] In contrast, Grant had resources to spare, used them sparingly (with limited exceptions) as long as he could, and lost a militarily tolerable 94,000 killed and wounded during the entire war.[13] Their total casualties, including missing and captured, are more difficult to calculate, but Lee's certainly exceeded Grant's.[14]

Perhaps the most revealing comparison of Grant and Lee is the different percentages of men killed and wounded in the battles they fought. According to McWhiney and Jamieson in *Attack and Die*, in the battles for which reliable statistics exist, Grant had an average of 18.1 percent of his men killed or wounded while killing or wounding about 20.7 percent of the enemy (a positive difference of 2.6 percent). On the other hand, Lee had an average of about 20.2 percent of his troops killed or wounded while killing or wounding about 15.4 percent of the enemy (a negative difference of 5.2 percent).[15] Amazingly, these statistics do not include the more than 78,000 Confederate troops who surrendered to Grant (14,000 at Fort Donelson, 29,500 at Vicksburg, and about 35,000 during the Appomattox Campaign).

In sharp contrast to Lee and McClellan, Grant rarely pleaded for reinforcements. Grant did the best he could with the resources he had—a trait he identified with, and probably acquired from, his Mexican War idol, Zachary Taylor.[16] Even when he could have used more troops, he made do with what he had. Lincoln confirmed this when he said, "General Grant is a copious worker and fighter, but a very meager writer or telegrapher. [Grant] doesn't worry and bother me. He isn't shrieking for reinforcements all the time. He takes what troops we can safely give him . . . and does the best he can with what he has got."[17]

Grant's armies incurred the bulk of their casualties in 1864 when he launched a deliberately aggressive offensive to emasculate Lee's army and end the war. During Grant's series of 1862 to 1863 successes, his forces suffered only 23,551 killed and wounded. When he fought in the East in 1864 to 1865, his killed and wounded totaled 70,620. Thus, his armies' total wartime killed and wounded were 94,171.[18] As indicated in Appendix III, Grant's total casualties (killed, wounded, and missing/captured) in Virginia in 1864 to 1865 were about 116,954.[19] However, that number compares favorably with the 143,925 Union casualties in the East before Grant arrived and the 91,400 Union casualties that had been incurred in just the seventeen days of fighting at Seven Days', Second Manassas, Antietam, Fredericksburg, Chancellorsville, and Gettysburg—with no concrete results to show for them.[20]

The classic example of Grant's aggressive, successful campaigns of maneuver that achieved great success with moderate casualties is his brilliant Vicksburg campaign of 1863, described by Weigley as "one of the masterpieces of military history."[21] Although that campaign "was built on speed and deception and military brilliance," Bruce Catton explained, "[Grant] . . . would be written off as a man with a bludgeon, a dull plodder who could win only when he had every advantage and need count no cost."[22]

Vicksburg was the culmination of Grant's offensive western campaigns. Catton summarized those campaigns: "The thrust which began at Cairo and was ending at Vicksburg had never been a matter of piling up overwhelming resources and trusting that something would break under the sheer weight of men and muscle.... This had been a business of finesse, of daring decisions and fast movement, of mental alertness and the ability to see and use an opening before it closed."[23] With a minimum of casualties, Grant deprived the Confederacy of much of Kentucky and Tennessee, made the Mississippi a Union highway, and cut off the western third of the Confederacy. Next, he saved a Union army trapped in Chattanooga and drove the Rebels out of Tennessee and on their heels toward Atlanta.

The pace toward victory, accompanied by an increase in casualties, quickened in 1864 as Grant aggressively pursued Lee and sought to ensure Lincoln's reelection. Meade's Army of the Potomac, under the personal supervision of Grant, did suffer high casualties during its drive to Petersburg and Richmond. However, it imposed an even higher percentage of casualties on Lee's army. Grant's determination to destroy Lee's army was demonstrated by three actions he took during and immediately after the Battle of the Wilderness, the first conflict of that campaign. Within a two-day period, he advised President Lincoln that there would be "no turning back," told his officers to focus on what they could do and not what Lee might do, and made the crucial decision to continue south after the bloody two-day Battle of the Wilderness. As historian Michael C. C. Adams explained, Grant, a westerner, was the first

Federal general in the East not intimidated by Lee and the myth of southern fighting superiority.[24]

Within less than seven weeks, Grant's army compelled Lee to retreat to a nearly besieged position at Richmond and Petersburg, which Lee had previously said would be the death-knell of his own army. Gregory A. Mertz concluded: "The campaign reached Richmond only because Lee retreated to the defenses of the capital city. When U.S. Grant became commander of all Union armies and chose to make his headquarters in the Eastern theater, he intended to take the war to the Army of Northern Virginia and pound Lee into submission. He battled the legendary Confederate leader and his army in the Wilderness and never looked back."[25]

At the same time, Grant was overseeing and facilitating a coordinated attack against Confederate forces all over the nation, particularly William T. Sherman's campaign from the Tennessee border to Atlanta. As he had hoped, Grant succeeded in keeping Lee from sending reinforcements to Georgia. Sherman took Atlanta and thus guaranteed the crucial reelection of Lincoln. Sherman ultimately broke loose on a virtually unimpeded sweep through Georgia and the Carolinas that doomed the Confederacy. Thus, in the words of Herman Hattaway, the war "was decided by Grant's superior strategy: the use of simultaneous advance in widely separated scenes of action."[26] Grant's 1864 nationwide coordinated offensive against the Rebel armies not only won the war but demonstrated that he was a national general with a broad vision, while Lee was a theater general suffering from Virginia myopia.

Furthermore, an analysis of the losses suffered by the four commanders' armies involved in the two major 1864 campaigns reveals that Grant's percentage of casualties, although higher than Sherman's, was better than those of the Confederate commanders:

Armies and Generals	Total Troops	Total Casualties
Army of Tennessee (Johnston/Hood)	66,000	35,000 (53%)[27]
Army of Northern Virginia (Lee)	70,000	42,000 (46%)[28]
Army of the Potomac, etc. (Grant)	122,000	50,000 (41%)[29]
Armies of the Tennessee, Ohio, and Cumberland (Sherman)	110,000	32,000 (29%)[30]

These numbers indicate not that Grant was a butcher, but rather that the Civil War had become savage. The bottom line is that vicious, aggressive fighting involving the significant movement of two large Union forces resulted in significant casualties on both sides in both theaters. By 1864, most combatants were using accurate rifled muskets (often breech-loading rifles), rifled artillery, and sometimes repeating weapons that required less reloading—which cumulatively resulted in more rapid and accurate firing. Soldiers had become expert at quickly creating field fortifications and making almost any assault extremely costly.

OVERVIEW OF GRANT'S CAMPAIGNS

One of the significant ramifications of Grant's butcher label is that Grant's successes have been seriously slighted.[31] He accepted the surrender of three entire Confederate armies—at Fort Donelson in 1862, Vicksburg in 1863, and Appomattox Court House in 1865. No other general on either side accepted the surrender of even one army until Sherman, with Grant's blessing, accepted the North Carolina capitulation of the remnants of the Army of Tennessee in mid-April 1865.

Also overlooked are Grant's numerous 1862 and 1863 successes in the West (Kentucky, Tennessee, and Mississippi). Acting on his own, he occupied Paducah, Kentucky, in early 1862 and then moved on to quickly capture Forts Henry and Donelson, gaining control of the Tennessee and Cumberland Rivers, and thereby putting a dagger in the left flank of the Confederacy. Shortly thereafter, at Shiloh, he recovered from a surprise Rebel attack, saved his army, and won a major victory.

The next year, Grant, again without approval from above, moved his army from the west bank across the Mississippi River to get below Vicksburg, took a daring gamble to feed his army off the countryside, won a series of five battles in eighteen days against total Confederate forces that outnumbered his, and accepted the surrender of Vicksburg and a 29,500-man army on July 4, 1863. James M. McPherson described this campaign's importance: "The capture of Vicksburg was the most important northern strategic victory of the war, perhaps meriting Grant's later assertion that 'the fate of the Confederacy was sealed when Vicksburg fell.'"[32] Russell Weigley discussed Grant's low casualty rate during the Vicksburg Campaign: "[Grant] waged successfully the kind of campaign of maneuver, and eventually of siege, at a low cost in lives, that McClellan had only hoped to wage."[33] The low cost was demonstrated by Grant's 9,400 casualties compared to his foes' 40,700.

As James Arnold concluded, the campaign was Napoleonic in Grant's logistical preparation, use of all available manpower, intelligent risk-taking, flexible adjustments to changing circumstances, and focus on the ultimate goal.[34] This almost flawless campaign resulted in splitting the Confederacy, opening the Mississippi to Union commerce, and impeding the flow of foodstuffs and imported goods from the Trans-Mississippi to Confederate armies east of that river. Just as significantly, the capture of Vicksburg and the simultaneous Union victory at Gettysburg had a combined dev-astating impact on morale throughout the South.

That autumn Lincoln called upon Grant to move into the "Middle Theater" of eastern Tennessee and save a Union army that was trapped in Chattanooga in southeastern Tennessee. When Grant arrived there, Union troops and their livestock were on the verge of starvation. Under his leadership, the Federal forces opened a new supply line, captured Lookout Mountain, carried Missionary Ridge, and drove the Rebel Army of Tennessee into the hills of northern Georgia. That November 1863 victory at Chattanooga set the stage for Sherman's 1864 campaign toward Atlanta, which split the remainder of the Confederacy in half.

Having cleared the Confederates from the Mississippi Valley and eastern Tennessee and having gained Lincoln's confidence in his willingness to fight and ability to win, Grant was summoned to the East in early 1864 to close out the war. He organized a coordinated national strategy, kept pressure on the Confederates on all fronts, and drove Lee's army back to Richmond in a bloody campaign through the Wilderness, Spotsylvania Court House, the North Anna River, Cold Harbor, and Petersburg.

Although this campaign proved costly to the Army of the Potomac, it was fatal for Lee's Army of Northern Virginia. Grant later put the Overland Campaign and its high casualties in perspective:

> The losses inflicted, and endured, were destined to be severe; but the armies now confronting each other had already been in deadly conflict for a period of three years, with immense losses in killed, by death from sickness, cap-

tured and wounded; and neither had made any real progress toward accomplishing the final end.... The campaign now begun was destined to result in heavier losses, to both armies, in a given time, than any previously suffered; but the carnage was to be limited to a single year, and to accomplish all that had been anticipated or desired at the beginning in that time. We had to have hard fighting to achieve this.[35]

Grant took advantage of the fact that Lee had vitiated his outnumbered army in 1862 and 1863, and he successfully conducted a campaign of adhesion against Lee's Army of Northern Virginia. Ever the national general, Grant was concerned all that year that Lee would send reinforcements to oppose Sherman's maneuvers toward and capture of Atlanta. In addition, with Lincoln's prospects in the coming election looking bleak and his reelection so critical to Union victory, Grant felt compelled to be more aggressive than ever to move the war toward an early conclusion. To this end, Grant successfully prevented the reinforcement of the Confederates facing Sherman and satisfied the northern need for a prominent campaign against Lee and Richmond.[36] When Atlanta fell on September 1, the critical reelection of Lincoln was probably assured, and the prospects for Confederate success dimmed considerably.

The following spring, Grant's troops cut off the last open railroad into Petersburg, broke through Lee's lines, outraced the fleeing Army of Northern Virginia, and compelled its surrender at Appomattox Court House on April 9, 1865. Executing Lincoln's policies toward the South, Grant was gracious in his acceptance of Lee's surrender and extended generous terms to Lee's officers and soldiers.

GRANT'S WINNING CHARACTERISTICS

Ulysses Grant won the Civil War. He was responsible for virtually all major Union victories in the West, the "Middle," and the East. What made him such a successful general?

Battling Alcohol Problems. Grant's battle against alcohol problems may have made him not only a better man but also a better general. Any discussion of Grant's traits must deal with his alcohol problem. Persistent rumors of his alleged drunkenness plagued Grant throughout the war. Although he may have inherited alcoholic tendencies from his grandfather, been greatly affected by a little alcohol, and had a drinking problem when separated from his family, Grant is never known to have been drinking—let alone drunk—during battle or at other than quiescent times during the war.[37] Recollections about Grant's drinking during the war may have been embellished by reporter Sylvanus Cadwallader, who was noted for inaccuracies and self-promoting exaggerations, and by John Rawlins, who wanted credit for being the watchdog over Grant's drinking.[38] James McPherson concluded that:

> [Grant's] predisposition to alcoholism may have made him a better general. His struggle for self-discipline enabled him to understand and discipline others; the humiliation of prewar failures gave him a quiet humility that was conspicuously absent from so many generals with a reputation to protect; because Grant had nowhere to go but up, he could act with more boldness and decision than commanders who dared not risk failure.[39]

Modesty. Grant's modesty was a distinguishing trait. One of his acquaintances described him as "a man who could remain silent in several languages." Adam Badeau, his military secretary, discussed his mix of humility and decisiveness:

> Not a sign about him suggested rank or reputation or power. He discussed the most ordinary themes with apparent interest, and turned from them in the same quiet tones, and without a shade of difference in his manner, to decisions that involved the fate of armies, as if great things and small were to him of equal moment. In battle, the sphinx awoke. The outward calm was even then not entirely broken; but the utterance was prompt, the ideas were rapid, the judgment was decisive, the words were those of command. The whole man became intense, as it were, with a white heat.[40]

Lucid Orders. Grant had many other traits that distinguished him from most other Civil War generals. Unlike Lee[41] and many other generals on both sides, Grant's orders were lucid and unambiguous—even when issued in the heat of battle.[42] General Meade's chief of staff commented that "there is one striking feature of Grant's orders; no matter how hurriedly he may write them on the field, no one ever has the slightest doubt as to their meaning, or even has to read them over a second time to understand them."[43] Horace Porter described Grant's drafting of a flurry of orders after his arrival at Chattanooga: "His work was performed swiftly and uninterruptedly, but without any marked display of nervous energy. His thoughts flowed as freely from his mind as the ink from his pen; he was never at a loss for an expression, and seldom interlined a word or made a material correction."[44] R. Steven Jones said, "Historians have always regarded Grant's orders as some of the clearest in the war, rarely leaving room for misunderstanding or misinterpretation."[45]

One reason that Grant's orders were lucid is that they were simple. His oral and written orders tended to be simple and goal-oriented with the means of execution left to the discretion of his subordinates. Jean Edward Smith concluded, "The genius of Grant's command style lay in its simplicity. Better than any Civil War general, Grant recognized the battlefield was in flux. By not specifying movements in detail, he left his subordinate commanders free to exploit whatever opportunities developed."[46] That approach reflected Grant's willingness to delegate discretionary authority to Sherman, Sheridan, Meade, and other subordinates.

Topographical Memory. Historian James McPherson concluded that Grant had a "topographical memory." McPherson said:

> He could remember every feature of the terrain over which he had traveled and find his way over it again. He could also look at a map and visualize the features of terrain he had never seen. Porter noted that any map "seemed to become photographed indelibly upon his brain, and he could follow its features without referring to it again." Grant could see in his mind the disposition of troops over thousands of square miles, visualize their relationship to roads and terrain, and know how and where to move them to take advantage of topography.[47]

Use of Staff. Grant made excellent use of his staff. While Lee's staff consisted mainly of lieutenant colonels who were not much more than glorified clerks, Grant's staff ultimately included some generals and, in T. Harry Williams' words, "was an organization of experts in the various phases of strategic planning."[48] A prime example of an excellent staff officer is Horace Porter, who served as Grant's aide-de-camp beginning in the spring of 1864. Grant used him as his personal emissary to Sherman in Georgia in late 1864 and relied upon him for advice in selecting the commander for the successful assault on Fort Fisher. Porter, who served Grant until 1872, described Grant as "direct, open, intelligent, offensive-minded, dedicated, and having 'singular mental powers which are rare military qualities.' "[49] Porter also pointed out that Grant "studiously avoided performing any duty which some one else could do as well or better than he, and in this respect demonstrated his rare powers of administration and executive methods."[50]

An exhaustive analysis of Civil War generals' use of personal staffs revealed that Porter was just one of several military professionals Grant used effectively as members of his personal staff— particularly in the second half of the war. By the time of the Overland Campaign, Grant had progressed, in the phrases of historian R. Steven Jones, from a "civilian staff" to an "accidental staff" to a "professional staff." As early as Shiloh, one of Grant's aides was positioning artillery, another herding troops to the right area, and two others trying to get Lew Wallace's Division into the fight. Throughout the Overland Campaign, Grant frequently sent members of his personal staff as his emissaries and even as his alter egos to far sectors of the battlefield and to other theaters, such as Georgia. Jones' study concluded that only Grant, among Civil War generals, took the lead in expanding the duties of personal staff, and that he developed something close to the Prussian system of delegation of responsibility.[51] He summarized Grant's role as a common-sense innovator in the use of staff:

> In Grant, all of the factors compatible with staff advancement came together: large armies, cooperative operations, and a willingness to experiment with staff improvements. Grant was not a staff reformer; he was a competent, intelligent

general looking for more efficient ways to fight a compli-
cated war. As such, he spent no time talking or writing about
staff work. He did not promote his innovations as a model
for the whole United States Army. He simply found a creative way to use an organizational element available to all
Civil War generals—the personal staff—and made it his right
hand of command.[52]

Perseverance. Dogged perseverance, including a disinclination to
retrace his steps, was an important aspect of Grant's character. He
displayed this trait when he persisted in his efforts to capture Vicksburg and launched his daring campaign across the Mississippi south
of Vicksburg instead of returning to Memphis to restart another
overland campaign from the north. During that campaign, James
R. Arnold stated, Grant "accepted war's uncertainty by flexibly
adjusting to new circumstances while maintaining a determined
focus on the main chance."[53]

Again, in 1864 to 1865, Grant demonstrated his perseverance
(Gordon Rhea called it "persistence") as he carried out his campaign of adhesion against Lee's Army of Northern Virginia and
achieved all his goals within a year.[54] As he explained in his official
reports, "The battles of the Wilderness, Spotsylvania, North Anna,
and Cold Harbor, bloody and terrible as they were on our side,
were even more damaging to the enemy, and so crippled him as to
make him wary ever after of taking the offensive."[55] That comment
was typical of Grant's "refusal to treat reverses as defeats."[56]

James R. Arnold summed up Grant's determination and focus
throughout the war: "Grant was a simple man who dealt with the
facts as he found them. While his contemporaries saw war in all its
complexities and too often took counsel of their fears, from Bel-

mont to Appomattox Grant saw the main chance, stuck to it, and thus led his armies to victory."[57]

Military Realism. A related characteristic was what Bruce Catton described as Grant's military realism. He learned as early as Belmont and Fort Donelson that in every hotly contested battle there is a critical time when both armies are exhausted and the battle is in the balance, and that "the one which can nerve itself for one more attack at such a time is very likely to win." Grant applied that lesson again at Shiloh, Champion's Hill, Chattanooga, Petersburg, and Appomatox Court House.[58]

Full Use of Superior Union Resources. Grant's effective recognition and utilization of the North's superior resources distinguished him from most other Union generals. Gary Gallagher said, "The North always enjoyed a substantial edge in manpower and almost every manufacturing category, but none of Grant's predecessors proved equal to the task of harnessing and directing that latent strength. Grant's ability to do so stands as one of his greatest achievements."[59] James Arnold added, "When he massed for battle he brought every available soldier to the field, sublimating those secondary considerations that so often consumed the attention and resources of weaker generals."[60] He concentrated his forces brilliantly in each Vicksburg Campaign battle and thereby negated the Confederates' overall numerical superiority in that theater.

In fact, Grant was rather unique in fighting uncomplainingly with the soldiers he had on hand. "He rarely complained, never asked for reinforcements, and went ahead and did the job with whatever resources were available."[61] Unlike McClellan, Grant did not grossly exaggerate the strength of his opponents in an effort to secure reinforcements, excuse inaction, or justify a potential defeat. Unlike Lee and McClellan, Grant rarely asked for reinforcements.[62] Lincoln told his Third Secretary, "[Grant] doesn't ask me to do impossibilities for him, and he's the first general I've had that didn't."[63] When Grant did ask for more troops, he did so in a subtle manner, such as, "The greater number of men we have, the shorter and less sanguinary will be the war. I give this entirely as my views and not in any spirit of dictation—always holding myself in readiness to use the material given me to the best advantage I know how."[64]

Minimizing Support Personnel. Ironically, the more successful Grant was in advancing into Confederate territory, consistent with the Union's strategic goals, the more manpower he needed to establish garrisons and to provide logistical support for his front-line troops.[65] By late 1863 and in 1864, Grant decided to deal with this problem by conducting army-size raids with little or no logistical support, destroying the Confederate infrastructure, and reducing the need for garrisons and supply lines in his rear.[66] His efficient move on Vicksburg, sending Sherman on his Meridian Campaign, approving Sherman's March to the Sea, and reducing the Washington, D.C. garrisons in 1864 all were consistent with this approach.

Fully Using Assigned Generals. Although Grant became frustrated with generals he perceived as lacking timely aggressiveness, and with incompetent political generals, he rehabilitated several eastern generals who had been shipped west after less than glowing careers in the East. Among these generals who served at least somewhat successfully under Grant were Joe Hooker, O. O. Howard, and Ambrose Burnside. This practice contrasted with that of Lee, who "dumped" his less successful generals on other theaters.

Decisiveness. Grant was decisive. Colonel James F. Rusling of the Quartermaster General's staff recalled an incident demonstrating Grant's deliberate decisiveness. In the winter of 1863 to 1864, a quartermaster officer approached Grant for approval of millions of dollars of expenditures for the coming Atlanta campaign, and Grant approved the expenditure after briefly examining the papers involved. Questioning Grant's swift decision, the officer asked him if he was sure he was right. Grant replied, "No, I am not, but in war anything is better than indecision. *We must decide*. If I am wrong we shall soon find it out and can do the other thing. But *not to decide* wastes both time and money and may ruin everything."[67] In discussing Grant's positive effect on the mind-set of the usually victorious Army of the Tennessee, Steven E. Woodworth pointed to his prompt and decisive counterattack at Shiloh: "Perhaps in part at least it was not so much that Grant infused confidence into his army as that he refrained from destroying—by timid campaigning—the confidence of men who knew they had survived the worst the enemy had to throw at them."[68]

Moral Courage. Another distinguishing feature of Ulysses Grant was what he himself called "moral courage." His friend William T. Sherman observed this trait in Grant:

> But I tell you where he beats me, and where he beats the world. He don't care a damn for what the enemy does out of his sight. . . . He uses such information as he has, according to his best judgment. He issues his orders and does his level best to carry them out without much reference to what is going on about him.[69]

As James McPherson pointed out, moral courage went beyond the physical courage that Grant and others had demonstrated while carrying out Mexican War attacks under the command of others:

> This was a quality different from and rarer than physical courage. . . . Moral courage involved a willingness to make

decisions and give the orders. Some officers who were phys-
ically brave shrank from this responsibility because decision
risked error and initiative risked failure. This was George B.
McClellan's defect as a commander; he was afraid to risk his
army in an offensive because he might be defeated. He lacked
the moral courage to act, to confront that terrible moment of
truth, to decide and to risk.[70]

General Fuller said, "In the Vicksburg campaign Grant's moral
courage has seldom been equaled, certainly seldom surpassed."[71] A
one-time subordinate, Major General Jacob D. Cox, said, "[Grant's]
quality of greatness was that he handled great affairs as he would
little ones, without betraying any consciousness that this was a
great thing to do."[72] T. Harry Williams noted that Grant's approach
was to "seek out the enemy and strike him until he is destroyed"—
an approach that required "a tremendous will and a dominant personality."[73] Grant had both; he had character.

Political Common Sense. Unlike McClellan, Beauregard, Joseph
Johnston, and many other Civil War generals, Grant made it his
business to get along with his president. That cooperation included
tolerating political generals, such as McClernand, Sigel, Banks, and
Butler, until Grant had given them enough rope to hang themselves.
Grant's political antennae also kept him from "retreating" back up
the Mississippi River to begin a fresh campaign against Vicksburg
or moving back toward Washington after Overland Campaign "setbacks" because of the negative public reaction and morale impact
such a regressive movement would provoke among his soldiers and
the public.[74]

Focus on Enemy Armies. Critical to Grant's success and Union
victory in the war was that Grant early in the war recognized the
need to focus, and thereafter stayed focused, on defeating, captur-

ing, or destroying opposing armies—not simply occupying geographic positions. This was evident at Fort Donelson, Vicksburg, and at Richmond. Instead he maneuvered his troops in such a way that he captured the enemy armies in addition to occupying important locations. Unlike McClellan, Hooker, and Meade, who ignored Lincoln's admonitions to pursue and destroy enemy armies, and Halleck, who was satisfied with his hollow capture of Corinth, Grant believed in and practiced that approach, which was so critical to Union victory.[75]

Maneuverability. Although he was consistently on the strategic offensive, Grant used the art of maneuver as much as possible. His Vicksburg Campaign, described by Thomas Buell as "the equivalent of a Second World War blitzkreig,"[76] was a classic surprise maneuver that caught his adversaries completely off-guard. It demonstrated that he was, according to Edwin Bearss, "daring and innovative."[77] At Chattanooga, he maneuvered on both of Bragg's flanks before the central attack on Missionary Ridge broke through. During his Overland Campaign, he kept maneuvering around Lee's right flank until he had forced Lee back to the lethal siege situation at Richmond/Petersburg. As Jean Edward Smith concluded, Grant's detaching a 115,000-man army from his foe and secretly crossing the James River "was a perilous maneuver and an incredible tactical accomplishment, and it in no way diminishes Patton's accomplishment [in changing fronts during the Battle of the Bulge in 1944] to say that it pales alongside Grant's withdrawal from Cold Harbor and his crossing of the James in June 1864."[78] The final word on this subject should go to General Fuller:

> Grant has gone down to history as a bludgeon general, a general who eschewed manoeuvre and who with head down, seeing red, charged his enemy again and again like a

bull: indeed an extraordinary conclusion, for no general, not excepting Lee, and few generals in any other war, made greater use of manoeuvre in the winning of his campaigns, if not of his battles. Without fear of contradiction, it may be said that Grant's object was consistent; strategically it was to threaten his enemy's base of operations, and tactically to strike at the rear, or, failing the rear, at a flank of his enemy's army.[79]

Intelligent Aggressiveness. Therefore, unlike most Union generals, who were reluctant to take advantage of the North's numerical superiority and unwilling to persistently invade the Confederacy that had to be conquered, Grant knew what had to be done and did it. Bruce Catton said it prosaically: "Better than any other Northern soldier, better than any other man save Lincoln himself, [Grant] understood the necessity for bringing the infinite power of the growing nation to bear on the desperate weakness of the brave, romantic, and tragically archaic little nation that opposed it. . . . "[80] General Cox, said, "[Grant] reminds one of Wellington in the combination of lucid and practical common-sense with aggressive bull-dog courage."[81] Grant advanced aggressively and creatively, and he attacked with vigor but usually avoided suicidal frontal attacks. In light of the large number of battles fought by his armies, the total of 94,000 killed and wounded suffered by his commands was surprisingly small—especially when considered in light of the 121,000 killed and wounded among the soldiers commanded by Robert E. Lee.

In a recent study of Grant's use of military intelligence, William Feis disagreed with Sherman's conclusion that his friend Grant "don't care a damn for what the enemy does out of his sight." After analyzing Grant's increasing use of intelligence throughout the war, Feis concluded, "In reality, he cared a great deal about what the enemy did on the 'other side of the hill,' but unlike Henry Halleck, George McClellan, or William Rosecrans, he refused to allow that concern to become an obsession in which the search for 'perfect' information became an end in itself, effectively stifling intuitive risk taking."[82]

A LOOK AT GRANT'S STATISTICS

General Fuller calculated that in the Overland Campaign, Grant's army suffered 34 percent casualties while imposing 43 percent casualties on Lee's army. He compared this to the somewhat similar Peninsular Campaign of 1862 when McClellan lost about 31 percent of his army and Lee lost 40 percent of his. McClellan, however, felt less pressure to advance and had the advantage of being on the tactical defensive during Lee's Seven Days' offensive. Fuller also pointed to Lee's high losses at Gettysburg and Malvern Hill.[83]

From those data, Fuller concluded, "If anything, *Lee* rather than Grant deserves to be accused of sacrificing his men."[84] Gordon Rhea similarly concluded that, "Judging from Lee's record, the rebel commander should have shared in Grant's 'butcher' reputation."[85] James McPherson compared the casualties of Lee and Grant: "Indeed, for the war as a whole, Lee's armies suffered a higher casualty rate than Grant's (and higher than any other army). Neither general was a 'butcher,' but measured by that statistic, Lee deserved the label more than Grant."[86]

Far from being the uncaring slaughterer of men, Grant again and again displayed his feelings about the contributions of the ordinary soldier. After Chattanooga, for example, he alone raised his hat in salute to a ragged band of Confederate prisoners through which Union generals and their staffs were passing, and at Hampton

Roads late in the war he spoke to a group of Rebel amputees about better artificial limbs that were being manufactured.[87]

In their thought-provoking book, *Attack and Die: Civil War Military Tactics and the Southern Heritage*, Gordon McWhiney and Perry D. Jamieson provided some astounding numbers related to Grant's major battles and campaigns. Their statistics demonstrate that the men under Grant's command generally survived to fight another day:

Battle or Campaign	Grant's Men	Grant's Losses (Killed and Wounded)
Fort Donelson (1862)	27,000	2,608 (10%)
Shiloh (1862)	62,682	10,162 (16%)
Champion's Hill (1863)	29,373	2,254 (8%)
Vicksburg (1863)	45,556	3,052 (7%)
Chattanooga (1863)	56,359	5,475 (10%)
Wilderness— Cold Harbor (1864)	c.122,000	c. 50,000 (41%)
The Mine at Petersburg (1864)	20,708	2,865 (14%)
Deep Bottom Run (1864)	27,974	2,180 (8%)
Weldon Railroad (1864)	20,289	1,303 (6%)
New Market Heights (1864)	19,639	2,682 (14%)
Boydton Plank Road (1865)	42,823	1,194 (3%)
Dabney's Mills (1865)	34,517	1,330 (4%)
Appomattox Campaign (1865)	112,992	9,066 (8%)
TOTALS	c. 621,912	94,171 (15%)[88]

These loss percentages are remarkably low—especially considering the fact that Grant was on the strategic and tactical offensive in most of these battles and campaigns. As indicated in the preface to this book, Grant's 15 percent killed and wounded compared quite favorably with those of Lee (20.2 percent), Bragg (19.5 percent), Hood (19.2 percent), and Beauregard (16.1 percent).

A fresh and comprehensive analysis of all the casualties (killed, wounded, and missing/captured) in all of Grant's campaigns and battles reinforces the brilliance of his accomplishments. Appendix II, "Casualties Resulting from the Campaigns and Battles of Ulysses S. Grant," contains a fairly exhaustive list of various historians' and other authorities' estimates of those casualties. This author has then made a best estimate of the casualties and, at the end of that appendix, created a table of best estimates of those casualties for the entire war. While Grant's armies were incurring a total of 153,642 casualties in those battles for which he was responsible and on which he had some effect, they were imposing a total of 190,760 casualties on the enemy. That positive total casualty differential of 37,118 should put to rest any negative analyses of Grant's performance.

CONCLUSIONS

Al W. Goodman, Jr. contended that Grant's Vicksburg Campaign played a significant role in establishing the U.S. Army's modern Air-Land Battle concept. He pointed to the four elements of that concept reflected in that campaign: (1) agility (quickly concentrating your units in a way that forces the enemy to strike blindly), (2) initiative (not allowing your opponent to take the initiative), (3) depth (gained by seizing territory needed to pin down the enemy while being able to maneuver your own forces), and (4) synchronization (bringing forces to bear on a particular point at a particular time).[89] Grant also demonstrated his mastery of these tenets at many other places, including Forts Henry and Donelson, Chattanooga, the Overland Campaign, and the Appomattox Campaign.

According to Eric J. Wittenberg, "Ulysses S. Grant was the master of the strategic raid."[90] Perhaps the most strategically effective cavalry raid of the entire war was Grierson's length-of-Mississippi incursion that disrupted transportation to Vicksburg and distracted Vicksburg's commander while Grant moved into position and began his amphibious crossing of the Mississippi that led to the fall of Vicksburg and the opening of the Mississippi. In May of 1864, Grant unleashed Sheridan on his raid toward Richmond that resulted in Jeb Stuart's death and distracted Lee from Grant's movement around Lee's right flank at Spotsylvania Court House.[91] Although Sheridan was unsuccessful in cutting off Lee's army during his June 1864 "Second Raid" and was defeated at Trevilian Station, it was Sheridan's raid-in-force that led to the crucial Union Victory at Five Forks and the breakdown of Lee's defenses, and ultimately his army, in April 1865.

Far from being a crude butcher, Grant was an inspired military leader with a genius for being self-effacing, issuing lucid orders, having a topographical memory, making excellent use of his staff, persevering, being a military realist, making full use of superior Union resources and assigned generals, minimizing support personnel, being decisive, having moral courage and political common sense, maneuvering his troops, and being intelligently aggressive. He determined what the North needed to do to win the war and did it. Grant's record of unparalleled success—Forts Henry and Donelson, Shiloh, Iuka, Corinth, Raymond, Jackson, Champion's Hill, Vicksburg, Chattanooga, the Overland Campaign, the James River crossing, Five Forks, Petersburg, and Appomattox—obtained with lower casualty rates than he imposed on the enemy establishes him as the greatest general of the Civil War and one of the greatest in history.

Appendix I

HISTORIANS' TREATMENT OF ULYSSES S. GRANT

*T*his appendix *merely scratches* the surface of the numerous Grant biographies (more than a hundred), Civil War histories, and other military histories that have examined the military career of Ulysses Grant. All cited works are listed in the bibliography at the end of this book.

A review of those writings must begin with mention of his autobiography. As he was dying from throat cancer, and in order to provide a secure financial future for his family, Grant wrote his remarkably lucid and revealing 275,000-word *Memoirs* in 1884 and 1885.[1] Edmund Wilson called that volume "the most remarkable work of its kind since the *Commentaries* of Julius Caesar."[2] British military historian John Keegan wrote, "If there is a single contemporaneous document which explains 'why the North won the Civil War,' that abiding conundrum of American historical inquiry, it is the *Personal Memoirs of U. S. Grant.*"[3]

After he was defrauded of his life's savings and desperately needed to earn money for his wife, Grant began his first writing about the war with four articles for the *Century* magazine series on "Battles and Leaders of the Civil War."[4] In mid-1884, he wrote articles on Shiloh, Vicksburg, Chattanooga, and the Wilderness. These articles formed the basis for the memoirs he wrote over the next year. Grant's friend Mark Twain, who had established his own publishing company, saved Grant from an unfair publishing arrangement by making Grant a generous offer. Given the choice of receiving 20 percent of the book's sales or 70 percent of its profits, Grant selected the latter as being fairer to Twain. The sales were so great that Grant's surviving family received $450,000 in royalties.[5]

James McPherson provided this insight into Grant and his memoirs:

> Grant's strength of will, his determination to do the best he could with what he had, his refusal to give up or to complain about the cruelty of fate help explain the success both of his generalship and his memoirs. These qualities were by no means typical among Civil War generals. Many of them spent more energy clamoring for reinforcements or explaining why they could not do what they were ordered to do than they did in trying to carry out their orders. Their memoirs are full of excuses for failure, which was always somebody else's fault.[6]

In his memoirs, Grant noted the southern historians who were creating the myth of "The Lost Cause":

> With us, now twenty years after the close of the most stupendous war ever known, we have writers—who profess devo-

tion to the nation—engaged in trying to prove that the Union forces were not victorious; practically, they say, we were slashed around from Donelson to Vicksburg and to Chattanooga; and in the East from Gettysburg to Appomattox, when the physical rebellion gave out from sheer exhaustion.[7]

In fact, several pro-Confederate writers attacked Grant as soon as the shooting stopped. One of those was Richmond newspaperman Edward Pollard, who, in *The Lost Cause: A New Southern History of the War of the Confederates* (1866), said that Grant "contained no spark of military genius; his idea of war was to the last degree rude—no strategy, the mere application of the vis inertia; he had none of that quick perception on the field of action which decides it by sudden strokes; he had no conception of battle beyond the momentum of numbers."[8]

Even northern historians criticized Grant. In 1866, *New York Times* war correspondent William Swinton wrote in his *Campaigns of the Army of the Potomac* that Grant relied "exclusively on the application of brute masses, in rapid and remorseless blows."[9] John C. Ropes told the Military Historical Society of Massachusetts that Grant suffered from a "burning, persistent desire to fight, to attack, in season and out of season, against intrenchments, natural obstacles, what not."[10]

Mediocre Confederate General Jubal Early led the way, along with incompetent Confederate General William Nelson Pendleton, in creating the Myth of the Lost Cause. In doing so, they felt compelled to belittle the accomplishments of Grant. In 1872, in a speech on Lee's birthday, Early said, "Shall I compare General Lee to his successful antagonist? As well compare the great pyramid which rears its majestic proportions in the Valley of the Nile, to a pygmy perched on Mount Atlas."[11] At least he admitted that Grant was successful.

Historian Gary Gallagher fairly recently criticized the selective-
ness and merits of Early's (and others') criticisms of Grant:

> Absent from Early's work, as well as that of other writers who
> portrayed Grant as a butcher, was any detailed treatment of
> Grant's brilliant campaign against Vicksburg, his decisive suc-
> cess at Chattanooga, or his other western operations. More-
> over, critics failed to grasp that Grant's tactics in 1864 went
> against his preferred style of campaigning. He fought Lee at
> every turn primarily because he wished to deny Jefferson Davis
> the option of shifting Confederate troops from Virginia to
> Georgia where they might slow Sherman's progress.[12]

In 1881, Jefferson Davis joined the parade of Grant critics when
he launched this criticism of Grierson's effective 1863 raid (which
barely affected civilians in Davis's native Mississippi): "Among the
expeditions for pillage and arson [Grierson's raid] stands prominent
for savage outrages against defenseless women and children, constituting a record alike unworthy a soldier and a gentleman."[13] The
1880s publication of *Battles and Leaders of the Civil War*, con-
taining the recollections of the war's participants, provided former
Confederates with an opportunity to impugn Grant. For example,
Lieutenant General Evander M. Law wrote, "What a part at least
of his own men thought about General Grant's methods was shown
by the fact that many of the prisoners taken during the [Overland]
campaign complained bitterly of the 'useless butchery' to which
they were subjected."[14]

Not surprisingly, Lee's former adjutant, Walter H. Taylor, elevated Lee at Grant's expense in his campaigning summary, *General
Lee: His Campaigns in Virginia 1861–1865 with Personal Reminiscences*, which was published in 1906. Of the Overland Cam-

paign, Taylor said: "It is well to bear in mind the great inequality between the two contending armies, in order that one may have a proper appreciation of the difficulties which beset General Lee in the task of thwarting the designs of so formidable an adversary, and realize the extent to which his brilliant genius made amends for the paucity of numbers, and proved more than a match for brute force, as illustrated in the hammering policy of General Grant." Later he essentially called Grant a butcher—but a justifiable one: "[Grant] certainly possessed a greater degree of pertinacity and put a lower estimate upon the value of human life than any of his predecessors; and in taking a calm retrospective view of the times, it must be conceded that in the possession of these traits he held the only key to the situation that promised success in any reasonable time."[15]

Some pro-Grant studies by former members of Grant's staff emerged after the war. One of those was Adam Badeau's *Military History of Ulysses S. Grant, from April, 1861, to April, 1865*, a three-volume work published in 1868. Badeau's work was a detailed insider's account of Grant's campaigns that particularly stressed the quickness and deception that kept the Confederates off-balance and outnumbered in each separate encounter during his Vicksburg campaign.[16] Another sympathetic appraisal of Grant was written by his former aide, Horace Porter. Porter's *Campaigning with Grant* originally appeared as articles in *Century Magazine* in the late 1880s and the 1890s. The book itself was published in 1897. Porter's synopsis of Grant's traits and successes reflects Porter's closeness to Grant:

> [Grant] was unquestionably the most aggressive fighter in the entire list of the world's famous soldiers.... For four years of bloody and relentless war he went steadily forward, replacing the banner of his country upon the territory where it had

been hauled down. He possessed in a striking degree every characteristic of the successful soldier. His methods were all stamped with tenacity of purpose, originality, and ingenuity.... He therefore adopted a more open order of battle, made an extensive use of skirmish-lines, employed cavalry largely as mounted infantry, and sought to cultivate the individuality of the soldier instead of making him merely an unthinking part of a compact machine. He originated the cutting loose from a base of supplies with large armies and living off the invaded country.[17]

Easterners, who controlled most of the newspapers and publishing houses, did not like Grant, "whom they saw as an uncouth westerner." In the wake of the numerous scandals in which his presidential appointees were involved, Grant's continuing support for the rights of African-Americans and Native Americans during his years as president, and intellectuals' revulsion at the materialism of the Industrial Age, many northerners joined southerners in glorifying Lee and his army and in attacking Grant as a butcher.[18] It is difficult to overestimate the damage to Grant that these writings caused and the virtual indelibility of the image they created of Grant the Butcher.

In fact, it was another Richmond newspaper reporter-turned-historian, Douglas Southall Freeman, who placed Lee on a pedestal at Grant's expense. In his four-volume treatise, *R.E. Lee*, Freeman idolized Lee in describing all the details of his generalship. Freeman criticized Grant for hammering Lee's forces instead of maneuvering more, but even Freeman did concede that Grant's efforts had not been in vain: "Lee did not lose the battles but he did not win the campaign. He delayed the fulfillment of Grant's mission, but he could not discharge his own. Lee found few opportunities of attacking the enemy in detail or on the march.... And in some subtle fashion General Grant infused into his well-seasoned troops a confidence they had never previously possessed."[19]

A pro-Lee disciple of Freeman's, Clifford Dowdey, was harder on Grant. In his 1960 *Lee's Last Campaign: The Story of Lee and His Men Against Grant*, Dowdey described Grant as a "boring-in type of attacker, who usually scorned finesse."[20] The anti-Grant tradition is not dead. It has been recently continued in Paul D. Casdorph's 1992 *Lee and Jackson: Confederate Chieftains* and Ernest B. Furgurson's 2000 *Not War But Murder: Cold Harbor 1864*. Casdorph grossly overestimated Grant's Cold Harbor casualties as including 13,000 killed ("dead or dying") and referred to "union hordes" and the "Yankee Goliath."[21]

Significant praise for Grant, other than from his subordinates and fellow officers, first came from overseas. British military historian and Major-General J. F. C. Fuller strongly endorsed the greatness of Grant in *The Generalship of Ulysses S. Grant* in 1929 and then in *Grant and Lee: A Study in Personality and Generalship* in 1932. Fuller concluded that Grant was a superior strategist, possessed common sense, recognized what needed to be done to win the war, and deserved the major credit for doing so. He compared Grant quite favorably to Lee, found that Lee consistently throughout the war lost a higher percentage of his troops than Grant or other adversaries he faced, and that Lee much more than Grant—and for no good reason—sacrificed his troops in frontal assaults and continued to do so until he had no more to sacrifice.

Another British military historian, John Keegan, also found cause to praise Grant. He did so in *The Mask of Command* (1987). There he discussed Grant in a chapter entitled "Grant and Unheroic Leadership." He praised Grant's fighting skills and concluded, "But in retrospect, great though Grant's generalship is seen to be, it is his comprehension of the nature of the war, and of what could and could not be done by a general within its defining conditions, that seems the more remarkable."[22]

The most comprehensive sympathetic treatment of Grant came with the works of Bruce Catton. He first wrote of Grant in the second and third volumes of the famous Civil War trilogy, *Mr. Lincoln's Army* (1951), *Glory Road* (1952), and the Pulitzer Prize–winning *A Stillness at Appomattox* (1953). Having come to admire Grant above other Civil War generals, Catton then proceeded to write *U.S. Grant and the American Military Tradition* (1954) (the bulk of which is entitled "The Great Commander"); *This Hallowed Ground: The Story of the Union Side in the Civil War* (1956); *Grant Moves South* (1960) (describing Grant's Civil War career through Vicksburg in glowing terms); and *Grant Takes Command* (1968) (taking him through the end of the war). The prolific Catton also produced *The Centennial History of the Civil War—The Coming Fury* (1961), *Terrible Swift Sword* (1963), and *Never Call Retreat* (1965). Like Grant himself, said Stephen W. Sears, Catton was "quiet and unassuming and unpretentious and business-like."[23]

A contemporary of Catton's, T. Harry Williams was a renowned Civil War scholar and a strong proponent of Grant. Williams found him superior to Lee and others in *Lincoln and His Generals* (1952), and superior to his fellow Union generals in *McClellan, Sherman and Grant* (1962). In the former book, Williams succinctly stated, "Grant was, by modern standards, the greatest general of the Civil War."[24]

Between 1958 and 1974, Shelby Foote, a former novelist, released the three volumes of his brilliant and lucid *The Civil War: A Narrative*. He fairly and accurately described Grant's assets and his liabilities. In a sentence summarizing public reaction to Grant's victories at Forts Henry and Donelson, Foote caught the essence of Grant: "People saw Grant as the author of this deliverance, the embodiment of the offensive spirit, the man who would strike and keep on striking until this war was won."[25]

In their exhaustive 1983 study of the war, *How the North Won: A Military History of the Civil War*, Herman Hattaway and Archer Jones concluded that Grant was responsible for recognizing the North's need to effectively use its superiority. Although they disclaimed any emphasis on turning points, they concluded that Grant's seizure of Forts Henry and Donelson and his approval of Sherman's March to the Sea were decisive events.

While he relied on Bruce Catton's work, William S. McFeely, however, treated Grant with much less sympathy in his 1981 *Grant: A Biography*. McFeely's Grant seemed uncaring about the death around him. This first "modern" biography of Grant reinforced earlier negative impressions with such characterizations of Grant as "a man of limited though by no means inconsequential talents to apply to whatever truly engaged his attention." McFeely made it appear that Grant's second-day offensive at Shiloh was a spur-of-the-moment idea conceived only that morning, and he then criticized Grant for failing to pursue the Rebels with his exhausted army. He claimed it was Grant's rivalry with McClernand that got him focused on Vicksburg. McFeely asserted, "Grant's strategy was to make sure more Southerners than Northerners were killed. It was a matter of simple arithmetic...." Of the Overland Campaign, he said, "In May 1864 Ulysses Grant began a vast campaign that was a hideous disaster in every respect save one—it worked. He led his troops into the Wilderness and there produced a nightmare of inhumanity and inept military strategy that ranks with the worst such episodes in the history of warfare." Jean Edward Smith later cited

McFeely's work as a biography written by an academic historian who was influenced by the Vietnam War and denigrated Grant's critical role in Union victory.[26]

A return to the Catton sympathetic approach marked the 1997 *Ulysses S. Grant: Soldier & President,* written by Geoffrey Perret, and the 2000 *Ulysses S. Grant: Triumph over Adversity, 1822–1865* by Brooks D. Simpson. Perret praised Grant's "military genius" and credited him with creating two concepts that the U.S. Army has been using ever since: the use of converging columns (Grant's 1864–1865 national strategy) and the wide envelopment (Grant's sweeping around Lee's flank throughout 1864 and 1865).[27] Simpson described a non-idealized Grant and praised his common sense, imagination, and perseverance. On the issue of Grant's tactics, Simpson concluded:

> He was less successful at shaking the perception that he was a ham-handed tactician who freely wasted the lives of his own men. This reputation was largely based on the pervasive impression of his generalship left by the 1864 campaign in Virginia. That during the Vicksburg and Chattanooga campaigns combined, Grant's forces suffered fewer losses than did Lee's troops at Gettysburg escaped most people's notice; that he was far more frugal with human life than his leading Confederate counterpart . . . is recognized by only a few. He preferred to take prisoners than to slay foes; he emphasized movement and logistics over slugging it out. Even his campaigns in Virginia show a general who . . . shifted units and probed for weaknesses, mixing assaults with marches, constantly seeking new approaches.[28]

In recent years, detailed studies of specific aspects of the Civil War have complimented the operations and practices of Grant. For example, R. Stephen Jones concluded in *The Right Hand of Command: Use & Disuse of Personal Staffs in the Civil War* (2000) that Grant had been unique in finding creative ways to assemble and fully utilize a professional personal staff in a manner that made them "his right hand of command."[29] Likewise, in his 2002 book, *Grant's Secret Service*, William Feis concluded that Grant viewed the uncertainty of war as a fertile ground for opportunity, used his own initiative to shift the burden of uncertainty onto the enemy, and, unlike George McClellan and others, was able to prevent his concern about what the enemy was doing from precluding his taking the offensive.[30]

Jean Edward Smith's 2001 book, entitled simply *Grant,* is an excellent, sympathetic biography of Grant. He pointed to Grant's decisiveness at Fort Donelson, his Vicksburg campaign's amphibious crossing, his moving forward after the Wilderness, and his surreptitious crossing of the James River as examples of Grant's greatness. He contended that Grant was the strategic master of his Confederate counterparts, had a lower casualty rate than Lee, and demonstrated his strategic skills by focusing on enemy armies rather than on mere geographic goals. Smith not only described the greatness of Grant as a Civil War general, but also the many overlooked positive aspects of his eight-year presidency. Smith detailed President Grant's efforts to protect Negroes' rights in the post-war South and Indians' rights in the West and said that "mainstream historians, unsympathetic to black equality, brutalized Grant's presidency."[31]

In the past several years, Grant's conduct of the Overland Campaign has received exhaustive and generally positive treatment at the hands of Gordon C. Rhea. His four books were *The Battle of the Wilderness* (1994), *The Battles for Spotsylvania Court House and the Road to Yellow Tavern* (1997), *To the North Anna River*

(2000), and *Cold Harbor* (2002). In those volumes and a series of contemporaneous articles, Rhea contended that Grant had been unfairly tagged as a "butcher," that his casualties were proportionately less than Lee's, and that Grant was an innovative and effective general who focused on and achieved his strategic objectives.[32]

During recent decades, several Civil War periodicals have provided new insights into Grant and many other aspects of the Civil War. They often contain articles by authors previewing their forthcoming books—many with better battle-maps than the books themselves. These publications include *North & South*, *Blue & Gray Magazine*, *Civil War Times Illustrated*, *America's Civil War*, *Military History Quarterly*, and the unfortunately defunct *Columbiad: A Quarterly Review of the War Between the States*.

An example of a cutting-edge article on Grant in one of these publications is James F. Epperson's "The Chance Battle in the Wilderness" (*Columbiad*), in which he effectively argued that Grant was not trying to rush through the Wilderness but rather was deliberately moving to directly engage Lee in battle.[33] Providing a fresh and definitive look at Lee's casualties during the Overland Campaign, which are critical to judgments about that campaign, was Alfred Young's "Numbers and Losses in the Army of Northern Virginia" in *North & South* in 2000.

In summary, Ulysses Grant got off to a bad start among post-war historians, but his military accomplishments have received increasing, if erratic, recognition since about 1930. Serious historical reestablishment of his multi-theater, war-winning record continues.

Appendix II

CASUALTIES IN GRANT'S
BATTLES AND CAMPAIGNS

etermination of the number of casualties is one of the most difficult issues in writing about the Civil War. Not only did the Union and the Confederacy calculate their casualties differently, but individual armies on both sides took different approaches to doing so. The deterioration of the Army of Tennessee in late 1864 and of the Army of Northern Virginia in 1864 and 1865 resulted in a dearth of complete and reliable Confederate records of their casualties for the last two calendar years of the war.

Defining casualties is another aspect of the problem. A full casualty count often includes killed, wounded, and missing/captured, but many records and writers include only killed and wounded. Distinctions between killed and wounded became difficult because of battle-related deaths that occurred during the days, weeks, and months after a battle. The missing category was particularly amorphous because it might or might not include soldiers who had wandered away or deserted under cover of battle—as well as those captured by the enemy.

Another problem has been determining the number of combatants on either side in order to calculate percentages of killed, wounded, or missing. The complexity of this chore can be demonstrated by the following description of three different ways that Union troops were counted:

> *Present:* Including all personnel for whom rations had to be issued;

> *Present for Duty:* Excluding personnel on sick call or recuperating from wounds and those under arrest, but including musicians, teamsters, hospital personnel, and other uniformed non-combatants; and

> *Present for duty equipped:* Including only combat-ready enlisted men and their officers; the number of men armed and ready to fight, excluding field musicians, teamsters, hospital personnel, and other uniformed non-combatants.[1]

The Confederates used the first two categories but, instead of the third one, used "Effectives," which included only enlisted men present and under arms.[2]

In 1883, Frederick Phisterer made the first significant attempt at summarizing Civil War casualties (especially Union casualties) in his *Statistical Record of the Armies of the United States*.[3] He was followed in 1888 by William F. Fox, whose years of labor resulted in the comprehensive *Regimental Losses in the American Civil War* with its Union regiment-by-regiment breakdown of casualties.[4] The foremost authority on civil war casualties was Thomas L. Livermore, whose *Numbers & Losses in the Civil War in America, 1861–1865* (1901) has been the starting point, and often the finishing point, for many later writers and statisticians. Livermore's entire concise tome explains how he derived his numbers. Unfortunately, his work contains few late-war Confederate statistics.

In his 1933 classic, *Grant and Lee: A Study in Personality and Generalship*, Major General J. F. C. Fuller included a valuable appendix listing the strength, killed, wounded, and missing of both sides in fifty-eight Civil War battles. About two-thirds of his numbers were taken from Livermore, but he expanded some of the lesser-known Confederate numbers. He also analyzed those figures and came to some startling conclusions. First, in their respective (and separate) 1862–1863 battles, Lee had 16 percent of his men killed or wounded while Grant's losses were only 10 percent. Second, Grant's 1864–1865 losses against Lee were 10 percent, and Lee's 1864–1865 losses are unknown. Third, where both sides' losses are known in the battles listed, the Federals lost 11 percent and the Confederates 12 percent—both higher than Grant's overall total of 10 percent and lower than Lee's 1862–1863 total of 16 percent, even though the Confederate totals include Lee's own numbers. In other words, Fuller found that Grant lost a smaller percentage of his troops than Lee; that Grant lost a smaller percentage of his troops than other Union generals, and that Lee lost a greater percentage of his troops than other Confederate generals.[5]

The culmination of these statistical analyses is found in Grady McWhiney's and Perry D. Jamieson's *Attack and Die: Civil War Military Tactics and the Southern Heritage* (1982). In their opening chapter, "It Was Not War—It Was Murder," they assembled an illuminating series of statistical tables analyzing the casualties (killed and wounded only) incurred by Union and Confederate commanders. The following significant statistical nuggets come from the tables in *Attack and Die*:

- ∿ Grant lost an average of 18 percent of his troops per battle while imposing a 21 percent loss on his opponents;
- ∿ Before 1864, Grant lost 23,551 of his 220,970 men (11 percent) in his major battles and campaigns;
- ∿ In 1864 to 1865, Grant lost 70,620 of his 400,942 men (18 percent);
- ∿ For the whole war, Grant lost 94,171 of 621,912 (15 percent).[6]

Even the detailed analyses of McWhiney and Jamieson result in a range between 15 and 18 percent for Grant's losses.

Any analysis that only includes the killed and wounded understates the impact of a general, such as Grant, who successfully trapped and captured three enemy armies. Also, the "missing/captured" numbers often included men who actually died in battle but whose deaths were not confirmed by their commands. Therefore, in the following tables, this author has attempted to reconstruct the *total* casualties on both sides in battles and campaigns involving Grant.

The following tables contain comprehensive lists of various historians' and other authorities' estimates of either or both sides' casualties in most of Ulysses Grant's campaigns and battles. Several observations are in order:

- ∿ There is considerable dependence on the numbers developed by Livermore.
- ∿ The numbers provided by directly interested parties, such as Ulysses Grant and Jefferson Davis, are biased and inaccurate.

∼ The numbers are fairly consistent with each other (perhaps due to use of Livermore and similar early sources).

∼ There are overlaps, gaps, and inconsistencies because different sources calculate the dates of certain battles and campaigns differently.

∼ The exact numbers of casualties cannot be known; some respectable authors and sources provide varying statistics for the same battle.

∼ For the last year of the war, Confederate statistics are incomplete or missing because there are inadequate Confederate records for that period.

∼ Some recent exhaustive studies (such as Young, "Numbers and Losses") provide the best available information on certain battles or campaigns.

At the end of each campaign and battle is my estimate of the total casualties on both sides. I have based my estimates on what I deemed to be the most reliable sources cited—both long-respected sources that have not been disproved and more recent sources that reflect detailed and conscientious research. The final table contains my estimates of the war-long total casualties incurred and imposed by Grant's armies when they were under his command and control. (The Shenandoah Valley and Arkansas Post, for example, did not meet that standard.) That summary table reveals that Grant's armies in the West, including the "Middle Theater" at Chattanooga, imposed 84,187 casualties while incurring only 36,688. It also shows that his aggressive eastern campaign to end the war resulted in his armies' inflicting 106,573 casualties on the Confederates while themselves suffering 116,954. For the entire war, therefore, his armies imposed 190,760 casualties on the enemy while incurring 153,642. Thus, Grant's armies imposed 37,118 more casualties on their opponents than they incurred themselves.

In summary, Grant succeeded for two years in the West with amazingly minimal casualties—particularly when compared with those of his foes. His later casualties in the East were militarily acceptable considering that the presidential election demanded swift and aggressive action and that he defeated Lee, captured his army, and took Petersburg and Richmond—in less than one year after initiating the Overland Campaign. These numbers disprove the canard that Grant was a butcher.

Casualties Resulting from Campaigns and Battles of Ulysses S. Grant

Unless otherwise noted, the numbers are the total of killed and wounded on each side. An asterisk (*) indicates the number includes missing/captured, as well as killed and wounded.

BELMONT (November 7, 1861)

Source	Confederate	Union
Arnold, *Armies of Grant*[7]	105 killed 419 wounded 117 missing	90 killed 400 wounded 100 captured
Buell, *Warrior Generals*[8]		600+ *
Current, *Encyclopedia*[9]	105 killed 409 wounded 117 missing	80 killed 322 wounded 99 missing
Foote, *Civil War*[10]	600+ *	600+ *
Fox, *Regimental Losses*[11]	105 killed 419 wounded 117 missing/captured	80 killed 322 wounded 99 missing/captured
Fuller, *Grant and Lee*[12]	105 killed 419 wounded 117 missing	79 killed 289 wounded 117 missing
Grant, *Memoirs*[13]	642*	425*
Hattaway and Jones, *How the North*[14]	641*	607*

Source	Confederate	Union
Heidlers, *Encyclopedia*[15]	641* (105 killed)	607* (120 killed)
Phisterer, *Statistics*[16]	966* 173 wounded 235 missing	90 killed
Roberts, "Belmont"[17]	641*	610*
Smith, *Grant*[18]	642*	607* (19%)
Author's Best Estimate:	**105 killed** **419 wounded** **117 missing/captured**	**80 killed** **322 wounded** **99 missing/captured**

FORT DONELSON (February 13–16, 1862)

Source	Confederate	Union
Arnold, *Armies of Grant*[19]	16,500 captured	
Badeau, *Grant*[20]	2,500+ killed/wounded 14,623 captured	425 killed 1,616 wounded/missing
Beringer et al, *Why the South Lost*[21]	16,623* (79%)	2,832* (10.5%)
Buell, *Warrior Generals*[22]	2,832* (10%)	
Cooling, "Forts"[23]	15,000 captured	
Foote, *Civil War*[24]	c. 2,000 plus 12,000+ captured	c. 3,000*
Fox, *Regimental Losses*[25]	466 killed 1,534 wounded 13,829 captured	500 killed 2,108 wounded 224 missing/captured
Fuller, *Grant and Lee*[26]	11,500 surrendered and 2,000 killed/wounded 14,623 captured/missing	3,000* 500 killed 2,108 wounded 224 missing
Heidlers, *Encyclopedia*[27]	1,500–3,500 killed and wounded 15,000 captured	500 killed 2,108 wounded 221 captured/missing
Jones, "Military Means"[28]	16,600*	3,800*
Livermore, *Numbers*[29]	2,000 killed/wounded 14,623 captured/missing	500 killed 2,108 wounded 224 missing
McPherson, *Battle Cry*[30]	500 killed 1,000+ wounded 12,000–13,000 captured	

Source	Confederate	Union
McWhiney & Jamieson, *Attack*[31]		2,608
Phisterer, *Statistics*[32]	15,067*	446 killed 1,735 wounded 150 missing
Simon, *Papers of Grant*[33]	12,000–17,750 captured	
Smith, *Grant*[34]	14,000 captured	3,000 (11%)
Williams, *Lincoln Finds*[35]	c. 2,000 killed/wounded 12,000–15,000 captured	2,608 killed/wounded
Author's Best Estimate:	**466 killed 1,534 wounded 14,000 captured**	**500 killed 2,108 wounded 224 missing/captured**

SHILOH (PITTSBURG LANDING) (April 6–7, 1862)

Source	Confederate	Union
Allen, "Shiloh!"[36]	1,728 killed 8,012 wounded 959 missing	1,754 killed 8,408 wounded 2,885 missing
Arnold, *Armies of Grant*[37]	10,700*	13,700*
Badeau, *Grant*[38]	1,728 killed 8,012 wounded 957 missing	1,700 killed 7,495 wounded 3,022 missing
Beauregard,"Shiloh"[39]	10,699*	
Beringer et al, *Why the South Lost*[40]	10,600* (26.5%)	13,000* (20.7%)
Buell, *Warrior Generals*[41]	10,694* (27%)	13,047* (21%)
Catton, *Grant Moves South*[42]	10,000+ *	13,000+ *
Current, *Encyclopedia*[43]	10,694*	13,047*
Daniel, *Shiloh*[44]	*(Confederate records incomplete)* 1,728 killed 8,012 wounded 959 missing	1,754 killed 8,408 wounded 2,885 missing
Davis, *Rise and Fall*[45]	*(Union figures are for first day only)* 1,728 killed 8,012 wounded 959 missing	1,500 killed 6,634 wounded 3,086 missing
Donald et al, *Civil War*[46]	10,699*	13,047*
Esposito, *West Point Atlas*[47]	10,700*	13,700*
Feis, *Grant's Secret Service*[48]		13,047*

Source	Confederate	Union
Foote, *Civil War*[49]	1,723 killed 8,012 wounded 959 missing	1,754 killed 8,408 wounded 2,885 captured
Fox, *Regimental Losses*[50]	1,723 killed 8,012 wounded 959 missing/captured	1,754 killed 8,408 wounded 2,885 missing/captured
Fuller, *Generalship of Grant*[51]	10,699*	13,573*
Fuller, *Grant and Lee*[52]	1,723 killed 8,012 wounded 959 missing	1,754 killed 8,408 wounded 2,885 missing
Grant, "Shiloh"[53]	1,728–4,000 killed 8,012 wounded 959 missing	1,754 killed 8,408 wounded 2,885 missing
Hattaway and Jones, *How the North*[54]	10,699*	13,047*
Heidlers, *Encyclopedia*[55]	1,700+ killed 8,000+ wounded	1,700+ killed 8,000+ wounded
Jones, "Military Means"[56]	10,600*	13,000*
Livermore, *Numbers*[57]	1,723 killed 8,012 wounded 959 missing	1,754 killed 8,408 wounded 2,885 missing
Lowe, "Field Fortifications"[58]	9,740	10,160
Martin, *Shiloh*[59]	10,699*	13,047*
McFeely. *Grant*[60]	1,723 killed	1,754 killed
McWhiney & Jamieson, *Attack*[61]	9,735 (24%)	10,162 (16%)
Nevins, *Ordeal of the Union*[62]	10,699*	13,047*
Phisterer, *Statistics*[63]	10,699*	1,735 killed 7,882 wounded 3,956 missing
Sherman, *Memoirs*[64]		1,700 killed 7,495 wounded 3,022 captured
Smith, *Grant*[65]	1,728 killed 8,012 wounded 959 missing	1,754 killed 8,408 wounded 2,885 missing
Williams, *Lincoln Finds*[66]	1,723 killed 8,012 wounded 959 missing/captured	1,754 killed 8,508 wounded 2,885 missing/captured
Author's Best Estimate:	**1,723 killed 8,012 wounded 959 missing/captured**	**1,754 killed 8,508 wounded 2,885 missing/captured**

IUKA (September 19, 1862)

Source	Confederate	Union
Allen, "Crossroads"[67]	86 killed 496 wounded 40 missing	144 killed 598 wounded
Badeau, *Grant*[68]	1,438*	
Cozzens, *Darkest Days*[69] *(Confederate and Union wounded estimates of Confederate casualties differed considerably.)*	85 killed 410 wounded 157 missing and 385–520 killed 692–1,300 wounded 181–361 captured	141 killed 613 36 missing
Foote, *Civil War*[70]	535*	790*
Fox, *Regimental Losses*[71]	86 killed 408 wounded 199 missing/captured	141 killed 613 wounded 36 missing/captured
Fuller, *Grant and Lee*[72]	782*	144 killed 598 wounded 40 missing
Hattaway and Jones, *How the North*[73]	1,500*	800*
Heidlers, *Encyclopedia*[74]	1,516*	782*
Lamers, *Edge of Glory*[75]	385 killed 692 wounded 361 captured	141 killed 613 wounded 36 missing
Phisterer, *Statistics*[76]	1,516*	144 killed 598 wounded 40 missing
Smith, *Grant*[77]	535*	790*
Snead, "With Price"[78]	86 killed 408 wounded 200 abandoned	141 killed 613 wounded 36 missing
Suhr, "Iuka"[79]	1,500*	800*
Author's Best Estimate:	**400 killed 1,000 wounded 200 missing/captured**	**141 killed 613 wounded 36 missing/captured**

CORINTH (October 3–4, 1862) (Grant not present[80])

Source	Confederate	Union
Allen, "Crossroads"[81]	505 killed 2,150 wounded 2,183 missing	355 killed 1,841 wounded 324 missing
Badeau, *Grant*[82] *(Union reports)*	1,423 killed 2,225 captured 232 missing/captured	315 killed 1,812 wounded
Catton, *Grant Moves South*[83]	Almost 5,000*	2,500*
Cozzens, *Darkest Days*[84] *(Confederate numbers include Hatchie River, Oct. 5.)*	505 killed 2,150 wounded 1,657 missing/captured	355 killed 1,841 wounded 324 missing
Current, *Encyclopedia*[85]	594 killed 2,162 wounded 2,102 missing/captured	315 killed 1,812 wounded 232 missing/captured
Foote, *Civil War*[86]	4,233*	2,520*
Fox, *Regimental Losses*[87] *(Includes Hatchie River, Oct. 5)*	505 killed 2,150 wounded 2,183 missing/captured	401 killed 2,334 wounded 355 missing/captured
Fuller, *Grant and Lee*[88]	473 killed 1,197 wounded 1,763 missing	355 killed 1,841 wounded 324 missing
Grant, *Memoirs*[89]	1,423 killed ? wounded 2,225 captured	315 killed 1,812 wounded 232 missing
Hattaway and Jones, *How the North*[90]	473 killed 1,197 wounded 1,763 missing	355 killed 1,841 wounded 324 missing
Heidlers, *Encyclopedia*[91]	1,423 killed 5,692 wounded 2,268 captured	315 killed 1,812 wounded 232 captured/missing
Lamers, *Edge of Glory*[92]	1,423 killed 5,000 wounded 2,268 missing/captured	355 killed 1,841 wounded 324 missing
Livermore, *Numbers*[93]	473 killed 1,997 wounded 1,763 missing	355 killed 1,841 wounded 324 missing
Phisterer, *Statistics*[94]	14,221*	315 killed 1,812 wounded 232 missing

Source	Confederate	Union
Rosecrans, "Corinth"[95]	1,423 killed c.5,000 wounded 2,268 captured	355 killed 1,841 wounded 324 captured
Smith, *Grant*[96]	5,000*	2,000*
Williams, *Lincoln Finds*[97]	2,470 killed/wounded 1,763 missing	2,196 killed/wounded 324 missing
Author's Best Estimate:	505 killed 3,500 wounded 2,183 missing	355 killed 1,841 wounded 324 missing

HATCHIE RIVER (October 5, 1862) (Grant not present)

Source	Confederate	Union
Cozzens, *Darkest Days*[98]	9 killed 30 wounded 300 captured	570*
Foote, *Civil War*[99]	c. 600*	c. 600*
Phisterer, *Statistics*[100]	500*	400*
Williams, *Lincoln Finds*[101]	605*	570*
Author's Best Estimate:	9 killed 30 wounded 300 captured	100 killed 400 wounded 100 missing/captured

CHICKASAW BAYOU AND BLUFFS (December 26–29, 1862)
(Grant not present)

Source	Confederate	Union
Badeau, *Grant*[102]	63 killed 134 wounded 10 missing	175 killed 930 wounded 43 missing
Bearss, *Vicksburg*[103]	58 killed 119 wounded 10 missing	213 killed 1,016 wounded 561 missing
Beringer et al, *Why the South Lost*[104]	207*	1,776*
Fox, *Regimental Losses*[105]	57 killed 120 wounded 10 missing/captured	208 killed 1,005 wounded 563 missing/captured
Fuller, *Grant and Lee*[106]	63 killed 134 wounded 10 missing	208 killed 1,005 wounded 563 missing
Hattaway and Jones, *How the North*[107]	207*	1,776*

Source	Confederate	Union
Livermore, *Numbers*[108]	63 killed 134 wounded 10 missing	208 killed 1,005 wounded 563 missing
Morgan, "Chickasaw Bluffs"[109]	63 killed 134 wounded 10 missing	208 killed 1,005 wounded 563 missing
Phisterer, *Statistics*[110]	207*	191 killed 982 wounded 756 missing
Author's Best Estimate:	**57 killed 120 wounded 10 missing/captured**	**208 killed 1,005 wounded 563 missing/captured**

ARKANSAS POST (Post Of Arkansas, Fort Hindman) (January 11, 1863) (Grant not present)

Source	Confederate	Union
Arnold, *Grant Wins*[111]	150 killed 4,791 captured	
Bearss, *Vicksburg*[112]	60 killed 73 wounded 80 missing 4,791 captured	134 killed 898 wounded 29 missing
Fox, *Regimental Losses*[113]		134 killed 898 wounded 29 missing/captured
Livermore, *Numbers*[114]	28 killed 81 wounded 4,791 captured	134 killed 898 wounded 29 missing
Phisterer, *Statistics*[115]	5,500*	129 killed 831 wounded 17 missing
Sherman, *Memoirs*[116]	c. 150 killed 440+ wounded 4,791 captured	79+ killed
Author's Best Estimate:	**60 killed 73 wounded 80 missing 4,791 captured**	**134 killed 898 wounded 29 missing**

PORT GIBSON (May 1, 1863)

Source	Confederate	Union
Arnold, *Grant Wins*[117] *(Confederate reports incomplete)*	400+ killed/wounded 387–580+ captured/missing	850 killed/wounded 25 missing
Badeau, *Grant*[118]	448 killed/wounded 650 captured	130 killed 718 wounded
Bearss, *Vicksburg*[119]	60 killed 340 wounded 387 missing	131 killed 719 wounded 25 missing
Current, *Encyclopedia*[120]	60 killed 340 wounded 387 missing	131 killed 719 wounded 25 missing
Fuller, *Grant and Lee*[121]	1,650*	130 killed 718 wounded 5 missing
Grant, *Memoirs*[122]		131 killed 719 wounded 25 missing
Heidlers, *Encyclopedia*[123]	About 800	About 800
Martin, *Vicksburg*[124]	787*	849*
"Opposing Forces," *Battles and Leaders*[125]		131 killed 719 wounded 25 missing/captured
Phisterer, *Statistics*[126]	1,650*	130 killed 718 wounded 5 missing
Smith, *Grant*[127]	832*	875*
Winschel, "Grant's Beachhead"[128] *(Incomplete Confederate Reports)*	68+ killed 380+ wounded 384+ missing	131 killed 719 wounded 25 missing
Author's Best Estimate:	**68+ killed 380+ wounded 384+ missing/captured**	**131 killed 719 wounded 25 missing/captured**

RAYMOND (May 12, 1863)

Source	Confederate	Union
Arnold, *Grant Wins*[129] *(incomplete Confederate reports)*	515+ *	442*
Badeau, *Grant*[130]	100 killed 305 wounded 15+ captured/missing	69 killed 341 wounded 30 missing
Bearss, *Vicksburg*[131]	73 killed 252 wounded 190 missing	68 killed 341 wounded 37 missing
Foote, *Civil War*[132]	514*	442*
Fox, *Regimental Losses*[133]	73 killed 252 wounded 190 missing/ captured	66 killed 339 wounded 37 missing/captured
Grant, *Memoirs*[134]	100 killed 305 wounded 415 captured	66 killed 339 wounded 37 missing
Hattaway and Jones, *How the North*[135]	c. 500*	c. 500*
Heidlers, *Encyclopedia*[136]	72 killed 252 wounded 190 missing and 100 killed 305 wounded 415 captured	66 killed 339 wounded 37 missing and 66 killed 339 wounded 37 missing
Martin, *Vicksburg*[137]	505*	432*
"Opposing Forces"[138]		66 killed 339 wounded 37 missing/captured
Author's Best Estimate:	**100 killed 305 wounded 415 missing/captured**	**66 killed 339 wounded 37 missing/captured**

JACKSON (May 14, 1863)

Source	Confederate	Union
Arnold, Grant Wins[139]	c. 845*	300*
Badeau, *Grant*[140]	845*	41 killed 249 wounded
Bearss, *Vicksburg*[141] *(Confederate reports incomplete)*	17+ killed 64+ wounded 7+ missing	42 killed 251 wounded 118 missing
Current, *Encyclopedia*[142]	Under 400*	300*
Foote, *Civil War*[143]	200+ *	48 killed 273 wounded 11 missing
Fox, *Regimental Losses*[144]		42 killed 251 wounded 7 missing/captured
Grant, *Memoirs*[145]	845*	42 killed 251 wounded 7 missing
Martin, *Vicksburg*[146]	800+ captured	
"Opposing Forces"[147]		42 killed 251 wounded 7 missing/captured
Author's Best Estimate:	**100 killed** **300 wounded** **100 missing/captured**	**42 killed** **251 wounded** **7 missing/captured**

CHAMPION'S HILL (Champion Hill) (May 16, 1863)

Source	Confederate	Union
Arnold, *Armies of Grant*[148] *(Confederate reports incomplete)*	3,800+ *	410 killed 1,844 wounded 187 missing (7% total casualties)
Arnold, *Grant Wins*[149] *(Confederate reports incomplete)*	381+ killed 1,018+ wounded 2,411+ missing	410 killed 1,844 wounded 187 missing
Badeau, *Grant*[150]	3,000–4,000 killed/wounded Almost 3,000 captured	26 killed 1,842 wounded 189 missing
Bearss, "Grant Marches West"[151]	381+ killed 1,018+ wounded 2,441+ missing	410 killed 1,944 wounded 187 missing

Source	Confederate	Union
Bearss, *Vicksburg*[152] (Confederate reports incomplete)	381+ killed 1,081+ wounded 2,441+ missing	396 killed 1,838 wounded 187 missing
Buell, *Warrior Generals*[153]	3,851* (19%)	2,441* (8%)
Catton, *Grant Moves South*[154]	3,800*	2,400+ *
Editors, *Great Battles*[155]	4,300*	2,400*
Esposito, *West Point Atlas*[156]	3,851*	2,441*
Foote, *Civil War*[157]	3,624*	2,441*
Fox, *Regimental Losses*[158]	380 killed 1,018 wounded 2,441 missing/captured	410 killed 1,844 wounded 187 missing/captured
Fuller, *Generalship of Grant*[159]	4,082*	2,438*
Fuller, *Grant and Lee*[160]	381 killed 1,800 wounded 1,670 missing	410 killed 1,844 wounded 187 missing
Grant, *Memoirs*[161]		410 killed 1,844 wounded 2,500+ captured 187 missing
Hattaway and Jones, *How the North*[162]	381 killed 1,800 wounded 1,670 missing	410 killed 1,844 wounded 187 missing
Heidlers, *Encyclopedia*[163]	About 3,800*	About 2,400*
Heidlers, *Encyclopedia*[164]	3,624*	2,441*
Livermore, *Numbers*[165]	381 killed c.1,800 wounded c.1,670 missing	410 killed 1,844 wounded 187 missing
Martin, *Vicksburg*[166]	400 killed 1,000 wounded 200 missing	400 killed 1,800 wounded 2,400 missing
McPherson, *Battle Cry*[167]	3,800*	2,400*
McWhiney & Jamieson, *Attack*[168]		2,254*
Miers, *Web of Victory*[169]	3,624*	2,500*
"Opposing Forces"[170]		410 killed 1,844 wounded 187 missing
Phisterer, *Statistics*[171]	4,300*	426 killed 1,842 wounded 189 missing
Smith, *Grant*[172]	3,840*	2,441*

Source	Confederate	Union
Williams, *Lincoln Finds*[173]	3,851*	2,441*
Author's Best Estimate:	381 killed 1,800 wounded 1,670 missing/captured	410 killed 1,844 wounded 187 missing/captured

BIG BLACK RIVER (Big Black River Bridge) (May 17, 1863)

Source	Confederate	Union
Arnold, *Grant Wins*[174] *(one Confederate division only)*	3 killed 9 wounded 473 missing	39 killed 237 wounded 3 missing
Badeau, *Grant*[175]	1,751 captured	29 killed 242 wounded
Barton, "Charge"[176]		279*
Bearss, *Vicksburg*[177] *(Confederate reports incomplete)*	4+ killed 16+ wounded 1,019+ missing	39 killed 237 wounded 3 missing
Civil War Times, *Great Battles*[178]	1,752 captured	39 killed 237 wounded
Foote, *Civil War*[179]	1,751*	276 killed/wounded 3 missing
Fox, *Regimental Losses*[180]		39 killed 237 wounded 3 missing/captured
Freeman, "Big Black River"[181]	1,751*	279*
Goodman, "Decision"[182]	? killed ? wounded 1,151 prisoners	39 killed 237 wounded 3 missing
Grant, *Memoirs*[183]	1,751 captured	39 killed 237 wounded 3 missing
Heidlers, *Encyclopedia*[184]	1,024* and 1,751*	under 300* and 279*
Martin, *Vicksburg*[185]	1,800 captured	Under 300*
"Opposing Forces"[186]		39 killed 237 wounded 3 missing/captured
Smith, *Grant*[187]	1,751*	200*
Author's Best Estimate:	3 killed 9 wounded 1,000 missing/captured	39 killed 237 wounded 3 missing/captured

VICKSBURG ASSAULT (May 19, 1863)

Source	Confederate	Union
Arnold, *Grant Wins*[188]	c. 200*	157 killed 777 wounded 8 missing
Bearss, *Vicksburg*[189] *(Confederate reports incomplete)*	8+ killed 62+ wounded 2+ missing	157 killed 777 wounded 8 missing
Civil War Times, *Great Battles*[190]	c. 250* 777 wounded 8 missing	157 killed
Fox, *Regimental Losses*[191]		157 killed 777 wounded 8 missing/captured
Martin, *Vicksburg*[192]	Under 100*	Under 1,000*
"Opposing Forces"[193]		157 killed 777 wounded 8 missing/captured
Trudeau, "Climax at Vicksburg"[194]	About 200*	157 killed 777 wounded 8 missing
Winschel, "Siege"[195]		942*
Author's Best Estimate:	**40 killed 160 wounded 0 missing/captured**	**157 killed 777 wounded 8 missing/captured**

VICKSBURG ASSAULT (May 22, 1863)

Source	Confederate	Union
Arnold, *Grant Wins*[196]		3,199*
Badeau, *Grant*[197]		3,000 killed/wounded
Bearss, *Vicksburg*[198] *(Confederate reports incomplete)*	82+ killed 242+ wounded 0+ missing	502 killed 2,550 wounded 147 missing
Buell, *Warrior Generals*[199]		3,199* (7%)
Esposito, *West Point Atlas*[200]		3,200*
Fox, *Regimental Losses*[201]		502 killed 2,550 wounded 147 missing/captured
Fuller, *Grant and Lee*[202]		502 killed 2,550 wounded 147 missing

Source	Confederate	Union
Hattaway and Jones, *How the North*[203]	Under 500*	502 killed 2,550 wounded 147 missing
Heidlers, *Encyclopedia*[204]		Over 3,000*
Livermore, *Numbers*[205]		502 killed 2,550 wounded 147 missing
Lowe, "Field Fortifications"[206]	500	3,200
Martin, *Vicksburg*[207]	500*	3,200*
McFeely, *Grant*[208]		3,200*
"Opposing Forces"[209]		502 killed 2,550 wounded 147 missing/captured
Smith, *Grant*[210]		3,000+ *
Trudeau, "Climax at Vicksburg"[211]	500*	502 killed 2,550 wounded 147 missing
Winschel, "Siege"[212]	Under 500*	3,199*
Author's Best Estimate:	**100 killed** **400 wounded** **0 missing/captured**	**502 killed** **2,550 wounded** **147 missing/captured**

VICKSBURG TRENCHES AFTER TWO ASSAULTS (May 23–July 4, 1863)

Source	Confederate	Union
Arnold, *Grant Wins*[213] *(incomplete Confederate reports)*	805 killed 1,938 wounded 129 missing	104 killed 419 wounded 7 missing
Bearss, *Vicksburg*[214] *(Confederates May 18–July 4/ incomplete)* *(Union June 23–July 4)*	817+ killed 1,952+ wounded 164+ missing	91 killed 391 wounded 118 missing
Fox, *Regimental Losses*[215]		147 killed 613 wounded 9 missing/captured
Hattaway and Jones, *How the North*[216] *(includes the two assaults)*	2,872*	4,910*
"Opposing Forces"[217]		104 killed 419 wounded 7 missing/captured

Source	Confederate	Union
Phisterer, *Statistics*[218] *(May 18–July 4, 1863)*	31,277*	545 killed 3,688 wounded 303 missing
Trudeau, "Climax at Vicksburg"	875 killed 2,169 wounded 158 missing	104 killed 419 wounded 119 missing
Author's Best Estimate	**805 killed** **1,938 wounded** **129 missing/captured**	**104 killed** **419 wounded** **118 missing/captured**

VICKSBURG CAMPAIGN (May 1–July 4, 1863)

Source	Confederate	Union
Arnold, *Armies of Grant*[219]	8,000+ 29,491 captured	1,514 killed 7,395 wounded 453 missing
Arnold, *Grant Wins*[220] *(including Port Hudson)*	47,625*	14,846*
Badeau, *Grant*[221]	12,000 killed/wounded 42,000 captured	1,243 killed 7,095 wounded 535 missing
Chambers, *Oxford Companion*[222]	10,000 killed/wounded 29,396 surrendered	9,000 killed/wounded
Davis, *Rise and Fall*[223]	5,632* 28,000 surrendered	8,875*
Esposito, *West Point Atlas*[224]		9,362*
Fox, *Regimental Losses*[225]		1,514 killed 7,395 wounded 453 missing
Fuller, *Generalship of Grant*[226]	10,000 killed/wounded 37,000 captured	1,243 killed 7,095 wounded 535 missing
Fuller, *Grant and Lee*[227]	10,000 killed/wounded 37,000 captured	1,243 killed 7,095 wounded 535 missing
Grant, *Memoirs*[228]	31,600 surrendered	
Hattaway and Jones, *How the North*[229]	29,396 captured	
Heidlers, *Encyclopedia*[230]	29,396 captured	
Livermore, *Numbers*[231]	29,396 surrendered	
McPherson, *Battle Cry*[232] *(May 1–18 only)*	7,200*	4,300*

Source	Confederate	Union
McWhiney & Jamieson, *Attack*[233]	29,396* (100%)	3,052 (7%)
"Opposing Forces"[234] *(incomplete Confederate reports)*	1,260 killed 3,572 wounded 33,718 missing/captured	1,514 killed 7,395 wounded 453 missing/captured
Poulter, Keith, "Stop Insulting"[235]	38,000+ *	10,142*
Sherman, *Memoirs*[236]	10,000 killed/wounded 3,000 missing 43,000 captured	1,243 killed 7,095 wounded 535 missing
Trudeau, "Climax at Vicksburg"[237]	29,491 captured	
Weigley, *American Way of War*[238]	About 39,000*	About 9,400*
Williams, *Lincoln Finds*[239]	29,396 captured	1,514 killed 7,395 wounded 453 missing/captured
Author's Best Estimate:	**2,000 killed 5,000 wounded 33,718 missing/captured**	**1,514 killed 7,395 wounded 453 missing/captured**

RETURN TO JACKSON, MISSISSIPPI (July 9–16, 1863) (Grant not present)

Source	Confederate	Union
Badeau, *Grant*[240]	71 killed 504 wounded 1,000+ captured	Under 1,000*
Current, *Encyclopedia*[241]	600*	1,132*
Fox, *Regimental Losses*[242]	71 killed 504 wounded 765 missing/captured	129 killed 762 wounded 231 missing/captured
Martin, *Vicksburg*[243]	c. 1,300	c. 1,100
Author's Best Estimate:	**71 killed 504 wounded 765 missing/captured**	**129 killed 762 wounded 231 missing/captured**

BROWN'S FERRY (October 27, 1863)

Source	Confederate	Union
Sword, "Battle Above Clouds"[244]		21
Author's Best Estimate:	**Unknown**	**3 killed 18 wounded**

WAUHATCHIE (October 29, 1863) (Grant not present)

Source	Confederate	Union
Grant, *Memoirs*[245]	150+ killed 100+ captured	416 killed/wounded
Cozzens, *Shipwreck*[246]	356*	216*
Sword, "Battle Above Clouds"[247]	356*	216*
Author's Best Estimate:	75 killed 200 wounded 80 missing/captured	50 killed 150 wounded 16 missing/captured

LOOKOUT MOUNTAIN (November 24, 1863)

Source	Confederate	Union
Sword, "Battle Above Clouds"[248]	1,251	
Author's Best Estimate:	1,251	Unknown

CHATTANOOGA (November 23–25, 1863)

Source	Confederate	Union
Arnold, *Armies of Grant*[249]	6,667*	5,824*
Buell, *Warrior Generals*[250]		5,824* (10%)
Catton, *Grant Takes Command*[251]		5,824* (under 10%)
Cozzens, *Shipwreck*[252]	361 killed 2,180 wounded 6,142 captured	684 killed 4,329 wounded 322 missing/captured
David et al, *Civil War*[253]	6,667*	5,824*
Davis, *Rise and Fall*[254] *"Our loss in killed and wounded was much less."*		757 killed 4,529 wounded 337 missing
Esposito, *West Point Atlas*[255]	6,667*	5,824*
Foote, *Civil War*[256]	361 killed 2,160 wounded 4,146 captured/missing	753 killed 4,722 wounded 349 captured/missing
Fox, *Regimental Losses*[257]	361 killed 2,160 wounded 4,146 missing/captured	687 killed 4,346 wounded 349 missing/captured 752 killed 4,713 wounded 349 missing/captured

Source	Confederate	Union
Fuller, *Grant and Lee*[258]	361 killed 2,160 wounded 4,146 missing/captured	753 killed 4,722 wounded 349 missing/captured
Grant, "Chattanooga"[259]	361 killed 6,100+ captured	752 killed 4,713 wounded 350 missing/captured
Grant, *Memoirs*[260]	6,142 captured	757 killed 4,529 wounded 330 missing
Hattaway and Jones, *How the North*[261]	6,667*	5,824*
Heidlers, *Encyclopedia*[262]	About 6,900*	About 5,400*
Livermore, *Numbers*[263]	361 killed 2,160 wounded 4,146 missing	753 killed 4,722 wounded 349 missing
McWhiney & Jamieson, *Attack*[264]	2,521 (6%)	5,475 *(10%)*
Phisterer, *Statistics*[265]	8,684*	757 killed 4,529 wounded 330 missing
Smith, *Grant*[266]	Under 2,700 4,146 missing/captured	5,475 349 missing/captured
Author's Best Estimate:	**361 killed 2,160 wounded 4,146 missing/captured**	**752 killed 4,713 wounded 349 missing/captured**

KNOXVILLE ASSAULT (November 29, 1863) (Grant not present)

Source	Confederate	Union
Foote, *Civil War*[267]	129 killed 458 wounded 226 captured	8 killed 5 wounded
Heidlers, *Encyclopedia*[268]	800+ *	
Author's Best Estimate:	**129 killed 458 wounded 226 missing/captured**	**8 killed 5 wounded 0 missing/captured**

KNOXVILLE CAMPAIGN (November–December 1863) (Grant not present)

Source	Confederate	Union
Foote, *Civil War*[269]	1,142*	693*
Heidlers, *Encyclopedia*[270]	1,296*	681*
Author's Best Estimate:	**1,219***	**687***

MERIDIAN CAMPAIGN (February 1864) (Grant not present)

SHERMAN'S MARCH

Source	Confederate	Union
Hattaway, "Hard War"[271]		21 killed
		61 wounded
	400 captured	81 missing

WILLIAM SOOY SMITH'S ANCILLARY CAVALRY MOVEMENT

Source	Confederate	Union
Hattaway, "Hard War"[272]	25 killed	54 killed
	75 wounded	179 wounded
		155 missing
Castel, "History in Hindsight"[273]	144 total	2 killed
		386 wounded/missing
Author's Best Estimate (Cumulative)	**50 killed**	**50 killed**
	175 wounded	**240 wounded**
	450 missing/captured	**236 missing/captured**

WILDERNESS (May 5–7, 1864)

Source	Confederate	Union
Buell, *Warrior Generals*[274]		17,666* (17%)
Catton, *Grant Takes Command*[275]		2,265 killed
		10,220 wounded
		2,902 missing
Catton, *Stillness*[276]		c. 15,000*
Civil War Times, *Great Battles*[277]	c. 11,400*	15,000+ *
Current, *Encyclopedia*[278]	c. 7,500*	17,666*
Esposito, *West Point Atlas*[279]	7,750–11,400*	15,000–18,000*
Foote, *Civil War*[280]	7,800*	17,666*
Fox, *Regimental Losses*[281]		2,246 killed
		12,037 wounded
		3,383 missing/captured
Freeman, *Lee*[282]	Less than 7,666*	17,666*
Fuller, *Generalship of Grant*[283]	11,400*+	17,666*
Fuller, *Grant and Lee*[284]	7,750+ *	17,666*
		and
		2,246 killed
		12,037 wounded
		3,383 missing/captured

Source	Confederate	Union
Hassler, *Commanders*[285]	8,000+ *	17,666*
Hattaway, "Changing Face"[286]	7,500+ *	2,246 killed 2,037 wounded 3,383 missing
Hattaway and Jones, *How the North*[287]	c. 7,500*	17,666*
Heidler, *Encyclopedia*[288]	10,000*	18,000*
Livermore, *Numbers*[289]	c.7,750*	2,246 killed 12,037 wounded 3,383 missing
McPherson, *Battle Cry*[290]	Under 10,500*	17,500*
Mertz, "Wilderness II,"[291]	11,000*	17,666*
Phisterer, *Statistics*[292]	11,400*	5,597 killed 21,463 wounded 10,677 missing
Rhea, "'Butcher' Grant"[293]	11,000*	18,000*
Smith, *Grant*[294]	11,000* (18%)	17,666* (18%) 2,246 killed 12,037 wounded 3,383 missing/captured
Steere, *Wilderness*[295]	8,700*	2,246 killed 12,037 wounded 3,383 missing
Taylor, *Lee*[296]		17,666*
U.S. War Department[297]		2,261 killed 8,785 wounded 2,902 missing
Young, "Numbers and Losses"[298]	1,495 killed 7,690 wounded 238 wounded/captured 1,702 missing	
Author's Best Estimate:	**1,495 killed 7,928 wounded 1,702 missing/captured**	**2,246 killed 12,037 wounded 3,383 missing/captured**

SPOTSYLVANIA COURT HOUSE (May 8–21, 1864)

Source	Confederate	Union
Civil War Times, *Great Battles*[299] 17,000+ *		
Current, *Encyclopedia*[300]	c. 10,000*	17,500*
Esposito, *West Point Atlas*[301]	9,000–10,000*	17,000–18,000*
Fox, *Regimental Losses*[302]		2,725 killed 13,416 wounded 2,258 missing/captured
Fuller, *Generalship of Grant*[303]	c. 12,000*	14,322*

(May 8–12 only)

Source	Confederate	Union
Fuller, *Grant and Lee*[304] *May 10 assault*		753 killed 3,347 wounded
May 12 assault	5,500? killed/wounded 4,000 missing	6,020 killed/wounded 800 missing
Hassler, *Commanders*[305]		18,399*
Heidlers, *Encyclopedia*[306]	About 12,000*	About 18,000*
Livermore, *Numbers*[307] *(May 10 & 12)*	800 missing	10,120 killed/wounded
Lowe, "Field Fortifications"[308]	8,000	16,100
Phisterer, *Statistics*[309]	9,000*	4,177 killed 19,687 wounded 2,577 missing
Rhea, "'Butcher' Grant,"[310]	12,500*	18,000*
Taylor, *Lee*[311]		18,399*
U.S. War Department[312]		2,271 killed 9,360 wounded 1,970 missing
Young, "Numbers and Losses"[313]	1,467 killed 4,783 wounded 452 wounded/captured 5,719 missing	
Author's Best Estimate:	**1,467 killed** **6,235 wounded** **5,719 missing/captured**	**2,725 killed** **13,416 wounded** **2,258 missing/captured**

NORTH ANNA, TOTOPOTOMOY, BETHESDA CHURCH AND SHERIDAN'S CAVALRY RAID (May 23–June 1, 1864) (Grant present at North Anna only)

Source	Confederate	Union
Fox, *Regimental Losses*[314]		591 killed 2,734 wounded 661 missing/captured
Fuller, *Grant and Lee*[315]	2,000? killed/wounded	223 killed 1,460 wounded 290 missing
Phisterer, *Statistics*[316]	2,000*	223 killed 1,460 wounded 290 missing
Rhea, " 'Butcher' Grant"[317] *(North Anna only)*	1,600*	2,600*
Taylor, *Lee*[318]		3,986*
U.S. War Department[319] *(North Anna & Totopotomoy only)*		285 killed 1,150 wounded 217 missing
Young, "Numbers and Losses"[320]	460 killed 1,918 wounded 109 wounded/captured 1,279 missing	
Author's Best Estimate:	**460 killed** **2,027 wounded** **1,279 missing/captured**	**591 killed** **2,734 wounded** **661 missing/captured**

COLD HARBOR (May 31–June 12, 1864)

Source	Confederate	Union
Arnold, *Armies of Grant*[321]		13,153* and Almost 6,000
Beringer et al, *Why the South Lost*[322]	1,500*#	7,000*#
Buell, *Warrior Generals*[323]		12,000* (11%)
Casdorph, *Lee and Jackson*[324]		13,000*#
Catton, *Grant Takes Command*[325]	Under 1,500*#	7,000+ *#
Catton, *Stillness*[326]		7,000*#
Current, *Encyclopedia*[327]	1,500*#	7,000*#
Esposito, *West Point Atlas*[328]	1,500*#	7,000*#

Source	Confederate	Union
Fox, *Regimental Losses*[329]		1,844 killed 9,077 wounded 1,816 missing/captured
Freeman, *Lee*[330]	1,200–1,500*#	7,000*#
Fuller, *Generalship of Grant*[331] (June 1–12)	1,300*#	1,100 killed# 4,517 wounded# and 12,737*
Fuller, *Grant and Lee*[332] 1,700?* killed/wounded		1,100 killed# 4,517 wounded# 1,400? missing# and 1,905 killed 10,570 wounded 2,546 missing
Hassler, *Commanders*[333]	1,700*#	12,737*
Heidlers, *Encyclopedia*[334]	1,500*#	7,000*#
Jones, *Right Hand*[335]	1,500*#	7,000*#
"Lee and Grant, 1864"[336]	1,500*#	about 7–8,000*#
Livermore, *Numbers*[337] (June 1–3)		c.12,000 killed/wounded
Lowe, "Field Fortifications"[338]	1,500#	3,000–3,500#
Lowry, *No Turning Back*[339]		7,000*#
O'Beirne, "Valley"[340]		5,500*#
Phisterer, *Statistics*[341]	1,700*	1,905 killed 10,570 wounded 2,456 missing
Rhea, "'Butcher' Grant"[342]	5,000*	13,000*
Rhea, "Cold Harbor"[343]	1,500*#	6,000*#
Rhea, *Cold Harbor*[344]	1,000–1,500*#	6,000+ *#
Taylor, *Lee*[345]	12,738*	
U.S. War Department[346] (May 31–June 12)		1,769 killed 6,752 wounded 1,537 missing
Young, "Numbers and Losses"[347]	83 killed 3,313 wounded 67 wounded/captured 1,132 missing	
# These numbers are for June 3 only		
Author's Best Estimate:	83 killed 3,380 wounded 1,132 missing/captured	1,844 killed 9,077 wounded 1,816 missing/captured

TREVILIAN RAID (June 7–24, 1864) (Grant not present)

Source	Confederate	Union
Fox, *Regimental Losses*[348]		141 killed 709 wounded 579 missing/captured
Phisterer, *Statistics*[349] *(June 11–12 at* *Trevelian Station only)*	370*	85 killed 490 wounded 160 missing
Taylor, *Lee*[350]		1,512*
Young, "Numbers and Losses"[351]	83 killed 380 wounded 1 wounded/captured 318 missing	
Author's Best Estimate:	83 killed 381 wounded 318 missing/captured	141 killed 709 wounded 579 missing/captured

OVERLAND (Richmond) Campaign (Wilderness To Petersburg) (May–June, 1864)

Source	Confederate	Union
Casdorph, *Lee and Jackson*[352]	32,000*	50,000*
Dana, *Recollections*[353]		7,621 killed 38,339 wounded 8,966 missing/captured
Davis, *Rise and Fall*[354]		Almost 100,000*
Donald et al, *Civil War*[355]	24,000*	55,000*
Esposito, *West Point Atlas*[356]	20,000–40,000*	55,000*
Fuller, *Generalship of Grant*[357]	c. 33,000* (43%)	c. 55,000* (34%)
Freeman, *Lee*[358]	c. 30,000*	c. 64,000*
Grant, *Memoirs*[359]		32,633*
Groom, *Shrouds of Glory*[360]		54,000*
Hassler, *Commanders*[361]	20,000*	60,000*
Heidlers, *Encyclopedia*[362]		c. 50,000*
Heidlers, *Encyclopedia*[363]	c. 33,500*	Almost 55,000*
McPherson, *Battle Cry*[364]	35,000+ *	c. 65,000*
McWhiney & Jamieson, *Attack*[365]	c. 32,000 (46%)	c. 50,000 (41%)
Miers, *Last Campaign*[366]	32,000*	50,000*
Rhea, *Spotsylvania*[367] *(Through May 12 only)*	23,000* (33%)	33,000+ * (28%)

Source	Confederate	Union
Smith, *Grant*[368]	35,000*	Almost 65,000*
Taylor, *Lee*[369]		54,926*
U.S. War Department[370]		6,586 killed 26,047 wounded 6,626 missing
Weigley, *American Way of War*[371]	32,000*	55,000*
Young, "Numbers and Losses"[372]	32,631* 4,206 killed 17,705 wounded 859 wounded/captured 9,861 missing	
Author's Best Estimate:	**4,206 killed** **18,564 wounded** **9,861 missing/captured**	**7,621 killed** **38,339 wounded** **8,966 missing/captured**

PETERSBURG ASSAULTS (June 15–18,1864) (Grant not present)

Source	Confederate	Union
Buell, *Warrior Generals*[373]	8,150* (13%)	
Current, *Encyclopedia*[374]	c. 4,000*	10,586*
Fox, *Regimental Losses*[375]		1,688 killed 8,513 wounded 1,185 missing/captured
Fuller, *Grant and Lee*[376]		8,150*
Livermore, *Numbers*[377]		8,150*
Lowe, "Field Fortifications"[378]	4,000	10,000
Phisterer, *Statistics*[379]		1,298 killed 7,474 wounded 1,814 missing
Trudeau, *The Last Citadel*[380]	4,000*	8,150 killed/wounded 1,814 missing
Author's Best Estimate:	**200 killed** **2,900 wounded** **900 missing/captured**	**1,688 killed** **8,513 wounded** **1,185 missing/captured**

WILSON–KAUTZ RAID (June 22–30, 1864) (Grant not present)

Source	Confederate	Union
Fox, *Regimental Losses*[381]		71 killed 262 wounded 1,119 missing/captured
Phisterer, *Statistics*[382]	300*	76 killed 265 wounded 700 missing
Trudeau, *Last Citadel*[383]		81 killed 261 wounded 1,113 missing/captured
Author's Best Estimate:	**300***	**81 killed** **261 wounded** **1,113 missing/captured**

FIRST DEEP BOTTOM RUN/STRAWBERRY PLAINS (July 26–29, 1864)

Source	Confederate	Union
Suderow, "Glory Denied"[384]	471 killed/wounded 208 captured	62 killed 340 wounded 86 missing
Fox, *Regimental Losses*[385]		62 killed 340 wounded 86 missing
Author's Best Estimate:	**80 killed** **391 wounded** **208 missing/captured**	**62 killed** **340 wounded** **86 missing/captured**

THE CRATER (The Mine), Petersburg (July 30, 1864)

Source	Confederate	Union
Catton, *Grant Takes Command*[386]		c. 4,000*
Catton, *Stillness*[387]		3,798*
Civil War Times, *Great Battles*[388]	c. 1,500	c. 4,400*
Current, *Encyclopedia*[389]	1,500*	4,000*
Esposito, *West Point Atlas*[390]		4,400*
Fox, *Regimental Losses*[391]		504 killed 1,881 wounded 1,413 missing/captured
Freeman, *Lee*[392]	c. 1,500*	
Fuller, *Grant and Lee*[393]		2,864 killed/wounded 929 missing

Source	Confederate	Union
Hassler, *Commanders*[394]	1,200*	4,000+ *
Livermore, *Numbers*[395] (Confederate reports incomplete)	619+ killed/wounded 563+ missing	2,864 killed/wounded 929 missing
McPherson, *Battle Cry*[396]	Under 2,000*	4,000*
McWhiney & Jamieson, *Attack*[397]		2,865
Phisterer, *Statistics*[398]	1,200*	419 killed 1,679 wounded 1,910 missing
Trudeau, *Last Citadel*[399]	361+ killed 727+ wounded 403+ missing	504 killed 1,881 wounded 1,413 missing
Author's Best Estimate:	**200 killed 900 wounded 400 missing/captured**	**504 killed 1,881 wounded 1,413 missing/captured**

SECOND DEEP BOTTOM RUN/STRAWBERRY PLAINS (August 14–19, 1864)

Source	Confederate	Union
Buell, *Warrior Generals*[400]		2,901* (10%)
Fox, *Regimental Losses*[401]		327 killed 1,851 wounded 721 missing/captured
Livermore, *Numbers*[402]		328 killed 1,852 wounded 721 missing
McWhiney & Jamieson, *Attack*[403]		2,180
Phisterer, *Statistics*[404]	1,100*	400 killed 1,755 wounded 1,400 missing
Suderow, "Nothing But a Miracle"[405]	1,100 killed/wounded 400 captured	2,180 killed/wounded 721 captured
Trudeau, *Last Citadel*[406]	1,000*	328 killed 1,852 wounded 721 missing/captured
Author's Best Estimate:	**200 killed 900 wounded 400 missing/captured**	**327 killed 1,851 wounded 721 missing/captured**

WELDON RAILROAD (Six Mile House) (August 18–21, 1864) (Grant not present)

Source	Confederate	Union
Arnold, *Armies of Grant*[407]	720*	592 killed/wounded 2,150 captured
Current, *Encyclopedia*[408]	c. 1,600*	4,455*
Fox, *Regimental Losses*[409]		251 killed 1,148 wounded 2,897 missing/captured
Fuller, *Grant and Lee*[410]	1,200? killed/wounded 419 missing	198 killed 1,105 wounded 3,152 missing
Hassler, *Commanders*[411]		4,455*
Livermore, *Numbers*[412]	211 killed 990 wounded 419 missing	198 killed 1,105 wounded 3,152 missing
McWhiney & Jamieson, *Attack*[413]		1,303
Phisterer, *Statistics*[414]	4,000*	212 killed 1,155 wounded 3,176 missing
Author's Best Estimate:	**211 killed 990 wounded 419 missing/captured**	**251 killed 1,148 wounded 2,897 missing/captured**

REAM'S STATION (Reams Station) (August 25, 1864) (Grant not present)

Source	Confederate	Union
Fox, *Regimental Losses*[415]		140 killed 529 wounded 2,073 missing/captured
Phisterer, *Statistics*[416]	1,500*	127 killed 546 wounded 1,769 missing
Trudeau, *Last Citadel*[417]	814*	117+ killed 439+ wounded 2,046+ missing/captured

NEW MARKET HEIGHTS/CHAFFIN'S FARM AND
FORTS HARRISON AND GILMER (September 28–30, 1864)

Source	Confederate	Union
Fox, *Regimental Losses*[418]		383 killed 2,299 wounded 645 missing
Fuller, *Grant and Lee*[419]		783 killed 4,328 wounded 645 missing
Hassler, *Commanders*[420]	2,000*	3,327*
Livermore, *Numbers*[421]		383 killed 2,299 wounded 645 missing
McWhiney and Jamieson, *Attack*[422]		2,682
Phisterer, *Statistics*[423]	2,000*	400 killed 2,029 wounded
Trudeau, *Last Citadel*[424] (includes Peebles Farm)	c. 3,000*	6,322*
Author's Best Estimates:	**250 killed 1,250 wounded 500 missing/captured**	**383 killed 2,299 wounded 645 missing/captured**

DARBYTOWN ROAD (Oct. 7, 1864)

Source	Confederate	Union
Fox, *Regimental Losses*[425]		49 killed 253 wounded 156 missing
Trudeau, "Unerring Firearm"[426]	600–1,000*	458*

HATCHER'S RUN/BURGESS MILL/BOYDTON PLANK ROAD (Oct. 27–28, 1864)

Source	Confederate	Union
Current, *Encyclopedia*[427]		1,758*
Fox, *Regimental Losses*[428]		166 killed 1,028 wounded 564 missing
Fuller, *Grant and Lee*[429]		166 killed 1,028 wounded 564 missing
Hassler, *Commanders*[430]		1,758*

Source	Confederate	Union
Heidlers, *Encyclopedia*[431]	Under 1,000*	Over 1,700*
Livermore, *Numbers*[432]		166 killed 1,028 wounded 564 missing
McWhiney and Jamieson, *Attack*[433]		1,194
Phisterer, *Statistics*[434]	1,000*	156 killed 1,047 wounded 699 missing
Trudeau, *Last Citadel*[435]	1,416*	3,428*
Author's Best Estimates:	**125 killed** **625 wounded** **250 missing**	**166 killed** **1,028 wounded** **564 missing**

DABNEY'S MILLS/HATCHER'S RUN (Feb. 5–7, 1865)

Source	Confederate	Union
Bergeron, "Hatcher's Run"[436]	1,000*	171 killed 1,181 wounded 187 missing
Current, *Encyclopedia*[437]	1,300+ *	
Fox, *Regimental Losses*[438]		171 killed 1,181 wounded 187 missing/captured
Livermore, *Numbers*[439]		170 killed 1,160 wounded 182 missing
McWhiney and Jamieson, *Attack*[440]		1,330
Phisterer, *Statistics*[441]	1,200*	232 killed 1,062 wounded 186 missing
Trudeau, *Last Citadel*[442]	c. 1,000*	171 killed 1,181 wounded 187 missing/captured
Author's Best Estimate:	**125 killed** **625 wounded** **250 missing/captured**	**171 killed** **1,181 wounded** **187 missing/captured**

FORT STEDMAN (Steadman) (March 25, 1865)

Source	Confederate	Union
Current, *Encyclopedia*[443]	4,400–5,000*	
Esposito, *West Point Atlas*[444]	5,000*	
Fox, *Regimental Losses*[445]		72 killed 450 wounded 522 missing/captured
Freeman, *Lee*[446]	Almost 4,800–5,000*	
Fuller, *Generalship of Grant*[447]	4,000*	2,080*
Fuller, *Grant and Lee*[448]	4,000?*	2,080*
Hassler, *Commanders*[449]	4,000*	2,000*
Heidlers, *Encyclopedia*[450]	2,500–3,500	72 killed 450 wounded 522 missing/captured
Marvel, "Retreat"[451]	3,000*	1,000*
McPherson, *Battle Cry*[452]	Almost 5,000*	2,000
Phisterer, *Statistics*[453] *(Federal counterattack)*	2,681* and 834*	68 killed 337 wounded 506 missing and 103 killed 864 wounded 209 missing
Smith, *Grant*[454]	5,000*	under 1,500*
Trudeau, *Last Citadel*[455] *(includes later Federal counterattack)*	2,681–4,000*	2,134*
Author's Best Estimate:	**600 killed 2,400 wounded 1,000 missing/captured**	**72 killed 450 wounded 522 missing/captured**

WHITE OAK ROAD (March 31, 1865) (Grant not present)

Source	Confederate	Union
Fox, *Regimental Losses*[456]		177 killed 1,134 wounded 556 missing/captured
Phisterer, *Statistics*[457]	1,235*	177 killed 1,134 wounded 556 missing
Author's Best Estimate:	**Unknown**	**177 killed 1,134 wounded 556 missing/captured**

DINWIDDIE COURT HOUSE (March 31, 1865) (Grant not present)

Source	Confederate	Union
Fox, *Regimental Losses*[458]		67 killed 354 wounded
Crawford, "Dinwiddie Court House"[459]	800–1,000*	400*
Fuller, *Grant and Lee*[460] *(including White Oak Road)*	1,050*?	2,198 killed/wounded 583 missing
Livermore, *Numbers*[461] *(March 29–31, including White Oak Road)*		2,198 killed/wounded 583 missing
Author's Best Estimate:	125 killed 625 killed 250 missing/captured	67 killed 354 wounded 30 missing/captured

FIVE FORKS (April 1, 1865) (Grant not present)

Source	Confederate	Union
Calkins, "Five Forks"[462]	545 killed and wounded 2,000–2,400 captured 57 missing	104 killed 670 wounded
Catton, *Grant Takes Command*[463]	4,500 captured	
Current, *Encyclopedia*[464]	4,500+ *	Under 1,000*
Esposito, *West Point Atlas*[465]	4,500 captured	
Fox, *Regimental Losses*[466]		124 killed 706 wounded 54 missing/captured
Freeman, *Lee*[467]	3,244 captured	
Marvel, "Retreat"[468]	5,000 captured	
Phisterer, *Statistics*[469]	8,500*	124 killed 706 wounded 54 missing
Trudeau, *Storm*[470]	605 killed/wounded 2,400 captured	103 killed 670 wounded 57 missing
Author's Best Estimate:	100 killed 445 wounded 4,500 captured	104 killed 670 wounded 57 missing

PETERSBURG BREAK–THROUGH (April 2, 1865)

Source	Confederate	Union
Current, *Encyclopedia*[471]		3,300–4,100*

Source	Confederate	Union
Fox, *Regimental Losses*[472]		296 killed 2,565 wounded 500 missing/captured
Fuller, *Grant and Lee*[473]		625 killed 3,189 wounded 326 missing
Livermore, *Numbers*[474]		625 killed 3,189 wounded 326 missing
Phisterer, *Statistics*[475]	3,000*	296 killed 2,565 wounded 500 missing
Author's Best Estimate:	**3,000***	**625 killed 3,189 wounded 326 missing**

PETERSBURG CAMPAIGN (June 15, 1864–April 3, 1865)

Source	Confederate	Union
Current, *Encyclopedia*[476]	At least 28,000*	42,000*
Trudeau, *Last Citadel*[477]	c. 28,000	c. 42,000
Author's Best Estimate:	**28,000***	**42,000***

SAILOR'S (SAYLER'S) CREEK (April 6, 1865) (Grant not present)

Source	Confederate	Union
Calkins, "Final Bloodshed"[478]	7,700 captured	
Fox, *Regimental Losses*[479]		166 killed 1,014 wounded
Freeman, *Lee*[480]	7,000–8,000*	
Glynn, "Black Thursday"[481]	c. 8,000 captured	
Heidlers, *Encyclopedia*[482]	c. 7,700 captured	
McPherson, *Battle Cry*[483]	6,000 captured	
Phisterer, *Statistics*[484]	7,000*	166 killed 1,014 wounded
Smith, *Grant*[485]	2,000 killed/wounded 6,000 captured	
Trudeau, *Last Citadel*[486]	6,000–7,000 captured	
Trudeau, *Storm*[487]	8,000*	1,180 killed/wounded
Author's Best Estimate:	**400 killed 1,600 wounded 7,000 captured**	**166 killed 1,014 wounded**

APPOMATTOX CAMPAIGN (April 2–9, 1865)

Source	Confederate	Union
Buell, *Warrior Generals*[488] (March 29–April 9, 1865)		10,780* (10%)
Civil War Times, *Great Battles*[489]	28,231 surrendered	
Current, *Encyclopedia*[490]	28,000* and Almost 30,000 surrendered	9,000*
Fuller, *Grant and Lee*[491]	22,349 surrendered	1,316 killed 7,750 wounded 1,714 missing
Hassler, *Commanders*[492]	28,000 surrendered	10,780*
Heidlers, *Encyclopedia*[493]	c. 28,000 surrendered	
Livermore, *Numbers*[494]	6,266	1,316 killed 7,750 wounded 1,714 missing
Marvel, *Lee's Last Retreat*[495] (March 25–April 9)	26,000* 28,000 surrendered 14,400–20,400 deserted	
McWhiney and Jamieson, *Attack*[496]	6,666 *(14%)*	9,066 *(8%)*
Phisterer, *Statistics*[497]	26,000 surrendered	
Porter, *Campaigning*[498] (March 29–April 9)	1,200 killed 6,000 wounded 75,000 captured	1,316 killed 7,750 wounded 1,714 missing/captured
Simpson, *Hood's Texas Brigade*[499]	28,231 surrendered	
Author's Best Estimate:	**1,111 killed 5,555 wounded 35,000 captured**	**1,316 killed 7,750 wounded 1,714 missing/captured**

Summary Table
of Author's Best Estimates of Casualties Incurred by Both Sides in Major Campaigns and Battles of Ulysses S. Grant

Campaign/Battle	Total Confederate Casualties	Total Union Casualties
Belmont	641	501
Fort Donelson	16,000	2,832
Shiloh	10,694	13,147
Iuka	1,600	790
Corinth/ Hatchie River	6,527	3,120
Vicksburg Campaign	40,718	9,362
Return to Jackson	1,340	1,122
Chattanooga	6,667	5,814
Western Totals	**84,187**	**36,688**
Wilderness	11,125	17,666
Spotsylvania Court House	13,421	18,399
North Anna River, etc.	3,766	3,986
Cold Harbor	4,595	12,737
Petersburg Assaults	4,000	11,386
Petersburg Siege/Campaign	28,000	42,000
Appomattox Campaign	41,666	10,780
Eastern Totals	**106,573**	**116,954**
TOTALS (killed, wounded, missing/captured)	**190,760**	**153,642**
Net Difference	**37,118**	

Appendix III

THE CRITICAL ELECTION OF 1864:
HOW CLOSE WAS IT?[1]

*U*lysses *Grant's aggressive* Overland Campaign of 1864, in combination with Sherman's Atlanta Campaign, was critical to producing battlefield success that would help ensure the reelection of Abraham Lincoln. His reelection was crucial to Union victory in the war.

Whether Abraham Lincoln could have been defeated in the presidential election of 1864 is an important issue in the ongoing debate about whether and how the Confederacy could have won the Civil War. The commonly accepted version of that election is that Lincoln won a landslide victory over the Democratic candidate, twice-sacked Major General George McClellan, and that it was an election Lincoln could not have lost. At first glance, the election returns seem to confirm this analysis, but an in-depth look reveals a different story.

Out of about four million votes, Lincoln received 2,218,388 (55 percent) while McClellan garnered 1,812,807 (45 percent). These votes resulted in a smashing 212 to 21 electoral vote victory for Lincoln. In the twelve states where military ballots were counted separately, Lincoln received 78 percent of them (119,754 to 34,291)—compared to his 53 percent of the civilian vote in those states.[2]

Election of 1864[3]

	Popular Vote	Electoral Votes
Lincoln	2,218,388 *(55%)*	212
McClellan	1,812,807 *(45%)*	21
Totals	4,031,195	233

But the election results were not so pre-ordained as these numbers appear to indicate. Lincoln was vulnerable because the North was divided on the issues of war, the draft, and slavery. There had been draft riots in New York City, anti-war "Copperhead" sentiment flourished in the Midwest, and the Democrats adopted a Peace Platform at their convention. Just after McClellan's nomination, Secretary of the Navy Gideon Welles worried that "McClellan will be supported by War Democrats and Peace Democrats, by men of every shade and opinion; all discordant elements will be made to harmonize, and all differences will be suppressed." The next day, however, he took a contrary position: "Notwithstanding the factious and petty intrigues of some professed friends ... and much mismanagement and much feeble management, I think the President will be reelected, and I shall be surprised if he does not have a large majority."[4]

"Increasingly, Confederate leaders and people, including the soldiers, looked to the Union presidential election of 1864 as the crucial time when the North could have a referendum on whether or not to continue the war."[5] As early as May 1863, Confederate Chief of Ordnance Josiah Gorgas noted in his diary the vulnerability of the North to political defeat: "No doubt that the war will go on until at least the close of [Lincoln's] administration. How many more lives must be sacrificed to the vindictiveness of a few unprincipled men! For there is no doubt that with the division of sentiment existing at the North the administration could shape its policy either for peace or for war."[6]

As the armies looked ahead to the crucial campaigns of 1864, Confederate General James Longstreet (commander of the First Corps in Lee's Army of Northern Virginia) on March 27 prophetically wrote, "Lincoln's re-election seems to depend upon the result of our efforts during the present year. If he is re-elected, the war must continue, and I see no way of defeating his re-election except by military success."[7] Longstreet also saw the connection between Grant's progress, or lack thereof, and the election as he explained, "If we can break up the enemy's arrangements early, and throw him back, he will not be able to recover his position or his morale until the Presidential election is over, and then we shall have a new President to treat with."[8]

During the summer of 1864, many northerners were upset by the Army of the Potomac's large number of casualties as its soldiers carried out their Overland Campaign from the Rappahannock River across the James River. Ever attacking, they suffered mounting losses at the Wilderness, Spotsylvania Court House, the North Anna River, Cold Harbor, and Petersburg.

Union casualty figures were being published daily in northern newspapers. In addition, many northerners were frustrated by the failure of Union armies to capture either Richmond or Atlanta—which were perceived to be the respective targets of Grant and

Sherman. Newspaper editors and Republican Party leaders urged Lincoln not to run again—to step aside for someone who could win. New York editor Horace Greeley wrote, "Mr. Lincoln is already beaten. He cannot be elected."[9] In July, he asked Lincoln to open peace negotiations with the Confederacy because "our bleeding, bankrupt, almost dying country longs for peace." Then in August, politico Thurlow Weed said, "The people are wild for peace. . . . Lincoln's reelection an impossibility."[10] On August 23, *New York Times* owner and editor and Republican National Executive Committee Chairman Henry J. Raymond advised Lincoln that if the election were held then Lincoln would lose several important states, including New York itself, by 50,000 votes.[11]

Lincoln himself was doubtful about his election prospects. That August he told a friend, "You think I don't know I am going to be beaten, but I do and unless some great change takes place, badly beaten."[12] In fact, on August 23 Lincoln reduced his pessimism to writing. At a Cabinet meeting, he wrote: "This morning, as for some days past, it seems exceedingly probable that this administration will not be re-elected. Then it will be my duty to so cooperate with the President-elect as to save the Union between the election and the inauguration, as he will have secured his election on such ground that he cannot possibly save it afterward."[13] Lincoln had each of his Cabinet members sign the document. As late as September 2, Greeley and two other New York newspaper editors appealed to northern governors to support a movement to replace Lincoln with another candidate.[14]

Lincoln's dim reelection prospects brought hope to Confederates. For example, on August 26, Jedediah Hotchkiss (Stonewall Jackson's famed cartographer) wrote to his wife, "The signs are brightening, and I still confidently look for a conclusion of hostilities with the ending of 'Old Abe's' reign."[15] James McPherson concluded: "If the election had been held in August 1864 instead of November, Lincoln would have lost. He would thus have gone down in history as an also ran, a loser unequal to the challenge of the greatest crisis in the American experience."[16]

The Democrats adopted a peace platform that spoke of "four years of failure" and called for a halt of fighting "with a view to an ultimate convention" to resolve the major issues dividing the nation. Especially after the fall of Atlanta, McClellan was compelled to back off from what too many would deem an unacceptable surrender to the South. Thus he issued a September 9 letter setting forth his position; he rejected the "four years of failure" language, but he conceded that, when the southern states were interested in returning to the Union on any terms, he would negotiate with them.[17]

Democrats emphasized the issue of race. One of their campaign posters read: "ELECT LINCOLN and the BLACK REPUBLICAN TICKET. You will bring on NEGRO EQUALITY, more DEBT, HARDER TIMES, and another DRAFT! Universal Anarchy, and Ultimate RUIN! ELECT McCLELLAN and the whole Democratic Ticket. You will defeat NEGRO EQUALITY, restore Prosperity, re-establish the UNION! In an Honorable, Permanent and Happy PEACE."[18] Two Democratic editors published a spurious pamphlet, supposedly a Republican document, that supported interracial marriage.[19]

Late August was Lincoln's nadir, but three military developments changed everyone's perspective. The first was the fall of Mobile Bay. On August 5, Admiral David Farragut made his "Damn the torpedoes—Full speed ahead" charge into Mobile Bay. On August 26, his forces captured Fort Morgan at the mouth of the harbor and thus deprived the Confederates of their last port in the Gulf of Mexico.

The second significant development was Phil Sheridan's September and October defeats of Jubal Early in the Shenandoah Valley. Finally, the third major event changing people's attitudes and minds—the "great change" Lincoln needed for reelection—was the fall of Atlanta. Grant had contributed to its fall by maintaining pressure on Lee to keep him from reinforcing the Confederates defending Atlanta. General Fuller emphasized the importance of these military victories: "These battles were not only of great value to Grant in furthering the war, but of immense importance to Lincoln in gaining his election, without which the war would in all probability have collapsed."[20]

Taking no chances, Lincoln pressured military commanders to provide adequate leave for soldiers from Indiana and other states that did not allow absentee balloting so that they could presumably vote for their commander-in-chief.[21] With all these positive military developments occurring shortly before the election, it is no wonder that Lincoln won. But what *is* amazing is that a shift of less than one percent of the popular vote (29,935 out of 4,031,195) could have given McClellan an additional 97 electoral votes—just enough to provide him with the total 118 electoral votes he needed to win the election.

As shown in the accompanying table, McClellan needed fewer than 30,000 more popular votes in six critical states to win the election. He could have picked up the huge states of Pennsylvania and New York—and their 59 electoral votes—with a swing of fewer than 13,000 voters. The additional 38 electoral votes he would have needed could have been found in any number of smaller states where he had significant percentages of the vote.

Additional Votes Needed by McClellan to Win

State	McClellan's Percent	Lincoln Votes Needed by McClellan	Electoral Votes
Connecticut	48.6%	1,195 of 44,673	6
Illinois	45.6%	5,395 of 189,512	16
Indiana	46.5%	9,829 of 149,887	13
New York	49.5%	3,375 of 368,735	33
Oregon	46.1%	716 of 9,888	3
Pennsylvania	48.4%	9,425 of 296,292	26
		29,935	97

Other Closely Contested States

State	McClellan's Percent	Lincoln Votes Needed by McClellan	Electoral Votes
Maryland	44.9%	3,708 of 40,153	7
Michigan	44.9%	8,494 of 91,133	8
New Hampshire	47.4%	1,782 of 36,596	5
Wisconsin	44.1%	8,788 of 83,458	8
		22,772	28[22]

Is it a farfetched possibility that such an outcome could have occurred? Consider the following:

~ On September 10, a week after Atlanta had fallen, the *London Daily News* correspondent wrote, "I think of Lincoln's chances at this moment as five to three."[23]

~ On October 13, Lincoln himself created a two-column list of possible state-by-state results in the coming election. By including New York, Pennsylvania, Illinois, and Maryland on the "Copperhead" side of his equation, he calculated that the Union/Republican electoral vote could be 117 (not counting the yet-to-be-admitted State of Nevada with its three electoral votes) and the Democratic/Copperhead vote of 114![24]

∾ As late as October 17, his fellow Illinoisian, Congressman Washburne, wrote to Lincoln, "It is no use to deceive ourselves.... There is imminent danger of our losing the State."[25]

Defeating Lincoln in 1864 was the Confederacy's best opportunity for victory. McClellan's well-documented respect for southern "property rights" could have led to some sort of settlement short of the total Union victory that included abolition of slavery—and perhaps to a cease-fire and de facto southern independence while the peace terms were being negotiated. In a recent study of the war, David Donald, Jean Baker, and Michael Holt concluded that "Lincoln's reelection ensured that the conflict would not be interrupted by a cease-fire followed by negotiations, and in that sense was as important a Union victory as any on the battlefield...."[26]

What is surprising is how close Lincoln came to losing—especially after the positive military developments that immediately preceded the election. The closeness of that election demonstrates how important it had been for Grant to launch an aggressive nationwide offensive only two months after he became the Union Commander-in-Chief. Without the capture of Atlanta, victory in the Shenandoah Valley, and the siege of Petersburg/Richmond, Lincoln's chances of reelection were slim to none.

GRANT INSIDERS

Close colleagues, aides, and associates of Grant

Grenville M. Dodge

James B. McPherson

Ely S. Parker

Horace Porter

John A. Rawlins

Philip H. Sheridan

William T. Sherman

Charles F. Smith

GRANT'S MAJOR OPPONENTS

Confederate generals who commanded armies against Grant

Robert E. Lee

Joseph E. Johnston

P. G. T. Beauregard

John C. Pemberton

GRANT'S UNION HANDICAPS

Union generals who hampered Grant's efforts

Henry W. Halleck

Benjamin F. Butler

James H. Ledlie

Franz Sigel

WARTIME VIEWS

Chattanooga, Tennessee, during the Civil War.

Union steamboats on the Tennessee River at Chattanooga with warehouses
and Lookout Mountain behind them.

Transport steamer "Bridgeport," used to supply Grant's army at Chattanooga via the Tennessee River.

View from Lookout Mountain over the Tennessee River near Chattanooga.

200 lb. battery, Missionary Ridge, Chattanooga.

Grant and some of his officers at City Point, Virginia.

Landing supplies on the James River.

Pontoon across the James River at Deep Bottom, 1864–65.

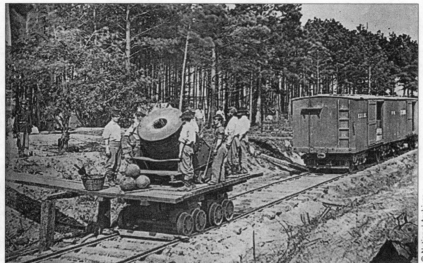

Mortar "Dictator" mounted on railroad car, U.S. Military R.R., Petersburg, Virginia.

Union troops in Virginia.

Ruins of Richmond, Virginia, 1865.

Dead Conferate and Union soldiers, Ft. Mahoney, Petersburg, Virginia.

Union artillery crosses the Rappa-hannock River at start of Overland Campaign, May 1864.

Grant, standing, leans over General Meade's shoulder to read map at Massaponnox Church, Virginia, in May 1864.

Appomattox Court House, Virginia.

CIVIL WAR TIMELINE

Selected campaigns and battles

	1861	**1862**
WESTERN THEATER	Belmont *(Nov. 7)*	Forts Henry and Donelson *(Feb. 6–16)*
		Shiloh *(April 6–7)*
		Iuka *(Sept. 19)*
		Corinth *(Oct. 3–4)*
MIDDLE THEATER		Perryville *(Oct. 8)*
		Stones River (Murfreesboro) *(Dec. 31, 1862–Jan. 2, 1863)*
EASTERN THEATER	First Bull Run (Manassas) *(July 21)*	Peninsula Campaign *(March 17–July 1)*
	Ball's Bluff *(Oct. 21)*	Seven Days' *(June 25–July 1)*
		Second Bull Run (Manassas) *(Aug. 28–30)*
		Antietam *(Sept. 17)*
		Fredericksburg *(Dec. 13)*

1863	**1864**	**1865**
Vicksburg Campaign *(March 31–July 4)*		
Tullahoma Campaign *(June 23–July 3)*	Atlanta Campaign *(May 1–Sept. 2)*	Sherman's March through the Carolinas *(Jan. 19–April 26)*
Chickamauga *(Sept. 19–20)*	Battles of Atlanta *(July 20–Sept. 1)*	Bentonville *(March 19–21)*
Chattanooga Campaign *(Oct. 24–Nov. 25)*	Sherman's March to the Sea *(Nov. 15–Dec. 21)*	
	Hood's Tennessee Campaign *(Nov. 29–Dec. 27)*	
Chancellorsville *(May 1–5)*	Overland Campaign (Wilderness, Spotsylvania Court House, North Anna River, Cold Harbor) *(May 4–June 12)*	Appomattox Campaign *(April 1–9)*
Gettysburg *(July 1–3)*	Petersburg Campaign *(June 15, 1864–April 3, 1865)*	

BIBLIOGRAPHY

MEMOIRS, LETTERS, PAPERS, AND OTHER PRIMARY DOCUMENTS

Alexander, Edward Porter. *Fighting for the Confederacy: The Personal Recollections of General Edward Porter Alexander* ed. by Gary W. Gallagher. Chapel Hill: University of North Carolina Press, 1989.

———. *The Military Memoirs of a Confederate.* New York: Charles Scribner's Sons, 1907.

Badeau, Adam. *Military History of Ulysses S. Grant, from April, 1861, to April, 1865.* 3 vols. New York: D. Appleton and Company, 1868.

Basler, Roy P. (ed.). *The Collected Works of Abraham Lincoln.* 8 vols. New Brunswick: Rutgers University Press, 1953.

Blackford, William Willis. *War Years with Jeb Stuart.* Baton Rouge and London: Louisiana State University Press, 1945. 1993 Reprint.

Cadwallader, Sylvanus. *Three Years with Grant.* New York: Alfred A. Knopf, 1956. Published version of 1896 manuscript entitled inaccurately *Four Years with Grant.*

Cox, Jacob Dolson. *Military Reminiscences of the Civil War.* 2 vols. New York: Charles Scribner's Sons, 1900.

Dana, Charles A. *Recollections of the Civil War.* New York: Collier Books, 1893, 1963.

Davis, Jefferson. *The Rise and Fall of the Confederate Government.* 2 vols. New York: Da Capo Press, Inc., 1990. Reprint of 1881 edition.

Dowdey, Clifford and Manarin, Louis H. (eds.). *The Wartime Papers of R.E. Lee.* New York: Bramhall House, 1961.

Freeman, Douglas Southall and McWhiney, Grady. (eds.) *Lee's Dispatches: Unpublished Letters of General Robert E. Lee, C.S.A., to Jefferson Davis and the War Department of the Confederate States of America 1862–65*. Baton Rouge and London: Louisiana State University Press, 1957, 1994. Update of Freeman's original 1914 edition.

Gaff, Alan D. *On Many a Bloody Field: Four Years in the Iron Brigade*. Bloomington and Indianapolis: Indiana University Press, 1996.

Gibbon, John. *Personal Recollections of the Civil War*. New York and London: G. P. Putnam's Sons, 1928.

Gordon, John B. *Reminiscences of the Civil War*. Baton Rouge and London, Louisiana State University Press, 1993. Reprint of New York: Charles Scribner's Sons, 1903.

Gorgas, Josiah. *The Civil War Diary of General Josiah Gorgas* ed. by Frank E. Vandiver Birmingham: University of Alabama Press, 1947.

Grant, Ulysses S. *Memoirs and Selected Letters: Personal Memoirs of U.S. Grant, Selected Letters 1839–1865*. Reprint. New York: Literary Classics of the United States, Inc., 1990.

Johnson, Robert Underwood and Buel, Clarence Clough (eds.). *Battles and Leaders of the Civil War*. 4 vols. New York: Thomas Yoseloff, Inc., 1956. Reprint of Secaucus, New Jersey: Castle, 1887–8.

Jones, J.B. *A Rebel War Clerk's Diary at the Confederate States Capital*. 2 vols. Philadelphia: J.B. Lippincott & Co., 1866. 1982 reprint.

Jones, J. William. *Personal Reminiscences of General Robert E. Lee*. Richmond: United States Historical Society Press, 1989. Reprint.

Longstreet, James. *From Manassas to Appomattox: Memoirs of the Civil War in America*. New York: SMITHMARK Publishers, Inc., 1994.

Nicolay, John G. *The Outbreak of Rebellion*. New York: Charles Scribner's Sons, 1881. Reprint of Harrisburg: The Archive Society, 1992.

Porter, Horace. *Campaigning with Grant*. New York: SMITHMARK Publishers, Inc., 1994. Reprint of 1897 edition.

Rhodes, Robert Hunt (ed.). *All for the Union: The Civil War Diary and Letters of Elisha Hunt Rhodes*. New York: Orion Books, 1991. Originally published by Andrew Mowbray Incorporated in 1985.

Sherman, William Tecumseh. *Memoirs of General W. T. Sherman*. New York: Literary Classics of the United States, Inc., 1990. Reprint of 1885 second edition.

Simon, John Y. (ed.). *The Papers of Ulysses Grant*. 24 vols. Carbondale and Edwardsville: Southern Illinois University Press, 1967–2000.

Stoddard, William O., Jr. *William O. Stoddard: Lincoln's Third Secretary*. New York: Exposition Press, 1955.

Taylor, Walter H. *General Lee: His Campaigns in Virginia 1861–1865 with Personal Reminiscences*. Lincoln and London: University of Nebraska Press, 1994. Reprint of Norfolk: Nusbaum Books, 1906.

Tower, R. Lockwood (ed.). *Lee's Adjutant: The Wartime Letters of Colonel Walter Herron Taylor, 1862–1865*. Columbia: University of South Carolina Press, 1995.

The War of Rebellion: A Compilation of the Official Records of the Union and Confederate Armies. 128 vols. Washington: Government Printing Office, 1880–1901.

Watkins, Sam. R. *"Co. Aytch," Maury Grays, First Tennessee Regiment; or, A Side Show of the Big Show.* Wilmington, N.C.: Broadfoot Publishing Company, 1987. Reprint of 1952 edition and of Nashville: Cumberland Presbyterian Publishing House, 1882.

Welles, Gideon. *Diary of Gideon Welles.* 3 vols. Boston and New York: Houghton Mifflin Company, 1911.

Wiggins, Sarah Woolfolk (ed.). *The Journals of Josiah Gorgas 1857–1878.* Tuscaloosa and London: The University of Alabama Press, 1995.

Woodward, C. Vann (ed.). *Mary Chestnut's Civil War.* New Haven and London: Yale University Press, 1981.

STATISTICAL ANALYSES

Fox, William F. *Regimental Losses in the American Civil War, 1861–1865: A Treatise on the Extent and Nature of the Mortuary Losses in the Union Regiments, with Full and Exhaustive Statistics Compiled from the Official Records on File in the State Military Bureaus and at Washington.* Dayton, Morningside House, Inc., 1985. Reprint of Albany: Brandow Printing Company, 1898.

Livermore, Thomas L. *Numbers & Losses in the Civil War in America: 1861–1865.* Millwood, New York: Kraus Reprint Co., 1977. Reprint of Bloomington: Indiana University Press, 1957.

Phisterer, Frederick. *Statistical Record: A Treasury of Information about the U.S. Civil War.* Carlisle, Pennsylvania: John Kallmann, Publishers, 1996. Reprint of *Statistical Record of the Armies of the United States* (1883), a supplementary volume to Scribner's Campaigns of the Civil War series.

ATLASES

Cobb, Hubbard. *American Battlefields: A Complete Guide to the Historic Conflicts in Words, Maps, and Photos.* New York: MACMILLAN, 1995.

Davis, George B.; Perry, Leslie J., and Kirkley, Joseph W. *Atlas To Accompany the Official Records of the Union and Confederate Armies.* Washington: Government Printing Office, 1891–95.

Esposito, Vincent J. (ed.) *The West Point Atlas of American Wars.* 2 vols. New York, Washington, London: Frederick A. Praeger, Inc., 1959.

Greene, A. Wilson and Gallagher, Gary W. *National Geographic Guide to the Civil War Battlefield Parks.* Washington, D.C.: The National Geographic Society, 1992.

McPherson, James M. (ed.). *The Atlas of the Civil War.* New York: Macmillan, Inc., 1994.

Nelson, Christopher. *Mapping the Civil War: Featuring Rare Maps from the Library of Congress.* Golden, Colorado: Fulcrum Publishing, 1992.

CHRONOLOGIES

Bishop, Chris and Drury, Ian. *1400 Days: The Civil War Day by Day.* New York: Gallery Books, 1990.

Bowman, John S. (ed.). *The Civil War Almanac.* New York: World Almanac Publications, 1983.

Mosocco, Ronald A. *The Chronological Tracking of the American Civil War Per the Official Records of the War of the Rebellion.* Williamsburg: James River Publications, 1994.

ENCYCLOPEDIAS

Chambers, John Whiteclay, II. *The Oxford Companion to American Military History.* Oxford: Oxford University Press, 1999.

Current, Richard N. (ed.), *Encyclopedia of the Confederacy.* 4 vols. New York: Simon & Schuster, 1993.

Faust, Patricia L. (ed.). *Historical Times Illustrated Encyclopedia of the Civil War.* New York: HarperPerennial, 1991.

Heidler, David S. and Heidler, Jeanne T. (ed.). *Encyclopedia of the American Civil War: A Political, Social, and Military History.* New York and London: W.W. Norton & Company, 2002.

Wagner, Margaret E., Gallagher, Gary W., and Finkelman, Paul (ed.). *The Library of Congress Civil War Desk Reference.* New York: Simon & Schuster, 2002.

OTHER BOOKS

Abbazia, Patrick. *The Chickamauga Campaign, December 1862–November 1863.* New York: Wieser & Wieser, Inc., 1988.

Alexander, Bevin. *How Great Generals Win.* New York and London: W. W. Norton & Co., 1993.

Ambrose, Stephen E. *Halleck: Lincoln's Chief of Staff.* Baton Rouge and London: Louisiana State University Press, 1962, 1990.

———. *Upton and the Army.* Baton Rouge: Louisiana State University Press, 1993.

Arnold, James R. *The Armies of U.S. Grant.* London: Arms and Armour Press, 1995.

———. *Grant Wins the War: Decision at Vicksburg.* New York: John Wiley & Sons, Inc., 1997.

Bearss, Edwin Cole. *Unvexed to the Sea: The Campaign for Vicksburg.* 3 vols. Dayton: Morningside House, Inc., 1991. Reprint of 1986 edition.

Beringer, Richard E.; Hattaway, Herman; Jones, Archer; and Still, William N., Jr. *Why the South Lost the Civil War.* Athens: University of Georgia Press, 1986.

Black, Robert C., III. *The Railroads of the Confederacy.* Chapel Hill and London: University of North Carolina Press, 1998.

Bonekemper, Edward H., III, *Grant and Lee: Victorious American and Vanquished Virginian.* (Westport, CT: Praeger/Greenwood, 2008).

———. *How Robert E. Lee Lost the Civil War.* Fredericksburg, Virginia: Sergeant Kirkland's Press, 1998.

Boritt, Gabor S. (ed.). *Lincoln's Generals.* New York and Oxford, Oxford University Press, 1994.

———. *Lincoln, the War President.* New York and Oxford: Oxford University Press, 1992.

——— (ed.). *Why the Confederacy Lost.* New York and Oxford: Oxford University Press, 1992.

Botkin, B.A. (ed.). *A Civil War Treasury of Tales, Legends and Folklore*. New York: Promontory Press, 1960.

Bridges, Hal. *Lee's Maverick General: Daniel Harvey Hill*. Lincoln and London: University of Nebraska Press, 1991. Reprint of New York: McGraw-Hill, c1961.

Buell, Thomas B. *The Warrior Generals: Combat Leadership in the Civil War*. New York: Crown Publishers, Inc., 1997.

Bushong, Millard Kessler. *Old Jube: A Biography of General Jubal A. Early*. Shippensburg, Pennsylvania: White Mane Publishing Company, Inc., 1955, 1990.

Castel, Albert E. *Decision in the West: The Atlanta Campaign of 1864*. Lawrence: University Press of Kansas, 1992.

———.Castel, Alber, "Vicksburg: Myths and Realities," *North & South*, Vol 6, No. 7 (Nov. 2003), 62-69.

Catton, Bruce. *The American Heritage New History of the Civil War*. New York: Penguin Books USA Inc., 1996.

———. *The Army of the Potomac: Glory Road*. Garden City, New York: Doubleday & Company, Inc., 1952.

———. *The Army of the Potomac: Mr. Lincoln's Army*. Garden City, New York: Doubleday & Company, Inc., 1951, 1962.

———. *The Army of the Potomac: A Stillness at Appomattox*. Garden City, New York: Doubleday & Company, Inc., 1953.

———. *Grant Moves South*. Boston: Little, Brown and Company, 1960.

———. *Grant Takes Command*. Boston: Little, Brown and Company, 1969.

———. *Terrible Swift Sword*. Garden City, New York: Doubleday & Company, Inc., 1963.

———. *This Hallowed Ground: The Story of the Union Side of the Civil War*. Garden City, New York: Doubleday & Company, Inc., 1956, 1962.

———. *U.S. Grant and the American Military Tradition*. Boston: Little, Brown and Company, 1954.

Civil War Times Illustrated. *Great Battles of the Civil War*. New York: W. H. Smith, Inc., 1984.

Clark, John E., Jr. *Railroads in the Civil War: The Impact of Management on Victory and Defeat*. Baton Rouge: Louisiana State University Press, 2001.

Coburn, Mark. *Terrible Innocence: General Sherman at War*. New York: Hippocrene Books, 1993.

Commager, Henry Steele (ed.). *The Blue and the Gray. Two Volumes in One. The Story of the Civil War as Told by Participants*. New York: The Fairfax Press, 1982. Reprint of Indianapolis: Bobbs-Merrill, c. 1950.

Congressional Quarterly, Inc. *Presidential Elections, 1789–1996*. Washington: Congressional Quarterly, Inc., 1997.

Connelly, Thomas Lawrence. *Army of the Heartland: The Army of Tennessee, 1861–1862*. Baton Rouge and London: Louisiana State University Press, 1967.

———. *Autumn of Glory: The Army of Tennessee, 1862–1865*. Baton Rouge and London: Louisiana State University Press, 1971, 1991.

———. *The Marble Man: Robert E. Lee and His Image in American Society*. New York: Alfred A. Knopf, 1977.

———— and Bellows, Barbara R. *God and General Longstreet: The Lost Cause and the Southern Mind*. Baton Rouge: Louisiana State University Press, 1982.

———— and Jones, Archer. *The Politics of Command: Factions and Ideas in Confederate Strategy*. Baton Rouge: Louisiana State University Press, 1973.

Cooling, Benjamin Franklin. *Forts Henry and Donelson: The Key to the Confederate Heartland*. Knoxville: The University of Tennessee Press, 1987.

Cozzens, Peter. *The Darkest Days of the War: The Battles of Iuka and Corinth*. Chapel Hill and London: The University of North Carolina Press, 1997.

————. *The Shipwreck of Their Hopes: The Battles for Chattanooga*. Urbana and Chicago: University of Illinois Press, 1994.

Davis, Burke. *The Long Surrender*. New York: Vintage Books, 1985.

Davis, William C. *The Cause Lost: Myths and Realities of the Confederacy*. Lawrence: University Press of Kansas, 1996.

————. *Jefferson Davis: The Man and His Hour*. Baton Rouge, Louisiana State University Press, 1991.

————. *The Orphan Brigade: The Kentucky Confederates Who Couldn't Go Home*. Mechanicsburg, Pennsylvania: Stackpole Books, 1993.

Dew, Charles B. *Apostles of Disunion: Southern Secession Commissioners and the Causes of the Civil War*. Charlottesville: University Press of Virginia, 2001.

Donald, David Herbert (ed.). *Why the North Won the Civil War*. New York: Macmillan Publishing Co., 1962.

Donald, David Herbert. *Lincoln*. New York: Simon & Schuster, 1995.

Donald, David Herbert; Baker, Jean Harvey; and Holt, Michael F. *The Civil War and Reconstruction*. New York and London: W.W. Norton & Company, 2001.

Dowdey, Clifford. *Lee*. Gettysburg: Stan Clark Military Books, 1991. Reprint of 1965 edition.

————. *Lee's Last Campaign: The Story of Lee and His Men Against Grant—1864*. Wilmington, North Carolina: Broadfoot Publishing Company, 1988. Reprint of New York: Little, Brown and Company, 1960.

Eicher, David J. *The Civil War in Books: An Analytical Bibliography*. Urbana and Chicago: University of Illinois Press, 1997.

Feis, William B. *Grant's Secret Service: The Intelligence War from Belmont to Appomattox*. Lincoln, Nebraska and London: University of Nebraska Press, 2002.

Fellman, Michael. *Citizen Sherman: A Life of William Tecumseh Sherman*. New York: Random House, 1995.

Fishel, Edwin C. *The Secret War for the Union: The Untold Story of Military Intelligence in the Civil War*. Boston and New York: Houghton Mifflin, 1996.

Foote, Shelby (ed.). *Chickamauga and Other Civil War Stories*. New York: Dell Publishing, 1993.

————. *The Civil War: A Narrative*. 3 vols. New York: Random House, 1958–1974.

Freeman, Douglas Southall. *Lee's Lieutenants: A Study in Command*. 3 vols. New York: Charles Scribner's Sons, 1942–4 (1972 reprint).

————. *R.E. Lee*. 4 vols. New York and London: Charles Scribner's Sons, 1934–5.

Fuller, J.F.C. *The Generalship of Ulysses S. Grant*. Bloomington: Indiana University Press, 1958. Reprint of 1929 edition.

———. *Grant and Lee: A Study in Personality and Generalship*. Bloomington: Indiana University Press, 1957. Reprint of 1933 edition.

Furgurson, Ernest B. *Ashes of Glory: Richmond at War*. New York: Alfred A. Knopf, 1996.

———. *Not War But Murder: Cold Harbor 1864*. New York: Alfred A. Knopf, 2000.

Gallagher, Gary W. *Lee and His Generals in War and Memory*. Baton Rouge: Louisiana State University, 1998.

———(ed.). *Lee the Soldier*. Lincoln and London, University of Nebraska Press, 1996.

———(ed.). *The Spotsylvania Campaign*. Chapel Hill and London: University of North Carolina Press, 1998.

———(ed.). *The Wilderness Campaign*. Chapel Hill and London: University of North Carolina Press, 1997.

Gienapp, William E. (ed.). *The Civil War and Reconstruction: A Documentary Collection*. New York and London: W.W. Norton & Company, 2001.

Glatthaar, Joseph T. *Partners in Command: The Relationships Between Leaders in the Civil War*. New York: Macmillan, Inc., 1994.

Gott, Kendall D. *Where the South Lost the War: An Analysis of the Fort Henry–Fort Donelson Campaign, February 1862* (Mechanicsburg, Pennsylvania: Stackpole Books, 2003).

Grant, Susan–Mary and Parish, Peter J. (eds.), *Legacy of Disunion: The Enduring Significance of the American Civil War* (Baton Rouge: Louisiana State University Press, 2003).

Griffith, Paddy. *Battle Tactics of the Civil War*. New Haven and London: Yale University Press, 1996.

Groom, Winston. *Shrouds of Glory. From Atlanta to Nashville: The Last Great Campaign of the Civil War*. New York: The Atlantic Monthly Press, 1995.

Guernsey, Alfred H. and Alden, Henry M. (eds.). *Harper's Pictorial History of the Civil War*. New York: The Fairfax Press, 1977. Reprint of *Harper's Pictorial History of the Great Rebellion in the United States*. New York: Harper & Brothers, 1866.

Hagerman, Edward. *The American Civil War and the Origins of Modern Warfare: Ideas, Organization, and Field Command*. Bloomington and Indianapolis: Indiana University Press, 1992.

Harsh, Joseph L. *Confederate Tide Rising: Robert E. Lee and the Making of Southern Strategy, 1861–1862*. Kent, Ohio and London: The Kent State University Press, 1998.

Hassler, Warren W., Jr. *Commanders of the Army of the Potomac*. Baton Rouge: Louisiana State University Press, 1962.

Hattaway, Herman and Jones, Archer. *How the North Won: A Military History of the Civil War*. Urbana and Chicago: University of Illinois Press, 1991. Reprint of 1983 edition.

Heleniak, Roman J. and Hewitt, Lawrence L. (ed.). *The Confederate High Command & Related Topics: The 1988 Deep Delta Civil War Symposium*. Shippensburg, Pennsylvania: White Mane Publishing Co., Inc., 1990.

Hughes, Nathaniel Cheairs, Jr. *General William J. Hardee: Old Reliable*. Baton Rouge and London: Louisiana State University Press, 1965.

Hurst, Jack. *Nathan Bedford Forest: A Biography*. New York: Alfred A. Knopf, 1993.

Johnson, Clint. *Civil War Blunders*. Winston-Salem: John F. Blair, 1997.

Jones, Archer. *Civil War Command & Strategy: The Process of Victory and Defeat*. New York, The Free Press, 1992.

———. *Confederate Strategy from Shiloh to Vicksburg*. Baton Rouge and London: Louisiana State University Press, 1991.

Jones, R. Steven. *The Right Hand of Command: Use & Disuse of Personal Staffs in the Civil War*. Mechanicsburg, Pennsylvania: Stackpole Books, 2000.

Jones, Terry L. *Lee's Tigers: The Louisiana Infantry in the Army of Northern Virginia*. Baton Rouge and London: Louisiana State University Press, 1987.

Jordan, David M. *Winfield Scott Hancock: A Soldier's Life*. Bloomington and Indianapolis, Indiana University Press, 1996.

Judge, Joseph. *Season of Fire: The Confederate Strike on Washington*. Berryville, Virginia: Rockbridge Publishing Co., 1994.

Katcher, Philip. *The Army of Robert E. Lee*. London: Arms and Armour Press, 1994.

Keegan, John. *The Mask of Command*. New York: Viking, 1987.

Kennett, Lee. *Marching Through Georgia: The Story of Soldiers and Civilians During Sherman's Campaign*. New York: HarperCollins, 1995.

Ketchum, Richard M. *The American Heritage Picture History of the Civil War*. 2 vols. New York: American Heritage Publishing Co., Inc., 1960.

Kiper, Richard L. *Major General John Alexander McClernand: Politician in Uniform*. Kent, Ohio and London: Kent State University Press, 1999.

Lamers, William M. *The Edge of Glory: A Biography of General William S. Rosecrans, U.S.A.* Baton Rouge: Louisiana State University Press, 1999. Reprint and expansion of New York: Harcourt, Brace & World, 1961.

Lawson, Melinda. *Patriot Fires: Forging a New American Nationalism in the Civil War North*. Lawrence: University Press of Kansas, 2002.

Lee, Fitzhugh. *General Lee: A Biography of Robert E. Lee*. New York: Da Capo Press, 1994. Reprint of Wilmington, North Carolina: Broadfoot Publishing Company, 1989 and New York: D. Appleton and Company, 1894.

Lewis, Lloyd. *Captain Sam Grant*. Boston: Little, Brown and Company, 1950.

Lewis, Thomas A. *The Guns of Cedar Creek*. New York: Harper & Row, 1988.

Long, David E. *The Jewel of Liberty: Abraham Lincoln's Re-election and the End of Slavery*. New York: Da Capo Press, 1997. Reprint of Mechanicsburg, Pennsylvania: Stackpole Books, 1994.

Longacre, Edward G. *Grant's Cavalryman: The Life and Wars of General James H. Wilson*. Mechanicsburg, Pennsylvania: Stackpole Press, 1996. Originally *From Union Stars to Top Hat*, 1972.

Lossing, Benson. *A History of the Civil War, 1861–65, and the Causes That Led up to the Great Conflict*. New York: The War Memorial Association, 1912.

Lowry, Don. *Fate of the Country: The Civil War from June—September 1864*. New York: Hippocrene Books, 1992.

———. *No Turning Back: The Beginning of the End of the Civil War: March–June, 1864*. New York: Hippocrene Books, 1992.

Marvel, William. *Lee's Last Retreat: The Flight to Appomattox*. Chapel Hill and London: University of North Carolina Press, 2002.

Matloff, Maurice (ed.). *American Military History*. Washington, D.C.: U.S. Army Center of Military History, 1985.

McDonough, James Lee. *Chattanooga: A Death Grip on the Confederacy*. Knoxville: The University of Tennessee Press, 1984.

McFeely, William. *Grant: A Biography*. New York and London: W.W. Norton & Company, 1981.

McKenzie, John D. *Uncertain Glory: Lee's Generalship Re-Examined*. New York: Hippocrene Books, 1997.

McMurry, Richard M. *Two Great Rebel Armies: An Essay in Confederate Military History*. Chapel Hill and London: The University of North Carolina Press, 1989.

McPherson, James M. *Battle Cry of Freedom: The Civil War Era*. New York: Ballantine Books, 1988.

McWhiney, Grady and Jamieson, Perry D. *Attack and Die: Civil War Military Tactics and the Southern Heritage*. Tuscaloosa: The University of Alabama Press, 1982.

Marszalek, John F. *Sherman: A Soldier's Passion for Order*. New York: Macmillan, Inc., 1993.

———. *The Shiloh Campaign, March–April 1862*. New York: Wieser & Wieser, Inc., 1987.

———. *The Vicksburg Campaign, April, 1862–July, 1863*. New York: Wieser & Wieser, Inc., 1990.

Marvel, William. *Lee's Last Retreat: The Flight to Appomattox*. Chapel Hill and London: University of North Carolina Press, 2002.

Meade, Robert Douthat. *Judah P. Benjamin: Confederate Statesman*. Baton Rouge: Louisiana State University Press, 1943, 2001.

Miers, Earl Schenck. *The Web of Victory: Grant at Vicksburg*. Baton Rouge: Louisiana State University Press, 1984. Reprint of New York: Alfred Knopf, 1955.

———. *The Last Campaign: Grant Saves the Union*. Philadelphia and New York: J.B. Lippincott Company, 1972.

Miller, William J. *Mapping for Stonewall: The Civil War Service of Jed Hotchkiss*. Washington: Elliott & Clark Publishing, 1993.

Mitchell, Joseph B. *Decisive Battles of the Civil War*. New York: Ballantine Books, 1955.

Morris, Roy, Jr. *Sheridan: The Life and Wars of General Phil Sheridan*. New York: Crown Publishers, Inc., 1992.

Neely, Mark E., Jr.; Holzer, Harold; and Boritt, Gabor S. *The Confederate Image: Prints of the Lost Cause*. Chapel Hill and London: The University of North Carolina Press, 1987.

Nevins, Alan. *Ordeal of the Union*. 8 vols. New York and London: Charles Scribner's Sons, 1947–50.

Nicolay, Helen. *The Boys' Life of Ulysses S. Grant*. New York: The Century Co., 1909.

Nolan, Alan T. *Lee Considered: General Robert E. Lee and Civil War History*. Chapel Hill and London: University of North Carolina Press, 1991.

Osborne, Charles C. *Jubal: The Life and Times of General Jubal A. Early, CSA, defender of the Lost Cause*. Baton Rouge and London: Louisiana State University Press, 1992.

Perret, Geoffrey. *A Country Made by War: From the Revolution to Vietnam—the Story of America's Rise to Power*. New York: Random House, 1989.

———. *Ulysses S. Grant: Soldier & President*. New York: Random House, 1997.

Pfanz, Donald C. *Richard S. Ewell: A Soldier's Life*. Chapel Hill and London: University of North Carolina Press, 1998.

Piston, William Garrett. *Lee's Tarnished Lieutenant: James Longstreet and His Place in Southern History*. Athens and London: The University of Georgia Press, 1987.

Pollard, Edward A. *The Lost Cause. A New Southern History of the War of the Confederates*. New York: Gramercy Books, 1994. Reprint of New York: E.B. Treat & Company, 1866.

Rhea, Gordon C. *The Battle of the Wilderness May 5–6, 1864*. Baton Rouge and London: Louisiana State University Press, 1994.

———. *The Battles for Spotsylvania Court House and the Road to Yellow Tavern, May 7–12, 1864*. Baton Rouge and London: Louisiana State University Press, 1997.

———. *Cold Harbor: Grant and Lee May 26–June 3, 1864*. Baton Rouge: Louisiana State University Press, 2002.

———. *To the North Anna River: Lee and Grant May 13–25, 1864*. Baton Rouge: Louisiana State University Press, 2000.

———. "The Truce at Cold Harbor," *North & South*, Vol. 7, No. 1 (Jan. 2004), 76-85

Robertson, James I., Jr. *General A.P. Hill: The Story of a Confederate Warrior*. New York: Random House, 1987.

Ross, Ishbel. *The General's Wife: The Life of Mrs. Ulysses S. Grant*. New York: Dodd, Mead and Company, 1959.

Rowland, Thomas J. *George B. McClellan and Civil War History in the Shadow of Grant and Sherman*. Kent, Ohio and London: The Kent State University Press, 1998.

Royster, Charles. *The Destructive War: William Tecumseh Sherman, Stonewall Jackson, and the Americans*. New York: Vintage Books, 1993.

Scott, Robert Garth. *Into the Wilderness with the Army of the Potomac*. Bloomington: Indiana University Press. 1985.

Sears, Stephen W. *The Civil War: The Best of American Heritage*. New York: American Heritage Press, 1991.

———. *Controversies & Commanders: Dispatches from the Army of the Potomac*. Boston and New York: Houghton Mifflin Company, 1999.

Simpson, Brooks D. *Ulysses S. Grant: Triumph Over Adversity, 1822–1865*. Boston and New York: Houghton Mifflin Company, 2000.

Simpson, Harold B. *Hood's Texas Brigade: Lee's Grenadier Guard*. Fort Worth: Landmark Publishing, Inc., 1970. Vol. 2 of four-volume set on Hood's Texas Brigade.

Smith, Gene. *Lee and Grant: A Dual Biography*. New York: Promontory Press, 1984.

Smith, Jean Edward. *Grant*. New York: Simon & Schuster, 2001.

Steere, Edward. *The Wilderness Campaign*. New York: Bonanza Books, 1960.

Stern, Philip Van Doren. *Robert E. Lee: The Man and the Soldier*. New York: Bonanza Books, 1963.

Stoddard, William O., Jr. *William O. Stoddard: Lincoln's Third Secretary*. New York: Exposition Press, 1955.

Swinton, William. *Campaigns of the Army of the Potomac*. New York: Richardson, 1866.

Thomas, Emory M. *Robert E. Lee: A Biography*. New York and London: W.W. Norton & Company, 1995.

Tidwell, William A.; Hall, James O.; and Gaddy, David Winfred. *Come Retribution: The Confederate Secret Service and the Assassination of Lincoln*. Jackson and London: University Press of Mississippi, 1988.

Trudeau, Noah Andre. *Bloody Roads South: The Wilderness to Cold Harbor, May–June 1864*. Boston, Toronto, London: Little, Brown and Co., 1989.

———. *The Last Citadel: Petersburg, Virginia June 1864—April 1865*. Baton Rouge: Louisiana State University Press, 1991.

———. *Out of the Storm: The End of the Civil War, April–June 1865*. Boston, New York, Toronto, London: Little, Brown and Company, 1994.

Wallace, Willard M. *Soul of the Lion: A Biography of General Joshua L. Chamberlain*. Gettysburg: Stan Clark Military Books, 1991. Reprint of Edinburgh, New York and Toronto: Thomas Nelson & Sons, 1960.

Ward, Geoffrey C.; Burns, Ric, and Burns, Ken. *The Civil War: An Illustrated History*. New York: Alfred A. Knopf, Inc., 1990.

Warner, Ezra J. *Generals in Blue: Lives of the Union Commanders*. Baton Rouge and London: Louisiana State University Press, 1964.

———. *Generals in Gray: Lives of the Confederate Commanders*. Baton Rouge and London: Louisiana State University Press, 1959.

Waugh, John C. *The Class of 1846: From West Point to Appomattox: Stonewall Jackson, George McClellan and Their Brothers*. New York: Warner Books, Inc., 1994.

———. *Reelecting Lincoln: The Battle for the 1864 Presidency*. New York: Crown Publishers, Inc., 1997.

Weber, Thomas. *The Northern Railroads in the Civil War, 1861–1865*. Bloomington and Indianapolis: Indiana University Press, 1999. Reprint of 1952 edition.

Weigley, Russell F. *The American Way of War: A History of United States Military Strategy and Policy*. New York: Macmillan Publishing Co., Inc., 1973.

———. *A Great Civil War: A Military and Political History, 1861–1865*. Bloomington and Indianapolis, Indiana University Press, 2000.

Weir, William. *Fatal Victories*. Hamden, Connecticut: Archon Books, 1993.

Werstein, Irving. *Abraham Lincoln Versus Jefferson Davis*. New York: Thomas Y. Crowell Company, 1959.

Wert, Jeffrey D. *A Brotherhood of Valor: The Common Soldiers of the Stonewall Brigade, C.S.A., and the Iron Brigade, U.S.A.* New York: Simon & Schuster, 1999.

———. *Custer: The Controversial Life of George Armstrong Custer*. New York: Simon & Schuster, 1996.

———. *General James Longstreet: The Confederacy's Most Controversial Soldier—A Biography*. New York: Simon & Schuster, 1993.

———. *From Winchester to Cedar Creek: The Shenandoah Campaign of 1864*. Carlisle, Pennsylvania: South Mountain Press, Inc., 1987.

———. *Mosby's Rangers*. New York: Simon & Schuster, 1990.

———. *On Fields of Fury: From the Wilderness to the Crater: An Eyewitness History*. New York: HarperCollins Publishers, 1991.

Wiley, Bell Irvin. *The Life of Billy Yank: The Common Soldier of the Union*. Baton Rouge and London: Louisiana State University Press, 1952, 1991.

———. *The Life of Johnny Reb: The Common Soldier of the Confederacy*. Baton Rouge and London: Louisiana State University Press, 1943, 1991.

———. *The Road to Appomattox*. Baton Rouge and London: Louisiana State University Press, 1994. Reprint of Memphis: Memphis State College Press, 1956.

Wilkinson, Warren. *Mother, May You Never See the Sights I Have Seen: The Fifty-seventh Massachusetts Veteran Volunteers in the Army of the Potomac, 1864–1865*. New York: Harper & Row, 1990.

Williams, Kenneth P. *Grant Rises in the West*. 2 vols. Lincoln: University of Nebraska Press, 1997. Originally vols. 3 and 4 of *Lincoln Finds a General: A Military Study of the Civil War*, New York: Macmillan, 1952.

———. *Lincoln Finds a General: A Military Study of the Civil War*. Vol. 1. Bloomington: Indiana University Press, 1985. Reprint of 1949 edition.

———. *Lincoln Finds a General: A Military Study of the Civil War*. Vols. 2 and 5 (Prelude to Chattanooga). New York: The Macmillan Company, 1959. Reprint of 1949 edition.

Williams, T. Harry. *Lincoln and His Generals*. New York: Alfred A. Knopf, Inc., 1952.

———. *McClellan, Sherman and Grant*. New Brunswick: Rutgers University Press, 1962.

Wills, Brian Steel. *A Battle from the Start: The Life of Nathan Bedford Forrest*. New York: HarperPerennial, 1992.

Wilson, Harold S. *Confederate Industry: Manufacturers and Quartermasters in the Civil War*. Jackson: University of Mississippi Press, 2002.

Winders, Richard Bruce. *Polk's Army: The American Military Experience in the Mexican War*. College Station: Texas A&M University Press, 1997.

Winik, Jay. *April 1865: The Month That Saved America*. New York: HarperCollins, 2001.

Woodworth, Steven E. (ed.). *Civil War Generals in Defeat*. Lawrence: University of Kansas Press, 1999.

——— (ed.). *Davis and Lee at War*. Lawrence: University of Kansas Press, 1995.

——— (ed.). *Grant's Lieutenants from Cairo to Vicksburg*. Lawrence: University of Kansas Press, 2001.

———. *Jefferson Davis and His Generals: The Failure of Confederate Command in the West*. Lawrence: University Press of Kansas, 1990.

PERIODICAL ARTICLES

Allen, Stacy D. "Corinth, Mississippi: Crossroads of the Western Confederacy," *Blue & Gray Magazine*, XIX, Issue 6 (Summer 2002), pp. 6–24, 36–51.

⸺. "Shiloh! The Campaign and First Day's Battle," *Blue & Gray Magazine*, XIV, No. 3 (Feb. 1997), pp. 6–27, 46–64.

⸺. "Shiloh! The Second Day's Battle and Aftermath," *Blue & Gray Magazine*, XIV, No. 4 (April 1997), pp. 6–27, 45–55.

Alexander, Ted. "McCausland's Raid and the Burning of Chambersburg," *Blue & Gray Magazine*, XI, Issue 6, pp. 10–18, 46–61.

Anderson, Kevin. "Grant's Lifelong Struggle with Alcohol: Examining the Controversy Surrounding Grant and Alcohol," *Columbiad: A Quarterly Review of the War Between the States*, Vol. 2, No. 4 (Winter 1999), pp. 16–26.

Arnold, James R. "Grant Earns a License To Win," *Columbiad: A Quarterly Review of the War Between the States*, Vol. 1, No. 2 (Summer 1997), pp. 31–41.

"The Battles at Spotsylvania Court House, Virginia May 8–21, 1864," *Blue & Gray Magazine*, I, Issue 6 (June–July 1984), pp. 35–48.

Barton, Dick. "Charge at Big Black River," *America's Civil War*, Vol. 12, No. 4 (Sept. 1999), pp. 54–61.

Bearss, Ed. "The Vicksburg Campaign: Grant Marches West: The Battles of Champion Hill and Big Black Bridge," *Blue & Gray Magazine*, XVIII, Issue 5 (June 2001), pp. 6–24, 44–52.

⸺. "The Vicksburg Campaign: Grant Moves Inland," *Blue & Gray Magazine*, XVIII, Issue 1 (October 2000), pp. 6–22, 46–52, 65.

Bergeron, Arthur W., Jr. "The Battle of Mobile Bay and the Campaign for Mobile, Alabama, 1864–65," *Blue & Gray Magazine*, XIX, Issue 4 (April 2002), pp. 6–20, 46–54.

⸺. "Three-day Tussle at Hatcher's Run," *America's Civil War*, Vol. 16, No. 1 (March 2003), pp. 30–7.

Bolte, Philip L. "An Earlier 'Bridge Too Far'," *North & South*, Vol. 3, No. 6 (Aug. 2000), pp. 26–32.

Bonekemper, Edward H., III. "Lincoln's 1864 Victory Was Closer Than It Looked," *Washington Times*, July 15, 2000, p. B3.

Bounds, Steve and Milbourn, Curtis. "The Battle of Mansfield," *North & South*, Vol. 6, No. 2 (February 2003), pp. 26–40.

Bradley, Mark L. "Last Stand in the Carolinas: The Battle of Bentonville, March 19–21, 1865," *Blue & Gray Magazine*, XIII, Issue 2 (December 1995), pp. 8–22, 56–69.

"Old Reliable's Finest Hour: The Battle of Averasboro, North Carolina, March 15–16, 1865," *Blue & Gray Magazine*, XVI, No. 1 (Oct. 1998), pp. 6–20, 52–7.

Broome, Doyle D., Jr. "Daring Rear-guard Defense," *America's Civil War*, Vol. 6, No. 5 (Nov. 1993), pp. 34–40.

Bruce, George A. "Strategy of the Civil War," *Papers of the Military Historical Society of Massachusetts*, 13, 1913, pp. 392–483.

Calkins, Chris M. "The Battle of Five Forks: Final Push for the South Side," *Blue & Gray Magazine*, IX, Issue 4 (April 1992), pp. 8–22, 41–52.

⸺. "Final Bloodshed at Appomattox," *America's Civil War*, Vol. 14, No. 2 (May 2001), pp. 34–40.

Campbell, Eric A. "Slept in the mud, Stood in the mud, Kneeled in the mud," *America's Civil War*, Vol. 15, No. 6 (January 2003), pp. 50–5.

Case, David. "The Battle That Saved Washington," *Civil War Times Illustrated*, XXXVII, No. 7 (Feb. 1999), pp. 46–56.

Clark, John E., Jr. "Reinforcing Rosecrans by Rail: The movement of the Federal Eleventh and Twelfth Corps from Virginia was a wonder of strategy, logistics, and engineering," *Columbiad: A Quarterly Review of the War Between the States*, Vol. 3, No. 3 (Fall 1999), pp. 74–95.

"Common Soldier: Dr. John Kennerly Farris, Confederate Surgeon, Army of Tennessee," *Blue & Gray Magazine*, XVII, Issue 2 (December 1999), pp. 46–7.

Connelly, Thomas Lawrence. "Robert E. Lee and the Western Confederacy: A Criticism of Lee's Strategic Ability," *Civil War History*, 15 (June 1969), pp. 116–32.

"Controversy: Was Butler 'Bottled Up'?," *Blue & Gray Magazine*, VII, No. 1 (Oct. 1989), pp. 27–9.

Cooling, Benjamin Franklin. "Forts Henry & Donelson: Union Victory on the Twin Rivers," *Blue & Gray Magazine*, IX, Issue 3 (Feb. 1992), pp. 10–20, 45–53.

———. "Monocacy: The Battle That Saved Washington," *Blue & Gray Magazine*, X, Issue 2 (Dec. 1992), pp. 8–18, 48–60.

Cozzens, Peter. "Moving into Dead Men's Shoes: The Fight for Battery Robinett at the Battle of Corinth, Mississippi," *Civil War Times Illustrated*, XXXVI, No. 2 (May 1997), pp. 24–33, 47–49.

Crawford, Mark J. "Dinwiddie Court House: Beginning of the End," *America's Civil War*, Vol. 12, No. 1 (March 1999), pp. 50–6.

Daniel, Larry J. "The South Almost Won by Not Losing: A Rebuttal," *North and South*, Vol. 1, No. 3 (Feb. 1998), pp. 44–51.

Davis, Stephen. "Atlanta Campaign. Hood Fights Desperately. The Battles for Atlanta: Events from July 10 to September 2, 1864," *Blue & Gray Magazine*, VI, Issue 6 (August 1989), pp. 8–39, 45–62.

Dew, Charles B. "Apostles of Secession," *North & South*, Vol. 4, No. 4 (April 2001), pp. 24–38.

Dolzall, Gary W. "Enemies Front and Rear," *America's Civil War*, Vol. 16, No. 2 (May 2003), pp. 38–45.

———. "Muddy, Soggy Race to Campbell's Station," *America's Civil War*, Vol. 15, No. 3 (July 2002), pp. 26–32, 80.

———. "O.O. Howard's Long Road to Redemption," *America's Civil War*, Vol. 14, No. 5 (Nov. 2001), pp. 38–44.

Durham, Roger S. "The Man Who Shot John Sedgwick: The Tale of Charles D. Grace— A Sharpshooter in the Doles-Cook Brigade, CSA," *Blue & Gray Magazine*, XIII, Issue 2 (Dec. 1995), pp. 24–9.

———. "Savannah: Mr. Lincoln's Christmas Present," *Blue & Gray Magazine*, VIII, Issue 3 (Feb. 1991), pp. 8–18, 42–53.

Epperson, James F. "Grant Story Flawed" [letter to editor], *Columbiad: A Quarterly Review of the War Between the States*, Vol. 3, No. 2 (Summer 1999), pp. 8–9.

———. "The Chance Battle in the Wilderness," *Columbiad: A Quarterly Review of the War Between the States*, Vol. 2, No. 1 (Spring 1998), pp.77–96.

Evans, E. Chris. "'I Almost Tremble at Her Fate': When Sherman came to Columbia, South Carolina, secession's hotbed became a bed of coals," *Civil War Times Illustrated*, XXXVII, No. 5 (Oct. 1998), pp. 46–51, 60–7.

———. "Return to Jackson: Finishing Stroke to the Vicksburg Campaign, July 5–25, 1863," *Blue & Gray Magazine*, XII, Issue 6 (Aug. 1995), pp. 8–22, 50–63.

Feis, William B. "Charles S. Bell: Union Scout," *North & South*, Vol. 4, No. 5 (June 2001), pp. 26–37.

———. "'He Don't Care a Damn for What the Enemy Does out of His Sight': A Perspective on U.S. Grant and Military Intelligence," *North & South*, Vol. 1, No. 2 (Jan. 1998), pp. 68–81.

Fonvielle, Chris. "The Last Rays of Departing Hope: The Fall of Wilmington, Including the Campaigns Against Fort Fisher," *Blue & Gray Magazine*, XII, Issue 2 (Dec. 1994), pp. 10–21, 48–62.

Freeman, Kirk. "Big Black River," *Military Heritage*, Vol. 2, No. 3 (Dec. 2000), pp. 76–85.

Furqueron, James R. "The 'Best Hated Man' in the Army, Part II," *North & South*, Vol. 4, No. 5 (June 2001), pp. 66–79.

Garavaglia, Louis A. "Sherman's March and the Georgia Arsenals," *North & South*, Vol. 6, No. 1 (Dec. 2002), pp. 12–22.

Gilbert, Thomas D. "Mr. Grant Goes to Washington," *Blue & Gray Magazine*, XII, Issue 4 (April 1995), pp. 33–7.

Glynn, Gary. "Black Thursday for Rebels," *America's Civil War*, Vol. 4, No. 5 (Jan. 1992), pp. 22–9.

Goodman, Al W., Jr. "Decision in the West (Part IV): Between Hell and the Deep Sea: Pemberton's Debacle at Big Black River Bridge," *North & South*, Vol. 1, No. 5 (June 1998), pp. 74–9.

———. "Grant's Mississippi Gamble," *America's Civil War*, Vol. 7, No. 3 (July 1994), pp. 50–6.

"Grant and Lee, 1864: From the North Anna to the Crossing of the James," *Blue & Gray Magazine*, XI, Issue 4 (April 1994), pp. 11–22, 44–58.

Greene, A. Wilson. "April 2, 1865: Day of Decision at Petersburg," *Blue & Gray Magazine*, XVIII, Issue 3 (Feb. 2001), pp. 6–24, 42–53.

Guttman, Jon. "Jeb Stuart's Last Ride," *America's Civil War*, Vol. 7, No. 2 (May 1994), pp. 34–40, 79–80.

Hattaway, Herman. "The Changing Face of Battle," *North & South*, Vol. 4, No. 6 (Aug. 2001), pp. 34–43.

———. "Dress Rehearsal for Hell: In early 1864, Mississippi was a proving ground for the 'total war' that would make Sherman infamous—and victorious," *Civil War Times Illustrated*, XXXVII, No. 5 (Oct. 1998), pp. 32–9, 74–5.

Hinze, David C. "'At All Hazards': Ulysses S. Grant's instructions to Benjamin M. Prentiss left little doubt as to the importance of the Hornets' Nest at Shiloh," *Columbiad: A Quarterly Review of the War Between the States*, Vol. 3, No. 3 (Fall 1999), pp. 19–38.

Holsworth, Jerry W. "VMI at the Battle of New Market and, Sigel's Defeat in the Shenandoah Valley," *Blue & Gray Magazine*, XVI, Issue 4 (April 1999), pp. 6–24, 40–52.

Hudson, Leonne. "Valor at Wilson's Wharf," *Civil War Times Illustrated*, XXXVII, No. 1 (March 1998), pp. 46–52.

Jamieson, Perry D. "Background to Bloodshed," *North & South*, Vol. 4, No. 6 (Aug. 2001), pp. 24–31.

Kelly, Dennis. "Atlanta Campaign. Mountains to Pass, A River to Cross: The Battle of Kennesaw Mountain and Related Actions from June 10 to July 9, 1864," *Blue & Gray Magazine*, VI, Issue 5 (June 1989), pp. 8–30, 46–58.

Kendall, Drew J. ""'Murder' at Malvern Hill," *Military History*, Vol. 19, No. 3 (Aug. 2002), pp. 42–8.

King, Curtis S. "'Reconsider, Hell!'," *MHQ: The Quarterly Journal of Military History*, Vol. 13, No. 4 (Summer 2000), pp. 88–95.

Leonard, Phillip A.B. "Forty-seven Days. Constant bombardment, life in bomb shelters, scarce food and water, and rapidly accumulating filth were the price of resistance for the resolute Confederate citizens of besieged Vicksburg, Mississippi," *Civil War Times Illustrated*, XXXIV, No. 4 (Aug. 2000), pp. 40–9, 68–9.

Leyden, John G. "Grant Wins Last Battle by Finishing Memoirs," *The Washington Times*, March 23, 2002, p. B3.

Long, David E. "Cover-up at Cold Harbor," *Civil War Times Illustrated*, XXXVI, No. 3 (June 1997), pp. 50–9.

Lowe, David W. "Field Fortifications in the Civil War," *North & South*, Vol. 4, No. 6 (Aug. 2001), pp. 58–73.

Lutz, Stephen D. "General Orders, No. 11, Grant's Ignoble Act," *America's Civil War*, XII, No. 7 (misprinted as 6) (March 2000), pp. 50–6.

Malone, Jeff. "Melee in the Underbrush," *America's Civil War*, Vol. 5, No. 5 (Nov. 1992), pp. 26–32.

Matter, William D. "The Battles of Spotsylvania Court House, Virginia, May 18–21, 1864," *Blue & Gray Magazine*, I, Issue 6 (June–July 1984), pp. 35–48.

Marvel, William. "Many Have Offered Excuses for the Confederate Retreat to Appomattox, Perhaps Beginning with Robert E. Lee," *America's Civil War*, Vol. 14, No. 3 (July 2001), pp. 62–70.

———. "Retreat to Appomattox," *Blue & Gray Magazine*, XXXVIII, Issue 4 (April 2001), pp. 6–24, 46–54.

———. "Thorn in the Flesh," *Civil War Times Illustrated*, XLI, No. 3 (June 2002), pp. 42–9, 60–2.

McGehee, Larry. "U.S. Grant Had a Career of Many Hills and Valleys," *Potomac News & Manassas Journal & Messenger* [Virginia], Sept. 8, 2001, p. A6.

McMurry, Richard M. "Atlanta Campaign. Rocky Face to the Dallas Line: The Battles of May 1864," *Blue & Gray Magazine*, VI, Issue 4 (April 1989), pp. 10–23, 46–62.

McPherson, James M. "The Unheroic Hero," *The New York Review of Books*, XLVI, No. 2 (February 4, 1999), pp. 16–19.

Mertz, Gregory A. "No Turning Back: The Battle of the Wilderness," *Blue & Gray Magazine*, XII, Issue 4 (April 1995), pp. 8–23, 47–53; Issue 5 (June 1995), pp. 8–20, 48–50.

————. "Upton's Attack and the Defense of Doles' Salient, Spotsylvania Court House, May 10, 1864," *Blue & Gray Magazine*, XVIII, Issue 6 (Summer 2001), pp. 6–25, 46–52.

Meyers, Christopher C. "'Two Generals Cannot Command This Army': John A. McClernand and the Politics of Command in Grant's Army of the Tennessee," *Columbiad: A Quarterly Review of the War Between the States*, Vol. 2, No. 1 (Spring 1998), pp. 27–41.

Miller, J. Michael. "Strike Them a Blow: Lee and Grant at the North Anna River," *Blue & Gray Magazine*, X, Issue 4 (April 1993), pp. 12–22, 44–55.

Morgan, Michael, "Digging to Victory," *America's Civil War*, Vol. 16, No. 3 (July 2003), pp. 22–9.

Naisawald, L. VanLoan. "'Old Jubilee' Saves Lynchburg," *America's Civil War*, Vol. 16, No. 2 (May 2003), pp. 30–6, 72.

Nofi, Albert A. "Calculating Combatants," *North & South*, Vol. 4, No. 2 (January 2001), pp. 68–9.

O'Beirne, Kevin M. "Into the Valley of the Shadow of Death: The Corcoran Legion at Cold Harbor," *North & South*, Vol. 3, No. 4 (April 2000), pp. 68–81.

Owens, Richard H. "An Astonishing Career," *Military Heritage*, Vol. 3, No. 2 (Oct. 2001), pp. 64–73.

Poggiali, Leonard. "Conditional Surrender: The Death of U.S. Grant, and the Cottage on Mount McGregor," *Blue & Gray Magazine*, X, Issue 3 (Feb. 1993), pp. 60–5.

————. "Lost Opportunity in the Wilderness," *Columbiad: A Quarterly Review of the War Between the States*, Vol. 3, No. 2 (Summer 1999), pp. 21–37.

Popowski, Howard J. "'We've Met Once before . . . in Mexico'," *Blue & Gray Magazine*, I, Issue 6 (June–July 1984), pp. 9–13.

Poulter, Keith. "Decision in the West: The Vicksburg Campaign, Part 1: The Entering Wedge," *North & South*, Vol. 1, No. 2 (Jan. 1998), pp. 18–25.

————. "Decision in the West: The Vicksburg Campaign, Part II: Running the Batteries," *North & South*, Vol. 1, No. 3 (Feb. 1998), pp. 68–75.

————. "Decision in the West: The Vicksburg Campaign, Part III," *North & South*, Vol. 1, No. 4 (April 1998), pp. 77–83.

————. "Stop Insulting Robert E. Lee!," *North & South*, Vol. 1, No. 5 (1998), p. 6.

Powles, James M. "New Jersey's Western Warriors," *America's Civil War*, Vol. 14, No. 4 (Sept. 2001), pp. 46–52.

"Reconsidering Grant and Lee: Reputations of Civil War Generals Shifting," Associated Press, http://www.cnn.com/2003/SHOWBIZ/books/01/08/wkd.Grant.vs.Lee.ap/index.html.

Rhea, Gordon C. "'Butcher' Grant and the Overland Campaign," *North & South*, Vol. 4, No. 1 (Nov. 2000), pp. 44–55.

————. "Butchery at Bethesda Church," *America's Civil War*, Vol. 14, No. 6 (Jan. 2002), pp. 48–54, 80.

————. "Cold Harbor: Anatomy of a Battle," *North & South*, Vol. 5, No. 2 (Feb. 2002), pp. 40–62.

————. "'The Hottest Place I Ever Was In': The Battle of Haw's Shop, May 28, 1864," *North & South*, Vol. 4, No. 4 (April 2001), pp. 42–57.

————. "Last Union Attack at Spotsylvania: The belief that one more hard blow would shatter the Confederate line at Spotsylvania may have been one of Ulysses S. Grant's greatest miscalculations.," *Columbiad: A Quarterly Review of the War Between the States*, Vol. 3, No. 4 (Winter 2000), pp. 111–39.

————. "'They Fought Confounded Plucky': The Battle of Harris Farm, May 19, 1864," *North & South*, Vol. 3, No. 1 (Nov. 1999), pp. 48–66.

————. "Robert E. Lee, Prescience , and the Overland Campaign," *North & South*, Vol. 3, No. 5 (June 2000), pp. 40–50; Rollins, Richard; Sears, Stephen, and Simon, John Y. "What Was Wrong with the Army of the Potomac?," *North & South*, Vol. 4, No. 3 (March 2001), pp. 12–8.

————. "Spotsylvania: The Battles at Spotsylvania Court House, Virginia, May 8–21, 1864," *Blue & Gray Magazine*, I, Issue 6 (June–July 1984), pp. 35–48.

Riggs, Derald T. "Commander in Chief Abe Lincoln," *America's Civil War*, Vol. 13, No. 03 (July 2000), pp. 34–40.

Roberts, Donald J. II. "Belmont: Grant's First Battle," *Military Heritage*, Vol. 2, No. 6 (June 2001), pp. 40–9.

Roth, Dave. "Grierson's Raid: A Cavalry Raid at Its Best, April 17–May 2, 1863," *Blue & Gray Magazine*, X, Issue 5 (June 1993), pp. 12–24, 48–65.

Scaife, William R. "Sherman's March to the Sea: Events from September 3 to December 21, 1864, Including the Occupation of Atlanta, More Battles with the Unpredictable John Bell Hood, the Burning of Atlanta, 'Marching Through Georgia,' and the Fall of Savannah," *Blue & Gray Magazine*, VII, Issue 2 (Dec. 1989), pp. 10–42.

Schiller, Herbert M. "Beast in a Bottle: Bermuda Hundred Campaign, May 1864," *Blue & Gray Magazine*, VII, Issue 1 (Oct. 1989), pp. 8–26.

Sears, Stephen W. "All the Trumpets Sounded. Bruce Catton: An Appreciation," *North & South*, Vol. 3, No. 1 (November 1999), pp. 24–32.

————. "The Dahlgren Papers Revisited," *Columbiad: A Quarterly Review of the War Between the States*, Vol. 3, No. 2 (Summer 1999), pp. 63–87.

————. "Gouverneur Kemble Warren and Little Phil," *North & South*, Vol. 1, No. 5 (June 1998), pp. 56–72.

Skoch, George F. "Miracle of the Rails," *Civil War Times Illustrated*, XXXI, No. 4 (Sept.–Oct. 1992), pp. 22–4, 56–9.

Smith, David M. "Too Little Too Late at Vicksburg," *America's Civil War*, Vol. 13, No. 2 (May 2000), pp. 38–44.

Smith, Timothy B. "The Forgotten Battle of Davis' Bridge," *North & South*, Vol. 2, No. 5 (June 1999), pp. 68–79.

Suderow, Bryce A. "Glory Denied: The First Battle of Deep Bottom, July 27th–29th, 1864," *North & South*, Vol. 3, No. 7 (Sept. 2000), pp. 17–32.

————. "'Nothing But a Miracle Could Save Us': Second Battle of Deep Bottom, Virginia, August 14–20, 1864," *North & South*, Vol. 4, No. 2 (Jan. 2001), pp. 12–32.

————. "War Along the James," *North & South*, Vol. 6, No. 3 (April 2003), pp. 12–23.

Suhr, Robert Collins. "Attack Written Deep and Crimson," *America's Civil War*, Vol. 4, No. 3 (Sept. 1991), pp. 46–52.

———. "Old Brains' Barren Triumph," *America's Civil War*, Vol. 14, No. 2 (May 2001), pp. 42–9.

———. "Saving the Day at Shiloh," *America's Civil War*, XII, No. 6 (January 2000), pp. 34–41.

———. "Small But Savage Battle of Iuka," *America's Civil War*, XII, No. 2 (May 1999), pp. 42–9.

Swift, Gloria Baker and Stephens, Gail. "Honor Redeemed: Lew Wallace's Military Career and the Battle of Monocacy," *North & South*, Vol. 4, No. 2 (Jan. 2001), pp. 34–46.

Sword, Wiley. "The Battle Above the Clouds," *Blue & Gray Magazine*, XVIII, Issue 2 (Dec. 2000), pp. 6–20, 43–56.

Trinque, Bruce A. "Battle Fought on Paper," *America's Civil War*, Vol. 6, No. 2 (May 1993), pp. 30–6.

Trudeau, Noah Andre. "Climax at Vicksburg," *North & South*, Vol. 1, No. 5 (June 1998), pp. 80–9.

———. " 'A Frightful and Frightening Place'," *Civil War Times Illustrated*, XXXVIII, No. 2, pp. 42–56.

———. "That 'Unerring Volcanic Firearm'," *Military History Quarterly*, Vol. 7, No. 4 (Summer 1995).

Wilson, John. "Miracle at Missionary Ridge," *America's Civil War*, XII, No. 7 (misprinted as 6) (March 2000), pp. 42–9.

Winschel, Terrence. "Grant's March Through Louisiana: 'The Highest Examples of Military Energy and Perseverance'," *Blue & Gray Magazine*, XIII, Issue 5 (June 1996), pp. 8–22.

———. "Grant's Beachhead for the Vicksburg Campaign: The Battle of Port Gibson, May 1, 1863," *Blue & Gray Magazine*, XI, Issue 3 (Feb. 1994), pp. 8–22, 48–56.

———. "The Siege of Vicksburg," *Blue & Gray Magazine*, XX, Issue 4 (Spring 2003), pp. 6–24, 47–50.

———. "Vicksburg: 'Thank God. The Father of Waters again goes unvexed to the sea.'," *America's Civil War*, Vol. 16, No. 3 (July 2003), pp. 18–9.

Wittenberg, Eric J. "Roadblock En Route to Washington," *America's Civil War*, Vol. 6, No. 5 (Nov. 1993), pp. 50–6, 80–2.

———. "Sheridan's Second Raid and the Battle of Trevilian Station," *Blue & Gray Magazine*, XIX, Issue 3 (Feb. 2002), pp. 8–24, 45–50.

Woodworth, Steven E. "The Army of the Tennessee and the Element of Military Success," *North & South*, Vol. 6, No. 4 (May 2003), pp. 44–55.

———. "Shiloh's Harsh Training Ground," *America's Civil War*, Vol. 15, No. 2 (May 2002), pp. 34–40.

Young, Alfred C., "Numbers and Losses in the Army of Northern Virginia," *North & South*, Vol. 3, No. 3 (March 2000), pp. 14–29.

Zentner, Joe and Syrett, Mary. "Confederate Gibralter," *Military History*, Vol. 19, No. 6 (February 2003), pp. 26–32, 73.

ACKNOWLEDGMENTS

This book would not have been possible without the support and assistance of many people. My wife, Susan, has been a constant pillar of support and tolerated my long hours of Civil War research, reading, travel, discussion, and writing. My mother, the late Marie H. Bonekemper, taught me how to read and gave me a love of reading before I entered school. My father, the late Edward H. Bonekemper, II, taught me the typesetting, printing, and newspaper businesses in my early and mid teens. My late father-in-law, Al Weidemoyer, strongly encouraged my Civil War writing.

I was fortunate to receive an eye-opening liberal arts education at Muhlenberg College in Allentown, Pennsylvania. Especially noteworthy was the History Department faculty, which included such stalwarts as Doctors Ed Baldrige, Joanne Mortimer, and the late doctors John Reed, Katherine Van Eerde, and Victor Johnson. All of them were inspirational. Particularly significant to me has been the support of former History

Department Chairman and Acting Dean, Dr. Ed Baldrige, who has encouraged my writing on Grant and Lee despite his abiding affection for Robert E. Lee. Also indispensable to me were Dr. Harold Wilson and the history faculty at Old Dominion University in Norfolk, Virginia, where I received my M.A. in history.

Special credit for his lucid maps goes to my cartographer, David Deis of Dreamline Cartography of Northridge, California. His professionalism, promptness, and patience are remarkable.

The following readers of my manuscript provided me with critical comments and advice. Due to their diligence and knowledge, the book's quality was vastly improved and many errors were avoided. Jim Mac-Donald, my dedicated fellow retired Coast Guard officer, did his usual exhaustive, substantive, and editorial review, which has proven to be indispensable; he also corrected my mapping errors. My former Department of Transportation lawyer colleagues, Elaine Joost, Mary Crouter, and Steve Farbman, provided reader-friendly suggestions so necessary for clarity and understanding. Serendipitously, Brian Jones' journalism skills proved to be just perfect for smoothing rough edges throughout the book. My former Coast Guard bosses, Jim Brown and Dore' Hunter, gave me the kind of incisive and constructive feedback for which they are well known. The late British/Bermudian Civil War buff John Faram, insightful Professor Baldrige, military buff Spencer Fisher, and well-informed and healthily skeptical Bill Schmidt all provided meaningful comments that helped me immeasurably. I am indebted to Ardelia Cassetta for her technical assistance.

Finally, I want to thank Harry Crocker, Vice President and Executive Editor of Regnery, for his confidence in my work.

NOTES

PREFACE: THE GREATEST CIVIL WAR GENERAL

1. Donald, David Herbert, *Lincoln* (New York: Simon & Schuster, 1995) , p. 515; Welles, Gideon, *Diary of Gideon Welles* (Boston and New York: Houghton Mifflin, 1911) (3 vols), II, pp. 44–5; Hattaway, Herman, "The Changing Face of Battle, *North & South*, Vol. 4, No. 6 (Aug. 2001), 34–43, "Changing Face, 42.

2. Pollard, Edward A., *The Lost Cause: A New Southern History of the War of the Confederates* (New York: Gramercy Books, 1994) (reprint of New York: E.B. Treat & Co., 1866), 669; Swinton, William, *Campaigns of the Army of the Potomac* (New York: Richardson, 1866), 440; Ropes, John C., "Grant's Campaign in Virginia in 1864," *Papers of the Military Historical Society of Massachusetts*, Vol. 4, 495, quoted in Rhea, Gordon C., *Cold Harbor: Grant and Lee May 23–June 6, 1864* (Baton Rouge: Louisiana State University Press, 2002), xii.

3. Gallagher, Gary W., "'Upon Their Success Hang Momentous Interests: Generals, in Boritt, *Why the Confederacy Lost*, 79–108 at 90–1, quoting

Early, Jubal A., *The Campaigns of Gen. Robert E. Lee. An Address by Lieut. General Jubal A. Early, before Washington and Lee University, January 19th, 1872* (Baltimore: Murphy, 1872), 44; Law, E. M., "From the Wilderness to Cold Harbor" in Johnson, Robert Underwood and Buel, Clarence Clough (eds.), *Battles and Leaders of the Civil War* (New York: Thomas Yoseloff, Inc., 1956) (reprint of Secaucus, New Jersey: Castle. 1887–8) (4 vols.) IV, 118–44 at 143.

4. Taylor, Walter H., *General Lee: His Campaigns in Virginia 1861–1865 with Personal Reminiscences* (Lincoln and London: University of Nebraska Press, 1994) (reprint of Norfolk: Nusbaum Books, 1906), 231, 241.

5. Dowdey, Clifford, *Lee* (Gettysburg: Stan Clark Military Books, 1991) (reprint of New York: Little, Brown and Company, 1965), 433; Meade, Robert Douthat, *Judah P. Benjamin: Confederate Statesman* (Baton Rouge: Louisiana State University Press, 1943, 2001), 284–5; Catton, Bruce, *The Army of the Potomac: A Stillness at Appomattox* (Garden City: Doubleday & Company, Inc., 1953) dust-jacket; Miller, J. Michael, "Strike Them a Blow: Lee and Grant at the North Anna River," *Blue & Gray Magazine*, Issue 4 (April 1993), 12–22, 44–55.

   Elsewhere Dowdey described Grant as a "boring-in type of attacker, who usually scorned finesse." Dowdey, Clifford, *Lee's Last Campaign: The Story of Lee and His Men Against Grant 1864* (Wilmington, N.C.: Broadfoot Publishing Company, 1988) (reprint of New York: Little, Brown and Company, 1960), 93.

6. Mertz, Gregory A. "No Turning Back: The Battle of the Wilderness," *Blue & Gray Magazine*, XII, Issue 5 (June 1995), 8–20, 48–50 at 50.

7. McGehee, Larry, "U.S. Grant Had a Career of Many Hills and Valleys," *Potomac News & Manassas Journal & Messenger* [Woodbridge, Virginia], September 8, 2001; Von Drehle, David, "Welcome to the Democrats, Misreading: How the Liberal Elite Keep Losing Big Elections to the 'Regular' Guys Like Bush and Reagan," *Washington Post*, November 10, 2002. Grant actually graduated 21st in his 1843 class of 39.

8. Lowry, Don, *No Turning Back: The Beginning of the End of the Civil War: March–June 1864* (New York: Hippocrene Books, 1962), 519;

Rhea, *Cold Harbor*, xi; Long, E. B., "Ulysses S. Grant for Today," in Wilson David L. and Simon, John Y. (eds.), *Ulysses S. Grant: Essays and Documents* (Carbondale: University of Illinois Press, 1981), 22; "Reconsidering Grant and Lee: Reputations of Civil War General Shifting," Associated Press, Jan. 8, 2003. Denigrating Grant in comparison to Lee has a long history.

9. Simpson, Brooks D. *Ulysses Grant: Triumph Over Adversity, 1822-1865* (New York: Houghton Mifflin, 2000), 458.

10. McWhiney, Grady and Jamieson, Perry D., *Attack and Die: Civil War Military Tactics and the Southern Heritage* (Tuscaloosa and London: The University of Alabama Press, 1982), 19–24, 158 (see Appendix II, "Casualties in Grant's Battles and Campaigns"); *Washington Post*, May 28, 2001. The 214,938 American battle deaths ranked behind the 291,557 in World War II, but ahead of 53,402 in World War I, 47,410 in the Vietnam War, 33,686 in the Korean War, 4,435 in the American Revolution, 2,260 in the War of 1812, 1,733 in the Mexican War, 1,000 in the Indian Wars, 385 in the Spanish-American War, and 148 in the Gulf War. Ibid.

11. Rhea, Gordon; Rollins, Richard; Sears, Stephen, and Simon, John Y., "What Was Wrong with the Army of the Potomac?," *North & South*, Vol. 4, No. 3 (March 2001), 12–18 at 18.

CHAPTER 1: LIVING A TROUBLED LIFE

1. Warner, Ezra J., *Generals in Blue: Lives of the Union Commanders* (Baton Rouge and London: Louisiana State University Press, 1964), 183; Grant, Ulysses S., *Memoirs and Selected Letters: Personal Memoirs of U.S. Grant, Selected Letters 1839–1865* (New York: Literary Classics of the United States, Inc., 1990) (reprint of 1885 edition), 20–21, 1121; Simon, *Papers of Grant*, I, xxxvii.

2. Grant, *Memoirs*, 20–1, 1121–1122; Simon, *Papers of Grant*, I, xxxvii; Lewis, Lloyd, *Captain Sam Grant* (Boston: Little, Brown and Company, 1950), 31–33.

3. Grant, *Memoirs*, 27.

4. Ibid., 28–29, 1122; Warner, *Generals in Blue*, 183–184; Simon, *Papers of Grant*, I, 3–4; Smith, Jean Edward, *Grant* (New York: Simon & Schuster,

2001), 25; Catton, Bruce, *U.S. Grant and the American Military Tradition* (Boston: Little, Brown and Company, 1954),15, 19. Congressman Thomas Hamer appointed Ulysses to the Military Academy at the request of Jesse Grant, despite the fact that an 1832 political dispute had led Grant to attack Hamer in the appropriately named Georgetown, Ohio. *The Castigator* (Sept. 25, 1832) (". . .he would at any time sacrifice a tried personal friend, to buy over two enemies, who will answer present purpose: That he cares not who sinks as long as he swims, and that he is alike faithless in his political principles, and his personal attachments."). Smith, *Grant*, 25.

5. Grant to R. McKinstry Griffith, Sept. 22, 1839, in Simon, *Papers of Grant*, I, 4–6 at 6. [As a West Point cadet and Mexican War officer, Grant had not mastered grammar or spelling. His writing later improved but never was perfect grammatically. Even with errors, his writing usually was quite lucid. I have tried to reproduce all quotes accurately; all edits are indicated.]

6. Grant, *Memoirs*, 129.

7. Ibid., 31–35, 1122–1123; Warner, *Generals in Blue*, 184.

8. Smith, *Grant*, 28.

9. Grant, *Memoirs*, 34–35.

10. Lewis, *Captain Sam Grant*, 108; Anderson, Kevin, "Grant's Lifelong Struggle with Alcohol: Examining the Controversy Surrounding Grant and Alcohol," *Columbiad: A Quarterly Review of the War Between the States*, Vol. 2, No. 4 (Winter 1999).

11. Grant, *Memoirs*, 36–39, 1123; Warner, *Generals in Blue*, 184; Simon, *Papers of Grant*, I, xxxvii.

12. Simon, *Papers of Grant*, I, xxxvii.

13. Grant, *Memoirs*, 41–42. It should be noted that Grant's statements of opposition to the Mexican War primarily occurred decades later when it was convenient to attack the war brought on by a Democratic president. Winders, Richard Bruce, *Polk's Army: The American Military Experience in the Mexican War* (College Station: Texas A&M University Press, 1997), 204–206.

14. McWhiney and Jamieson, *Attack and Die*, 156.

15. Grant, *Memoirs*, 50.

16. Smith, *Grant*, 42, 52–53.

17. Grant, *Memoirs*, 65, 81, 1124; Smith, *Grant*, 56.

18. Grant to Julia Dent, May 11, 1846, Simon, *Papers of Grant*, I, 84–87 at 86.

19. McPherson, James N., "The Unheroic Hero," *The New York Review of Books*, LXVI, No. 2 (Feb. 4, 1999).

20. Grant, *Memoirs*, 69–70. "Back of the famous soldier who was to go slouching off to the supreme moment of his career at Appomattox Courthouse wearing a private's blouse, mud-stained pants and boots and no sword at all, stood somewhere the remembered example of Old Rough-and-Ready, who would have done it just the same way." Catton, *Grant*, 28.

21. McPherson, "Unheroic Hero", 16; Grant, *Memoirs*, 83–85; Catton, *Grant*, 37. Polk's treatment of Taylor backfired: "General Taylor's victory at Buena Vista, February 22d, 23d, and 24th, 1847, with an army composed almost entirely of volunteers who had not been in battle before, and over a vastly superior force numerically, made his nomination for the Presidency by the Whigs a foregone conclusion." Grant, *Memoirs*, 85.

22. Smith, *Grant*, 67.

23. Ibid., 152.

24. Ibid., 64.

25. Ibid., 36, 64, 69.

26. Grant, *Memoirs*, 1125–1126.

27. Anderson, "Grant's Struggle with Alcohol;" Simon, *Papers of Grant*, I, 195.

28. Grant, *Memoirs*, 130–131, 1125–1126.

29. Grant to Julia Dent Grant, July 1, 1852. Grant wrote this letter about his unsuccessful trip to Washington while staying at Washington's Willard Hotel, where he would arrive under more favorable circumstances about twelve years later. Simon, *Papers of Grant*, I, 242–245, 245–246; Grant, *Memoirs*, 1126.

30. Grant to Julia Dent Grant, Aug. 9, 1852, Simon, *Papers of Grant*, I, 251–253.

31. Anderson, "Grant's Struggle with Alcohol;" Grant, *Memoirs*, 1126.

32. Simon, *Papers of Grant*, I, 311–315; Anderson, "Grant's Struggle with Alcohol."

33. Grant to Julia Dent Grant, Feb. 2, 1854, Simon, *Papers of Grant*, I, 316–318.

34. Grant to Julia Dent Grant, Feb. 6, 1854, Ibid., 320–322.

35. Grant to Julia Dent Grant, Mar. 6 and 25, 1854, Ibid., 322–324, 326–328.

36. Ibid., 328–333. There is considerable dispute about whether Grant was drunk while serving as a paymaster at Humboldt, California. See Epperson, James F., Letter to Editor, *Columbiad*, Vol. 3, No. 2 (Summer 1999), citing the following from Charles Ellington's *The Trial of U.S. Grant*: "At this date, so far removed from the time in question, it is impossible to know whether the payroll episode did indeed take place." Jean Edward Smith concludes that circumstantial evidence indicates that the "story rings true." Smith, *Grant*, 87.

37. Anderson, "Grant's Struggle with Alcohol." "Grant had served in the Army for fifteen years, performed well, and gained valuable experience. During those fifteen years, he had occasionally indulged in periods of drinking, but these generally had been confined to social occasions or when he had little to occupy his time and was separated from his family. There is no indication that prior to his resignation Grant drank more than was typical for a man of the time. Unfortunately, Grant incautiously allowed others to see him when inebriated, and he left the Army with a reputation as a heavy drinker." Ibid., 21.

38. Ibid., 1126–1127; Warner, *Generals in Blue*, 184. Drinking problems may have been the immediate cause of Grant's resignation, and he may have had no more than a few off-duty drinking bouts during the Civil War. He had no drinking problem when he was with his wife, and when Grant was away from her, his friend and chief-of-staff, John Rawlins, usually kept him from drinking. McPherson, "Unheroic Hero," 19.

39. Grant, *Memoirs*, 141–142, 1127–1128; Simon, Papers of Grant, I, 336–345; Warner, *Generals in Blue*, 184.

40. Grant, *Memoirs*, 1128; Warner, *Generals in Blue*, 184; Anderson, "Grant's Struggle with Alcohol."

CHAPTER 2: 1861: SEEKING A CHANCE TO FIGHT

1. Grant, *Memoirs*, 143–52. Support for Grant's perception that slavery was the driving force behind secession is found in the secession ordinances of South Carolina, Mississippi, and Alabama, as well as the declarations of

Georgia and Texas concerning the reasons for their secession. Heidler, David S. And heidler, Jeanne T. (eds.), *Encyclopedia of the American Civil War: A Political, Social, and Military History* (New York and London: W.W. Norton & Company, 2002), 2240–52. Also, a pronounced emphasis on supporting slavery permeated the letters, speeches and writings of the commissioners sent by the early-seceding Confederate states to other states urging them to join the Confederacy. Dew, Charles B., "Apostles of Secession," *North & South (Vol. 4, No. 4, Apr. 2001)*, 24–38; Dew, Charles B., *Apostles of Disunion* (Charlottesville: University Press of Virginia, 2001).

2. Historian James M. McPherson provided this handy guide to Civil War army units:

CIVIL WAR UNION UNITS: Regiment—colonel—10 companies (1,000 men); Brigade—brigadier general—4 regiments (4,000 men); Division—brigadier or major general—3 or 4 brigades (12,000 men); Corps—major general—2 or more divisions (24,000 or more men); Army—major general—several corps. But he cautioned that most Union units were at one-third to one-half strength throughout the war. CIVIL WAR CONFEDERATE UNITS: Divisions were commanded by lieutenant generals. Because divisions often contained four brigades and Corps often contained four divisions, Confederate divisions and corps often were larger than their Union counterparts. McPherson, James M., *Battle Cry of Freedom: The Civil War Era* (New York: Ballantine Books, 1988), 330, note 23.

3. Grant, *Memoirs*, 152–155, 1128–1129; Smith, *Grant*, 100–105.

4. Grant, *Memoirs*, 157–159; Anderson, "Grant's Struggle with Alcohol;" Smith, *Grant*, 105–107.

5. Fuller, J. F. C., *Grant and Lee: A Study in Personality and Generalship* (Bloomington: University of Indiana Press, 1957) (reprint of 1932 edition), 59.

6. Grant, *Memoirs*, 160–162, 1129; Smith, *Grant*, 107–108.

7. Orders No. 7, June 18, 1861, Simon, *Papers of Grant*, II, 45–46.

8. Smith, *Grant*, 108–109.

9. Ibid.,111.

10. Grant, *Memoirs*, 163–165.

11. Ibid., 168–171, 1129. Grant's appointment as brigadier general was back-dated to May 17, 1861, making him thirty-fifth in seniority in the U.S. Army (headed by Winfield Scott). Smith, *Grant*, 113.

12. Grant to Captain Speed Butler, August 23, 1861, Simon, *Papers of Grant*, II, 131. The "Pillow" reference is to Confederate Brigadier General Gideon J. Pillow, who gained notoriety in the Mexican War for having a ditch dug on the wrong side of his fortifications.

13. Smith, *Grant*, 116.

14. Grant, *Memoirs*, 171–173, 1129; Smith, *Grant*, 117–118.

15. Roberts, Donald J., II, "Belmont: Grant's First Battle," *Military Heritage*, Vol. 2, No. 6 (June 2001).

16. Grant, *Memoirs*, 172–175, 1129; Smith, *Grant*, 118–120. In addition to notifying Fremont of his intended move on Paducah, Grant also sent a telegram to the speaker of the Kentucky legislature advising him of the Confederate occupation of Columbus in violation of that Common-wealth's neutrality. Grant, *Memoirs*, 176; Smith, *Grant*, 119.

17. Feis, William, *Grant's Secret Service: The Intelligence War from Belmont to Appomattox* (Lincoln, Nebraska and London: The University of Nebraska Press, 2002), 21–25.

18. Grant, *Memoirs*, 177; Smith, *Grant*, 120–122.

19. Feis, *Grant's Secret Service*, 48–52; Foote, Shelby, *The Civil War: A Narrative* (New York: Random House, 1958–1974) (3 vols.), 149.

20. Roberts, "Belmont." Polk's son described the effect of Grant's deceptions: "Polk had been deterred from sending in the first instance a larger force to meet Grant's attack by the reports which his scouts made of the move-ments of the transports upon the river, and of the position and numbers of the columns from Fort Holt and Paducah, all tending to show that the landing upon the opposite shore of the river was a mere feint, while the real design was an attack on Columbus." Polk, William M., "General Polk and the Battle of Belmont," *Battles and Leaders*, I, 349.

21. Roberts, "Belmont;" Grant, *Memoirs*, 177–184; Smith, *Grant*, 128–130; McFeely, William S., *Grant: A Biography* (New York and London: W.W. Norton & Company, 1981), 93.

22. Wallace, Lew, "The Capture of Fort Donelson," *Battles and Leaders*, I, 404.

23. Smith, *Grant*, 133–134.

24. Fox, William F., *Regimental Losses in the American Civil War, 1861–1865: A Treatise on the Extent and Nature of the Mortuary Losses in the Union Regiments, with Full and Exhaustive Statistics Compiled from the Official Records on File in the State Military Bureaus and at Washington* (Dayton: Morningside House, Inc., 1985) (Reprint of Albany: Brandow Printing Company, 1898), 543, 549. For details on casualties in this and later battles and campaigns, see Appendix II, "Casualties Resulting from Campaigns and Battles of Ulysses S. Grant." There I have listed others' estimates of casualties and then made my own best estimate of those casualties—generally by selecting the estimates I found most reliable.

25. Grant, *Memoirs*, 185–186; Roberts, "Belmont;" Smith, *Grant*, 130–132; Hattaway and Archer, *How the North Won*, 53.

CHAPTER 3: WINTER 1862: CAPTURING FORTS HENRY AND DONELSON

1. Grant, *Memoirs*, 188; Feis, *Grant's Secret Service*, 63.

2. Grant, *Memoirs*, 189; Smith, *Grant*, 135–40; McFeely, *Grant*, 96–97; Catton, Bruce, *Grant Moves South* (Boston: Little, Brown and Company, 1960), 123–125, 129–132; Grant to Halleck, January 28 and 29, 1862, Simon, *Papers of Grant*, IV, 99–102. Grant's problems in dealing with Halleck have been ascribed by British Major-General and military histo-rian J. F. C. Fuller to Halleck's being a "cautious, witless pedant who had studied war, and imagined that adherence to certain strategical and tacti-cal maxims constituted the height of generalship." Fuller added, "It may be said, without fear of contradiction, that throughout the war Halleck was worth much more than the proverbial army corps to the Confederate forces." Fuller, J. F. C., *The Generalship of Ulysses S. Grant* (New York: Da Capo Press, Inc., 1991) (reprint of 1929 edition), 79.

3. Smith, *Grant*, 140–141.

4. Grant, *Memoirs*, 189–190; Cooling, Benjamin Franklin, "Forts Henry and Donelson: Union Victory on the Twin Rivers," *Blue & Gray Maga-zine*, IX, Issue 3 (Feb. 1992); Smith, *Grant*, 141.

5. Feis, *Grant's Secret Service*, 66–67.

6. Cooling, Benjamin Franklin, *Forts Henry and Donelson: The Key to the Confederate Heartland* (Knoxville: The University of Tennessee Press, 1987), 101–111; 13–17; Smith, *Grant*, 147. The artillerist at Fort Henry said that General Tilghman held a war council the prior day, decided that withdrawing his "green" troops under fire would be difficult, and told his commanders to "rejoin your commands and hold them in readiness for instant motion." The artillerist proudly stated that his gunners held out for two hours (instead of the one requested) and never did state when the 4,000 defenders retreated to Fort Donelson. Taylor, Jesse, "The Defense of Fort Henry," *Battles and Leaders*, I, 368–372.

7. Cooling, *Forts*, 20.

8. Smith, *Grant*, 153.

9. Grant, *Memoirs*, 190–195; Cooling, *Forts*, 17; Smith, *Grant*, 148; Cooling, *Forts*, 113–115.

10. Cooling, *Forts*, 20.

11. Smith, *Grant*, 149.

12. Grant, *Memoirs*, 196–197. The Fort Donelson operation marked the beginning of the great partnership between Grant and Sherman, which is discussed in Glatthaar, Joseph T., *Partners in Command: The Relationships Between Leaders in the Civil War* (New York: The Free Press, 1994), 135–161.

13. Cooling, *Forts*, 140–146, 45–46; Wallace, "Donelson," 411–412.

14. Cooling, *Forts*, 147–160, 46–47; Wallace, "Donelson," 413–414.

15. Cooling, *Forts*, 166–183, 47–48; Wallace, "Donelson," 415–421. Lew Wallace later rhetorically asked, "Why did [Floyd] not avail himself of the dearly bought opportunity, and march his army out?" Ibid., 418.

16. Wallace, "Donelson," 421–422.

17. Grant, *Memoirs*, 205.

18. Cooling, *Forts*, 183–199; 48–49; Smith, *Grant*, 157–160.

19. Smith, *Grant*, 160.

20. Grant, *Memoirs*, 197–207; Cooling, *Forts*, 200–223, 51–52; Smith, *Grant*, 160–161; Wallace, "Donelson." 425–426.

21. Grant, *Memoirs*, 207–211; Smith, *Grant*, 165–166; Wallace, "Donelson," 426–428; Grant to Buckner, Feb. 16, 1862, Simon, *Papers of Grant*, IV, 218; Buckner to Grant, Feb. 16, 1862, Ibid.

22. Williams, *McClellan, Sherman and Grant*, 88.

23. Cooling, *Forts*, 49.

24. Ibid., 52.

25. Davis, William C., *Jefferson Davis: The Man and His Hour* (Baton Rouge: Louisiana State University Press, 1991), 398–399; Fuller, *Generalship of Grant*, 93–94.

26. Grant to Brigadier General George W. Cullum, Simon, *Papers of Grant*, IV, 223.

27. Foote, *Civil War*, I, 214–215.

28. Jones, J. B., *A Rebel War Clerk's Diary at the Confederate States Capital* (Philadelphia: J.B. Lippincott & Co., 1866) (1982 reprint) (2 vols.), I, 111.

29. Grant, *Memoirs*, 214; Cooling, *Forts*, 53; Smith, *Grant*, 151–152, 164, 166.

30. Catton, Bruce, *Terrible Swift Sword* (Garden City, New York: Doubleday & Company, Inc., 1963), 163.

31. Hattaway, Herman, and Jones, Archer, *How the North Won: A Military History of the Civil War* (Urbana and Chicago: University of Illinois Press, 1983, 1991), xv. In fact, a recent analysis of that campaign by Kendall D. Gott is entitled *Where the South Lost the War: An Analysis of the Fort Henry–Fort Donelson Campaign, February 1862* (Mechanicsburg, Pennsylvania: Stackpole Books, 2003).

32. Fox, *Regimental Losses*, 543, 549; McWhiney and Jamieson, *Attack and Die*, 158.

CHAPTER 4: SPRING 1862: SALVAGING A VICTORY AT SHILOH

1. Smith, *Grant*, 168–171; Buell, Thomas B., *The Warrior Generals: Combat Leadership in the Civil War* (New York: Crown Publishers, Inc., 1997), 168–70.

2. Grant, *Memoirs*, 219–220; McFeely, *Grant*, 104; Grant, Ulysses S., "The Battle of Shiloh," *Battles and Leaders*, I, 465–466; Halleck to Grant, March 4, 1862, Simon, *Papers of Grant*, IX, 319 note.

3. Grant, *Memoirs*, 220; Badeau, Adam, *Military History of Ulysses S. Grant, from April, 1861, to April, 1865* (New York: D. Appleton and Company, 1868) (3 vols.), I, 60.

4. Williams, *McClellan, Sherman and Grant*, 90–91; Grant, *Memoirs*, 220–221; Allen, Stacy D., "Shiloh! The Campaign and First Day's Battle," *Blue & Gray Magazine*, Vol. XIV, Issue 3 (Feb. 1997); Smith, *Grant*, 172–177; Simon, *Papers of Grant*, IV, 319–359; Badeau, *Grant*, 60–68.

5. Grant, *Memoirs*, 222–233.

6. Williams, *McClellan, Sherman and Grant*, 92; Grant, *Memoirs*, 223.

7. Grant, *Memoirs*, 224–225.

8. For details and comprehensive battle-maps of the Battle of Shiloh, see Daniel, Larry J., *Shiloh: The Battle That Changed the Civil War* (New York: Simon & Schuster, 1997), 143–292; Allen, "Shiloh! I"; Allen, Stacy D., "Shiloh! The Second Day's Battle and Aftermath," *Blue & Gray Magazine*, XIV, No. 4 (April 1997). Also see Johnson and Buel, *Battles and Leaders*, I, 464–610.

9. Allen, "Shiloh! I," 24; Grant to Halleck, April 5, 1862, Simon, *Papers of Grant*, V, 13; Grant to Halleck, Ibid., 14.

10. Allen, "Shiloh! I."

11. Ibid.

12. Grant, *Memoirs*, 225–226; Allen, "Shiloh! II."

13. Grant, *Memoirs*, 226; Swift, Gloria Baker and Stephens, Gail, "Honor Redeemed: Lew Wallace's Military Career and the Battle of Monocacy," *North & South*, Vol. 4, No. 2 (Jan. 2001). In a long footnote in his memoirs, Grant described a letter written by General Lew Wallace on April 4, 1862, that Grant had received after writing the first version of his chapter on Shiloh. Based on that letter, Grant concluded that Wallace had mistakenly taken the wrong road, the road he took might have gotten him to a helpful position if the front had not changed as the battle proceeded, and Wallace had erred only in continuing on that road when the sounds of battle had fallen off in the area toward which he was marching. Grant, *Memoirs*, 236. See the following footnote and accompanying text concerning Grant's footnote on this subject. The 1862 letter and other relevant documents on this controversy may be found in Johnson and Buel,

Battles and Leaders, I, 607–610. For more on the Grant/Wallace miscommunication and dispute, see " 'If He Had Less Rank': Lewis Wallace," in Woodworth, Steven E. (ed.), *Grant's Lieutenants from Cairo to Vicksburg* (Lawrence: University Press of Kansas, 2001), 63–89.

14. Swift & Stephens, "Honor Redeemed," [editorial note by Keith Poulter]; June 21, 1885 note of Ulysses S. Grant in Grant, "Shiloh," 468–469; Allen, "Shiloh! II."

15. Woodworth, Steven E., "Shiloh's Harsh Training Ground," *America's Civil War*, 34–40. Those three generals' divisions lost almost 7,000 of the nearly 11,000 casualties Grant's forces incurred at Shiloh. Ibid., 39.

16. Allen, "Shiloh! I."

17. Ibid., 24–27.

18. Grant, *Memoirs*, 227.

19. Allen, "Shiloh! I."

20. Ibid.; Johnston, William Preston, "Albert Sydney Johnston at Shiloh," *Battles and Leaders*, 564–565.

21. Allen, "Shiloh I."

22. Hinze, David C., " 'At All Hazards': Ulysses S. Grant's instructions to Benjamin M. Prentiss left little doubt as to the importance of the Hornets' Nest at Shiloh," *Columbiad*, Vol. 3, No. 3 (Fall 1999).

23. Ibid.

24. Ibid., quoting R. W. Hurdle, *Reminiscences of the Boys in Gray* (Mamie Yarey, ed.) (New Orleans: Dante Publishing, 1912), 368.

25. Ibid.

26. Ibid.

27. Ibid.; Grant, *Memoirs*, 228.

28. Hinze, " 'At All Hazards';" Woodworth, "Shiloh's Training Ground;" Allen, "Shiloh! I."

29. Hattaway, "Changing Face."

30. Hinze, " 'At All Hazards';" Woodworth, "Shiloh's Training Ground;" Allen, "Shiloh I." Grant may have thought that Prentiss had unnecessarily sacrificed his command by literally following Grant's order to "maintain that position at all hazards." Woodworth, "Shiloh's Training Ground."

31. Allen, "Shiloh! I."

32. Hinze, "'At All Hazards';" Woodworth, "Shiloh's Training Ground."

33. Grant, *Memoirs*, 230–231.

34. Grant, "Shiloh," I, 474; Grant, *Memoirs*, 231.

35. Grant, "Shiloh," 474–475; Beauregard, P. G. T., "The Campaign of Shiloh," *Battles and Leaders*, I, 590; McWhiney and Jamieson, *Attack and Die*, 112; Suhr, Robert Collins, "Saving the Day at Shiloh," *America's Civil War*, XII, No. 6 (January 2000), 34–41.

36. Allen, "Shiloh! II." Jean Edward Smith pointed out many similarities between how Wellington won at Waterloo against Napoleon and how Grant fought on the first day at Shiloh: Both stood on the defensive all day, their lines bent but did not break, late-day enemy charges were repelled, both received late-day reinforcements, and total casualties (including missing) were 24 percent in both battles (when the second day of Shiloh is included). Smith, *Grant*, 204.

37. Grant, *Memoirs*, 232–233, 243–244; Allen, "Shiloh! I."

38. Grant, *Memoirs*, 233–234. When Grant had ordered Nelson's division to proceed from Savannah to Pittsburg Landing on the morning of April 6, Grant was not aware that Buell had arrived at Savannah and failed to report to Grant. Buell proceeded to hold Nelson's division at Savannah until 1 p.m., when Buell was personally satisfied that its advance was appropriate. Allen, "Shiloh! I;" "Shiloh! II."

39. Allen, "Shiloh! II."

40. Allen, "Shiloh! I."

41. Grant, *Memoirs*, 234.

42. Allen, "Shiloh! II."

43. Smith, *Grant*, 204.

44. Allen, "Shiloh! II."

45. Ibid.

46. Grant, *Memoirs*, 235–236; Allen, "Shiloh! II;" Feis, *Grant's Secret Service*, 100–101; Grant, "Shiloh," 478.

47. Allen, "Shiloh! II;" Weigley, *American Way of War*, 139.

48. Grant, "Shiloh," 479.

49. McWhiney and Jamieson, *Attack and Die*, 8, 19–20, 158; Allen, "Shiloh! II."

50. Smith, *Grant*, 204.

51. Allen, "Shiloh! II."

52. Daniel, *Shiloh*, 304–309; Allen, "Shiloh! II;" Buell, *Warrior Generals*, 178–179; Foote, *Civil War*, I, 351; Anderson, "Grant's Struggle with Alcohol." Under the watchful eye of Major John Rawlins, Grant drank but stayed sober until late 1862. Rawlins denied the false accusations that Grant had been drinking during the Battle of Shiloh. Anderson, "Grant's Struggle with Alcohol." For a typical example of postwar nitpicking and backstabbing among generals (even on the same side), see Buell, Don Carlos, "Shiloh Reviewed," *Battles and Leaders*, I, 487–539. Buell was faint in his praise of Grant and vicious in attacking Sherman as a liar and incompetent.

CHAPTER 5: 1862–1863: SURVIVING FRUSTRATION UPON FRUSTRATION

1. General Orders No. 16, Department of the Mississippi; Captain Nathaniel H. McLean to Grant, April 14, 1862, Simon, *Papers of Grant*, V, 48–49.

2. Halleck to Grant, April 14, 1862, *The War of Rebellion: A Compilation of the Official Records of the Union and Confederate Armies*, series one (Washington: Government Printing Office, 1880–1901) (128 vols.), X, part 2, 106; Grant, *Memoirs*, 247.

3. Weigley, *American Way of War*, 139; Special Orders No. 35, Department of the Mississippi, April 30, 1862, Simon, *Papers of Grant*, V, 105.

4. Allen, Stacy D., "Corinth, Mississippi: Crossroads of the Western Confederacy," *Blue & Gray* magazine, XIX, Issue 6 (Summer 2002).

5. Grant, *Memoirs*, 250–252; Cozzens, Peter, *The Darkest Days of the War: The Battles of Iuka & Corinth* (Chapel Hill and London: University of North Carolina Press, 1997), 17. Grant was unaware that, in the aftermath of Shiloh, Lincoln was resisting suggestions that he remove Grant by saying, "I can't spare this man; he fights." Williams, *McClellan, Sherman and Grant*, 96.

6. Allen, "Crossroads;" Watkins, Sam R., *"Co. Aytch": Maury Grays, First Tennessee Regiment or a Side Show of the Big Show* (Wilmington, N.C.: Broadfoot Publishing Company, 1987) (Reprint of 1882 and 1952 editions), 71.

7. Grant, *Memoirs*, 252–255; Allen, "Crossroads;" Cozzens, *Darkest Days*, 31–33.

8. Grant, *Memoirs*, 250–255; Suhr, Robert Collins, "Old Brains' Barren Triumph," *America's Civil War*, Vol. 14, No. 2 (May 2001), 49.

9. Grant, *Memoirs*, 255–257.

10. Weigley, *American Way of War*, 136.

11. Grant, *Memoirs*, 262–263.

12. Williams, *McClellan, Sherman and Grant*, 94.

13. Feis, *Grant's Secret Service*, 109; Cozzens, *Darkest Days*, 35.

14. Feis, *Grant's Secret Service*, 114.

15. Allen, "Crossroads." For details on the Battle of Iuka, see Suhr, Robert Collins, "Small But Savage Battle of Iuka," *America's Civil War*, Vol. 12, No. 2 (May 1999), 42–49; Cozzens, *Darkest Days*, 66–134.

16. Snead, Thomas L., "With Price East of the Mississippi," in Johnson and Buel, *Battles and Leaders*, II, 731–732; Suhr, "Iuka;" Allen, "Crossroads."

17. Suhr, "Iuka; Allen, "Crossroads."

18. Suhr, "Iuka." Acoustic shadows had similar effects at other Civil War battles: Fort Donelson, Tennessee (1862); Gaines' Mill, Virginia (1862); Perryville, Kentucky (1862); Rappahannock Station, Virginia (1863); and Drewry's Bluff, Virginia (1864). Suhr, "Iuka;" Schiller, Herbert M., "Beast in a Bottle: Bermuda Hundred Campaign, May 1864," *Blue & Gray* magazine, VII, Issue 1 (Oct. 1989); Smith, *Grant*, 157, 218. Rosecrans' sympathetic biographer William M. Lamers contended that the sounds of battle were heard in the vicinity of Grant and Ord, their failure to attack may have been due to Grant's drunkenness or mistake, and Rosecrans did not have sufficient troops to safely block the Rebels' escape route. Lamers, William M., *The Edge of Glory: A Biography of General William S. Rosecrans, U.S.A.* (Baton Rouge: Louisiana State University Press, 1999) (Reprint and update of New York: Harcourt, Brace & World, 1961), 102–130. It is hard to believe that Grant would knowingly have passed up an opportunity to attack, especially in a planned pincers movement situation.

19. Grant, *Memoirs*, 263–277; Suhr, "Iuka;" Allen, "Crossroads."

20. Suhr, "Iuka;" Cozzens, *Darkest Days*, 133.

21. Allen, "Crossroads;" Suhr, Robert Collins, "Attack Written Deep and Crimson," Vol. 4, No. 3 (Sept. 1991), *pp.* 46–52. As Price's aide-de-camp, John Tyler, heard Price and Van Dorn debate the proposed attack on Rosecrans, "It was becoming clear to Tyler why Rosecrans had graduated fifth in the West Point class of 1842 and Van Dorn fifth from the bottom." Cozzens, *Darkest Days*, 139.

22. Cozzens, *Darkest Days*, 159–270, 305–306; Allen, "Crossroads;" Suhr, "Attack;" Cozzens, Peter, "Moving into Dead Men's Shoes: The Fight for Battery Robinett at the Battle of Corinth, Mississippi," *Civil War Times Illustrated*, XXXVI, No. 2 (May 1997); Smith, *Grant*, 219.

23. Allen, "Crossroads;" Cozzens, *Darkest Days*, 274–277; Foote, *Civil War*, I, 725.

24. Grant, *Memoirs*, 278–80.

25. For details of the battle of Davis' Bridge, see Smith, Timothy B., "The Forgotten Battle of Davis' Bridge," *North & South*, Vol. 2, No. 5 (June 1999).

26. Grant, *Memoirs*, 280–282; Allen, "Crossroads;" Cozzens, *Darkest Days*, 280–290.

27. Smith, "Davis' Bridge." The deteriorating relationship between Grant and Rosecrans was described in Gordon, Lesley J., " 'I Could Not Make Him Do As I Wished': The Failed Relationship of William S. Rosecrans and Grant" in Woodworth, *Grant's Lieutenants*, 109–127.

28. Grant, *Memoirs*, 280–281; Cozzens, *Darkest Days*, 298–304. In his version of Corinth, Rosecrans described his telegrams to Grant seeking permission to continue the pursuit and Grant's denial, and said, "Confederate officers told me afterward that they never were so scared in their lives as they were after the defeat before Corinth." Rosecrans, William S., "The Battle of Corinth," in *Battles and Leaders*, II, 754–756. Those officers may have been referring to Corinth's immediate aftermath, when Rosecrans disobeyed Grant's orders to pursue immediately.

29. Grant, *Memoirs*, 281; Allen, "Crossroads."

30. Grant, *Memoirs*, 281–282; Feis, *Grant's Secret Service*, 123.

31. Allen, "Crossroads."

32. Grant, *Memoirs*, 283.

33. Weigley, *American Way of War*, 139.

34. Grant, *Memoirs*, 283; Grant to Halleck, Nov. 2, 1862, Simon, *Papers of Grant*, VI, 243.
35. Grant, *Memoirs*, 283–286; Meyers, Christopher C., " 'Two Generals Cannot Command This Army': John A. McClernand and the Politics of Command in Grant's Army of the Tennessee," *Columbiad*, Vol. 2, No. 1 (Spring 1998).
36. Grant, *Memoirs*, 286–288.
37. Ibid., 287; Grant to Sherman, Dec. 8, 1862, Simon, *Papers of Grant*, VI, 406–407.
38. Grant, *Memoirs*, 289. Actually, Winfield Scott's army had lived off the countryside in Mexico.
39. Ibid., 289–293.
40. Ibid., 289–91.
41. Ibid., 291. The same point was made in Badeau, *Grant*, I, 140–141.
42. Grant, *Memoirs*, 289, 292; Morgan, George W., "The Assault on Chickasaw Bluffs," in *Battles and Leaders*, III, 462–471; Fox, *Regimental Losses*, 23, 544, 550; Bearss, Edwin Cole, *Unvexed to the Sea: The Campaign for Vicksburg* (Dayton, Ohio: Morningside House, Inc., 1985, 1991) (3 vols.), I, 192–229. It was during this same period of time, specifically December 17, 1862, that Grant issued his ignominious General Orders No. 11, which provided: "The Jews, as a class violating every regulation of trade established by the Treasury department and also department orders, are hereby expelled from the department within twenty-four hours from receipt of this order. Post commanders will see that all of this class of people be furnished passes and required to leave, and any one returning after such notification will be arrested and held in confinement until an opportunity occurs of sending them out as prisoners, unless furnished with permit from headquarters. No passes will be given these people to visit headquarters for the purpose of making personal application for trade permits." Grant apparently issued this order, which shortly was countermanded by President Lincoln, in an angry reaction to his own father's appearance at his Holly Springs, Mississippi camp with three Jewish merchant partners and a scheme to participate in the cotton speculation that was flourishing through Grant's lines. Lutz, Stephen D.,

"General Orders, No. 11: Grant's Ignoble Act," *America's Civil War*, XII, No. 7 (misprinted as 6) (March 2000), 50–56.

43. Grant, *Memoirs*, 292–293; Meyers, "Two Generals."

44. Grant, *Memoirs*, 293–295.

45. Grant, *Memoirs*, 296.

46. Grant, *Memoirs*, 296–297.

47. Bearss, *Vicksburg*, I, 431–450; Grant, *Memoirs*, 297–298; Groom, Winston, *Shrouds of Glory From Atlanta to Nashville: The Last Great Campaign of the Civil War* (New York: The Atlantic Monthly Press, 1995), 89.

48. Bearss, *Vicksburg*, I, 467–478; Grant, *Memoirs*, 298–299.

49. Bearss, *Vicksburg*, I, 479–548; Grant, *Memoirs*, 299–301.

50. Bearss, *Vicksburg*, I, 549–595; Grant, *Memoirs*, 301–302; Groom, *Shrouds of Glory*, 89–90.

51. Grant, *Memoirs*, 303–305.

52. Arnold, James R., *Grant Wins the War: Decision at Vicksburg* (New York: John Wiley & Sons, Inc., 1997), 52

53. Meyers, "Two Generals."

54. The general, unlike his brother, spelled his name without an "e" on the end.

55. Smith, *Grant*, 230–231.

56. Fuller, *Generalship of Grant*, 134.

CHAPTER 6: MAY–JULY 1863: VANQUISHING VICKSBURG

1. McPherson, "Unheroic Hero,"18; Williams, *McClellan, Sherman and Grant*, 95; Goodman, Al W., Jr., "Grant's Mississippi Gamble," *America's Civil War*, Vol. 7, No. 3 (July 1994), 54; Winschel, Terrence J., "Vicksburg: 'Thank God. The Father of Waters again goes unvexed to the sea.'" *America's Civil War*, Vol. 16, No. 3 (July 2003), 19. Grant's version of the Vicksburg Campaign is in Grant, Ulysses S., "The Vicksburg Campaign" in *Battles and Leaders*, III, 493–539 and in Grant, *Memoirs*, 303–383.

2. Winschel, Terrence J., "Grant's March Through Louisiana: 'The Highest Examples of Military Energy and Perseverance," *Blue & Gray* magazine, XIII, Issue 5 (June 1996).

3. Fuller, *Generalship of Grant*, 137.

4. Winschel, "Grant's March."

5. Grant, *Memoirs*, 305–306.

6. Grant, *Memoirs*, 306–308; Catton, *Grant Moves South*, 411–415; Winschel, "Grant's March;" Poulter, Keith, "Decision in the West: The Vicksburg Campaign, Part II: Running the Batteries," *North & South*, Vol. 1, No. 3 (Feb. 1998).

7. Bearss, *Vicksburg*, II, 53–74; Arnold, *Grant Wins*, 78.

8. Grant, *Memoirs*, 306–308; Catton, *Grant Moves South*, 411–415; Winschel, "Grant's March;" Poulter, "Decision Part II."

9. Smith, *Grant*, 236–237; Arnold, *Grant Wins*, 78–79.

10. Grant, *Memoirs*, 309, 16–19; Nevins, Alan, *Ordeal of the Union* (New York and London: Charles Scribner's Sons, 1947–50) (8 vols.), VI, 415. Ever innovative, Grant had tried building a canal (the Duckport Canal) to assist in the movement from Hard Times to New Carthage, but the effort was unsuccessful. Winschel, "Grant's March."

11. Although the Union corps officially were numbered with Roman numerals (e.g., XVIII), I have used more reader-friendly English words or Arabic numerals (e.g., Second or 18th) to describe them.

12. Bearss, Vicksburg, II, 74–82; Grant, *Memoirs*, 310–314; Smith, *Grant*, 237; Arnold, *Grant Wins*, 79–81.

13. Arnold, *Grant Wins*, 81–82.

14. Feis, *Grant's Secret Service*, 144–145.

15. Williams, Kenneth P., *Grant Rises in the West* (Lincoln: University of Nebraska Press, 1997) (2 vols.) (Originally vols. 3 and 4 of Lincoln Finds a General: A Military Study of the Civil War New York: Macmillan, 1952), II, 339; Roth, Dave, "Grierson's Raid: A Cavalry Raid at Its Best, April 17–May 2, 1863," *Blue & Gray* magazine, X, Issue 5 (June 1993); Grant to Hurlbut, Feb. 13, 1863, Simon, *Papers of Grant*, VII, 317. For more details on Grierson's raid, see Bearss, *Vicksburg*, II, 187–236.

16. Roth, "Grierson's Raid."

17. Feis, William B., "Charles S. Bell, Union Scout," *North & South*, Vol. 4, No. 5 (June 2001); Roth, "Grierson's Raid." Thereafter, Bell apparently scouted ahead of Grierson to advise him where it was safe to go without encountering significant Confederate forces. Ibid., 28.

18. Roth, "Grierson's Raid."

19. Ibid.

20. Arnold, *Grant Wins*, 87; Williams, *Grant Rises in the West*, II, 345.

21. Weigley, Russell F., *A Great Civil War: A Military and Political History, 1861–1865* (Bloomington and Indianapolis: Indiana University Press, 2000), 265; Roth, "Grierson's Raid;" Foote, *Civil War*, II, 334; Smith, *Grant*, 239; Arnold, *Grant Wins*, 87.

22. Feis, *Grant's Secret Service*, 146; Roth, "Grierson's Raid."

23. Grant, *Memoirs*, 318; Weigley, *Great Civil War*, 265; Catton, *Grant Moves South*, 422–424; Winschel, "Grant's March."

24. Feis, *Grant's Secret Service*, 158; Winschel, "Grant's March;" Dana, Charles A., *Recollections of the Civil War* (New York: Collier Books, 1898, 1963), 56–58; Arnold, *Grant Wins*, 87–89.

25. Grant, *Memoirs*, 315–317; Winschel, "Grant's March."

26. Grant, *Memoirs*, 317–321; Poulter, "Decision Part II."

27. Grant, *Memoirs*, 321.

28. Winschel, "Grant's March."

29. Winschel, Terrence J., "Grant's Beachhead for the Vicksburg Campaign: The Battle of Port Gibson, May 1, 1863," *Blue & Gray* magazine, XI, Issue 3 (Feb. 1994).

30. Arnold, *Grant Wins*, 98.

31. For details and battle maps of the Battle of Port Gibson, see Winschel, "Grant's Beachhead;" Arnold, *Grant Wins*, 101–118; and Bearss, *Vicksburg*, II, 353–407. For battle maps of the battles of Port Gibson, Raymond, and Jackson, see Poulter, Keith, "Decision in the West: The Vicksburg Campaign, Part III," *North & South*, Vol. 1, No. 4 (April 1998).

32. Grant, *Memoirs*, 321–4; Winschel, "Grant's Beachhead;" Bearss, Ed, "The Vicksburg Campaign: Grant Moves Inland," *Blue & Gray* magazine, XVIII, Issue 1 (October 2000); Goodman, "Grant's Gamble." Even after the fall of Port Gibson, General Pemberton in Vicksburg had no idea what Grant was doing. He telegraphed his local commander, "Is it not probable that the enemy will himself retire tonight?" Goodman, "Grant's Gamble."

33. Winschel, "Grant's Beachhead."

34. Ibid.; Arnold, *Grant Wins*, 116–7; Ballard, Michael B., "Misused Merit: The Tragedy of John C. Pemberton," in Woodworth, Steven E. (ed.), *Civil War Generals in Defeat* (Lawrence: University of Kansas Press, 1999), 157.

35. Poulter, "Decision Part III."

36. E. M. Stanton to C. M. Dana, May 6, 1863, in Dana, *Recollections*, 66.

37. Grant, *Memoirs*, 324–327; Bearss, "Grant Moves Inland;" Weigley, *Great Civil War*, 265.

38. On May 3, Grant wrote to Halleck of Grierson's raid and concluded: "He has spread excitement throughout the State, destroyed railroads, trestle works, bridges, burning locomotives & rolling stock taking prisoners destroying stores of all kinds [sic]. To use the expression of my informant 'Grierson has knocked the heart out of the State.' " Grant to Halleck, May 3, 1863, Simon, *Papers of Grant*, VIII, 144.

39. Grant, *Memoirs*, 326–328; Bearss, "Grant Moves Inland;" Weigley, *Great Civil War*, 266.

40. Grant to Halleck, May 3, 1863, Simon, *Papers of Grant*, VIII, 147–8.

41. Poulter, "Decision III."

42. Grant, *Memoirs*, 328–329; Bearss, "Grant Moves Inland."

43. Williams, *McClellan, Sherman and Grant*, 95.

44. Buell, *Warrior Generals*, 247.

45. Grant, *Memoirs*, 328, 330; Bearss, "Grant Moves Inland." On May 9, Grant wrote to Sherman: "I do not calculate upon the possibility of supplying the Army with full rations from Grand Gulf. I know it will be impossible without constructing additional roads. What I do expect however is to get up what rations of hard bread, coffee & salt we can and make the country furnish the balance.... A delay would give the enemy time to reinforce and fortify." Grant to Sherman, May 9, 1863, Simon, *Papers of Grant*, VIII, 183–4. On May 10, Grant rejected a complaint from McClernand about "a very small number of teams" and pointed out that each corps had been provided with equal transportation. Grant to McClernand, May 10, 1863, Simon, *Papers of Grant*, VIII, 193.

46. Feis, *Grant's Secret Service*, 160.

47. Fuller, *Generalship of Grant*, 140–146.

48. Trudeau, Noah Andre, "Climax at Vicksburg," *North & South*, Vol. 1, No. 5 (June 1998).

49. For details on the Battle of Raymond, see Bearss, Vicksburg, II, 483–517.

50. Grant, *Memoirs*, 330–331; Bearss, "Grant Moves Inland;" Arnold, *Grant Wins*, 129–136; Fox, *Regimental Losses*, 544, 550.

51. Bearss, "Grant Moves Inland;" Smith, *Grant*, 245; Davis, *Jefferson Davis*, 501–504. For General Johnston's critique of Davis's involvement in the defense of Vicksburg, and particularly his refusal to provide reinforcements from west of the Mississippi, see Johnston, Joseph E., "Jefferson Davis and the Mississippi," in *Battles and Leaders*, III. Johnston was responding to Davis's criticism of Johnston's conduct of the campaign in Davis, Jefferson, *The Rise and Fall of the Confederate Government* (New York: Da Capo Press, 1990) (reprint of 1881 edition) (2 vols.), II, 333–355. There Davis found no fault with Pemberton's conduct but stated that Johnston failed to act at all, let alone promptly, to come to Pemberton's and Vickburg's relief.

52. Grant, *Memoirs*, 332; Bearss, "Grant Moves Inland;" Feis, "Charles S. Bell;" Grant to McClernand, McPherson, and Sherman (three dispatches), May 12, 1863, Simon, *Papers of Grant*, VIII, 204–208; Grant to McClernand (two dispatches), May 13, 1863, Ibid., 208–209. Grant's entire order to Sherman after the battle at Raymond reflects Grant's decision to take Jackson and the pithiness that Grant often used, especially in dealing with Sherman: "After the severe fight of today at Raymond and repulse of the enenemy [*sic*] towards Clinton and Jackson, I have determined to move on the latter place by way of Clinton, and take the Capitol of the state and work from there westward. McPherson is ordered to march at day light to Clinton. You will march at 4. A. M. in the morning and follow McPherson. McClernand will follow you with three Divisions, and send his fourth back to old Auburn, to await the arrival of trains now on the road [from Grand Gulf], and Blairs Division to conduct them after the Enemy." Grant to Sherman, May 12, 1863, Ibid., 207–208.

53. Grant, *Memoirs*, 333; Bearss, "Grant Moves Inland."

54. Feis, *Grant's Secret Service*, 161.

55. For details on the Battle of Jackson, see Bearss, *Vicksburg*, II, 519–558.

56. Grant, *Memoirs*, 334–338; Bearss, "Grant Moves Inland;" "The Opposing Forces in the Vicksburg Campaign," in *Battles and Leaders*, III, 549; Weigley, *Great Civil War*, 267; Wilson, Harold S., *Confederate Industry: Manufacturers and Quartermasters in the Civil War* (Jackson: University of Mississippi Press, 2002), 192–193.

57. Feis, "Charles S. Bell." Sherman's men tore up railroad ties and rails, set the ties on fire, heated the rails on those fires, and then bent the rails around trees and telegraph poles in what became known as "Sherman necklaces." Bearss, "Grant Moves Inland."

58. Grant, *Memoirs*, 338–340; Bearss, "Grant Moves Inland;" Feis, *Grant's Secret Service*, 162.

59. Grant, *Memoirs*, 340–341; Feis, *Grant's Secret Service*, 163; Bearss, Ed, "The Vicksburg Campaign. Grant Marches West: The Battles of Champion Hill and Big Black Bridge," *Blue & Gray* magazine, XVIII, Issue 5 (June 2001). The Bearss article contains excellent maps of both those battles. For more details and battle maps on the Battle of Champion Hill, see Arnold, *Grant Wins*, 147–199 and Bearss, *Vicksburg*, II, 559–651.

60. Bearss, "Grant Marches West."

61. Ibid.

62. Ibid.; Arnold, *Grant Wins*, 158–169.

63. Bearss, "Grant Marches West;" Arnold, *Grant Wins*, 170–178.

64. Bearss, "Grant Marches West;" Arnold, *Grant Wins*, 178–192; Foote, *Civil War*, II, 372–373.

65. Bearss, "Grant Marches West."

66. Grant, *Memoirs*, 342–348; Livermore, Thomas L., *Numbers & Losses in the Civil War in America: 1861–1865* (Millwood, New York: Kraus reprint Co., 1977) (reprint of Bloomington: Indiana University Press, 1957), 99–100; Bearss, "Grant Marches West."

67. Arnold, *Grant Wins*, 197–199; Foote, *Civil War*, II, 375; Grant, *Memoirs*, 349.

68. Grant, *Memoirs*, 349–350; Bearss, "Grant Marches West;" Freeman, Kirk, "Big Black River," *Military Heritage*, Vol. 2, No. 3 (Dec. 2000), 76–85; Goodman, Al W., Jr., "Decision in the West (Part IV): Between

Hell and the Deep Sea: Pemberton's Debacle at Big Black River Bridge," *North & South*, Vol. 1, No. 5 (June 1998).

69. For details and battle maps of the Battle of the Big Black River, see Freeman, "Big Black River;" Goodman, "Decision;" Arnold, *Grant Wins*, 225–332; and Bearss, *Vicksburg*, II, 653–89.

70. Grant, *Memoirs*, 350–353; Bearss, "Grant Marches West;" Freeman, "Big Black River;" Goodman, "Decision;" Barton, Dick, "Charge at Big Black River," *America's Civil War*, Vol. 12, No. 4 (Sept. 1999), 54–61.

71. Grant, *Memoirs*, 350–354; Bearss, "Grant Marches West."

72. Grant, *Memoirs*, 354. In fact, Sherman had verbally and by letter urged Grant before the crossing of the Mississippi not to undertake the risky campaign with no base or line of supply. Grant was more concerned about the impact in the North if he appeared to be retreating by returning to Memphis to restart a presumably safer overland campaign against Vicksburg. As soon as Vicksburg was besieged, Sherman himself revealed his earlier opposition. But Grant was fully forgiving: "[Sherman's] untiring energy and great efficiency during the campaign entitle him to a full share of all the credit due for its success. He could not have done more if the plan had been his own." Grant, *Memoirs*, 364.

73. Weigley, *American Way of War*, 139–140; Bearss, "Grant Marches West," (emphasis added).

74. Grant, *Memoirs*, 354–356; Bearss, *Vicksburg*, III, 753–873. *Chicago Times* reporter Sylvanus Cadwallader observed and said of McClernand's May 22 attack: "McClernand had commenced his attack. He expected to succeed. But that he ever carried any part of the fortifications on his front, as he signaled Grant he had already done, was absolutely false." Cadwallader, Sylvanus, *Three Years with Grant* (New York: Alfred A. Knopf, 1956), 92. Sherman agreed that McClernand had lied and thereby caused many additional casualties. Sherman, William Tecumseh, *Memoirs of General W. T. Sherman* (New York: Literary Classics of the United States, Inc., 1990) (reprint of 1885 second edition), 352–353.

75. Grant, *Memoirs*, 588–589.

76. Fuller, *Generalship of Grant*, 154; Livermore, *Numbers and Losses*, 100; Grant, *Memoirs*, 358.

77. Lee to Davis, May 28, 1863, Freeman, Douglas Southall (ed.), *Lee's Dispatches: Unpublished Letters of General Robert E. Lee, C.S.A. to Jefferson Davis and the War Department of The Confederate States of America, 1862–65* (Baton Rouge and London: Louisiana State University Press, 1994) (reprint of 1914 edition), 98 (emphasis added).

78. Cadwallader, *Three Years*, 70–71, 103–105; Anderson, "Grant's Struggle with Alcohol;" McFeely, *Grant*, 133–135; Epperson, James F., Letter to Editor, *Columbiad*, Vol. 3, No. 2 (Summer 1999); Jones, R. Steven, *Right Hand of Command: Use & Disuse of Personal Staffs in the Civil War* (Mechanicsburg, Pennsylvania: Stackpole Books, 2000), 113–116. On June 6, Chief of Staff John Rawlins wrote a letter to Grant asking to be relieved from duty if Grant did not stop drinking. Rawlins thoughtfully left a copy of the letter for posterity, along with a similar letter from another occasion when Rawlins incorrectly thought that Grant had been drinking. Apparently, Rawlins wanted the historical record to show that he had been Grant's "alcohol nanny." Ibid., 114–116. "With a defender like Rawlins, Grant had no need of any enemies." Ibid., 116, quoting Bruce Catton.

79. Botkin, B.A. (ed.), *A Civil War Treasury of Tales, Legends and Folklore* (New York: Promontory Press, 1960), 243–244.

80. Grant, *Memoirs*, 359–360, 1134; Arnold, James R., *The Armies of U.S. Grant* (London: Arms and Armour Press, 1995), 127; Evans, E. Chris, "Return to Jackson: Finishing Stroke to the Vicksburg Campaign, July 5–25, 1863" *Blue & Gray* magazine, XII, Issue 6 (Aug. 1995); Trudeau, "Climax at Vicksburg."

81. Smith, David M. "Too Little Too Late at Vicksburg," *America's Civil War*, Vol. 13, No. 2 (May 2000), 38–44; Williams, *Grant Rises in the West*, II, 452–453.

82. Grant, *Memoirs*, 359–360, 1134; Evans, "Return to Jackson;" Trudeau, "Climax at Vicksburg;" Bearss, *Vicksburg*, III, 875–881. McClernand's termination was due to "a rather long list of vexatious shortcomings which had been constantly accumulating against him for months, and his uncontrollable itching for newspaper notoriety" as well as his costly and dubious claims of initial success during the May 22 assault on Vicksburg's fortifications. Cadwallader, *Three Years*, 92.

83. Grant, *Memoirs*, 368; Evans, "Return to Jackson."

84. Grant, *Memoirs*, 369–370; Leonard, Phillip A. B., "Forty–seven Days. Constant bombardment, life in bomb shelters, scarce food and water, and rapidly accumulating filth were the price of resistance for the resolute Confederate citizens of besieged Vicksburg, Mississippi," *Civil War Times Illustrated*, XXXIX, No. 4 (August 2000); Evans, "Return to Jackson;" Smith, "Too Little;" Hickenlooper, Andrew, "The Vicksburg Mine" in *Battles and Leaders*, III, 539–542. Vicksburg residents' primary meats were mules and rats. Anonymous, "Daily Life during the Siege of Vicksburg," in Gienapp, William E. (ed.), *The Civil War and Reconstruction: A Documentary Collection* (New York and London: W.W. Norton and Company, 2001), 159–162.

85. Morgan, Michael, "Digging to Victory," *America's Civil War*, Vol. 16, No. 3 (July 2003), 22–29; Arnold, *Grant Wins*, 298.

86. Grant, *Memoirs*, 374–375.

87. Grant, *Memoirs*, 384; Lockett, S. H., "The Defense of Vicksburg," in *Battles and Leaders*, III, 492. Lockett was the Confederate Chief Engineer at Vicksburg.

88. Grant, *Memoirs*, 375–382.

89. Bearss, *Vicksburg*, III, 1301–1310; Catton, Bruce, *This Hallowed Ground: The Story of the Union Side of the Civil War* (Garden City, New York: Doubleday & Company, Inc., 1956, 1962), 122; Arnold, *Grant Wins*, 298–299; Davis, *Jefferson Davis*, 508–509.

90. Evans, "Return to Jackson;" Feis, "Charles S. Bell." Feis's article contains the detailed and accurate order of battle that Bell had prepared on Johnston's force in Jackson and delivered to Sherman.

91. Arnold, *Grant Wins*, 301; Fuller, *Generalship of Grant*, 158.

92. See Appendix II.

93. Hattaway and Jones, *How the North Won*, 415.

94. Evans, "Return to Jackson." For the viewpoint that the capture of Vicksburg was not terribly significant, see Castel, Alber, "Vicksburg: Myths and Realities," *North & South*, Vol 6, No. 7 (Nov. 2003), 62–69.

95. Nevins, *Ordeal of the Union*, VI, 425.

96. Smith, *Grant*, 256.

97. Basler, Roy P. (ed.), *The Collected Works of Abraham Lincoln* (New Brunswick: Rutgers University Press, 1953) (8 vols.), VI, 326.

98. McWhiney and Jamieson, *Attack and Die*, 8, 19–21, 158.

99. "Opposing Forces;" Weigley, *American Way of War*, 140.

100. Jones, *Diary*, I, 374; Gorgas, Josiah, *The Civil War Diary of General Josiah Gorgas*, ed. by Frank E. Vandiver (Birmingham: University of Alabama Press, 1947), 55.

101. Feis, William B., "The War of Spies and Supplies: Grant and Grenville M. Dodge in the West, 1862–1864" in Woodworth, *Grant's Lieutenants*, 183–198 at 195–197.

102. Feis, *Grant's Secret Service*, 173–174.

103. Trudeau, "Climax at Vicksburg."

104. Steven Woodworth commented that "Twenty years later [President] Davis still did not understand that Grant had no supply–lines for the Confederates to cut or that Pemberton, in allowing himself to be bottled up in Vicksburg, had made the worst possible move." Woodworth, Steven E., *Jefferson Davis and His Generals: The Failure of Confederate Command in the West* (Lawrence: University Press of Kansas, 1990), 310.

105. Bearss, *Vicksburg*, III, 1311.

Chapter 7: Autumn 1863: Saving Chattanooga

1. Smith, *Grant*, 261–262; Grant, *Memoirs*, 388. Grant later complained that, as had happened after Corinth the prior year, Halleck broke up Grant's army and sent his troops where they "would do the least good." Ibid., 389.

2. Grant, *Memoirs*, 390; Anderson, "Grant's Struggle with Alcohol."

3. Catton, *Grant Moves South*, 489.

4. Wilson, John, "Miracle at Missionary Ridge," *America's Civil War*, XII, No. 7 (misprinted as 6) (March 2000), 42–44.

5. Grant, *Memoirs*, 389, 403; McDonough, James Lee, *Chattanooga: A Death Grip on the Confederacy* (Knoxville: The University of Tennessee Press, 1984), 49.

6. McDonough, *Chattanooga*, 45; Feis, *Grant's Secret Service*, 177. Grant's descriptions of the Chattanooga Campaign are in Grant, Ulysses S.,

"Chattanooga," in *Battles and Leaders*, III, 679–711 and Grant, *Memoirs*, 403–462.

7. Clark, John E., Jr., "Reinforcing Rosecrans by Rail: The movement of the Federal Eleventh and Twelfth Corps from Virginia was a wonder of strategy, logistics, and engineering," *Columbiad*, Vol. 3, No. 3 (Fall 1999); Skoch, George F., "Miracle of the Rails," *Civil War Times Illustrated*, XXXI, No. 4 (Oct. 1992); Clark, John E., Jr., *Railroads in the Civil War: The Impact of Management on Victory and Defeat* (Baton Rouge: Louisiana State University, 2001), 146–209; Weber, Thomas, *The Northern Railroads in the Civil War, 1861–1865* (Bloomington and Indianapolis: Indiana University Press, 1952, 1999), 181–186. The move to the West opened career opportunities for Howard, who proved his value during Chattanooga, Knoxville, and the march to Atlanta, and then was selected by Sherman (over the more senior Joseph Hooker) to replace Major General James McPherson as Commander of the Army of the Tennessee when he was killed outside Atlanta. Dolzall, Gary W., "O. O. Howard's Long Road to Redemption," *America's Civil War*, Vol. 14, No. 5 (Nov. 2001), 38–44. The two transferred corps commanders, Howard and Slocum, later commanded the two wings of Sherman's army marching through Georgia and the Carolinas.

8. Grant, *Memoirs*, 411–412; McDonough, *Chattanooga*, 53–54.

9. Grant, *Memoirs*, 413–418; McDonough, *Chattanooga*, 54–58, 76–85; Cozzens, Peter, *The Shipwreck of Their Hopes: The Battles for Chattanooga* (Urbana and Chicago: University of Illinois Press, 1994), 48–65; Sword, Wiley, "The Battle Above the Clouds," *Blue & Gray* magazine, XVIII, Issue 2 (Dec. 2000).

10. Catton, Bruce, *Grant Takes Command* (Boston: Little, Brown and Company, 1968, 1969), 55–56.

11. Grant, *Memoirs*, 418–419.

12. Grant, *Memoirs*, 419–420; McDonough, *Chattanooga*, 88–94; Cozzens, *Shipwreck*, 74–100; Sword, "Battle Above Clouds." Grant apparently got a laugh when the quartermaster in charge of the stampeding mules requested that they receive promotion to the rank of horses. Botkin, *Treasury*, 332–333.

13. Grant, *Memoirs*, 420.

14. Ibid., 420–421.

15. Ibid.; Bonekemper, Edward H., III, *How Robert E. Lee Lost the Civil War* (Fredericksburg: Sergeant Kirkland's Press, 1998), 142.

16. Cozzens, *Shipwreck*, 103–105; Wilson, "Miracle," 44–45; Bonekemper, *How Lee Lost*, 142–143; Connelly, Thomas Lawrence, "Robert E. Lee and the Western Confederacy: A Criticism of Lee's Strategic Ability," *Civil War History* 15 (June 1969); Wert, Jeffrey D., *General James Longstreet: The Confederacy's Most Controversial Soldier—A Biography* (New York: Simon & Schuster, 1993), 320–321. "Davis's suggestion that Bragg detach Longstreet was quixotic, reflecting both his lack of appreciation of the Union buildup at Chattanooga and the degree to which he was swayed by Robert E. Lee." Cozzens, *Shipwreck*, 103. For an analysis of the Knoxville expedition from the perspective of Hood's Texas brigade, see Simpson, Harold B., *Hood's Texas Brigade: Lee's Grenadier Guard* (Fort Worth: Landmark Publishing, Inc., 1970, 1999), 345–358.

17. Grant, *Memoirs*, 427–430; Sword, "Battle Above Clouds;" Cozzens, *Shipwreck*, 125.

18. Grant, *Memoirs*, 439–441; McDonough, *Chattanooga*, 106–120, 129–140; Cozzens, *Shipwreck*, 159–178; Wilson, "Miracle;" Sword, "Battle Above Clouds."

19. Marszalek, Sherman: *A Soldier's Passion for Order* (New York: The Free Press, 1993), 241–243.

20. Grant, *Memoirs*, 443–445; McDonough, *Chattanooga*, 143–160; Cozzens, *Shipwreck*, 199–244.

21. Wilson, "Miracle."

22. McDonough, *Chattanooga*, 161–180; Wilson, "Miracle."

23. McDonough, *Chattanooga*, 181–189; Morris, Roy, Jr., *Sheridan: The Life and Wars of General Phil Sheridan* (New York: Crown Publishers, Inc., 1992), 144–145; Wilson, "Miracle;" Catton, *Grant Takes Command*, 81–82.

24. Wilson, "Miracle;" Morris, *Sheridan*, 145; McDonough, *Chattanooga*, 167.

25. McDonough, *Chattanooga*, 182–185.

26. Wilson, "Miracle;" Morris, *Sheridan*, 146; Cozzens, *Shipwreck*, 289–299. One of the first soldiers to reach the top of Missionary Ridge was First Lieutenant Arthur MacArthur; for his heroism, he was awarded the Congressional Medal of Honor—an honor that was bestowed almost eighty years later on his son, Douglas MacArthur.

27. Grant, *Memoirs*, 445–446; Wilson, "Miracle;" Smith, *Grant*, 280; Morris, *Sheridan*, 148; Broome, Doyle D., Jr., "Daring Rear–guard Defense," *America's Civil War*, Vol. 6, No. 5 (Nov. 1993), pp. 34–40; Watkins, "Co. Aytch."

28. Smith, William Farrar, "Comments on General Grant's 'Chattanooga' " in *Battles and Leaders*, III, 717. Years later, when Grant was asked if Bragg had thought his position was impregnable, Grant responded with a smile, "Well, it *was* impregnable." Foote, *Civil War*, II, 859.

29. Williams, *McClellan, Sherman and Grant*, 100.

30. Dolzall, Gary W., "Muddy, Soggy Race to Campbell's Station," *America's Civil War*, Vol. 15, No. 3 (July 2002), 26–32, 80.

31. Cox, Jacob Dolson, *Military Reminiscences of the Civil War* (New York: Charles Scribner's Sons, 1900) (2 vols.), II, 20–41.

32. Lincoln to Grant, Nov. 25, 1863, Basler, *Works of Lincoln*, VII, 30; Grant, *Memoirs*, 452–458; Lincoln to Grant, Dec. 8, 1863, Basler, *Works of Lincoln*, VII, 53; Simpson, *Hood's Texas Brigade*, 359–381. On activity at Knoxville, see *Battles and Leaders*, III, 731–752.

33. Wilson, "Miracle."

34. Foote, *Civil War*, II, 859.

35. John Kennerly Farris to Mary Farris, December 26, 1863, quoted in "Common Soldier: Dr. John Kennerly Farris, Confederate Surgeon, Army of Tennessee," *Blue & Gray* magazine, XVII, Issue 2 (December 1999), 47, from "Letters to Mary: The Civil War Diary of Dr. John Kennerly Farris," *Franklin County Historical Review*, Vol. XXV, Winchester, Tennessee (1964).

36. Davis, *Jefferson Davis*, 527–531.

37. Feis, *Grant's Secret Service*, 189.

38. Livermore, *Numbers & Losses*, 106–108; Fox, *Regimental Losses*, 23, 546, 551.

39. McWhiney and Jamieson, *Attack and Die*, 157–158. See Appendix II of this book, *Casualties Resulting from Campaigns and Battles of Ulysses S. Grant*, especially the summary table at the end.

CHAPTER 8: EARLY 1864: PLANNING A NATIONAL CAMPAIGN

1. Catton, *Grant Takes Command*, 93; Grant to Halleck, Dec. 7, 1863, Simon, *Papers of Grant*, IX, 500–501.
2. Waugh, John C., *Reelecting Lincoln: The Battle for the 1864 Presidency* (New York: Crown Publishers, Inc., 1997), 121; Basler, *Works of Lincoln*, VIII, 339.
3. Smith, *Grant*, 284. Winfield Scott had received a brevet (or honorary, but not an official) promotion to lieutenant general.
4. Grant, *Memoirs*, 458–466.
5. Hattaway, Herman, "Dress Rehearsal for Hell: In early 1864, Mississippi was a proving ground for the 'total war' that would make Sherman infamous—and victorious," *Civil War Times Illustrated*, XXXVII, No. 5 (Oct. 1998), 32–39, 74–75; Fuller, *Generalship of Grant*, 181; Marszalek, *Sherman*, 253–254.
6. Grant, *Memoirs*, 469; Smith, *Grant*, 284–287.
7. Jones, *Right Hand*, 192.
8. Simon, John Y., "Grant, Lincoln, and Unconditional Surrender," in Boritt, Gabor S. (ed.), *Lincoln's Generals* (New York and Oxford: Oxford University Press, 1994), 164.
9. Grant, *Memoirs*, 469.
10. Ibid.
11. Historian Gordon Rhea quoted in "Reconsidering Grant and Lee."
12. Rhea, " 'Butcher' Grant," 46.
13. Catton, *Stillness*, 39–40.
14. Campbell, Eric A., " 'Slept in the mud, stood in the mud, kneeled in the mud," *America's Civil War*, Vol. 15, No. 6 (January 2003), 54–55.
15. Reid, Brian Holden, "Civil-Military Relations and the Legacy of the Civil War" in Grant, Susan-Mary and Parish, Peter J. (eds.), *Legacy of Disunion: The Enduring Significance of the American Civil War* (Baton Rouge: Louisiana State University Press, 2003), 157.

16. Grant, *Memoirs*, 470–471.

17. Smith, *Grant*, 292–294.

18. Grant, *Memoirs*, 480–481.

19. Jones, *Right Hand*, 59–60, 191–192, 219.

20. Simon, "Grant, Lincoln," 168–169.

21. Catton, *Stillness*, 37, 44–49.

22. Grant, *Memoirs*, 478–479.

23. Simon, "Grant, Lincoln," 168; Grant to Sherman, April 4, 1864, Simon, *Papers of Grant*, X, 253.

24. Hattaway and Jones, *How the North Won*, 516–533; Grant to Meade, April 9, 1864, Simon, *Papers of Grant*, X, 274; Bonekemper, *How Lee Lost*, 145–146.

25. Connelly, Thomas Lawrence and Jones, Archer, *The Politics of Command: Factions and Ideas in Confederate Strategy* (Baton Rouge: Louisiana State University Press, 1973), 179–181.

26. In declining the White House dinner, Grant told Lincoln, "I appreciate the honor, but time is very important now, and I have had enough of this show business." The declination caused the *New York Herald* to exclaim, "We have found our hero." Smith, *Grant*, 294.

27. Grant, *Memoirs*, 471–473.

28. Smith, *Grant*, 296.

29. Connelly and Jones, *Politics of Command*, 180–181.

30. Marzalek, *Sherman*, 263.

31. Grant, *Memoirs*, 473.

32. Lincoln to Grant, April 30, 1864, Basler, *Works of Lincoln*, VII, 324; Johnson and Buel, *Battles and Leaders*, IV, 112.

33. Rhea, " 'Butcher' Grant."

34. Feis, *Grant's Secret Service*, 196–197.

35. Ibid., 197–200

36. Ibid., 200–201.

37. Ibid., 201–203.

38. Thomas, Emory M., *Robert E. Lee: A Biography* (New York and London: W.W. Norton & Company, 1995), 322; Lee to Davis, March 25, 1863, Freeman, *Lee's Dispatches*, 140–143.

39. Grant, *Memoirs*, 481–482; Feis, *Grant's Secret Service*, 203–205; Grant to Meade, April 9, 1864, Simon, *Papers of Grant*, X, 274.

40. Epperson, James F., "The Chance Battle in the Wilderness," *Columbiad*, Vol. 2, No. 1 (Spring 1998), 80–81.

41. Feis, *Grant's Secret Service*, 207.

42. Grant to Meade, April 9, 1864, Simon, *Papers of Grant*, X, 274.

43. Ibid., 275.

44. Smith, *Grant*, 303–304.

45. Beringer et al., *Why the South Lost*, 316.

46. Rhea, "'Butcher' Grant."

Chapter 9: Summer 1864: Attacking Lee's Army

1. Grant, *Memoirs*, 512.

2. Rhodes, Robert Hunt (ed.), *All for the Union: The Civil War Diary and Letters of Elisha Hunt Rhodes* (New York: Orion Books, 1991) (originally published by Andrew Mowbray Incorporated in 1985), 142.

3. Grant, *Memoirs*, 490–494; Schiller, "Beast in a Bottle." "[Butler] was perfectly safe against an attack; but, as [Chief Engineer General] Barnard expressed it, the enemy had corked the bottle and with a small force could hold the cork in place." Grant, *Memoirs*, 493–494. Also see "Controversy: Was Butler 'Bottled Up'?," *Blue & Gray* magazine, VII, Issue 1 (Oct. 1989), 27–29.

4. Warner, *Generals in Blue*, 448.

5. Holsworth, Jerry W., "VMI at the Battle of New Market and, Sigel's Defeat in the Shenandoah Valley," *Blue & Gray* magazine, XVI, Issue 4 (April 1999).

6. Bounds, Steve and Milbourn, Curtis, "The Battle of Mansfield," *North & South*, Vol. 6, No. 2 (Feb. 2003).

7. McMurry, Richard M., "Georgia Campaign: Rocky Face to the Dallas Line, The Battles of May 1864," *Blue & Gray* magazine, VI, Issue 4 (April 1989); Kelly, Dennis, "Atlanta Campaign. Mountains to Pass, A River to Cross, The Battle of Kennesaw Mountain and Related Actions from June 10 to July 9, 1864," *Blue & Gray* magazine, VI, Issue 5 (June 1989).

8. Jones, *Right Hand*, 194.

9. Ibid.; Porter, Horace, *Campaigning with Grant* (New York: SMITH-MARK Publishers, Inc.) (Reprint of 1897 edition), 37–38.

10. Grant's 1864 Overland Campaign is described in detail in Trudeau, Noah Andre, *Bloody Roads South: The Wilderness to Cold Harbor, May–June 1864* (Boston, Toronto, London: Little, Brown and Co., 1989); Lowry, *No Turning Back*; Lowry, Don, *Fate of the Country: The Civil War from June–September 1864* (New York: Hippocrene Books, 1992); Rhea, Gordon C., *The Battle of the Wilderness, May 5–6, 1864* (Baton Rouge and London: Louisiana State University Press, 1994); Rhea, Gordon C., *The Battles for Spotsylvania Court House and the Road to Yellow Tavern: May 7–12, 1864* (Baton Rouge and London: Louisiana State University, 1997); Rhea, Gordon C., *To the North Anna River: Grant and Lee, May 13–25, 1864* (Baton Rouge: Louisiana State University Press, 2000); Rhea, *Cold Harbor*; Wheeler, Richard, *On Fields of Fury: From the Wilderness to the Crater: An Eyewitness History* (New York: HarperCollins Publishers, 1991); and Law, "From the Wilderness to Cold Harbor."

11. Feis, *Grant's Secret Service*, 207.

12. Epperson, "Chance Battle."

13. Lee's strength was definitively calculated at 65,995 in Young, Alfred C., "Numbers and Losses in the Army of Northern Virginia," *North & South*, Vol. 3, No. 3 (March 2000).

14. Trudeau, Noah Andre, " 'A Frightful and Frightening Place'," *Civil War Times Illustrated*, XXXVIII, No. 2 (May 1999); Epperson, "Chance Battle."

15. Ibid.

16. For more details on the Battle of the Wilderness, see Rhea, *Wilderness*; Scott, Robert Garth, *Into the Wilderness with the Army of the Potomac* (Bloomington: Indiana University Press, 1985); Trudeau, "Frightful Place."

17. Grant to Meade, May 5, 1864, 8:24 a.m., Simon, *Papers of Grant*, X, 399.

18. Trudeau, "Frightful Place;" Epperson, "Chance Battle;" Mertz, Gregory A., "No Turning Back: The First Day of the Wilderness," *Blue & Gray* maga-

zine, XII, Issue 4 (April 1995). On the morning of May 5, Grant was aware
from his signal tower behind the Rapidan that Confederates were approaching but, because of Wilson's inadequate performance, was not aware of
Ewell's substantial and close presence on the Orange Turnpike. Demonstrating his intent to engage Lee, Grant issued orders changing the direction of
his troops from a westerly and southwesterly direction to a more westerly
approach to where he expected Lee to be. "Grant's orders clearly envisioned
a westward advance toward Lee. Contrary to many casual accounts of the
campaign, Grant was not trying to steal a march past Lee's flank, but was
turning to meet Lee's army." Epperson, "Chance Battle."

19. Trudeau, "Frightful Place;" Mertz, "Wilderness I." For more details on
the first day's fighting at the Wilderness, see Mertz, "Wilderness I;" Freeman, Douglas Southall, *R. E. Lee* (New York and London: Charles Scribner's Sons, 1934–1935) (4 vols.), III, 269–283. Epperson contends that
competent reconnaissance by Wilson would have discovered Ewell's late
May 4 position on the Orange Turnpike and enabled Grant to pounce on
the flank and front of his 17,200 men with a combined force of 51,000
men (the Fifth and Sixth corps and a division from Burnside's Ninth
Corps). Epperson, "Chance Battle."

20. Trudeau, "Frightful Place;" Mertz, "Wilderness I."

21. Ibid.

22. Rhea, *Wilderness*, 271.

23. Lowry, *No Turning Back*, 518.

24. Mertz, "Wilderness II." For more details on the second day's fighting at
the Wilderness, see Mertz, "Wilderness II;" Freeman, *R.E. Lee*, III,
283–303.

25. Freeman, *R.E. Lee*, III, 287–288; Mertz, "Wilderness II;" Trinque, Bruce
A., "Battle Fought on Paper," *America's Civil War*, Vol. 6, No. 2 (May
1993), 30–36; Trudeau, "Frightful Place;" Longstreet, James, *From Manassas to Appomattox: Memoirs of the Civil War in America* (New York:
SMITHMARK Publishers Inc., 1994), 562–565.

26. Trudeau, "Frightful Place."

27. Mertz, "Wilderness II."

28. Trudeau, "Frightful Place."

29. Livermore, *Numbers & Losses*, 110; Arnold, *Armies Grant*, 186; Mertz, "Wilderness II;" Fuller, *Generalship of Grant*, 239; Young, "Numbers and Losses;" Smith, *Grant*, 333.

30. McWhiney & Jamieson, *Attack and Die*, 108; Fuller, *The Generalship of Grant*, 362.

31. Mertz, "Wilderness II."

32. Gilbert, Thomas D., "Mr. Grant Goes to Washington," *Blue & Gray* magazine, XII, Issue 4 (April 1995); Porter, *Campaigning with Grant*, 69–70; Lowry, *No Turning Back*, 223.

33. Rhodes, *All for the Union*, 146.

34. Mertz, "Wilderness II."

35. Grant, *Memoirs*, 536–537.

36. "Grant kept fighting, even after some battles other generals would consider defeats." "Reconsidering Grant and Lee." Grant later said he was trying to get between Lee and Richmond and also to protect Butler against a possible counter-attack by Lee. Grant, *Memoirs*, 540.

37. Smith, *Grant*, 338.

38. Rhea et al., "What Was Wrong?"

39. Sherman, William T., "The Grand Strategy of the Last Year of the War," *Battles and Leaders*, IV, 248.

40. Foote, *Civil War*, III, 190–191.

41. Lee to James A. Seddon, May 8, 1864, Dowdey, Clifford and Manarin, Louis H. (eds.), *The Wartime Papers of R. E. Lee* (New York: Bramhall House, 1961), 724.

42. Mertz, "Wilderness II."

43. For details on the Battle of Spotsylvania Court House, see Rhea, Gordon C., "Spotsylvania: The Battles at Spotsylvania Court House, Virginia, May 8–21, 1864," *Blue & Gray* magazine, I, Issue 6 (June–July 1984).

44. Grant, *Memoirs*, 540–541; Lowry, *No Turning Back*, 518. Perhaps influenced by Sheridan's later removal of Warren from command at the end of the Battle of Five Forks in April 1865, Grant criticized Warren in his *Memoirs* for being slow to get to and reinforce Spotsylvania Court House. Grant also explained that he moved Warren from the right flank of his line past his other corps (which were closer to Spotsylvania) so that he

maintained a defensible line while leaving the Wilderness. Grant, *Memoirs*, 541–543.

45. Mertz, Gregory A., "Upton's Attack and the Defense of Doles' Salient, Spotsylvania Court House, Va., May 10, 1864," *Blue & Gray* magazine, May 10, 1864," XVIII, Issue 6 (Summer 2001); Guttman, Jon, "Jeb Stuart's Last Ride," *America's Civil War*, Vol. 7, No. 2 (May 1994), 34–40, 79–80; Rhea, *North Anna River*, 35–64. In his memoirs, Grant praised Sheridan's performance and seemed unfazed by his sixteen-day absence. Grant, *Memoirs*, 494–497.

46. Durham, Roger S., "The Man Who Shot John Sedgwick: The Tale of Charles D. Grace—A Sharpshooter in the Doles-Cook Brigade, CSA," *Blue & Gray* magazine, XIII, Issue 2 (Dec. 1995), 24–29; Warner, *Generals in Blue*, 431, 575.

47. Smith, *Grant*, 357–358.

48. Mertz, "Upton's Attack;" McWhiney and Jamieson, *Attack and Die*, 91.

49. Grant, *Memoirs*, 549–550; Mertz, "Upton's Attack,"16–25, 46–51; McWhiney and Jamieson, *Attack and Die*, 91–92; Ambrose, Stephen E., *Upton and the Army* (Baton Rouge: Louisiana State University Press, 1993), 30–34. Grant rewarded Upton with a battlefield promotion to brigadier general. Grant, *Memoirs*, 550.

50. Grant to Halleck, May 11, 1864, Simon, *Papers of Grant*, X, 422.

51. Grant to Meade, May 11, 1864, Simon, *Papers of Grant*, X, 427; Grant to Burnside, May 11, 1864, Ibid., 424–425.

52. McWhiney & Jamieson, *Attack and Die*, 116; Freeman, *R. E. Lee*, III, 315–316, 433; Smith, *Grant*, 349–350. "Never had Lee made a more egregious miscalculation." Rhea, Gordon C., "Robert E. Lee, Prescience, and the Overland Campaign," *North & South*, Vol. 3, No. 5 (June 2000). Rhea's article summarized the major decisions of Lee (and some by Grant) in the Overland Campaign.

53. Grant, *Memoirs*, 553; McWhiney and Jamieson, *Attack and Die*, 92–93.

54. Warren's refusal to promptly execute Meade's order for him to attack in support of Hancock's primary assault led Grant to tell Meade, "If Warren fails to attack promptly send Humphreys to command his corps, and relieve him." Grant to Meade, May 12, 1864, Simon, *Papers of Grant*, X,

433; Grant, *Memoirs*, 554. This incident and a similar refusal to attack at Mine Run the prior November constituted the first two strikes against Warren, and he was "struck out" by Phil Sheridan (with Grant's blessing) after unfairly perceived hesitance at the Battle of Five Forks in April 1865. Sears, Stephen W., *Controversies and Commanders: Dispatches from the Army of the Potomac* (Boston and New York: Houghton Mifflin Company, 1999), 253–287 [chapter entitled "Gouverneur Kemble Warren and Little Phil"]. The same material is in Sears, Stephen W., "Gouverneur Kemble Warren and Little Phil," *North & South*, Vol. 1, No. 5 (1998).

55. Catton, *Stillness*, 125, 126–127.

56. Grant, *Memoirs*, 553–555. On the severed oak tree, see Matter, William D., "The Oak Tree at Spotsylvania," *Blue & Gray* magazine, I, Issue 6 (June–July, 1984).

57. Smith, *Grant*, 354–355.

58. Grant, *Memoirs*, 555–558; Rhodes, *All for the Union*, 153.

59. Grant, *Memoirs*, 560–561; Rhea, Gordon C., "Last Union Attack at Spotsylvania: The belief that one more hard blow would shatter the Confederate line at Spotsylvania may have been one of Ulysses S. Grant's greatest miscalculations.," *Columbiad*, Vol. 3, No. 4 (Winter 2000); Grant to Meade, May 18, 1864, Simon, *Papers of Grant*, X, 464. Believing that he had more artillery than he could use, Grant sent over a hundred guns back to Washington. Grant, *Memoirs*, 560.

60. Rhea, Gordon C., " 'They Fought Confounded Plucky': The Battle of Harris Farm, May 19, 1864," *North & South*, Vol. 3, No. 1 (Nov. 1999); Rhea, *North Anna River*, 164–189.

61. Rhea, "Harris Farm," 52–66; Rhea, *North Anna River*, 167–189.

62. Bonekemper, *How Lee Lost*, 156; Fuller, *Generalship of Grant*, 255.

63. Law, "From the Wilderness to Cold Harbor." Law added that ". . . Grant's constant 'hammering' with his largely superior force had, to a certain extent, a depressing effect upon both officers and men." Ibid., 144.

64. Miller, "Strike Them;" Foote, *Civil War*, III, 223; Smith, *Grant*, 355.

65. Colonel Theodore Lyman to Elizabeth Russell Lyman, May 18, 1864, quoted in McWhiney and Jamieson, *Attack and Die*, 75, citing Agassiz, George R. (ed.), *Meade's Headquarters*, 1863–1865 (Boston, 1922).

66. Ibid., 75–76.

67. Grant, *Memoirs*, 560–561.

68. Grant, *Memoirs*, 562–564; Miller, "Strike Them." This encounter also was known as the Battle of Henagan's Redoubt.

69. Robertson, James I., Jr. *General A.P. Hill: The Story of a Confederate Warrior* (New York: Random House, 1987), 276; Trudeau, "Question of Time," in Gallagher, Gary W. (ed.), *Lee the Soldier* (Lincoln and London: University of Nebraska Press, 1996), 533.

70. Grant, *Memoirs*, 567.

71. Dowdey, *Lee*, 464; Miller, "Strike Them." General Ledlie somehow managed to get promoted to division commander and performed miserably and drunkenly again at the Battle of the Crater on June 30. General Fuller hypothesized that it was Lee's prior heavy loss of manpower, not illness, that precluded him from attacking Grant's divided forces at the North Anna River. Fuller, *Generalship of Grant*, 267.

72. Lowry, *No Turning Back*, 424, 518; Miller, "Strike Them."

73. Hudson, Leonne, "Valor at Wilson's Wharf," *Civil War Times Illustrated*, XXXVII, No. 1 (March 1998). Lee's threat concerning treatment of the Black troops was a thinly veiled reference to Nathan Bedford Forrest's slaughter of surrendering Black soldiers at Fort Pillow, Tennessee, six weeks before. Also, there was a rumor in the Union camp that Confederates had executed two Black soldiers they had captured on May 21. Ibid., 50.

74. "Grant and Lee, 1864: From the North Anna to the Crossing of the James," *Blue & Gray* magazine, XI, Issue 4 (April 1994); Grant to Halleck, May 26, 1864, Simon, *Papers of Grant*, X, 491.

75. "Grant and Lee, 1864," pp. 12–3; Grant to Halleck, May 26, 1864, Simon, Papers of Grant, X, pp. 490–1.

76. Rhea, *Cold Harbor*, 388.

77. "Grant and Lee, 1864;" Malone, Jeff, "Melee in the Underbrush," *America's Civil War*, Vol. 5, No. 5 (Nov. 1992). For a detailed study of the Battle of Haw's Shop, see Rhea, "'The Hottest Place I Ever Was in," *North & South*, Vol. 4, No. 4 (April 2001); Rhea, *Cold Harbor*, 61–91.

78. "Grant and Lee, 1864."

79. "Grant and Lee, 1864;" Rhea, Gordon C., "Butchery at Bethesda Church," *America's Civil War*, Vol. 14, No. 6 (January 2002), 48–54, 80. For details of the Battle of Bethesda Church, also see Rhea, *Cold Harbor*, 139–151.

80. Grant, *Memoirs*, 568–575; "Grant and Lee, 1864;" Rhea, *Cold Harbor*, 159–160.

81. Welles, *Diary*, II, 44–45.

82. Fellman, Michael, *Citizen Sherman: A Life of William Tecumseh Sherman* (New York: Random House, 1995), 177.

83. Rhea, *Cold Harbor*, 392.

84. "Grant and Lee, 1864."

85. Ibid.

86. Ibid. Union soldiers had similarly pinned their names on their uniforms before an apparent assault (which was cancelled) at Mine Run the prior November. Ibid., 54.

87. Ibid.; Rhea, Gordon C., "Cold Harbor: Anatomy of a Battle," *North & South*, Vol. 5, No. 2 (Feb. 2002). For a detailed description of the Battle of Cold Harbor, see Rhea, *Cold Harbor*, 318–364. For a description of one Irish brigade's decimation at Cold Harbor, see O'Beirne, Kevin M., "Into the Valley of the Shadow of Death: The Corcoran Legion at Cold Harbor," *North & South*, Vol. 3, No. 4 (April 2000).

88. Rhea, *Cold Harbor*, 390.

89. Grant to Halleck, June 3, 1864, 2 p.m., Simon, *Papers of Grant*, XI, 9.

90. Long, David E., "Cover-up at Cold Harbor," *Civil War Times Illustrated*, XXXVI, No. 3 (June 1997).

91. Grant, *Memoirs*, 584–585.

92. Ernest B. Furgurson's book on Cold Harbor is *Not War But Murder: Cold Harbor 1864* (New York: Alfred A. Knopf, 2000). Ironically, Confederate Major General Daniel Harvey Hill earlier used the phrase, "It was not war—it was murder," to describe Lee's assault on Malvern Hill at the end of the Seven Days' Campaign in 1862. Hill, Daniel H., "McClellan's Change of Base and Malvern Hill," in *Battles and Leaders*, 394; Kendall, Drew J., " 'Murder' at Malvern Hill," *Military History*, Vol. 19, No. 3 (Aug. 2002), 42–48.

93. Simpson, *Hood's Texas Brigade*, 419–420.

94. Grant, *Memoirs*, 588.

95. A typical summary is "Cold Harbor, for example, cost Grant seven thousand men in a charge that lasted less than an hour." Groom, *Shrouds of Glory*, 9. Likewise, "Grant had lost . . . seven thousand in less than an hour of June 3 at Cold Harbor . . . ." Fellman, *Citizen Sherman*, 195. On the high side is the statement, "Grant's assault was finally canceled when thirteen thousand Union troopers lay dead or dying." Casdorph, Paul D., *Lee and Jackson: Confederate Chieftains* (New York: Paragon House, 1992), 401.

96. Rhea, *Cold Harbor*, 386; "Reconsidering Grant and Lee."

97. "Lee and Grant, 1864."

98. Rhea, *Cold Harbor*, 382, 386; Rhea, "Cold Harbor."

99. Dana, *Recollections*, 187.

100. Rhodes, *All for the Union*, 158.

101. Smith, *Grant*, 365–366. Adams belonged to the famous presidential Adams family of Massachusetts.

102. Cox, Jacob D., *Military Reminiscences*, II, 224.

103. William T. Sherman to Ellen Boyle Ewing, May 20, 1864, cited in McWhiney and Jamieson, *Attack and Die*, 106–107.

104. Catton, *Stillness*, 171.

105. McFeely, *Grant*, 171–173; Lowry, *No Turning Back*, 518–519. For details of the unseemingly dispute over aiding the wounded between the lines, see Rhea, Gordon C., "The Truce at Cold Harbor," *North & South*, Vol. 7, No. 1 (Jan. 2004), 76-85

106. McWhiney and Jamieson, *Attack and Die*, 116; Freeman, Douglas Southall, *Lee's Lieutenants: A Study in Command* (New York: Charles Scribner's Sons, 1942–1944, 1972) (3 vols.), III, 512–513; Bonekemper, *How Lee Lost*, 158.

107. Smith, *Grant*, 368.

108. Grant to Halleck, June 5, 1864, Simon, *Papers of Grant*, XI, 19. As to the morale of his army, Grant told Halleck, "The feeling of the two Armies now seems to be that the rebels can protect themselves only by strong intrenchments, whilst our Army is not only confidant [*sic*] of pro-

tecting itself, without intrenchments, but that it can beat and drive the enemy whenever and wherever he can be found without this protection." Ibid., 20.

109. Ibid.

110. "Lee and Grant, 1864;" Wittenberg, Eric J., " Sheridan's Second Raid and the Battle of Trevilian Station," *Blue & Gray* magazine, XIX, Issue 3 (Feb. 2002).

111. "Lee and Grant, 1864."

112. Alexander, Edward Porter, *Fighting for the Confederacy: The Personal recollections of General Edward Porter Alexander* ed. by Gary W. Gallagher (Chapel Hill: University of North Carolina Press, 1989), 420.

113. Smith, *Grant*, 370.

114. Trudeau, Noah Andre, *The Last Citadel: Petersburg, Virginia June 1864–April 1865* (Baton Rouge: Louisiana State University Press, 1991), 22–25.

115. Alexander, *Fighting for the Confederacy*, 422.

116. Fuller, *Generalship of Grant*, 285.

117. Lee to Beauregard, June 16, 1864, 10:30 a.m., Downey and Manarin, *Papers of Lee*, 784; Thomas, *Lee*, 337; Alexander, *Fighting for the Confederacy*, 429.

118. Lee to Beauregard, June 16, 1864, 4 p.m., Dowdey and Manarin, *Papers of Lee*, 785; Alexander, *Fighting for the Confederacy*, 429.

119. Lowry, *Fate of the Country*, 53; Freeman, *R. E. Lee*, III, 417; Alexander, *Fighting for the Confederacy*, 430.

120. Thomas, *Lee*, 337.

121. Lee to Beauregard, June 17, 1864, 4:30 p.m., Dowdey and Manarin, *Papers of Lee*, 789; Alexander, *Fighting for the Confederacy*, 430.

122. Foote, *Civil War*, III, 438; Lowry, *Fate of the Country*, 56; Freeman, *Lee's Lieutenants*, III, 534; Freeman, *R. E. Lee*, III, 421; Trudeau, *The Last Citadel*, 51; Alexander, *Fighting for the Confederacy*, 430–431; Lee to E. H. Gill [Superintendent, Richmond and Petersburg Railroad], June 18, 1864, 3:30 a.m., Dowdey and Manarin, *Papers of Lee*, 791.

123. Grant, *Memoirs*, 599–602; Hattaway and Jones, *How the North Won*, 589–590; Nolan, Alan T., *Lee Considered: General Robert E. Lee and*

Civil War History (Chapel Hill and London: University of North Carolina Press, 1991), 85.

124. Bonekemper, *How Lee Lost*, 163.

125. Heidler and Heidler, *Encyclopedia*, 1497.

126. Waugh, *Reelecting Lincoln*, 202.

127. See Appendix II, "Casualties in Grant's Battles and Campaigns."

128. Young, Alfred C., "Numbers and Losses in the Army of Northern Virginia," *North & South*, Vol. 3, No. 3 (March 2000).

129. Fox, *Regimental Losses*, 571–572; Warner, Ezra J., *Generals in Gray: Lives of the Confederate Commanders* (Baton Rouge and London: Louisiana State University Press, 1964).

130. Rhea, " 'Butcher' Grant."

131. Nolan, *Lee Considered*, 85.

132. McPherson, "Unheroic Hero."

133. Rhea, *Cold Harbor*, xii.

CHAPTER 10: 1864–1865: TIGHTENING THE NOOSE

1. One of the first of these raids was a late June 1864 raid on the Richmond & Danville and Southside railroads by Brigadier General James H. Wilson with 5,500 cavalrymen. Although Wilson succeeded in destroying sixty miles of railroad track and disrupting Lee's supply flow for a month, he took considerable losses in getting back to Union lines. Bolte, Philip L., "An Earlier 'Bridge Too Far'," *North & South*, Vol. 3, No. 6 (August 2000).

2. Grant, *Memoirs*, 605; Naisawald, L. VanLoan, " 'Old Jubilee' Saves Lynchburg," *America's Civil War*, Vol. 16, No. 2 (May 2003).

3. Case, David, "The Battle That Saved Washington," *Civil War Times Illustrated*, XXXVII, No. 7 (Feb. 1999). For details of Early's campaign, see Judge, Joseph, *Season of Fire: The Confederate Strike on Washington* (Berryville, Virginia: Rockbridge Publishing Co., 1994); Ambrose, Stephen E., *Halleck: Lincoln's Chief of Staff* (Baton Rouge and London: Louisiana State University Press, 1962, 1990), 179; Vandiver, Frank E., *Jubal's Raid: General Early's Famous Attack on Washington in 1864* (New York, etc.: McGraw-Hill Book Company, Inc., 1960).

4. Case, "Battle;" Cooling, Benjamin Franklin, "Monocacy: The Battle That Saved Washington," *Blue & Gray* magazine, X, Issue 2 (Dec. 1992).

5. Case, "Battle."

6. For details on the Battle of Monocacy, see Cooling, "Monocacy;" Judge, *Season of Fire*, 171–201; and Wittenberg, Eric J., "Roadblock En Route to Washington," *America's Civil War*, Vol. 6, No. 5 (Nov. 1993), 50–56, 80–82.

7. Case, "Battle;" Cooling, "Monocacy;" Swift and Stephens, "Honor Redeemed."

8. Grant, *Memoirs*, 605–607, 614; Alexander, Ted, "McCausland's Raid and the Burning of Chambersburg," *Blue & Gray* magazine, XI, Issue 6 (August 1994); Case, "Battle."

9. Hattaway and Jones, *How the North Won*, 604.

10. Alexander, *Fighting for the Confederacy*, 440. Another Confederate leader saw those same possibilities: Brigadier General Josiah Gorgas, Chief of Confederate Ordnance, wrote: "I still think that my notions were correct at the outset of Sherman's movement when I advocated the detachment of 10,000 men to Georgia, even at the risk of losing Petersburgh [sic] & the Southern R.R. It would have ruined Sherman, & with his ruin, gone far to make the north tired of the war." Wiggins, Sarah Woolfolk (ed.), *The Journals of Josiah Gorgas 1857–1878* (Tuscaloosa: and London: The University of Alabama Press, 1995), 143–144.

11. In his memoirs, Grant said of the change of command: "I know that both Sherman and I were rejoiced when we heard of the change." Grant, *Memoirs*, 632. In fact, Sherman had contemporaneously written to his wife, "I confess I was pleased at the change." Groom, *Shrouds of Glory*, 25.

12. Castel, Albert, *Decision in the West: The Atlanta Campaign of 1864* (Lawrence: University Press of Kansas, 1992), 362; Davis, Stephen, "Atlanta Campaign. Hood Fights Desperately. The Battles of Atlanta: Events from July 10 to September 2, 1864," *Blue & Gray* magazine, VI, Issue 6 (August 1989); Watkins, "Co. Aytch;" Groom, *Shrouds of Glory*, 25; Marszalek, *Sherman*, 277; Connelly, Thomas Lawrence, *Autumn of Glory: The Army of Tennessee, 1862–1865* (Baton Rouge and London:

Louisiana State University Press, 1971, 1991), 433; Hattaway and Jones, *How the North Won*, 609; Bonekemper, *How Lee Lost*, 166–170.

13. Powles, James M., " New Jersey's Western Warriors," *America's Civil War*, Vol. 14, No. 4 (Sept. 2001).

14. Grant, *Memoirs*, 607–612.

15. Grant to Meade, July 24, 1864, Simon, *Papers of Grant*, XI, 305–307 at 306; Grant, *Memoirs*, 612–613; Hattaway and Jones, *How the North Won*, 614–615; Livermore, *Numbers & Losses*, 116; Miller, "Strike Them," 53.

16. Suderow, Bryce A. "War Along the James," *North & South*, Vol. 6, No. 3 (April 2003), 12–23.

17. Suderow, Bryce A. "Glory Denied: The First Battle of Deep Bottom, July 27th–29th, 1864," *North & South*, Vol. 3, No. 7 (Sept. 2000).

18. Grant to Washburne, August 16, 1864, *Papers of Grant*, XII, 16.

19. Grant to Benjamin F. Butler, August 18, 1864, Ibid., 27.

20. Grant to William H. Seward, August 19, 1864, Ibid., 37–8 at 38.

21. Suderow, Bryce A., " 'Nothing But a Miracle Could Save Us': Second Battle of Deep Bottom, Virginia, August 14–20, 1864," *North & South*, Vol. 4, No. 2 (Jan. 2001), 12–32.

22. Halleck to Grant, Aug. 11, 1864, *Papers of Grant*, XI, 424–5 note; Grant to Halleck, August 15, 1864, Ibid., 424; Basler, *Works of Lincoln*, VII, 499; Lincoln to Grant, Aug. 17, 1864, Simon, *Papers of Grant*, XI, 225 note; Basler, Works of Lincoln, VII, 499.

23. Groom, *Shrouds of Glory*, 53.

24. Ibid., 54.

25. Grant to Sherman, Sept. 12, 1864, Simon, *Papers of Grant*, XII, 154–155.

26. Grant, *Memoirs*, 614–615; Grant to Halleck, August 1, 1864, Simon, *Papers of Grant*, XI, 358.

27. Lincoln to Grant, August 3, 1864, Basler, *Works of Lincoln*, VII, 476; Grant, *Memoirs*, 615–616.

28. Grant, *Memoirs*, 616–617; Williams, *Lincoln and His Generals*, 331–333.

29. Grant, *Memoirs*, 617–618.

30. Grant, *Memoirs*, 602, 619; Wagner, Margaret E., Gallagher, Gary W., and Finkelman, Paul (ed.), *The Library of Congress Civil War Desk Reference*

(New York: Simon & Schuster, 2002), 311; McWhiney and Jamieson, *Attack and Die*, 19, 158.

31. Grant, *Memoirs*, 620–621. For details of the 1864 Shenandoah Valley Campaign, see Wert, Jeffrey D., *From Winchester to Cedar Creek: The Shenandoah Campaign of 1864* (Carlisle, Pennsylvania: South Mountain Press, Inc., 1987).

32. Grant, *Memoirs*, 622.

33. Ibid., 625.

34. Feis, *Grant's Secret Service*, 246–249; Trudeau, Noah Andre, "That 'Unerring Volcanic Firearm'," *Military History Quarterly*, Vol. 7, No. 4 (Summer 1995).

35. Grant, *Memoirs*, 628–630.

36. McPherson, *Battle Cry of Freedom*, 800. To accusations that Grant's no-exchange policy was the cause of many prison-camp deaths, Professor James Gillispie retorted that such a policy was the only security against a widespread Confederate policy of executing African-American prisoners and their white officers and that it also was intended to shorten the war by reducing the number of combatants, especially on the Rebel side. Gillispie, James, Letter to Editor, *North & South*, Vol. 5, No. 7 (Oct. 2002).

37. Bergeron, Arthur W., Jr., "The Battle of Mobile Bay and the Campaign for Mobile, Alabama," *Blue & Gray* magazine, XIX, Issue 4 (April 2002).

38. McPherson, *Battle Cry of Freedom*, 775.

39. Grant, *Memoirs*, 630; Heidler and Heidler, *Encyclopedia*, 496.

40. Grant, *Memoirs*, 630.

41. Congressional Quarterly, Inc., *Presidential Elections 1789–1996* (Washington: Congressional Quarterly, Inc., 1997), 94; Bonekemper, Edward H., III, "Lincoln's 1864 Victory Was Closer Than It Looked," *Washington Times*, July 15, 2000. See Appendix III, "The Critical Election of 1864: How Close Was It?"

42. Grant, *Memoirs*, 632–636; Grant to Sherman, Sept. 10, 1864, Simon, *Papers of Grant*, XII, 144; Sherman to Grant, Sept. 10, 1864, Ibid., 144; Grant to Sherman, Sept. 12, 1864, Ibid., 154–155. Porter described the visit in Porter, *Campaigning with Grant*, 287–296.

43. Sherman to Grant, 11 a.m., October 11, 1864, Simon, *Papers of Grant*, XII, 290 note; Grant, *Memoirs*, 816.

44. Grant to Sherman, 11:30 p.m., October 11, 1864, Simon, *Papers of Grant*, XII, 290 note.

45. Grant, *Memoirs*, 636–640. Of Sherman's proposal for his famous march, Grant later wrote: "His suggestions were finally approved, although they did not immediately find favor in Washington. Even when it came to the time of starting, the greatest apprehension, as to the propriety of the campaign he was about to commence, filled the mind of the President, induced no doubt by his advisers. This went so far as to move the President to ask me to suspend Sherman's march for a day or two until I could think the matter over. . . . I was in favor of Sherman's plan from the time it was first submitted to me. My chief of staff, however, was very bitterly opposed to it and, as I learned subsequently, finding that he could not move me, he appealed to the authorities at Washington to stop it." Grant, *Memoirs*, 652–653.

46. Grant, *Memoirs*, 631–638; Garavaglia, Louis A., "Sherman's March and the Georgia Arsenals," *North & South*, Vol. 6, No. 1 (Dec. 2002). For details of Sherman's March to the Sea, see Scaife, William R., "Sherman's March to the Sea: Events from September 3 to December, 1864, Including the Occupation of Atlanta, More Battles with the Unpredictable John Bell Hood, the Burning of Atlanta, 'Marching Through Georgia,' and the Fall of Savannah," *Blue & Gray* magazine, VII, Issue 2 (Dec. 1989). General Kilpatrick acquired his nickname, "Kill Cavalry," by virtue of his unnecessarily sacrificing his men in battle.

47. Grant, *Memoirs*, 648–650; Grant to Sherman, Dec. 3, 1864, Simon, *Papers of Grant*, XIII, 56.

48. Grant, *Memoirs*, 651–652; Durham, Roger S., "Savannah: Mr. Lincoln's Christmas Present," *Blue & Gray* magazine, VIII, Issue 3 (Feb. 1991).

49. Grant, *Memoirs*, 652.

50. Grant, *Memoirs*, 654–655; McWhiney and Jamieson, *Attack and Die*, 21; Groom, *Shrouds of Glory*, 156–224; Heidler and Heidler, *Encyclopedia*, 771–772.

51. A frustrated Grant had issued orders to relieve Thomas of command, but Lincoln and Halleck provided Thomas with enough time to attack before those orders could take effect. Williams, *Lincoln and His Generals*, 342–344.

52. Grant, *Memoirs*, 655–661; McWhiney and Jamieson, *Attack and Die*, 21; Groom, *Shrouds of Glory*, 224–275; Dolzall, Gary W., "Enemies Front and Rear," *America's Civil War,* Vol. 16, No. 2 (May 2003); Cox, *Reminiscences*, II, 358–374.

Chapter 11: Early 1865: Winning the War

1. Wiley, Bell Irvin, *The Road to Appomattox* (Baton Rouge and London: Louisiana State University Press, 1994) (Reprint of Memphis: Memphis State College Press, 1956), 85; Jones, "Military Means" in Boritt, Gabor S., *Why the Confederacy Lost* (New York and Oxford: Oxford University Press, 1992), 74; Beringer et al., *Why the South Lost*, 333; Connelly, "Lee and the Western Confederacy."

2. Lincoln to William H. Seward, Jan. 31, 1865, Basler, *Works of Lincoln*, VIII, 250–251; Lincoln to Grant, Feb. 1, 1865, Ibid., 252; Grant to Lincoln, Feb. 1, 1865, Ibid., 280 note and Simon, *Papers of Grant*, XIII, 344–345; Bergeron, Arthur W., Jr., "Three-day Tussle at Hatcher's Run," *America's Civil War*, Vol. 16, No. 1 (March 2003), 30. For all the relevant communications on this abortive conference, see Lincoln to the House of Representatives, Feb. 10, 1865, Basler, *Works of Lincoln*, VIII, 274–285. A month later, Lee tried to initiate discussions with Grant, who sought instructions and was told by Lincoln not to confer with Lee "unless it be for the capitulation of Gen. Lee's army, or on some minor, and purely, military matter." Lincoln to Grant, March 3, 1865, Ibid., 330–331 note.

3. Connelly, *Autumn of Glory*, 529.

4. Grant, *Memoirs*, 671–674. For example, the 10,000-man 23rd Corps was moved by river, rail, and sea from Clifton, Tennessee, to Wilmington in a rapid movement reminiscent of the late 1863 movement of the 11th and 12th corps from Virginia to Chattanooga. Report of Colonel Lewis B.

Parsons, *Official Records*, XLVII, part 2 [S#99]; Longstreet, *From Manassas to Appomattox*, 386–387.

5. Bradley, Mark L., "Last Stand in the Carolinas: The Battle of Bentonville, March 19–21, 1865," *Blue & Gray* magazine, XIII, Issue 2 (Dec. 1995).

6. Williams, *Lincoln and His Generals*, 347.

7. Grant to Sherman, December 18, 1864, Simon, *Papers of Grant*, XIII, 130; Coburn, Mark, *Terrible Innocence: General Sherman at War* (New York: Hippocrene Books, 1993), 191–192.

8. Thomas, *Lee*, 348.

9. Rhodes, *All for the Union*, 214–216.

10. Ibid., 349.

11. Wiley, *Road to Appomattox*, 72.

12. Marvel, William, *Lee's Last Retreat: The Flight to Appomattox* (Chapel Hill and London: The University of North Carolina Press, 2002), 5–6.

13. Ibid., 205.

14. Alexander, Bevin, *How Great Generals Win* (New York and London: W.W. Norton and Company, 1993), 167.

15. Glatthaar, Joseph T., "Black Glory" in Boritt, *Why the Confederacy Lost*, 160; Thomas, *Lee*, 347; Beringer et al., *Why the South Lost*, 373; Hattaway and Jones, *How the North Won*, 272.

16. Fonvielle, Chris, "The Last Rays of Departing Hope: The Fall of Wilmington Including the Campaigns Against Fort Fisher," *Blue & Gray* magazine, XII, Issue 2 (Dec. 1994); Zentner, Joe and Syrett, Mary, "Confederate Gibralter," *Military History*, Vol. 19, No. 6 (Feb. 2003); Grant to Sherman, Dec. 3, 1964, Simon, *Papers of Grant*, XIII, 56. When Davis designated Bragg to defend Wilmington, a Virginia newspaper opined, "Braxton Bragg has been ordered to Wilmington. Goodbye Wilmington."

17. Fonvielle, "Last Rays," 20–21, 48–52. "The Wilmington expedit[ion] has proven a gross and culpable failure." Grant to Lincoln, Dec. 28, 1864, Simon, *Papers of Grant*, XIII, 177.

18. Fonvielle, "Last Rays," 52–57.

19. Grant, *Memoirs*, 662–670, 680; Fonvielle, "Last Rays," 57–62; Zentner and Syrett, "Confederate Gibralter," 26–32, 73.

20. Fonvielle, "Last Rays," 62.

21. McPherson, *Battle Cry of Freedom*, 826.

22. Marszalek, *Sherman*, 320–321.

23. Grant, *Memoirs*, 675.

24. Sherman, *Memoirs*, 752.

25. Grant, *Memoirs*, 679–680.

26. Grant, *Memoirs*, 681–682. On the burning of Columbia, see Evans, E. Chris, " 'I Almost Tremble at Her Fate': When Sherman came to Columbia, South Carolina, secession's hotbed became a bed of coals," *Civil War Times Illustrated*, XXXVII, No. 5 (Oct. 1998). Sherman's comment on the burning of Columbia was, "Though I never ordered it and never wished it, I have never shed many tears over the event, because I believe it hastened what we all fought for, the end of the war." Ibid., 67.

27. Alexander, *How Great Generals Win*, 164.

28. Hattaway and Jones, *How the North Won*, 667.

29. Alexander, *How Great Generals Win*, 164–165, quoting Hart, Liddell, *Sherman: Soldier, Realist, American*, 356 and Sherman, *Memoirs*, 271.

30. Cox, *Military Reminiscences*, II, 431–444; Bradley, "Last Stand."

31. For details on the Battle of Averasboro, see Bradley, Mark L., "Old Reliable's Finest Hour: The Battle of Averasboro, North Carolina, March 15–16, 1865" *Blue & Gray* magazine, XVI, Issue 1 (Oct. 1998).

32. For full details and battle maps of the Battle of Bentonville, see Bradley, "Last Stand."

33. Alexander, *How Great Generals Win*, 166–167.

34. Marvel, *Lee's Last Retreat*, 7.

35. Bergeron, "Hatcher's Run."

36. Lowe, David W., "Field Fortifications in the Civil War," *North & South*, Vol. 4, No. 6 (Aug. 2001).

37. Ibid.

38. Grant, *Memoirs*, 691–693; McWhiney and Jamieson, *Attack and Die*, 165; Marvel, *Lee's Last Retreat*, 9–11; Lowe, "Field Fortifications," 72; Fox, *Regimental Losses*, 548.

39. Rhodes, *All for the Union*, 221–222.

40. Grant to Meade, March 24, 1865, Simon, *Papers of Grant*, 211.

41. Grant, *Memoirs*, 693; Grant to Meade, March 24, 1865, Simon, *Papers of Grant*, XIV, 211–4.

42. Sears, *Controversies*, 263–264; Calkins, Chris, "The Battle of Five Forks: Final Push for the South Side," *Blue & Gray* magazine, IX, No. 4 (April 1992).

43. Rhodes, *All for the Union*, 223.

44. Calkins, "Five Forks."

45. King, Curtis S., "Reconsider, Hell!," *MHQ: The Quarterly Journal of Military History*, Vol. 13, No. 4 (Summer 2001); Sears, *Controversies*, 269–271; Calkins, "Five Forks."

46. For details of the Battle of Dinwiddie Court House, see Crawford, Mark J., "Dinwiddie Court House: Beginning of the End," *America's Civil War*, Vol. 12, No. 1 (March 1999), 50–56.

47. Crawford, "Dinwiddie Court House;" Calkins, "Five Forks."

48. Rhodes, *All for the Union*, 224.

49. King, "Reconsider, Hell!;" Sears, *Controversies*, 272–274; Calkins, "Five Forks."

50. Calkins, "Five Forks."

51. Ibid.

52. King, "Reconsider, Hell!;" Sears, *Controversies*, 279–281; Crawford, "Dinwiddie Court House;" Calkins, "Five Forks;" Sears, "Warren and Little Phil."

53. King, "Reconsider, Hell!;" Sears, *Controversies*, 281; Marvel, William, "Retreat to Appomattox," *Blue & Gray* magazine, XXXVIII, Issue 4 (Spring 2001); Marvel, William, "Thorn in the Flesh," *Civil War Times Illustrated*, XLI, No. 3 (June 2002); Greene, A. Wilson, "April 2, 1865: Day of Decision at Petersburg," *Blue & Gray* magazine, XVIII, Issue 3 (Feb. 2001); Sears, "Warren and Little Phil." Many military and civilian observers believed that Sheridan had acted out of jealousy and fear that Warren would receive credit for the victory. For example, the well-known battlefield artist Alfred Waud wrote on the back of a sketch of Warren's attack at Five Forks, "Sheridan and the ring he belongs to intends to grab all laurels no matter at the cost of what injustice." Marvel, *Lee's Last Retreat*, 16.

Another view is that the firing of Warren was the final step in ridding the Army of the Potomac of McClellan loyalists: "[McClellanism's] final victim was Gouverneur Warren, sacked at the moment of victory at Five Forks in 1865 by Sheridan (at Grant's nod) because as a McClellan loyalist Warren represented all that was wrong with the Army of the Potomac." Rhea et al., "What Was Wrong?"

Warren spent the seventeen years after his relief trying to restore his reputation. His last words before his November 1881 death were, "I die a disgraced soldier." Sears, *Controversies*, 282–284. Unfortunately, it was three months after his death when Warren was exonerated by a court of inquiry appointed by President Rutherford B. Hayes. King, "Reconsider, Hell!" Grant had prevented the inquiry (presumably to protect Sheridan) while he was general-in-chief and then president. Sears, *Controversies*, 282–284. In his memoirs, Grant naturally supported Sheridan's relief of Warren (which Grant had authorized): "[Warren] could see every danger at a glance before he had encountered it. He would not only make preparations to meet the danger which might occur, but he would inform his commanding officer what others should do while he was executing his move." Grant, *Memoirs*, 702. Grant did not want hesitance; he wanted immediate action. As a result, Generals Gouverneur Warren and George Thomas, among others, earned Grant's wrath and criticism for what he perceived as their hesitance.

54. Smith, *Grant*, 399 note.
55. Calkins, "Five Forks;" Marvel, "Retreat."
56. Grant, *Memoirs*, 702–703; Greene, "April 2, 1864;" Calkins, "Five Forks."
57. Grant, *Memoirs*, 703–705; Greene, "April 2, 1864;" Davis, Burke, *The Long Surrender* (New York: Vintage Books, 1989), 21–32.
58. Greene, "April 2, 1865."
59. For details on the Appomattox Campaign, see Marvel, *Lee's Last Retreat*; Marvel, "Retreat" [includes battle maps].
60. William Marvel contended that the missing pontoon bridge delayed Lee more than any missing rations. He blamed both on poor headquarters communication. Marvel, *Lee's Last Retreat*, 44–51, 207–208; Marvel, William, "Many have offered excuses for the Confederate retreat to

Appomattox, perhaps beginning with Robert E. Lee," *America's Civil War*, Vol. 14, No. 3 (July 2001). He also attacked the "myth" of the missing rations' significance and laid the probable blame for their absence at the doorstep of Walter Taylor. Marvel, *Lee's Last Retreat*, 207–213; Marvel, "Many Have Offered."

61. Marvel, "Retreat."

62. Marvel, *Lee's Last Retreat*, 67–94; Glynn, Gary, "Black Thursday for Rebels," *America's Civil War*, Vol. 4, No. 5 (Jan. 1992); Marvel, "Retreat;" Calkins, "Final Bloodshed at Appomattox," *America's Civil War*, Vol. 14, No. 2 (May 2001); Fox, *Regimental Losses*, 549; Heidler and Heidler, *Encyclopedia*, 1710.

63. Marvel, "Retreat."

64. Marvel, "Retreat;" Lincoln to Grant, April 7, 1865, Basler, *Works of Lincoln*, VIII, 392.

65. Grant to Lee, April 7, 1865, Simon, *Papers of Grant*, XIV, 361.

66. Lee to Grant, April 7, 1865, Dowdey and Manarin, *Papers of Lee*, 931–932 and Simon, *Papers of Grant*, Vol. 14, page 361 note. Dowdey and Manarin made editorial corrections to Lee's papers to make them as perfect as possible, while Simon republished Grant's correspondence as it was written (including all the errors). Simon similarly maintained the original accuracy of Lee's correspondence that he quoted in notes to Grant's correspondence. The Lee texts quoted here and below are the unedited Simon versions.

67. Grant to Lee, April 8, 1865, Simon, *Papers of Grant*, XIV, 367.

68. Lee to Grant, April 8, 1865, Dowdey and Manarin, *Papers of Lee*, 932 and Simon, *Papers of Grant*, XIV, 367 note.

69. Freeman, *Lee's Lieutenants*, III, 721; Longstreet, *Memoirs*, 620.

70. Marvel, "Retreat;" Calkins, "Final Bloodshed."

71. Grant to Lee, April 9, 1865, Simon, *Papers of Grant*, XIV, 371.

72. Marvel, "Retreat."

73. Lee to Grant, April 9, 1865, Dowdey and Manarin, *Papers of Lee*, 932; Simon, *Papers of Grant*, XIV, 371 note.

74. Marvel, *Lee's Last Retreat*, 180. Several of Grant's officers immediately bought the McLean parlor furniture as souvenirs. Ibid.,181.

75. McWhiney and Jamieson, *Attack and Die*, 19, 158.
76. Marvel, *Lee's Last Retreat*, 184, 201–206; Marvel, "Many Have Offered."
77. Dana, *Recollections*, 210–211.

CHAPTER 12: GRANT'S WINNING CHARACTERISTICS

1. Welles, *Diary*, II, 44–45; Jones, *Right Hand*, 200; Groom, *Shrouds of Glory*, 9. A 1993 article in *Blue & Gray* magazine refers to the "butcher's bill" of the first two weeks of the Overland Campaign. Miller, "Strike Them," 13. On June 4, 1864, Navy Secretary Gideon Welles also wrote in his diary, "Still there is heavy loss, but we are becoming accustomed to the sacrifice. Grant has not great regard for human life." Welles, *Diary*, II, 45.
2. Weigley, *American Way of War*, 152.
3. Ibid., 142.
4. Dana, *Recollections*, 187–189.
5. Williams, *McClellan, Sherman and Grant*, 105; Fuller, *Grant and Lee*, 63, 68.
6. "Reconsidering Grant and Lee."
7. "The Confederacy only had to be defended to survive. As Federal General Henry W. Halleck pointed out: 'the North must conquer the South.'" McWhiney and Jamieson, *Attack and Die*, 6.
8. Smith, *Grant*, 213.
9. Williams, *Lincoln and His Generals*, 312–313.
10. McWhiney and Jamieson, *Attack and Die*, 19–23.
11. "Reconsidering Grant and Lee."
12. Perret, *Grant*, 332.
13. Ibid., 23, 158.
14. For a comprehension comparison of war-long casualties incurred and imposed by Grant and Lee's armies, see Bonekemper, Edward H., III, *Grant and Lee: Victorious American and Vanquished Virginian* (Westport, CT: Praeger/Greenwood, 2008), 267–322.
15. McWhiney and Jamieson, *Attack and Die*, 22–23. Here I have deleted from their calculations 29,396 Confederates captured at Vicksburg that

they used to further improve Grant's statistics. They point out that their numbers do not include some of Grant's Petersburg Campaign numbers because Confederate numbers are not available for comparison.

16. Grant, *Memoirs*, 69–70.

17. Williams, *McClellan, Sherman and Grant*, 97–98.

18. McWhiney and Jamieson, *Attack and Die*, 23, 158. Again, these numbers do not include late-war battles in which related Confederate casualties were not estimated by those authors.

19. This number includes killed and wounded in late-war battles not covered by the McWhiney and Jamieson estimates.

20. Dana, *Recollections*, 187–189; Rhea, "'Butcher' Grant." "No single day of Grant's pounding saw the magnitude of Union casualties that McClellan incurred in one day at Antietam, and no three consecutive days of Grant's warring proved as costly to the Union as Meade's three days at Gettysburg." Ibid.

21. Weigley, *Great Civil War*, 264.

22. Catton, *Grant*, 105.

23. Ibid., 104.

24. McMurry, Richard M., *Two Great Rebel Armies: An Essay in Confederate Military History* (Chapel Hill and London: University of North Carolina Press, 1989), 44–50, quoting Adams, Michael C.C., *Our Masters The Rebels: A Speculation on Union Military Failure in the East, 1861–1865* (Cambridge, Mass., 1978).

25. Mertz, "Wilderness II."

26. Hattaway, "Changing Face."

27. Groom, *Shrouds of Glory*, 54.

28. McWhiney and Jamieson, *Attack and Die*, 19. These are the casualties from Wilderness through Cold Harbor. Detailed Confederate statistics are unavailable after that point.

29. McWhiney and Jamieson, *Attack and Die*, 19, 158. Again, for consistency with Lee's numbers, these only include casualties from the Wilderness through Cold Harbor.

30. Groom, *Shrouds of Glory*, 54.

31. See discussions of this issue at the beginning of the preface, the beginning of this chapter, and Appendix I, "Historians' Treatment of Ulysses S. Grant."

32. McPherson, *Battle Cry*, 637.

33. Weigley, *American Way of War*, 140.

34. Arnold, *Grant Wins*, 4.

35. Grant, *Memoirs*, 512.

36. Fuller, *Generalship of Grant*; McMurry, *Two Armies*, 54–55.

37. Anderson, "Grant's Struggle with Alcohol;" Perret, Geoffrey, *Ulysses S. Grant: Soldier & President* (New York: Random House, 1997), 262. "There is no evidence that he was under the influence at any moment of decision or that the habit interfered with his generalship. But the suspicion was always there, and it cropped up at regular intervals." Williams, *McClellan, Sherman and Grant*, 89.

38. Jones, *Right Hand*, 113–116.

39. McPherson, *Battle Cry of Freedom*, 588.

40. Badeau, *Grant*, II, 21.

41. Bonekemper, *How Lee Lost*, 203.

42. McPherson, "Unheroic Hero."

43. Keegan, *Mask of Command*, 200. Grant probably modeled his orders on those of Zachary Taylor, of whom Grant wrote, "Taylor was not a conversationalist, but on paper he could put his meaning so plainly that there could be no mistaking it. He knew how to express what he wanted to say in the fewest well-chosen words." Grant, *Memoirs*, 95.

44. Porter, *Campaigning with Grant*, 7.

45. Jones, *Right Hand*, 111. Jones cites evidence that Grant wrote his own orders because he could write them more quickly than explain to a clerk or aide what he wanted written. Ibid., 111–112.

46. Smith, *Grant*, 202.

47. Porter, *Campaigning with Grant*, 66.

48. Williams, *Lincoln and His Generals*, 313.

49. Owens, Richard H., "An Astonishing Career," *Military Heritage*, Vol. 3, No. 2 (Oct. 2001), 64–73.

50. Porter, *Campaigning with Grant*, 250.

51. Jones, *Right Hand*, 86–122, 176–219.

52. Ibid.,219.

53. Arnold, *Grant Wins*, 4.

54. McPherson, "Unheroic Hero;" Rhea, *Cold Harbor*, 388.

55. *Official Records*, XLVI , part 1, 22.

56. Rhea, *Cold Harbor*, 388.

57. Arnold, *Armies of Grant*, 275.

58. Catton, *Grant Moves South*, 217; Arnold, *Armies of Grant*, 108.

59. Gallagher, "'Upon Their Success'."

60. Arnold, *Grant Wins*, 4.

61. Smith, *Grant*, 138; Fuller, *Grant and Lee*, 81.

62. Williams, *Lincoln and His Generals*, 271.

63. Stoddard, William O., Jr., *William O. Stoddard: Lincoln's Third Secretary* (New York: Exposition Press, 1955), 197–198.

64. Williams, *McClellan, Sherman and Grant*, 97.

65. Weigley, *American Way of War*, 130.

66. Hattaway and Jones, *How the North Won*, xvi.

67. Catton, *Grant Takes Command*, 105.

68. Woodworth, Steven E., "The Army of Tennessee and the Element of Military Success," *North & South*, Vol. 6, No. 4 (May 2003).

69. Williams, *McClellan, Sherman and Grant*, 59.

70. McPherson, "Unheroic Hero."

71. Fuller, *Generalship of Grant*, 190.

72. Cox, *Reminiscences*, II, 41.

73. Williams, *McClellan, Sherman and Grant*, 105–106.

74. Williams, T. Harry, "The Military Leadership of North and South" in Donald, David Herbert (ed.), *Why the North Won the Civil War* (New York: Collier Books, 1960), 50–52.

75. McPherson, James M., "Lincoln and the Strategy of Unconditional Surrender," in Boritt, Gabor S. (ed.), *Lincoln, the War President: The Gettysburg Lectures* (New York and Oxford: Oxford University Press, 1992), 45.

76. Buell, *Warrior Generals*, 247.

77. Bearss, *Vicksburg*, III, 1311.

78. Smith, *Grant*, 369.
79. Fuller, *Generalship of Grant*, 195.
80. Catton, *Grant Moves South*, 489.
81. Cox, *Reminiscences*, II, 41.
82. Feis, *Grant's Secret Service*, 267. Feis's conclusions appeared earlier in Feis, William B., "'He Don't Care a Damn for What the Enemy Does out of His Sight," *North & South*, Vol. 1, No. 2 (Jan. 1998), 68–81.
83. Fuller, *Generalship of Grant*, 371–372.
84. Ibid., 372.
85. Rhea, *Cold Harbor*, xii.
86. McPherson, "Unheroic Hero."
87. Williams, *McClellan, Sherman and Grant*, 100–101.
88. McWhiney and Jamieson, *Attack and Die*, 158. This table is borrowed virtually verbatim from that book except for the percentages, which have been calculated by the author of this book.
89. Goodman, "Grant's Gamble."
90. Wittenberg, " Sheridan's Second Raid."
91. Ibid.

Appendix I

1. "Personal Memoirs of U.S. Grant made a rich man of [publisher] Mark Twain and earned $450,000 for the Grant family. The two-volume, 1200-page edition sold over 300,000 copies in its first printing, making it one of the most successful books of the 19th century." Poggiali, Leonard, "Conditional Surrender: The Death of U.S. Grant, and the Cottage on Mount McGregor," *Blue & Gray*, X, Issue 3 (Feb. 1993), 60–5 at 63.
2. Wilson, Edmund, *Patriotic Gore* (London: Oxford University Press, 1962), 132, quoted in McPherson, "The Unheroic Hero," 16.
3. Keegan, John, *The Mask of Command* (New York: Viking, 1987) , 202.
4. These articles were later published in a four-volume series that has become a gold-mine (despite much of the mineral being fool's gold) for Civil war historians. Johnson & Buel, *Battles and Leaders*.
5. McPherson, "Unheroic Hero," 16; Leyden, John G., "Grant wins last battle by finishing memoirs," *Washington Times*, March 23, 2002.

6. McPherson, "Unheroic Hero," 16.

7. Grant, *Memoirs*, 115.

8. Pollard, *Lost Cause*, 510.

9. Swinton, *Campaigns*, 440.

10. Ropes, John C., "Grant's Campaign in Virginia in 1864," *Papers of the Military Historical Society of Massachusetts*, Vol. 4, 495, quoted in Rhea, *Cold Harbor*, xii.

11. Gallagher, "'Upon Their Success'." 90–91, quoting Early, Jubal A., *The Campaigns of Gen. Robert E. Lee*. An Address by Lieut. General Jubal A. Early, before Washington and Lee University, January 19th, 1872 (Baltimore: Murphy, 1872), 44.

12. Gallagher, "'Upon Their Success'," 91.

13. Davis, *Rise and Fall*, II, 335.

14. Law, "From the Wilderness to Cold Harbor," 143.

15. Taylor, *Lee*, 231, 241.

16. Badeau, *Grant*, I, 203–295.

17. Porter, *Campaigning with Grant*, 513.

18. McMurry, *Two Armies*, 50.

19. Freeman, *R.E.Lee*, III, 433–4, 447.

20. Dowdey, *Lee's Last Campaign*, 93.

21. Casdorph, *Lee and Jackson*, 401; Furgurson, *Not War But Murder*.

22. Keegan, *Mask of Command*, 229.

23. Sears, Stephen W., "All the Trumpets Sounded. Bruce Catton: An Appreciation," *North & South* (Vol. 3, No. 1, Nov. 1999), 24–32 at 30. Ironically, the dust jacket of Catton's Stillness was the location of an invidious comparison of Grant and Lee: "[The Army of the Potomac's] leader was General Ulysses S. Grant, a seedy little man who instilled no enthusiasm in his followers and little respect in his enemies. Opposing Grant . . . was Robert E. Lee, the last great knight of battle. He was a god to his men and scourge to his antagonists." Catton, *Stillness*, dust jacket.

24. Williams, *Lincoln and His Generals*, 312.

25. Foote, *Civil War*, I, 215.

26. McFeely, *Grant*, xii, 114–5, 122, 157, 165; Smith, *Grant*, 15.

27. Perret, *Grant*, 321–2.

28. Simpson, *Grant*, 463.

29. Jones, *Right Hand*, 176–219.

30. Feis, *Grant's Secret Service*, 267–8.

31. Smith, *Grant*, 14–5.

32. The full titles of Rhea's books and articles may be found in the bibliography of this book.

33. Epperson, "Chance Battle," 77–88.

Appendix II

1. Nofi, Albert A., "Calculating Combatants," *North & South*, Vol. 4, No. 2 (Jan. 2001), 68–69 at 69.

2. Ibid.

3. Phisterer, Frederick, *Statistical Record of the Armies of the United States* (Carlisle, Pennsylvania: John Kallman Publishers, 1996) (reprint of Edison, New Jersey: Castle Books, 1883).

4. Fox, *Regimental Losses*.

5. Fuller, *Grant and Lee*, 286–7.

6. McWhiney and Jamieson, *Attack and Die*, 23, 158.

7. Arnold, *Armies of Grant*, 31–2.

8. Buell, *Warrior Generals*, 147.

9. Current, Richard N. (ed.), *Encyclopedia of the Confederacy* (New York: Simon & Schuster, 1993) (4 vols.), I, 156.

10. Foote, *Civil War*, I, 152.

11. Fox, *Regimental Losses*, 543, 549.

12. Fuller, *Grant and Lee*, 286.

13. Grant, *Memoirs*, 185.

14. Hattaway and Jones, *How the North*, 53.

15. Heidler and Heidler, *Encyclopedia*, 208.

16. Phisterer, *Statistical Record*, 213.

17. Roberts, "Belmont," 49.

18. Smith, *Grant*, 130.

19. Arnold, *Armies of Grant*, 47.

20. Badeau, *Grant*, I, 51–2.

21. Beringer et al, *Why the South Lost*, 124.

22. Buell, *Warrior Generals*, 440.

23. Cooling, "Forts," 52.

24. Foote, *Civil War*, I, 215.

25. Fox, *Regimental Losses*, 543, 549.

26. Fuller, *Grant and Lee*, 144, 286.

27. Heidler and Heidler, *Encyclopedia*, 730.

28. Jones, "Military Means," 57.

29. Livermore, *Numbers & Losses*, 78.

30. McPherson, *Battle Cry*, 402.

31. McWhiney and Jamieson, *Attack and Die*, 158.

32. Phisterer, *Statistical Record*, 213.

33. Grant to Halleck, Feb. 16, 1862, Simon, *Papers of Grant*, 223–5 at 223, and 226 note.

34. Smith, *Grant*, 165.

35. Williams, *Grant Rises in the West*, I, 257–8.

36. Allen, "Shiloh! II," 48.

37. Arnold, *Armies of Grant*, 70.

38. Badeau, *Grant*, I, 91–2.

39. Beauregard, "Shiloh," 593.

40. Beringer et al, *Why the South Lost*, 131.

41. Buell, *Warrior Generals*, 440, 442.

42. Catton, *Grant Moves South*, 247.

43. Current, *Encyclopedia*, I, 338.

44. Daniel, *Shiloh*, 322.

45. Davis, *Rise and Fall*, II, 58.

46. Donald, David Herbert; Baker, Jean Harvey; and Holt, Michael F., *The Civil War and Reconstruction* (New York and London: W.W. Norton & Company, 2001), 201.

47. Esposito, Vincent J. (ed.), *The West Point Atlas of American Wars* (New York, Washington, London: Frederick A. Prager, Inc., 1959) (2 vols.), I, Map 38 text.

48. Feis, *Grant's Secret Service*, 101.

49. Foote, *Civil War*, I, 350.

50. Fox, *Regimental Losses*, 23, 543 and 549.

51. Fuller, *Generalship of Grant*, 116.

52. Fuller, *Grant and Lee*, 286.

53. Grant, "Shiloh," 485.

54. Hattaway and Jones, *How the North Won*, 169.

55. Heidler and Heidler, *Encyclopedia*, 1779.

56. Jones, "Military Means," 58.

57. Livermore, *Numbers & Losses*, 79-80.

58. Lowe, "Field Fortifications," 65.

59. Martin, David G., *The Shiloh Campaign, March–April 1862* (Bryn Mawr, Pennsylvania: Combined Books, 1987), 155.

60. McFeely, *Grant*, 115.

61. McWhiney and Jamieson, *Attack and Die*, 8, 158.

62. Nevins, *Ordeal of the Union*, VI, 85.

63. Phisterer, *Statistical Record*, 213.

64. Sherman, *Memoirs*, 268.

65. Smith, *Grant*, 204.

66. Williams, *Grant Rises in the West*, I, 394.

67. Allen, "Crossroads," 38.

68. Badeau, *Grant*, I, 115.

69. Cozzens, *Darkest Days*, 133.

70. Foote, *Civil War*, I, 720.

71. Fox, *Regimental Losses*, 23, 544, 550.

72. Fuller, *Grant and Lee*, 286.

73. Hattaway and Jones, *How the North Won*, 252.

74. Heidler and Heidler, *Encyclopedia*, 1052.

75. Lamers, *Edge of Glory*, 115.

76. Phisterer, *Statistical Record*, 214.

77. Smith, *Grant*, 218.

78. Snead, "With Price," 734.

79. Suhr, "Iuka," 49.

80. The designation "Grant not present" represents my subjective judgment that, although Grant had command responsibility for the battle, he was not sufficiently involved to have had a direct impact on the outcome of the battle.

81. Allen, "Crossroads," 46.

82. Badeau, *Grant*, I, 117.

83. Catton, *Grant Moves South*, 315.

84. Cozzens, *Darkest Days*, 305–6.

85. Current, *Encyclopedia*, I, 415.

86. Foote, *Civil War*, I, 724–5.

87. Fox, *Regimental Losses*, 23, 544, 550.

88. Fuller, *Grant and Lee*, 286.

89. Grant, *Memoirs*, 281.

90. Hattaway and Jones, How the North Won, 256.

91. Heidler and Heidler, *Encyclopedia*, 500.

92. Lamers, *Edge of Glory*, 154–5.

93. Livermore, *Numbers & Losses*, 94.

94. Phisterer, *Statistical Record*, 214.

95. Rosecrans, "Corinth," 756.

96. Smith, *Grant*, 219.

97. Williams, *Grant Rises in the West*, I, 104.

98. Cozzens, *Darkest Days*, 292.

99. Foote, *Civil War*, 725.

100. Phisterer, *Statistical Record*, 214.

101. Williams, *Grant Rises in the West*, I, 104.

102. Badeau, *Grant*, I, 145.

103. Bearss, *Vicksburg*, I, 224–9.

104. Beringer et al, *Why the South Lost*, 243.

105. Fox, *Regimental Losses*, 23, 544, 550.

106. Fuller, *Grant and Lee*, 286.

107. Hattaway and Jones, *How the North Won*, 314.

108. Livermore, *Numbers & Losses*, 96–7.

109. Morgan, "Chickasaw Bluffs," 468–9.

110. Phisterer, *Statistical Record*, 215.

111. Arnold, *Grant Wins*, 45.

112. Bearss, *Vicksburg*, I, 405, 415–9.

113. Fox, *Regimental Losses*, 23.

114. Livermore, *Numbers & Losses*, 98.

115. Phisterer, *Statistical Record*, 215.

116. Sherman, *Memoirs*, 325.

117. Arnold, *Grant Wins*, 116.

118. Badeau, *Grant*, I, 211.

119. Bearss, *Vicksburg*, II, 402–7.

120. Current, *Encyclopedia*, III, 1238.

121. Fuller, *Grant and Lee*, 386.

122. Grant, *Memoirs*, 358.

123. Heidler and Heidler, *Encyclopedia*, 1545.

124. Martin, David G., *The Vicksburg Campaign* (New York: Wieser and Wieser, Inc., 1990), 94.

125. "The Opposing Forces in the Vicksburg Campaign," in Battles and Leaders, III, 546–50 at 549. These numbers represent "the gist of all the data obtainable in the Official Records." Ibid., 546.

126. Phisterer, *Statistical Record*, 215.

127. Smith, *Grant*, 240.

128. Winschel, "Grant's Beachhead," 56.

129. Arnold, *Grant Wins*, 135.

130. Badeau, *Grant*, I, 236–7.

131. Bearss, *Vicksburg*, II, 515–7.

132. Foote, *Civil War*, II, 360.

133. Fox, *Regimental Losses*, 544, 550.

134. Grant, *Memoirs*, 331, 358.

135. Hattaway and Jones, *How the North Won*, 392.

136. Heidler and Heidler, *Encyclopedia*, 1611, 2022.

137. Martin, *Vicksburg*, 97.

138. "Opposing Forces," 549.

139. Arnold, *Grant Wins*, 140.

140. Badeau, *Grant*, I, 249.

141. Bearss, *Vicksburg*, II, 555–8.

142. Current, *Encyclopedia*, II, 838.

143. Foote, *Civil War*, 363.

144. Fox, *Regimental Losses*, 544.

145. Grant, *Memoirs*, 337, 358.

146. Martin, *Vicksburg*, 99.

147. "Opposing Forces," 549.

148. Arnold, *Armies of Grant*, 109.

149. Arnold, *Grant Wins*, 196.

150. Badeau, *Grant*, I, 269–70.

151. Bearss, "Grant Marches West," 45.

152. Bearss, *Vicksburg*, II, 642–51.

153. Buell, *Warrior Generals*, 440, 442.

154. Catton, *Grant Moves South*, 445.

155. Civil War Times Illustrated Editors (eds.), *Great Battles of the Civil War* (New York: Gallery Books, 1984), 342.

156. Esposito, West Point Atlas, I, Map 105 text.

157. Foote, *Civil War*, II, 374.

158. Fox, *Regimental Losses*, 544, 550.

159. Fuller, *Generalship of Grant*, 152.

160. Fuller, *Grant and Lee*, 286.

161. Grant, *Memoirs*, 347, 358.

162. Hattaway and Jones, *How the North Won*, 393.

163. Heidler and Heidler, *Encyclopedia*, 392.

164. Ibid., 2023–4.

165. Livermore, *Numbers & Losses*, 99–100.

166. Martin, *Vicksburg*, 110.

167. McPherson, *Battle Cry*, 630.

168. McWhiney & Jamieson, *Attack and Die*, 158.

169. Miers, Earl S., *The Web of Victory: Grant at Vicksburg* (Baton Rouge: Louisiana State University Press, 1984) (Reprint of New York: Alfred Knopf, 1955), 195.

170. "Opposing Forces," 549.

171. Phisterer, *Statistical Record*, 215.

172. Smith, *Grant*, 250.

173. Williams, *Grant Rises in the West*, II, 379.

174. Arnold, *Grant Wins*, 228–32.

175. Badeau, *Grant*, I, 278.

176. Barton, "Charge," 60.

177. Bearss, *Vicksburg*, II, 686–9.
178. Civil War Times, Great Battles, 344.
179. Foote, *Civil War*, II, 377.
180. Fox, *Regimental Losses*, 545.
181. Freeman, "Big Black River," 84–5.
182. Goodman, "Decision," 79.
183. Grant, *Memoirs*, 353, 358.
184. Heidler and Heidler, *Encyclopedia*, 2024, 228.
185. Martin, *Vicksburg*, 111.
186. "Opposing Forces," 549.
187. Smith, *Grant*, 251.
188. Arnold, *Grant Wins*, 245.
189. Bearss, *Vicksburg*, III, 773–80.
190. Civil War Times, Great Battles, 348.
191. Fox, *Regimental Losses*, 545.
192. Martin, *Vicksburg*, 118.
193. "Opposing Forces," 549.
194. Trudeau, "Climax at Vicksburg," 82.
195. Winschel, Terrence, "The Siege of Vicksburg," *Blue & Gray*, XX, Issue 4 (Spring 2003), 6–24, 47–50 at 12.
196. Arnold, *Grant Wins*, 256.
197. Badeau, *Grant*, I, 326–7.
198. Bearss, *Vicksburg*, III, 862–73.
199. Buell, *Warrior Generals*, 440.
200. Esposito, West Point Atlas, I, Map 106 text.
201. Fox, *Regimental Losses*, 545.
202. Fuller, *Grant and Lee*, 286.
203. Hattaway and Jones, *How the North Won*, 395.
204. Heidler and Heidler, *Encyclopedia*, 2025.
205. Livermore, *Numbers & Losses*, 100.
206. Lowe, "Field Fortifications," 65.
207. Martin, *Vicksburg*, 126.
208. McFeely, *Grant*, 132.
209. "Opposing Forces," 549.

210. Smith, *Grant*, 252.

211. Trudeau, "Climax at Vicksburg," 85.

212. Winschel, "Siege of Vicksburg," 14.

213. Arnold, *Grant Wins*, 298.

214. Bearss, *Vicksburg*, III, 957–68.

215. Fox, *Regimental Losses*, 545.

216. Hattaway and Jones, *How the North Won*, 411.

217. "Opposing Forces," 549.

218. Phisterer, *Statistical Record*, 215.

219. Trudeau, "Climax at Vicksburg," 88.

220. Arnold, *Armies of Grant*, 125.

221. Badeau, *Grant*, I, 386, 398–9.

222. Chambers, John Whiteclay, II, *The Oxford Companion to American Military History* (Oxford: Oxford University Press, 1999), 756.

223. Davis, *Rise and Fall*, II, 349.

224. Esposito, West Point Atlas, I, Map 107 text.

225. Fox, *Regimental Losses*, 23.

226. Fuller, *Generalship of Grant*, 158.

227. Fuller, *Grant and Lee*, 183, 286.

228. Grant, *Memoirs*, 384.

229. Hattaway and Jones, *How the North Won*, 411.

230. Heidler and Heidler, *Encyclopedia*, 2026.

231. Livermore, *Numbers & Losses*, 100–1.

232. McPherson, *Battle Cry*, 631.

233. McWhiney and Jamieson, *Attack and Die*, 8, 21, 158.

234. "Opposing Forces," 549–50.

235. Poulter, Keith, "Stop Insulting Robert E. Lee!," *North & South*, Vol. 1, No. 5 (1998), 6.

236. Sherman, *Memoirs*, 358.

237. Trudeau, "Climax at Vicksburg," 88.

238. Weigley, *American Way of War*, 140.

239. Williams, *Grant Rises in the West*, II, 420.

240. Badeau, *Grant*, I, 397.

241. Current, *Encyclopedia*, II, 838.

242. Fox, *Regimental Losses*, 545, 550.

243. Martin, *Vicksburg*, 180.

244. Sword, "Battle Above Clouds," 14.

245. Grant, *Memoirs*, 420.

246. Cozzens, *Shipwreck*, 100.

247. Sword, "Battle Above Clouds," 19.

248. Sword, "Battle Above Clouds," 54.

249. Arnold, *Armies of Grant*, 143.

250. Buell, *Warrior Generals*, 441.

251. Catton, *Grant Takes Command*, 91.

252. Cozzens, *Shipwreck*, 389.

253. Donald et al, *Civil War*, 369.

254. Davis, *Rise and Fall*, II, 365.

255. Esposito, West Point Atlas, I, Map 116 text.

256. Foote, *Civil War*, II, 858.

257. Fox, *Regimental Losses*, 546, 551, 23.

258. Fuller, *Grant and Lee*, 287.

259. Grant, "Chattanooga," 711.

260. Grant, *Memoirs*, 455.

261. Hattaway and Jones, *How the North Won*, 461–2.

262. Heidler and Heidler, *Encyclopedia*, 415.

263. Livermore, *Numbers & Losses*, 106–8.

264. McWhiney and Jamieson, *Attack and Die*, 20, 158.

265. Phisterer, *Statistical Record*, 215.

266. Smith, *Grant*, 281.

267. Foote, *Civil War*, II, 865.

268. Heidler and Heidler, *Encyclopedia*, 1133.

269. Foote, *Civil War*, II, 865.

270. Heidler and Heidler, *Encyclopedia*, 1133.

271. Hattaway, "Hard War," 75.

272. Ibid.

273. Castel, Albert, "History in Hindsight: Sherman and Sooy Smith. William Tecumseh Sherman's war of words with William Sooy Smith may have been merely a case of sour grapes," *Columbiad: A Quarterly*

review of the War Between the States, Vol. 3, No. 3 (Fall 1999), 56–75 at 71.

274. Buell, *Warrior Generals*, 441.

275. Catton, *Grant Takes Command*, 204.

276. Catton, *Stillness*, 91.

277. Civil War Times, *Great Battles*, 438.

278. Current, *Encyclopedia*, I, 338.

279. Esposito, West Point Atlas, I, Map 125 text.

280. Foote, *Civil War*, III, 188.

281. Fox, *Regimental Losses*, 23, 546.

282. Freeman, *R.E. Lee*, III, 428.

283. Fuller, *Generalship of Grant*, 238.

284. Fuller, *Grant and Lee*, 215.

285. Hassler, *Commanders*, 211.

286. Hattaway, "Changing Face," 41.

287. Hattaway and Jones, *How the North Won*, 545.

288. Heidler and Heidler, *Encyclopedia*, 2113.

289. Livermore, *Numbers & Losses*, 110–1.

290. McPherson, *Battle Cry*, 726.

291. Mertz, "Wilderness II," 49.

292. Phisterer, *Statistical Record*, 216.

293. Rhea, "Butcher' Grant," 48.

294. Smith, *Grant*, 333.

295. Steere, Edward, *The Wilderness Campaign* (New York: Bonanza Books, 1960), 463, 472.

296. Taylor, *Lee*, 249.

297. Smith, *Grant*, 365.

298. Young, "Numbers and Losses," 26. All of Young's "killed" numbers included those mortally wounded, for which he provided numbers. He also spelled out the numbers of wounded who subsequently died. His work is phenomenal.

299. Civil War Times, Great Battles, 447.

300. Current, *Encyclopedia*, I, 338.

301. Esposito, West Point Atlas, I, Map 133 text.

302. Fox, *Regimental Losses*, 23, 546.

303. Fuller, *Generalship of Grant*, 252.

304. Fuller, *Grant and Lee*, 287.

305. Hassler, *Commanders*, 216.

306. Heidler and Heidler, *Encyclopedia*, 1841.

307. Livermore, *Numbers & Losses*, 112.

308. Lowe, "Field Fortifications," 65.

309. Phisterer, *Statistical Record*, 216.

310. Rhea, "'Butcher' Grant," 49.

311. Taylor, *Lee*, 249.

312. Smith, *Grant*, 365.

313. Young, "Numbers and Losses," 26. Although Young's table shows a total of 12,451 casualties, his broken-down numbers total 12,421.

314. Fox, *Regimental Losses*, 23, 547.

315. Fuller, *Grant and Lee*, 287.

316. Phisterer, *Statistical Record*, 216.

317. Rhea, "'Butcher' Grant," 48.

318. Taylor, *Lee*, 249.

319. Smith, *Grant*, 365.

320. Young, "Numbers and Losses," 26–7. Although Young's tables for Sheridan's raid, North Anna, and Totopotomoy show a total of 3,757 casualties, his broken-down numbers total 3,766. The totals of his broken-down numbers for those three battles are 617, 1,558, and 1,591, respectively.

321. Arnold, *Armies of Grant*, 221.

322. Beringer et al, *Why the South Lost*, 349.

323. Buell, *Warrior Generals*, 441.

324. Casdorph, *Lee and Jackson*, 401.

325. Catton, *Grant Takes Command*, 267.

326. Catton, *Stillness*, 163.

327. Current, *Encyclopedia*, I, 367.

328. Esposito, West Point Atlas, I, Map 136 text.

329. Fox, *Regimental Losses*, 23, 547.

330. Freeman, *R.E. Lee*, III, 391.

331. Fuller, *Generalship of Grant*, 274.

332. Fuller, *Grant and Lee*, 221, 287.

333. Hassler, *Commanders*, 218.

334. Heidler and Heidler, *Encyclopedia*, 465.

335. Jones, *Right Hand*, 199.

336. "Lee and Grant, 1864," 56.

337. Livermore, *Numbers & Losses*, 114.

338. Lowe, "Field Fortifications," 65, 70.

339. Lowry, *No Turning Back*, 453.

340. O'Beirne, "Valley," 77.

341. Phisterer, *Statistical Record*, 216.

342. Rhea, "'Butcher' Grant," 49.

343. Rhea, "Cold Harbor," 60–1.

344. Rhea, *Cold Harbor*, 382.

345. Taylor, *Lee*, 249.

346. Smith, *Grant*, 365.

347. Young, "Numbers and Losses," 27. Although Young's table shows a total of 5,294 casualties, his broken-down numbers total 5,295.

348. Fox, *Regimental Losses*, 547.

349. Phisterer, *Statistical Record*, 217.

350. Taylor, Lee, 249.

351. Young, "Numbers and Losses," 27.

352. Casdorph, Lee and Jackson, 401.

353. Dana, *Recollections*, 188.

354. Davis, *The Rise and Fall of the Confederate Government*, II, 442.

355. Donald et al, *Civil War*, 378.

356. Esposito, West Point Atlas, I, Map 137 text.

357. Fuller, *Generalship of Grant*, 371.

358. Freeman, *R.E. Lee*, III, 446.

359. Grant, *Memoirs*, 597, quoting data from "A Statement of Losses Compiled in the Adjutant-General's Office."

360. Groom, *Shrouds of Glory*, 8.

361. Hassler, *Commanders*, 219.

362. Heidler and Heidler, *Encyclopedia*, 466.

363. Ibid., 1639.

364. McPherson, *Battle Cry*, 742.

365. McWhiney and Jamieson, *Attack and Die*, 19, 158.

366. Miers, Earl Schenck, *The Last Campaign: Grant Saves the Union* (Philadelphia and New York: J.B. Lippincott Company, 1972), 122.

367. Rhea, *Spotsylvania*, 319, 324.

368. Smith, *Grant*, 376.

369. Taylor, *Lee*, 249.

370. Smith, *Grant*, 365.

371. Weigley, *American Way of War*, 144.

372. Young, "Numbers and Losses," 27. If Kenon's Landing and Trevilian Station battles are included, Young's numbers increase to 33,508, 4,313, 18,153, 861, and 10,181, respectively.

373. Buell, *Warrior Generals*, 441.

374. Current, *Encyclopedia*, III, 1198.

375. Fox, *Regimental Losses*, 23, 547.

376. Fuller, *Grant and Lee*, 287.

377. Livermore, *Numbers & Losses*, 115.

378. Lowe, "Field Fortifications," 65.

379. Phisterer, *Statistical Record*, 217.

380. Trudeau, *The Last Citadel*, 55.

381. Fox, *Regimental Losses*, 547.

382. Phisterer, *Statistical Record*, 217.

383. Trudeau, *The Last Citadel*, 90.

384. Suderow, "Glory Denied," 31.

385. Fox, *Regimental Losses*, 547.

386. Catton, *Grant Takes Command*, 325.

387. Catton, Stillness, 253.

388. Editors, *Great Battles*, 469.

389. Current, *Encyclopedia*, III, 1200.

390. Esposito, West Point Atlas, I, Map 139 text.

391. Fox, *Regimental Losses*, 547.

392. Freeman, *R.E. Lee*, III, 477.

393. Fuller, *Grant and Lee*, 287.

394. Hassler, *Commanders*, 227.

395. Livermore, *Numbers & Losses*, 116–7.

396. McPherson, *Battle Cry*, 760.

397. McWhiney & Jamieson, *Attack and Die*, 158.

398. Phisterer, *Statistical Record*, 217.

399. Trudeau, *The Last Citadel*, 127.

400. Buell, *Warrior Generals*, 441.

401. Fox, *Regimental Losses*, 23, 547.

402. Livermore, *Numbers & Losses*, 117.

403. McWhiney & Jamieson, *Attack and Die*, 158.

404. Phisterer, *Statistical Record*, 217.

405. Suderow, "Nothing But a Miracle," 31.

406. Trudeau, *The Last Citadel*, 170.

407. Arnold, *Armies of Grant*, 246.

408. Current, *Encyclopedia*, III, 1200.

409. Fox, *Regimental Losses*, 547.

410. Fuller, *Grant and Lee*, 287.

411. Hassler, *Commanders*, 229.

412. Livermore, *Numbers & Losses*, 118.

413. McWhiney & Jamieson, *Attack and Die*, 158.

414. Phisterer, *Statistical Record*, 217.

415. Fox, *Regimental Losses*, 547.

416. Phisterer, *Statistical Record*, 217.

417. Trudeau, *The Last Citadel*, 189.

418. Fox, *Regimental Losses*, 548.

419. Fuller, *Grant and Lee*, 287.

420. Hassler, *Commanders*, 230.

421. Livermore, *Numbers & Losses*, 128.

422. McWhiney and Jamieson, *Attack and Die*, 158.

423. Phisterer, *Statistical Record*, 217.

424. Trudeau, *The Last Citadel*, 217.

425. Fox, *Regimental Losses*, 548.

426. Trudeau, "Unerring Firearm," 86.

427. Current, *Encyclopedia*, III, 1201.

428. Fox, *Regimental Losses*, 548.

429. Fuller, *Grant and Lee*, 287.

430. Hassler, *Commanders*, 231.

431. Heidler and Heidler, *Encyclopedia*, 946.

432. Ibid., 130–1.

433. McWhiney and Jamieson, *Attack and Die*, 158.

434. Phisterer, *Statistical Record*, 218.

435. Trudeau, *The Last Citadel*, 248, 250–1.

436. Bergeron, "Hatcher's Run," 37.

437. Current, *Encyclopedia*, III, 1201.

438. Fox, *Regimental Losses*, 548.

439. Livermore, *Numbers & Losses*, 133–4.

440. McWhiney and Jamieson, *Attack and Die*, 158.

441. Phisterer, *Statistical Record*, 218.

442. Trudeau, *The Last Citadel*, 322.

443. Current, *Encyclopedia*, III, 1201.

444. Esposito, West Point Atlas, I, Map 142 text.

445. Fox, *Regimental Losses*, 548.

446. Freeman, *R.E. Lee*, IV, 19.

447. Fuller, *Generalship of Grant*, 341.

448. Fuller, *Grant and Lee*, 287.

449. Hassler, *Commanders*, 239.

450. Heidler and Heidler, *Encyclopedia*, 753.

451. Marvel, "Retreat," 6.

452. McPherson, *Battle Cry*, 726.

453. Phisterer, *Statistical Record*, 218.

454. Smith, *Grant*, 393.

455. Trudeau, *The Last Citadel*, 353–4.

456. Fox, *Regimental Losses*, 549.

457. Phisterer, *Statistical Record*, 218.

458. Fox, *Regimental Losses*, 549.

459. Crawford, "Dinwiddie Court House," 55.

460. Fuller, *Grant and Lee*, 287.

461. Livermore, *Numbers & Losses*, 137.

462. Calkins, "Five Forks," 51.

463. Catton, *Grant Takes Command*, 445.

464. Current, *Encyclopedia*, III, 1201.

465. Esposito, *West Point Atlas*, I, Map

466. Fox, *Regimental Losses*, 549.

467. Freeman, *R.E. Lee*, IV, 40.

468. Marvel, "Retreat," 6.

469. Phisterer, *Statistical Record*, 218.

470. Trudeau, Noah Andre, *Out of the Storm: The End of the Civil War, April–June 1865* (Boston, New York, Toronto, London: Little, Brown and Company, 1994), 45.

471. Current, *Encyclopedia*, III, 1201.

472. Fox, *Regimental Losses*, 549.

473. Fuller, *Grant and Lee*, 287.

474. Livermore, *Numbers & Losses*, 138.

475. Phisterer, *Statistical Record*, 218.

476. Current, *Encyclopedia*, III, 1201.

477. Trudeau, *The Last Citadel*, 419.

478. Calkins, "Final Bloodshed," 36.

479. Fox, *Regimental Losses*, 549.

480. Freeman, *R.E. Lee*, IV, 91, 93.

481. Glynn, "Black Thursday," 29.

482. Heidler and Heidler, *Encyclopedia*, 1710.

483. McPherson, *Battle Cry*, 848.

484. Phisterer, *Statistical Record*, 218.

485. Smith, *Grant*, 398.

486. Trudeau, *The Last Citadel*, 414.

487. Trudeau, *Out of the Storm*, 115–6.

488. Buell, *Warrior Generals*, 441.

489. Civil War Times, *Great Battles*, 560.

490. Current, *Encyclopedia*, I, 48.

491. Fuller, *Grant and Lee*, 287.

492. Hassler, *Commanders*, 240.

493. Heidler and Heidler, *Encyclopedia*, 72.

494. Livermore, *Numbers & Losses*, 135–7.

495. Marvel, *Lee's Last Retreat*, 205.

496. McWhiney and Jamieson, *Attack and Die*, 19, 158. If the Confederate loss figure is supposed to be 6,266 (Livermore's number) instead of 6,666, the Confederate loss percentage would be 13 percent.

497. Phisterer, *Statistical Record*, 219.

498. Porter, *Campaigning with Grant*, 492.

499. Simpson, *Hood's Texas Brigade*, 466.

Appendix III

1. I earlier discussed this issue—with no votes tables—in Bonekemper, "Lincoln's 1864 Victory." For a strongly contrary view, see Daniel, Larry J., "The South Almost Won by Not Losing: A Rebuttal," *North & South*, Vol. 1, No. 3 (Feb. 1998), 44–51. Daniel contends that Lincoln would have won even if Atlanta had not fallen. The reader will have to examine the numbers and draw his own conclusion about whether Lincoln would have had enough votes to win if Atlanta and the Shenandoah had not fallen and Grant had not penned Lee's army up in Richmond/Petersburg.

2. McPherson, *Battle Cry*, 804.

3. *Congressional Quarterly*, Presidential Elections, 94.

4. Welles, *Diary, II*, 130, 132.

5. Jones, Archer, "Military Means, Political Ends," in Boritt, Gabor S. (ed.), *Why the Confederacy Lost*, 43–77 at 48.

6. Wiggins, *Journals of Gorgas*, 66.

7. Longstreet to Brigadier General Thomas Jordan, March 27, 1864, quoted in McPherson, *Battle Cry*, 721.

8. McPherson, *Battle Cry*, 721.

9. Donald et al, *Civil War*, 423, quoting *New York Sun*, June 30, 1889 (publishing documents on anti-Lincoln cabal of 1864).

10. McPherson, James M., "American Victory, American Defeat," in Boritt, *Why the Confederacy Lost*, 15–42, 40.

11. Lowry, *Fate of the Country*, 381.

12. Donald, *Lincoln*, 529.

13. Nevins, *Ordeal of the Union, VIII*, 92–3.

14. Donald et al, *Civil War*, 425.

15. Miller, William J., *Mapping for Stonewall: The Civil War Service of Jed Hotchkiss* (Washington: Elliott & Clark Publishing, 1993), 143.

16. McPherson, "American Victory," 39.

17. Nevins, *Ordeal of the Union, VIII*, 99–102.

18. Beringer et al, *Why the South Lost*, photo between 274–5.

19. Donald et al, *Civil War*, 425.

20. Fuller, *Generalship of Grant*, 330.

21. Beringer et al, *Why the South Lost*, 349. Three-quarters of the more than 250,000 troops who voted cast their ballots for Lincoln. Donald et al, *Civil War*, 426. On September 19, Lincoln urged Sherman to do anything he could "safely do" to allow Indiana soldiers to return home to vote in the October 11 state elections because of the effect those elections would have on the November election. Lincoln to Sherman, Sept. 19, 1864, Basler, *Works of Lincoln, VIII*, 11. On September 26, Lincoln wrote to Rosecrans to ensure that soldiers would be allowed to vote in Missouri and said, "Wherever the law allows soldiers to vote, their officers must allow it." Lincoln to Rosecrans, Sept. 26, 1864, Basler, *Works of Lincoln, VIII*, 24.

22. Numbers derived from *Congressional Quarterly*, Presidential Elections, 94.

23. Nevins, *Ordeal of the Union*, VIII, 103.

24. Estimated Electoral Vote in hand of President Lincoln, Oct. 13, 1864, Basler, *Works of Lincoln, VIII*, 46. On October 31, Lincoln issued a proclamation admitting Nevada (and its three electoral votes) to the Union. Proclamation Admitting Nevada into the Union, Oct. 31, 1864, Ibid., 83–4.

25. Fuller, *Generalship of Grant*, 330–1.

26. Donald et al, *Civil War*, 427.

INDEX

About the Author

ED BONEKEMPER received his B.A. *cum laude* in American history from Muhlenberg College, his M.A. in American history from Old Dominion University, and his J.D. from Yale Law School. He is adjunct lecturer in military history at Muhlenberg College, Allentown, PA, a frequent Civil War speaker, and the author of three other Civil War books: *How Robert E. Lee Lost the Civil War, McClellan and Failure: A Study of Civil War Fear, Incompetence and Worse*, and *Grant and Lee: Victorious American and Vanquished Virginian*. He and his wife of over forty-six years, Susan Weidemoyer Bonekemper, live in Willow Street, PA, with their cockapoo Ruby.